THE LETTERS OF RUDYARD KIPLING

Kipling in his study at Naulakha, 1895
(photograph by Arthur D. Wyatt, Brattleboro; Library of Congress).

The Letters of Rudyard Kipling

Volume 2
1890–99

Edited by

THOMAS PINNEY

University of Iowa Press, Iowa City

UNIVERSITY OF IOWA PRESS,
Iowa City 52242

International Standard Book Number 0–87745–306–3
Library of Congress Catalog Card Number 90–70525
First edition, 1990

Printed in Great Britain

Contents

List of Illustrations

Frontispiece: Kipling in his study at Naulakha, 1895: photograph by Arthur D. Wyatt, Brattleboro (Library of Congress).

Part One
The Man from Nowhere
1890–93

INTRODUCTION

To the English public 1890 was the year of Rudyard Kipling: he burst upon them as a wholly unexpected and marvellously precocious talent, "the man from nowhere" (J. M. Barrie's phrase), who gave them *Barrack-Room Ballads*, *The Courting of Dinah Shadd*, *The Light that Failed*, and the reprinted volumes of the Indian Railway Library in dazzling profusion. But for Kipling, the new year began as the old had ended, mixing together his public success and his private unhappiness in the gloom of a London winter. At the end of January he had some sort of physical and nervous collapse. The engagement to Caroline Taylor came to an end – the circumstances are not known – but then Kipling met by chance his old infatuation Florence Violet Garrard and was at once thrown into fresh turmoil. Kipling seems never to have had much pleasure in London during this first phase of his return to England. He encountered the city in a suspicious and defensive frame of mind: he was determined not to be cheated by publishers or exploited by editors or drawn in to the quarrels of the literary cliques of the city. In consequence, he behaved in a distinctly prickly way, with how much reason we cannot know now. But the attitudes that he cultivated in his first season of London success persisted in him to the end. He put all of his publishing arrangements in the hands of an agent within weeks of his arriving in England, and he studiously avoided all attempts to associate him with any literary party or group. He would be his own man. When the American firm of Harpers published some of his work without authorisation – as they were free to do before the passage of a copyright agreement between the United States and Britain – Kipling, naturally angry, did not hesitate to attack even such respectable names as those of Walter Besant, Thomas Hardy, and William Black when they seemed to defend what Harpers had done.

Kipling's life in London grew more agreeable after May of 1890, when his parents arrived to spend more than a year's leave there. Nor did his determination to keep clear of literary entanglements prevent him from making literary friends and acquaintances. He frequented the Savile Club, and saw much of such men as Andrew Lang, Edmund Gosse, Henry James, Thomas Hardy, Rider Haggard, and W. E. Henley. Indeed, if he is to be associated with any group, it would be with the group that gathered round Henley, then editor of the *Scots Observer*. Henley and Kipling were united in their admiration of the empire and their detestation of the "aesthetic" style in literature and life. It was

3

about this time that Kipling, provoked by the indifference or even hostility of the English at home to the work and values of the English abroad, determined to become the apostle of the Imperial gospel to the gentiles of England: "And what should they know of England who only England know?"

Of central importance to Kipling's life but almost undocumented is his acquaintance with a young American writer and publisher named Wolcott Balestier, who was in London as the representative of an American publisher and who was starting up his own firm to publish reprints of English literature on the continent. The two young men appear to have met within the first months of Kipling's residence in London, either late in 1889 or early in 1890. Kipling assigned the publication of his books in America to Balestier, and by the middle of 1890 was collaborating with Balestier on a novel, *The Naulahka*. Even more important in the long run, and equally undocumented, was Kipling's acquaintance with Balestier's sister Caroline, the woman whom Kipling was to marry, and whom he probably met in 1890 when she was in London assisting her brother in his publishing enterprises. The near-invisibility of the Balestiers, sister and brother, in Kipling's letters from this time strongly suggests that all correspondence between them has been destroyed.

In the late summer of 1891, after nearly two years of hard work in London, Kipling set out on a trip around the southern hemisphere of the world, calling in South Africa, New Zealand, Australia, and India. From his parents' house in Lahore, at Christmas time, he was summoned back to England by news of the sudden death of Wolcott Balestier. Kipling left at once (he was never to return to India), arrived in London in early January 1892, took out a special licence, and married Wolcott's sister, Caroline, to the surprise and wonder of all his friends.

The newly wed couple undertook a trip around the world as their honeymoon journey. It was evidently Kipling's intention to maintain a footloose style even though he had married, but circumstances dictated otherwise. First, when Kipling and his wife reached Japan, Kipling's bank failed: they were forced to abandon their tour and to retreat to her family's home in Brattleboro, Vermont. Then, his wife was pregnant: their first child, Josephine, was born at the end of the year. They then built a house near Brattleboro: before the end of 1893, Kipling was a husband, a father, and a householder. He would, in some sense, remain a man without a country for the rest of his life, but he could no longer think of himself as footloose.

To Caroline Taylor, 2 January 1890

Text: Copy, University of Sussex

[London]

Jan. 2:

Last night I dined with the money-editor of the *Times*.[1] Poor Chap, he has gone through great trouble of late and doesn't like being alone. None the less I could wish that he had *not* come up to my rooms and talked till 3. A.M. I feel tired and limp today in consequence. Did I tell you of my birthday visit. I went to tea in the "hoight av society" at a place in Stanhope Gate and was shown off to a lot of people. Among 'em three, Lady Wentworth,[2] Lords Pembroke[3] and Grosvenor[4] backed me into a corner and stood over me pouring melted compliments into my throat, one after the other. And through it all I kept thinking to myself: – "Unless it happened that I was the fashion for the moment – to be treated like a purple monkey on a yellow stick for just so long as I amuse you, you'd let me die of want on your doorsteps". So they would, but now, O its "dear Mr Kipling *please* come as often as you can and we'll talk," and on my mantlepiece are arriving cards to picture galleries, concerts and all manner o' tuppeny ha' penny shows [. . .][5] increasing and now I receive 200 dollars where before I got only 120. This ought to be soothing to us. As you very wisely point out we should have to go slow but not *so* slow. At least you won't have to get up and light fires or beat a help with a stick. If your father and a few friends of his had not constructed a fool of a tarrif living in America would be 40% cheaper than it is. However I suppose it must be the "land of the free" and expensive. My notion after I had heard my second cousin's American bride[6] discourse was a flat – janitor, lights of Edison, and so forth in any decent city which allows us escape in the summer. I should think Pittsburgh, out on the far side, and then kite away to the sea or somewhere when the weather gets hot. If this court knows itself Carrie is a person who wilts in great heat. But be it clearly understood O my queen that nothing in the aforesaid arrangement shall stop us bolting over to England just as often as ever we please. There's a lot of country in this island that is passing beautiful and we'll see it together. But here am I yarning away as tho' we were [the rest is missing].

Notes
1. Wynnard Hooper: see 3–25 December 1889.
2. Mary Caroline Stewart-Wortley (1848–1941), wife of Baron Wentworth.
3. George Robert Charles Herbert (1850–95), 13th Earl of Pembroke.
4. The current Lord Grosvenor, afterwards 2nd Duke of Westminster, was eleven years old at this time: who can RK mean?
5. Gap of indeterminate length in copy.

6. Perhaps RK means the wife of Teddy Bell (see 8–16 November 1889); Bell was the nephew of RK's uncle-by-marriage, Edward Poynter.

To Unidentified Recipient, 7 January 1890

ALS: The Athenaeum, London.

Embankment Chambers, / Villiers Street, Strand.

Dear Sir,

The author of those books you mention is up to his eyes in work but what interests him is this same Irish question in Frisco.[1] The stuff is by him waiting to be made up into a book.[2] If you care to give the instructions *viva voce* he will attend. Later he will be too raxed.[3]

Yours sincerely
Rudyard Kipling

7–1–90

Notes
1. RK wrote on the Irish in San Francisco politics in Letter 24 of *From Sea to Sea*.
2. This is perhaps an early notion for the book that RK planned under the title of *The Book of the Forty-Five Mornings* but did not publish. He may also have thought of republishing the "From Sea to Sea Letters" or of developing them along different lines. RK's mother wrote on 23 December 1889 that "From Sea to Sea will make a capital book, and I wonder how the Americans will like his clear analyzing of their political attitude, and its causes!" (to Mrs Hill: Copy, Sussex).
3. The word means to stretch or to reach out, and RK uses it in something like that sense in "Bread Upon the Waters" (*The Day's Work*). Here it appears to mean something different.

To Samuel Sidney McClure,[1] [January 1890]

Text: Extract, American Art Association Catalogue, 20 April 1925, item 163, with partial facsimile: ALS, 2pp. 16mo; dated Embankment Chambers, Villiers Street, Strand

I have had the pleasure of dealing with your association while in charge of a weekly in India, but if possible I should much like to see some of the printed schedules, tariffs and general arrangements of the Press. I am afraid short tales from my pen are all disposed of but I fancy the "fiction for youth notion" is workable. Thus, I have the notes and scaffolding of a book for boys, to be called "An Officer and a Gentleman."

It is merely the history of a lad serving the Queen in India – his troubles, war experiences [. . .][2] He fights on the Northern frontier, in Burma, where he leads his own detachment, gets a look in at Egypt and generally has a good time. That sort of life I know down to its bootheels and I fancy 'twould interest boys between fifteen and eighteen. There would be any amount of blood in the pages but the slaughtering should be of a practical kind and a large amount of rough-cast morality could be worked in. No one seems to care to tell the youngsters what life on foreign service and the handling of men really means. I think I could interest 'em. That sort of work might with advantage be syndicated in America.

If you think anything of the notion would you kindly give me (a) your most preferred size and (b) your rates. The story could be compressed or pulled out to suit.

> Yours sincerely
> Rudyard Kipling

Notes
1. McClure (1857–1949), American editor and magazine publisher, made his reputation beginning in 1884 through the invention and successful development of a literary syndicate, supplying newspapers round the world with stories and features. McClure was indefatigable in pursuing likely authors to write for the syndicate, and almost every well-known writer in the last part of the century, including RK, signed with him. *McClure's Magazine*, begun in 1893, was famous as the magazine of the Muckrakers.
2. The printed text in the catalogue ends here with an ellipsis. The rest of the text is from the accompanying facsimile.

To Samuel Alexander Hill,[1] [24 January 1890]

Text: Copy, University of Sussex

[London]

Can't write you anything this week. I'm better but my head is all queer and I am going to have it mended some day. Keep better than me.

Note
1. According to Mrs Hill's notes on the copy of this note, it was addressed to Mr Hill, was written in lead pencil, not dated, not signed, and "was the last thing that R.K. wrote when he went into that extreme illness in 1890". Mrs Hill states that it was posted 24 January 1890 at Charing Cross.

To William Ernest Henley,[1] [31 January? 1890]
ALS: Morgan Library

Embankment Chambers, / Villiers Street, Strand. / Friday

Dear Mr. Henley,

Thank you. It came yesterday. I'd like the book better had I not read it before. How in the world was I to know that you wrote "A book of verses"?[2] I read all the Hospital Sketches in India and also that maddening "Made in the hot weather" which should be read with the thermometer at 104° in the shade – to the greater glory of the author.

Since we be only islands shouting misunderstandings to each other across seas of speech or writing[3] I am going to say nothing. I take off my hat and drop my sword point. You have been where I have yet to go so I dare not ask you why you are so tired. When you get my stuff you will see how far I've walked, and where.[4]

Yes, men tell me I am young in this country but I have put seven years of India behind me and they do not make a man younger or more cheerful. Also, luckily, they don't lead him to believe the protestations of the disinterested publisher or the blandishments of the people to whom a new writer man is as a new purple monkey on a yellow stick. I live very largely alone and my wants are limited to a new fly-rod and some flies. *But,* you can do me immense service by sending in a memo of reminder if it seems to you that I am spinning out my guts too swiftly, at any time.

To a young man the temptation is strong and it is to no body's interest to tell him to go slow. Rather they want all he has at once and then he can go to the deuce, being squeezed dry. I've treated men in the same way when I was an Editor. I see now I was unkind.

I am ordered off for a month's idleness now 'cause of my head. If it is written I come to Edinburgh ere long and then I shall see you and – this is business – if you think it worth while you shall give me my riding orders by word of mouth and we will elaborate a Line of Work.

At present I am divided between the broken top-joint of my rod, and a reel that won't croon properly. Literature is a weariness of the flesh – all books are wicked and the only real thing in the world is a four pound bass coming up with the tide at the mouth of the Torridge,[5] my hook in the right hand top angle of his mouth.

Yours very sincerely
Rudyard Kipling

Notes
1. Henley (1849–1903), editor, critic, and poet, was at this time editor of the Edinburgh weekly, the *Scots Observer*.

2. Henley's first volume of poems, 1885, includes "In Hospital" and the ballade "Made in the Hot Weather". RK's copy of the book inscribed "Rudyard Kipling / 'Yussuf' / from the Author. / 29 / 1 / 90" is now at Wimpole Hall.
3. Perhaps the source of the passage in ch. 5 of *The Light that Failed* whose origins have so far baffled enquiry: "Who's the man that says that we're all islands shouting lies to each other across seas of misunderstanding?"
4. RK's first contribution to the *Scots Observer* was "The Explanation", 1 February; thereafter most of the "Barrack-Room Ballads" appeared in the paper, beginning on 22 February 1890.
5. At Bideford, just over the ridge from RK's school at Westward Ho!

To [Edmonia Hill], [*c.* early February 1890]
AL: Fragment, University of Sussex

Embankment Chambers, / Villiers Street, Strand.

[. . .] you do well to say that the half year has begun. It has and I have broken up. My head has given out and I am forbidden work and I am to go away somewhere. This is the third time it has happened – last time was on the Honam on the Canton river but this time is the completest.[1] I do not want, even if I deserved, your pity. I must go on alone now till the end of my time. I can do nothing to save myself from breaking up now and again.

I hope you are keeping well. I am physically in perfect health but I can neither work nor think nor read and have been in this state for – since the 20th of January – alone. You and the doctors always laughed but I knew that the smash would come some day. It's nobody's fault but my own. Thank Alick for his letter and tell him I'm not well.[2]

Notes
1. No doubt the first breakdown occurred during one of RK's years in Lahore – there is no way to tell when. The second, "on the Canton river", may be dated around 8 April 1889, when RK and the Hills journeyed from Hong Kong to Canton on the *Ho-Nam*. The terrified violence of RK's reaction to China (*From Sea to Sea*, Letter 10) does seem to suggest mental disturbance. Mrs Hill later said that RK was suffering from fever when they reached Canton (quoted in W. M. Carpenter, "RK's Allahabad Home", MS, Cornell, p. 24).
2. At some time near the date of this letter the engagement between RK and Caroline Taylor must have come to an end.

To Unidentified Recipient,[1] 6 March 1890
ALS: University of Sussex

Embankment Chambers, / Villiers Street, Strand. / Mar.6.90.

No, indeed no, and very many times no. You didn't understand, altogether, in spite of the beautiful sympathy and insight of your note (I've got a mother o' my own who is all but all the world to me and so, you see, I know).

It's the amazing selfishness of the White man that ruins your counsel of perfection. "Money fame and success" are to remain unto me? Surely 'tis just as selfish consciously and deliberately to work for that trinity as to lay siege to a woman or a glass of gin and porter! Where I come from they taught me (with whips of circumstance and the thermometer at 110° in the shade) that the only human being to whom a man is responsible is himself. His business is to do his work and sit still.

No man can be a power for all time or the tenth of it – else would some of my friends who have died at their posts be those powers. Least of all can a man do aught if he thinks about it, and tries to add cubits to his stature mental or physical. It's as bad as waltzing and counting the steps "one, two, three, one two three" under your breath. Surely the young man does best to pray to be delivered from "the public demand that walketh in the noonday and the cheque-book that destroyeth in the study."[2] For the rest, his business is to think as little about his soul as possible for that breeds self-consciousness and loss of power. The event is in God's hands absolutely and no hawking or clutching for fame or any other skittles is the least use.

Recollect I've tasted power – such power as I shall never get this side of the water – when I knew all the heads of the Indian Government – rulers administrators and kings – and saw how the machinery worked. Sunshine, colour, light, incident and fight I've had poured into my lap: and now the chastened amusements of this black place don't bite. (But, bless you for that hint about debt. It showed you were in earnest. It's all right, though). Wait till you've been shot at and bossed a hundred and seventy men and walked "with Death and morning on the silver horns"[3] in the Himalayas if you wish to know how far the smoking-room, the club and the music hall, and the cheap ormolu amourettes taste good.

This only do. Pray for me, since I am a lonely man in my life, that I do not take the sickness which for lack of understanding I should call love. For that will leave me somebody else's servant – instead of my own. My business at present, so far as I can feel, is to get into touch with the common folk here, to find out what they desire, hope or fear and then after the proper time to speak whatever may be given to me.

Also to do just enough fairly decent work to keep me going till I have found my calling and my voice. From this ideal I make no doubt I shall lamentably fall. Then I shall have to walk slowly through a Hell that I have been through once already. It's an awful thing to think that each soul has to work out its own salvation and more awful to know that if it sits down to think about that salvation it is in deep danger of losing it.

If the success comes my father's delight will be greater than mine. If the money comes my Mother will be more pleased than I. The two together may spoil my work and make me think less of waiting than getting more little pieces of newspapers and little cheques. Wherefore, once again, let us pray. You see I've answered at undue length. Here is *my* key-note. Don't believe in me one inch further than you can see. What's the use of pinning faith on things that one uses to write about? Please don't for I must do my own work in my own way and if my notions clashed with yours you'd be hurt for nothing. Look on it as an interesting study and let it go. I'm not going to set the Thames on fire. So I hope I shan't have occasion to get mired in the mud on its banks. Once more, thank you a thousand times.

Sincerely yours
Rudyard Kipling

P.S.   Those commission verses[4] have found a nest: *Scots Observer*, next Saturday. There will be some little explosion if the other side fight.

Notes
1. This letter is filed with those to E. K. Robinson at Sussex, but Robinson was still in India, and there are other reasons why he is extremely unlikely to have been the recipient of this letter. Professor Carrington suggests that the recipient may have been Wolcott Balestier (see to Robert Underwood Johnson [1890]).
2. Cf. Psalms 91:6.
3. Tennyson, *The Princess*, vii, 189.
4. "Cleared", *Scots Observer*, 8 March 1890: the verses are a response to the report of the Commission appointed to inquire into charges that Parnell and other Irish Members of Parliament had been implicated in the Phoenix Park murders. According to RK, both *The Times* and the *Fortnightly* rejected the verses before Henley took them (*Something of Myself*, p. 83).

To [Edmund? Yates][1] [April? 1890?]

ALS: Dalhousie University

[London]

Dear Mr Yates,

This is to announce that "Farmyard Topling"[2] is a Pig. He feels it acutely because he has done nothing for you – but if you went round to two or three other papers they'd say he was worse than a Pig.

He has now struck work and is maturing revenge against the whole American nation who have taken to giving away *free in book form* the whole of his *Plain Tales from the Hills* with their vile newspapers![3] If this isn't revenge of the Gods for not writing for you, the Gods only know what is.

Yours repentantly
Rudyard Kipling

P.S.   In all seriousness – give me a lead.[4]

Notes
1. Edmund Yates (1831–94), journalist and editor, founded *The World*, a weekly paper, in 1874. *The World* published a lengthy interview with RK in its series entitled "Celebrities at Home" on 2 April 1890, and I conjecture that Yates may have pressed RK for a contribution to the paper around that date. For a somewhat doubtful anecdote of Yates's "discovery" of RK, see Arthur Reed Kimball, "A Story of Rudyard Kipling", in Orel, *Rudyard Kipling: Interviews and Recollections*, I, 135–7.
2. That is, Rudyard Kipling.
3. The earliest American edition of *Plain Tales* is that published in Lovell's International Series dated 9 January 1890. In an undated letter to Elizabeth Bisland [1890?] RK says that a New York paper is giving away an edition of "the whole of Mulvaney and the Plain Tales" under the title of "Mulvaney the Musketeer and Plain Tales from the Hindoo Highlands" (ALS, Syracuse). No such title is on record.
4. Apart from the sonnet RK published in *The World* in 1882 (see 21 November 1884) nothing by him is known to have appeared in the paper.

To Edmund Gosse,[1] 2[6] May 1890

ALS: British Library

Embankment Chambers, / Villiers Street, Strand. / 24.5.90

Dear Misther Gosse
Your wingèd hoss
That crops Parnashiun grasses,

Was bred an' bitted
in Climes unfitted
For Oriental asses!

I thried to lead
My own poor steed
Up that same steep hill side, Sorr
But the rar*e*yfaction
Disthurbed his action –
My garron[2] nearly died, Sorr.

I tuck 'im down
To the crowded town
An' put 'im into a shtable
To run to order
Fornenst a Forder[3]
An' earn me all he's able.

But I sometimes think
From his desolate wink
An' the dhroopin' cock of his tail, Sir
That he looks wid sighs on
The blue horizon
   Where the strong-winged horses sail, Sorr.

Doggerel apart, dear Mr Gosse I'm charmed to have your book[4] and thank you many times for it.

                    Sincerely
                    Rudyard Kipling

Monday

Notes

1. (Sir) Edmund Gosse (1849–1928), poet, essayist, and critic; librarian to the House of Lords, 1904–14. Gosse, who knew everyone worth knowing and who kept a sharp eye on the literary scene, took an interest in RK at once.
2. Small Irish or Scottish horse.
3. A cab horse.
4. *On Viol and Flute* (1890), a new edition of Gosse's first book of poems (1873).

To William Ernest Henley, [June? 1890]

Text: Composite from John Connell, *W. E. Henley* (London, 1949) p. 183; and Sotheby's Catalogue, 21–2 July 1983, item 262

Oh thou that runnest over golden sands with feet of silver, I've got the *Views and Reviews*[1] and at the same time a notion of your strengths and weaknesses. You hold the notion of the Arabian Nights in the heel of your fist but – why the rest? seeing that these men for the most part be dead and pickled: and human souls being awesome lonely and independent see and insist upon seeing things according to their own lights. But as you know it's beautiful stuff and *therefore* you shouldn't ha' chucked it away on the repeated crambe – which is dumb crambo.[2] I'm getting my ballads into order and shall go slow. F.B.[3] has said nothing. The book about Ripon has come at last. Pater sends salaams.[4]

                                                                Ruddy

Notes
1. Henley's *Views and Reviews . . . Literature* (1890), a collection of his journalistic work over the last fourteen years, including items on the *Arabian Nights*, Rabelais, Sidney, Walton, Tourneur, and Herrick as well as many nineteenth-century writers. RK praised the *Arabian Nights* piece in *Something of Myself*, p. 82.
2. "Repeated crambe" = cabbage served up again, i.e. distasteful repetition (Juvenal, *Satires*, VII, 154); dumb crambo is a word-guessing game.
3. Probably Fitzroy Bell, a major backer of Henley's *Scots Observer*.
4. RK's parents, on furlough from India, had arrived in England in early May 1890 and were now living in London.

To William Canton,[1] [*c.* late June? 1890]

ALS: Berg Collection, New York Public Library

Embankment Chambers, / Villiers Street, Strand. / Monday

Once upon a time there was a Coffee-pot and Allah-al-Bari who is the greatest of all conjurors caused it to pour out sometimes coffee black as the pit; sometimes milk white as the feet of little children and sometimes wine red as the blood of a strong man.

And because Coffee pots do not often pour after the usages of the trinity Those who should Have Known Better surrounded that coffee pot as it went abroad on its occasions through the bazars thus:

[Illustration of a coffee-pot appears here

See Plate 7 in this volume]

And when it had poured wine they said "Pour milk" and when it had poured milk they said "pour coffee" and when it had done all these things they said: "Wah! Wah! Was there ever such a coffee pot." So they made its face shiny and polished its stomach and set it upon a large mat in the mid-doorway and they called strangers to do it honour. So that it was a saying among the tribes Dhámthatquoughphy Pot. And the coffee pot beat its stomach and was proud but neither the pot nor the others called once upon the name of God the Artificer but upon another God whom they called Djinnius and whose shrine they said was within the coffee pot.

Then Allah stooping down with his little finger troubled the concealed fittings of the coffee-pot so that the conjuring compartments fell inwards and the first was like the third and there was no second and the wine and the milk and the coffee made an evil vat of bilge water when next they bade the coffee pot pour. Those who should have known Better became aware of this mixture and they spat it out abusing the coffee-pot. And the coffee pot said: – "By Allah! what fault is it of mine?" Now because the coffee-pot had called on Allah, That Great One sent down none other than Jibrael to teach it wisdom and a three fold humility – being one humility for each compartment. And Jibrael resting upon a sword said these verses

"That which is in thee is in three and comes forth at
the appointed times of God whether it be dung,
urine or coffee.
Wilt thou be proud of the morning stool or exalt
thyself for the matter of a nose-blowing?

Or canst thou say which is the worthier in Our sight
the shred toe-nails of Mahommed Our messenger, or all
the Surahs of the Koran which we commanded him to
write.
For the one and the other are Ours and our balances
are hidden from the sight of men.

> Go now O coffee pot and remember these things lest
> we suddenly tie thee to the hinder tail of a
> dog and thou are haled clattering through the
> the gutter – empty and making lamentable music."

Whereat the coffee-pot laid its hand upon its three
compartments and sat still while Jibrael returned to his place:
And this is the legend of the coffee pot.

Tis but your notion drawn wire-thin but canst thou not see O my
good friend how I must keep the certainty of that knowledge before me
if I wish to get good work poured through me. I've cooked your letter
after laying it to heart. You've drunk bitter waters and you haven't
forgotten the taste. However men learn who have been fathers twice,
one very comforting fact tho' it's rather a brutal one. It's an awful thing
to see the made life die but we are only the links in the chain that keeps
the whole machinery going – and, within certain limits, we are not
responsible either for the death or what is worse the downward path of
the soul that we falsely imagine has come from us. But you of course
know this better than I and your wife, if I mistake not, better than you.

I'm very busy just now with a new yarn[2] – all bluggy.[3] Horrid bluggy.
Jock Learoyd has got into a mess with a girl and tells me about it. I
want to make these people understand that it has been given to me to
describe, when God chuses, country village rusticity in the North
whence I come; "for my birth and kin Ise Yorkshire and Stingo." I will
e'en return to the hammering out.

Your Indian extracts have made me sick. I know these papers. Can't
you imagine the hideous misgovernment of India when the registration
of one suspected criminal is made to do duty for a ghastly crime. And
if you knew the Indian court and heard the language of ordinary life
you'd appreciate the sensitive shrinking of a Hindu at the least abuse.
Poor creature! Talking of babies what do you think of the enclosed. I'd
have given something to have written it in something the same way.

All good luck be yours – and write me a line now and again if you're
not too busy. It seems as tho I knew you and your household well and
some day I'll come up to make sure.

Rudyard

Notes
1. Canton (1845–1926), at this time leader writer on the *Glasgow Herald*, came to London
   in 1891 to do editorial and managerial work for the publishing firm of Isbister; he was
   the author of poems and stories for children, and of the history of the Bible Society.
   He had evidently written RK more than one flattering letter.
2. "On Greenhow Hill" (*The Courting of Dinah Shadd*).
3. Jocular for "bloody".

To Margaret Clifford,[1] [early August 1890?]
ALS: Berg Collection, New York Public Library

[London]

Estimable Turk

This is the diplomatic or Sectarial Political way of beginning a letter. I write because I do not know what in the world to say and because your Mummy has gone to put on her things to come for a walk with me in the Park and *she* says writing to you might keep me out of mischief which *I* don't think it will and anyhow there's only one pen in the house fit to write with for all the rest are quills and the way they are worn at their noses is something awful [sketch of frayed pen nib]. That toothbrush was the best I could find till your Mummy gave me a jay which isn't much better.

I heard that you was (this is a new pen!) moloncoly when you went away[2] and for that I feel moloncoly too till I smelt the smell of stale secondhand London all up and down these stuffy streets then I invied you –

I see you now – with a wicked glare in your eye wandering through Clifton killing innocent cats with a meat chopper – exactly as you used to do in London [sketch of Margaret with hatchet, captioned: "This is not a saucepan. It is a hatchet"]. All I ask of you is don't – don't eat them on the hearthrug. The hair is fluffy and you'll only have to spit it out again. Never kill a cow just because it happens to be alone and unprotected, break as few windows as possible, and abstain from beating men about the head with both fists.

I am not very mad but the Mummy is such a time putting her things on that I'm paying you out for it.

Goodbye and love,
Ruddy

Notes

1. Margaret was the younger daughter of W. K. and Lucy Clifford; RK's pet name for her was Turkey. Her mother Lucy (d. 1929) was the widow of the mathematician and philosopher, William Kingdon Clifford; after his early death in 1879 she supported herself by her pen as a journalist, novelist, and playwright. She was much liked as a hostess, and was the friend of many well-known writers.
2. She was at Clifton.

To Margaret Clifford, [11 August 1890][1]
ALS: Berg Collection, New York Public Library

[London] Monday

Dear Turks,

I'se sorry but the blotting was because of the pen; the bad writing was because of the hurry and – there's no excuse for the nonsense. That was because of me. But let's talk seriously. I've seen the Mummy and she is well. Yesterday – no, day before, my Mummy went to call on her and they stayed talking for a long time. Last night which was Sunday I dined with your Mummy – fruit and cream and *good!* – I missed you at that table, but it's good to know you're out of this muggy, woolly hot weather. When you have learned lawn tennis you must let me know the exact weight of the racquet that fits you best and I'll get it you. My own notion is that you ought to be able to use a 16/oz racquet in a little time because – as I have good reason to know – your wrists are strong. There's nothing exciting to tell. Your Mummy has got a play on her brain and I've one on mine so you can imagine when we both talk at once about our own play, how pleasantly and intelligently we converse. Atop of the play I've got to give a book[2] to the printers on the 15th of this month and then and then I'm going to take a little fishing rod and leave no address and hunt for fish till its time to come back again, and do some more work. I'm very tired and awful worried and as hot as a baked apple at the back of the oven. If I wasn't so uncomfy I draw you a picture – only you'd say it was nonsense. You're awful growed up all of a sudden. Why can't you frivol and be a baby now and again as I am always

Keep well
Be fat
Grow Tall
Learn Tennis
and

believe
    me
       yours
         at
           twelve
             o clock
              of
                Monday
               morning
             which

                                        is
                              unusual
                    late
              for
        me
  to
        get
              up
                    but
                          I
                              couldn't
                                    help
                                          it
                                                    Sincerely
                                          yours
                              Ruddy.[3]

Notes
1. Dated from postmark.
2. Either *The Light that Failed* or *The Book of the Forty-Five Mornings*; both were finished at about the same time (see 15 August) but RK withdrew the second, which was never published.
3. The undulating closing line is flanked by sketches of birds.

To Margaret Clifford, 15 August 1890
ALS: Berg Collection, New York Public Library

Embankment Chambers, / Villiers Street, Strand. / 15/Aug. 90

Revered Turks

Your Mummy is kite well acause I has just seen her an' tomoworo we goes to Hazlemere to play wif Tennyson.[1] This means to the Pollocks[2] an' I spose I'll see Ethel.[3] Then I'll go fishing and as soon as I have a real live address I'll write or telegraph it to you, but just you go on writing to Embankment Chambers Villiers St. Strand and the letters will tumble in somehow.

I am nearly broked in two. I have done my two books an' I'm dead tired and frabjous an' muzzy about the head. Likewise polumneas and metheoligastical which are serious diseases.

Tomorrow I go. Oh joy! Go like this: – with mine coat tails flying [sketch of RK running]. There's nothing exciting to record. I am past excitement. I dance like this [sketch of dancing man with six arms and six legs]. The extra legs and arms are on account of my joy at being idle. Some day I shall catch a fish [sketch of angler catching fish with rod and reel]. Then I shall be happy but today

I am

> only
> yours
> very
> tiredly.
> Ruddy

P.S.   Don't you cry about the Mummy. She's all right. *My* Mummy has been rather ill.

P.S.   I sees you before the 6th.

Notes

1. Tennyson's house, named Aldworth, was near Haslemere, Surrey. Evidently RK did call on Tennyson: see [late April 1891]. RK says that he and Tennyson never met (*Something of Myself*, p. 90).
2. Sir Frederick Pollock (1845–1937), 3rd Baronet, was a distinguished lawyer and legal scholar, Professor of Jurisprudence at Oxford, 1883–1903. He was a close friend of the Cliffords and edited W. K. Clifford's *Lectures and Essays* with Leslie Stephen. Pollock had a country house at Hindhead, Surrey, near Haslemere.
3. Ethel (d. 1959), elder daughter of Lucy Clifford; afterwards Lady Fisher Wentworth Dilke.

To Thomas Nelson Page,[1] [August 1890]

ALS: Duke University

Embankment Chambers / Villiers Street

Dear Mr. Page,

I've received your book[2] and lost your address – so I'm sending this to McClure who knows all about the whereabouts of us all. I don't know whether I like Marse Chan or Meh Lady best but no matter: I like 'em all and the more since I've heard you speak in nig. dialect to show me how to deal with the spelling.

Come and see me here. I'm supposed to be on a holiday. That is why I am in town.

Sincerely
Rudyard Kipling

Notes
1. Page (1853–1922), lawyer and author, best known as a local colourist specialising in the life of northern Virginia. He was in London on business.
2. *In Ole Virginia* (1887), Page's first book; it contains both "Marse Chan" and "Meh Lady".

To William Canton, [17 September 1890]¹
ALS: Berg Collection, New York Public Library

Embankment Chambers

Very many thanks for your flying note – too long unacknowledged. I am not yet what one might call well but, some day perhaps, I may be.

Considering the size of one baby² it is amazing how it can spread, by merely being unfriendly with its innards, sorrow, blight, blackness and desolation for miles about. I've been down to the sea-side making love to an Ollendorfian dab-chick.³ She was three, and made of dresden China; talked French and English equally well, and I adored her. She *would* paddle; and then sat down fatly in at least two inches of raging ocean, gasping; – *Mon Dieu, Je suis mort*! I laughed too much to help her up.⁴

By the way I see my book of baby-tales⁵ (about babies) is on the market. Have you seen it yet?

With all regards and love to the little one –

Rudyard

Notes
1. Dated from postmark.
2. Canton's daughter Winifred Vida was born in the summer of this year.
3. Heinrich Godefroy Ollendorf (1803–65) was the author of a step-by-step "new method" for learning a foreign language, widely used in the nineteenth century. I suppose RK means that the child was talking in simple phrases.
4. RK describes this child again, in the same terms, in the second of his "Letters on Leave", *Pioneer*, 11 October 1890 (*Abaft the Funnel*).
5. *Wee Willie Winkie*, the first English edition.

To William Ernest Henley, [23 September 1890]
Text: John Connell, *W. E. Henley*, p. 194.

[Embankment Chambers]

Losh a'mighty! Call that rush of compliment a slating![1] It doesn't even give one what-for. Thank Whibley[2] for it, because it's more than I deserve or is good for me; but break him of that trick of trying to get behind my work and saying such a thing is probably intuition rather than observation and so forth.[3] The wharfo' of the man don't concern anybody – all the other papers tell me what I have seen and haven't seen, have experienced and have not experienced, and when they begin to lay down the bounds of the possible it makes me snigger, which is an unholy frame of mind. I am wondrous miserable just now, being in the dead water between two notions, but I ain't miserable enough not to crow and wax fat over your poem in this week.[4] It's gorgeous. It's grand. It's a heap o' nice things. BUT, now O critic, I have thee – why *pad*? It jars like a train going over facing points. Did you intend it that way? I'd give more than one sixpence just for those verses.

Ruddy

Notes
1. A review by Charles Whibley in the *Scots Observer*, 20 September 1890, of *In Black and White* and *The Story of the Gadsbys*.
2. Whibley (1859–1930) was Henley's assistant on the *Scots Observer*; he afterwards wrote for the *Pall Mall Gazette*, and then, for many years, *Blackwood's Magazine*. He published several collections of his critical and historical essays and did much editorial work.
3. "The knowledge of human feeling and human impulse he displays in *The Story of the Gadsbys* would be miraculous did we not reflect that it is intuitive: he probably knew as much at fifteen as he does at twenty-five."
4. "Night Piece", *Scots Observer*, 20 September. Reprinted as no. 3 of *Rhymes and Rhythms*.

To William Ernest Henley, [September? 1890]
ALS: Morgan Library

Embankment Chambers, / Villiers Street, Strand.

Dear Henley,
I am in trouble and furious. You know that I have written within the past few months some tales for MacM[illan's]. Mag and others. Harper and Co. bought the serial rights for America and paid me. The series in MacM. I intended to be one of twelve stories into which I purposed to put as good stuff as I could do, revise extensively and eventually

republish with a preface. Today I receive a note from Harpers (leading publishers) announcing that they have reprinted in book form *The Courting of Dinah Shadd*, the *Incarnation of Krishna Mulvaney*, *The Man Who Was*, and all the others.[1] They will give it their own title. (They have given it their own title). They have not had the decency to apprize me of their intention and to complete the insult they fling a £10 note (the wages of one New York road scavenger for one month) at my head. They call it an *honorarium*. Now I may turn out work too quickly. They are at perfect liberty to steal when I have done my work but the grotesque Yahoodom of nipping pieces off a half-presented foetus and slamming it into the market makes me jump. It isn't literature, it isn't honour. It is simply a piece of cowardly and huckstering sharp-practice to exploit a name that, for the time being, sells. Rather less than 12 months ago that firm in a letter one line and seven words long told me that they would not republish *Soldiers Three*, *The Gadsbys*, and all the rest.[2] What do you recommend me to do? I have of course returned the money and told them that I cannot authorize the thing which they call an "Edition." This month's Harpers magazine brings in an elaborate patronization of me in the Editors Receiving Shop.[3] Look at it. It completes the circle. I don't know who the man is but the whole notion of the article is intensely funny. The American, he says, lives in a "nimbler atmosphere" or something of the kind.[4] When the man was writing that his blasted owners were stealing my work. The critic himself was criticizing stolen work with adjectives stolen from England. I am much too wrath just now to write to the papers disclaiming the Edition, but I must blow off somehow so I go to you, who can see the insult of the burglary – the savage indecency and the utter disregard of anything except the dollars on the part of the leading publishing firm in America. Send me your notions on the matter. As a journalist, two years ago I should have lifted the scalp of Harpers and the amiable critic who "deplores" for me, and my vulgarity. It isn't the critic's fault that he lives, as every man must live, under the laws of his own life and environment, when he calls my stuff lacking in appreciation of the subtler values. The thing that makes it like a Gilbert–Sullivan operation is the raw, rank theft that runs through the "business" of his firm. When a burglar sits down on the front door steps to quarrel with the pattern of the silver-ware that he hath stolen he may be an authority on silver but he is first of all a thief and secondly he lacks a sense of humour. I suppose I shall be able to laugh at the business in a little time but at present I'm too savage to do more than swear.[5]

Ruddy

Notes
1. *The Courting of Dinah Shadd and Other Stories* (New York, Harper and Brothers, 1890).

RK's position was that he had sold only the serial rights, and that the Harpers' publication of the collected stories was a violation of the original agreement. Unluckily, there was as yet no copyright agreement between the US and Britain.
2. See 10 September 1889.
3. William Dean Howells, the editor, deplored the "fad" for RK, and spoke of the "knowingness and swagger of his performance" ("The Editor's Study", *Harper's*, LXXXI [October 1890] 801).
4. "The American . . . breathes a rarefied and nimble air full of shining possibilities and radiant promises" (ibid., 804).
5. The *Athenaeum* of 4 October published a note based on information from RK protesting the Harpers' publication and setting off a correspondence lasting into December: see [November] 1890.

To Oscar Browning,[1] [*c.* September? 1890?]
ALS: King's College, Cambridge

Embankment Chambers, / Villiers Street, Strand.

Dear Mr. Browning:

Very many thanks for your kind note and appreciation. You see I've been a rough and tumble journalist for seven years and all the slating is part of the day's work – to be given and taken as a matter of duty: the papers have very cleverly taken "vulgarity" for the note of attack.[2] You *cannot* combat that charge and it always leaves the critic a little bit above you. It's just the same as saying of a man in a club: – "Oh yes – but *is* he quite a – quite a gentleman y'know?"

I've got my own work to do in my own way and it will be queer if I do not get in the future some reviews and criticisms compared to which the notices of these days will be milk and water.

Sincerely yours
Rudyard Kipling

Notes
1. Browning (1837–1923), a historian, fellow of King's College, Cambridge; for many years a popular master at Eton; he was dismissed from the school in 1875. Returning to King's, he became an institution there. Browning was a notable lion-hunter; no doubt he hoped to add RK to his trophies.
2. Oscar Wilde, for example, had remarked on RK's "superb flashes of vulgarity" ("The True Function and Value of Criticism", *Nineteenth Century*, XXVIII [September 1890] 455).

To the Editor of the *Athenaeum,* [November] 1890
Text: *Athenaeum*, 8 November 1890, p. 627

I maintain that the paragraph which appeared in your issue of the 4th of October was absolutely true when it stated that Messrs. Harpers picked out of the magazines some six of my stories and produced them in book form without asking my permission, and without giving me a chance of revising them, and that they then tried to give me a ten-pound note as compensation for their action.

In their letter to the *Athenæum* of the 1st of November Messrs. Harper & Brothers write of my stories that "all of them save one, 'The Incarnation of Krishna Mulvaney,' had been previously published in *Harper's Weekly*. They were offered to us by Mr. Kipling or his business agent, and we paid for them in each case the price asked." This would lead any one not acquainted with the customs of the craft to suppose that Messrs. Harper & Brothers had purchased the book as well as the serial rights of the stories. This they did not do.

On the 11th of January last my agent, Mr. A.P. Watt, offered them through their London agent by word of mouth one tale entitled 'The Courting of Dinah Shadd,' distinctly stating that he was only selling them the serial rights. In due course Messrs. Harper & Brothers forwarded a cheque for the price asked. If the firm refer to Mr. Watt's letter to them, under date May 12th, they will there find that he thanked them for such and such a sum, "being the amount due for the American serial use of 'The Courting of Dinah Shadd.'"

On the 14th of March last another tale, called 'The Man who Was,' was offered in the same way under the same restrictions. Messrs. Harper & Brothers' cheque followed as before, and in Mr. Watt's letter of May 5th they will again find that he thanked them for such and such a sum as payment "for the serial use of Mr. Rudyard Kipling's 'The Man who Was' in America." The other three stories were offered by Mr. Watt by letter, and in each letter it is distinctly stated by him that he is only offering the serial use in America. The receipts recapitulate this restriction. Should Messrs. Harper & Brothers care to reread their 'Reply' in the light of these letters and receipts, I would inform them that the dates of the letters offering the stories are April 25th, May 17th, and August 1st. The dates of the receipts are June 10th, June 20th, and September 23rd. Reference to that file alone would amply prove that Messrs. Harper & Brothers bought, and knew that they were buying, nothing more than serial rights in five of my stories.

I hold, however, further proof. In a letter addressed to me under date August 27th they advise me of the production in book form of my stories – all carefully enumerated. They do not think it necessary to let me know what title they have given to the thing, but of five of the dragged-together stories they admit that they "were published in *Harper's Weekly* from advance sheets furnished by Mr. A. P. Watt, *to whom we made payment for such use, as agreed."*

To return to Messrs. Harper & Brothers' 'Reply' in last week's *Athenæum*. They inform you that "the additional payment of 10£ was tendered in acknowledgment for the story 'The Incarnation of Krishna Mulvaney.'" In their letter to me of August 27th Messrs. Harper & Brothers write as follows: "We have instructed our London agent, Mr. James R. Osgood, to pay you 10£ *in acknowledgment of our reprinting the stories in the 'Franklin Square Library.'"* There was only one ten-pound note mixed up with this sordid little farce, and that was the ten-pound note that it was not in my power to accept from Mr. James R. Osgood, London agent of Harper & Brothers.

Am I or am I not right in reaffirming that Messrs. Harper & Brothers appropriated my tales without asking my permission, had not the courtesy to allow me to revise proofs before jamming those tales into a job-work volume, and sent me a ten-pound note as a notification of outrage perpetrated?

Since Messrs. Harper & Brothers are so anxious to make clear to the English public that they possess a canon of commercial morality, it is hardly necessary to make clear both to public and pirate that the purchase of advance sheets of five stories does not confer the right of hastily hawking those five stories (and one other thrown in to make bulk) up and down the States in the shape of an unedited, unrevised, unfinished, disorderly abortion of botch-work.

The real trouble, of course, is not with this or that particular picaroon across the water. The high seas of literature are unprotected, and those who traffic on them must run their chance of being plundered. If Messrs. Harper & Brothers had not taken my stories, some other long or short firm would have done so. Only, a pretentiously moral pirate is rather more irritating than a genuine Paul Jones. The latter, at least, does not waste your time and ink.[1]

Rudyard Kipling.

Note

1. The Harpers withdrew "The Incarnation of Krishna Mulvaney" from the *Dinah Shadd* volume and substituted "The Record of Badalia Herodsfoot", which had earlier appeared in *Harper's Weekly*. At the same time they complained, with justice, that RK's attack was ungracious and self-defeating, since it would not prevent other publishers, who had paid him nothing, from reprinting his work in the US. RK later agreed with them. In a note dated 6 May 1898 he wrote: "As regards the Harper discussion, there is no sense in starting a newspaper argument with anyone under any circumstances. I should have taken their money and held my tongue but in those days I thought I did well to be angry. Never again" (Grolier Club, *Catalogue of the Works of Rudyard Kipling* [New York, 1930] p. 38).

To William Ernest Henley, [early December 1890]
ALS: National Library of Scotland

Embankment Chambers, / Charing Cross, / W.C.

Dear Henley:
    Would you kindly let me know at your convenience if the following is rot or what. I can't make it out and I don't seem to have been drunk when I did it:

                                                  Ruddy:

Twilight in the Abbey.[1]

(The Prayer of the Mark Master Mason)

If there was good in that I wrought
    Thy hand compelled it Master, Thine
If I have failed to meet Thy thought
    I know through Thee, the fault was mine

One moment's toil to Thee denied
    Stands all Eternity's offence
For aught I did with Thee to guide
    To Thee, through Thee, be excellence

Who lest all thought of God head fade
    Brings Eden to the craftsman's brain
Godlike to muse o'er his own trade
    And manlike stand with God again

Hard is the rule whereby I move:
    For thou hast set about my path
The praise that turneth man to love
    The blame that moveth men to wrath.

Wherefore, before the face of men
    Great Overseer, I bring my Mark –
Fair craft or foul – in mercy Thou
    Will that I die not in the dark.

And if I die as betters died
    Who railed not at thy high intent
Give me that heart, so long denied,
    Manlike to bear my punishment

> Or if forbid the weakling plan
> And if the darkness close indeed
> Help me to need no help from man
> That I may help such men as need.

N.B.   This seems to be the *first* verse:

> My new-cut finial takes the light
> Where crimson-dark the windows flare
> By my own work before the night
> Great Overseer, I make my prayer.

You can have it if you like or send it back to me with curses. Frankly I don't know what to make of it. If it's good for aught use it this week and don't be wrath.

RK

Note
1. Published under this title in the *National Observer*, 6 December 1890; collected, in much altered form, as "My New-Cut Ashlar" (*Songs from Books*).

To Caroline Taylor, [early December 1890][1]
Text: Copy, University of Sussex

[Embankment Chambers]

Dear Miss Taylor
   Would you care for me to come over between 8–8-30? And if I come would Mrs. Hill think fit to see me?

Sincerely yours
Rudyard Kipling

Note
1. Caroline Taylor and Mrs Hill were in London on their return to the United States following the death of Alex Hill in India on 23 September. The letter, though undated, was written on stationery with the Embankment Chambers letterhead (note on copy by W. M. Carpenter, who owned the now-lost original). Since RK could have had no such letterhead before Caroline Taylor and Mrs Hill left London for India on 25 October 1889, the letter must belong to one or the other of the dates on which Mrs Hill's diary records RK's calls on them at the Hotel Metropole in 1890: 1 December, "Mr. Kipling called"; 5 December, "Mr Kipling called on Carrie" (MS, Cornell). These were the last meetings between RK, Mrs Hill, and his former fiancée.

To Walter Besant, [December 1890?]
ALS: Dalhousie University

Embankment Chambers, / Charing Cross, / W.C.

Dear Mr. Besant:

Very many thanks for your kindness. Not a little step do I move down the ringing grooves of small change[1] till July next when the American copyright ought to be through.[2] After that a book on India might be worth vending:[3]

It is good to learn that Hardy isn't angry.[4] It shall not occur again.

Sincerely

Rudyard Kipling.

P.S.

I have a pig of a (Indian) publisher[5] who hasn't submitted any statement of accts for near 2 years. What will I do to him? Hand him up to the "Authors" or come to Portugal Street about it?

RK

Notes

1. Cf. Tennyson, "Locksley Hall", l. 182.
2. British authors received copyright protection in the United States by the act that came into force in July 1891.
3. Perhaps *The Book of the Forty-Five Mornings*. It was still being talked of as late as 3 October 1890 in the *St James's Gazette*. RK must have decided against publishing it not long after.
4. Presumably over the publication of "The Rhyme of the Three Captains", *Athenaeum*, 6 December 1890. This was RK's revenge on the Harpers for publishing the unauthorised *Dinah Shadd* (see [September? 1890] and [November] 1890) and on Walter Besant, William Black, and Thomas Hardy for publishing a letter in defense of the Harpers (*Athenaeum*, 22 November 1890, p. 701). RK condenses them into a triple pun at the end of the poem: "the bezant is hard, ay, and black".
5. Thacker, Spink and Co.

To Robert Underwood Johnson,[1] [1890][2]
ALS: Library of Congress

Embankment Chambers, / Villiers Street, Strand.

R. U. Johnstone Esq
Dear Sir

In reply to your letter 22nd ult—a "step-dance" is just a breakdown or walkround.[3] The Lancashire and Northern regiments pride themselves on their step dancing and superior performers are envied and respected. The word step-dance is used also in Music halls where it covers the word clog-dance. But though a clog-dance is a step-dance every step dance is not necessarily a clog-dance.

What Ortheris would do to impress the headman would be to dangle his hands loosely at his sides, backs of the hands outwards, begin to whistle his own accompaniment softly and double-shuffle heel and toe towards the Burman.

Since you broach the subject of words may I ask whether you are acquainted with a word suggested by my friend Mr Wolcott Balestier[4] in place of the clumsy phrase "telephonic despatch" etc. *viz. telepheme* which I believe was first put forward in the Rochester N.Y. Post-Express in 1881 and which Mr Balestier tells me is used by telephone exchanges on their bills and has gained a certain currency in the U.S.[5]

Sincerely
Rudyard Kipling.

Notes

1. Johnson (1853–1937) was associate editor of the *Century Magazine* until 1909 and then editor until 1913. He was a founder of the American Academy of Arts and Letters and its secretary until his death; Ambassador to Italy, 1920–1.
2. The internal evidence suggests that the letter comes from the first half of 1890, but it is impossible to be certain.
3. The reference is to "The Taking of Lungtungpen" in *Plain Tales*; at the end of the story Ortheris "began rowlin' his eyes an' crackin' his fingers an' dancin' a step-dance for to impress the Headman."
4. Balestier (1861–91), an American, was agent in London for the New York publisher John W. Lovell, with offices in the precincts of Westminster Abbey. He had also formed a partnership with William Heinemann to publish reprints of English language works on the continent, in direct competition with the established Tauchnitz editions. A man of powerful charm, Balestier was quickly established in London literary society just as RK himself was rising to fame. The friendship between RK and Balestier is not clearly documented, but it went back to the first months of RK's London career.
5. The first of only two instances of this word in the *OED* is by Balestier in the Rochester *Post-Express*, 5 August 1882. Balestier was a native of Rochester.

To the John W. Lovell Company,[1] [1890]

ALS: Facsimile, *Soldiers Three*, Authorized Edition, New York, John W. Lovell Co. [1890]

Gentlemen:

Your country takes the books of all of the other countries without paying for them. Your firm has taken some books of mine and has paid a certain price for them though it might have taken them for nothing.

I object to the system altogether but since I am helpless, authorize you to state that all editions of my property now in your hands have been overlooked by me.

Yours,
Rudyard Kipling.

Note
1. The firm of Lovell was represented in London by Wolcott Balestier, who was authorised to offer payment to British authors for the reprinting of their works in the US by his firm. Lovell was a notorious pirate, but he was now acting in anticipation of the passage of an international copyright agreement between Britain and the US, hoping to acquire a goodwill that would carry over into the new day of business affairs guaranteed by copyright. RK agreed to let Lovell's editions of his books carry the phrase "Authorized Edition", an agreement that probably testifies to the persuasive powers of Balestier. The first of RK's books to be published by Lovell in the US, *Plain Tales from the Hills*, is dated 9 January 1890, but such dates are unreliable.

To George Allen, [*c.* 5? January 1891]

ALS: Dalhousie University

Embankment Chambers, / Charing Cross, / W.C.

Dear Mr. Allen

That is a Royal gift – fit for a Prince. I shall have to remodel my general life to live up to it – but it hews paper like a sword. Very many thanks for it and more for your kind wishes that come atop of many kindnesses in the past.

I'd sell all my success just now for ten hours of hot sunshine. Therefore we are all going down to Brighton tomorrow[1] to see if the coast is clear. England is the vilest land alive. Mercifully I ought to be back in Lahore next September.[2]

May you have a happy (that is to say a warm) new year.

Yours affectionately
Ruddy.

Notes
1. "We" are RK and his parents. A letter from JLK to [Mrs Clifford], 6 January 1891, written from the Grand Hotel, Brighton, describes their walk along the King's Road, RK discoursing to his mother about "those blackguard Americans", watching a dog fight, and admiring a Christy minstrel performing for the crowd (ALS, Library of Congress).
2. This is perhaps early evidence of RK's intention to make the trip round the world that he began in August (see 23 July 1891); or perhaps he means that he intends to accompany his parents on their return to India.

To Norman MacColl,[1] 8 January 1891
ALS: British Library

Embankment Chambers, / Charing Cross, / W.C. / Thursday / 8.1.91

Dear Mr M'Coll

Mrs Clifford tells me something about a suggestion, from the *Athenæum*, of payment for my *Rhyme of the Three Captains*.[2] The affair was a matter, in part, of pure revenge, to the address of Harper and Co who by the way seem to have complicated their original sins by a couple of gratuitous lies in your paper. The thing isn't worth squabbling over, and I don't suppose for a moment that those Yank yahoos will see the drift of my rhymes. But inasmuch as I wrote the ballad on a matter touching my own honour, I should as soon think of accepting payment for it as of selling my own pistol at the beginning of an unpleasantness. Please don't trouble any more about it.

Sincerely
Rudyard Kipling

Notes
1. MacColl (1843–1904) was editor of the *Athenaeum*, 1871–1900.
2. See letter to Walter Besant [December 1890?].

To Hallam Tennyson,[1] 8 April 1891
ALS: Central Reference Library, Lincoln

Earls Court Road[2] / Ap: 8: 91

Dear Sir

When the commander in chief notices a private of the line the man does not say "thank you," but he never forgets the honour and it makes him fight better.[3] It would be impertinence on my part to thank your father for his message which is more than a decoration on the field to me. If there be any good in my verses he knows better than I, that that is due to no power of my own.

It's good to hear that your Irish gunners liked Lungtungpen.[4] Soldiers and children are the cruellest sort of critics – I've suffered from them both.

Sincerely yours
Rudyard Kipling

Notes
1. Tennyson (1852–1928), elder son and biographer of the poet, whom he succeeded as 2nd Baron. Until 1892 he acted as his father's private secretary.
2. The house where RK's parents had been living since 1890, after their return from India in May of that year. RK spent more and more of his time there, and though he kept his rooms in Embankment Chambers until about May of 1891, he came for all practical purposes to reside at 101 Earl's Court Road. Trix was there too without her husband, so that the "family square" was re-established for some months.
3. Lord Tennyson had praised RK's "The English Flag", published on 4 April, and Hallam wrote to RK to tell him so. See Hallam Tennyson, *Alfred Lord Tennyson* (1897) II, 392.
4. "The Taking of Lungtungpen", *Plain Tales from the Hills*.

To Unidentified Recipient, 30 April 1891
ALS: Syracuse University

101. Earls Court Road / S.W. / Ap: 30: 91

Dear Lady – for I do not know whether you are Miss or Mrs. – I have just received your very kind letter and write to thank you for it. It is good to be able to give people pleasure and it is nice to hear them say so. But why object so fiercely to Henry James? He's by way of being a personal friend of mine and I fancy that he has given me a very pretty send off in the collected edition which I gather you have been reading.[1] I haven't seen it yet – I never *do* see American versions of my books unless they come over by accident: – and some of the editions are anything but pretty and some of 'em contain stories that I do not recognize. However I would put up with a great deal from your curious book-devillers over there in exchange for so enthusiastic a letter as yours. I only wish I deserved a tithe of the praise you give so freely.

Very sincerely yours
Rudyard Kipling.

P.S.   I've put "Miss" on the envelope and it's all your fault if I'm wrong, because you didn't tell. However I've a notion that like myself, you are not so very old.

RK.

Note
1. *Mine Own People* (New York, 1891) contained twelve stories, six of them collected for the first time. Henry James contributed a "critical introduction" which did not appear in the English edition. By "collected edition" RK means the authorised reprints of his work being brought out in New York by the firm of Lovell.

To William Ernest Henley, [late April 1891]
ALS: Morgan Library

101. E[arl's]. C[ourt]. R[oad].

Dear Henley,
    Very many thanks for cheque. Hallam wrote to me direct. I have been there calling once last summer,[1] and I suppose they knew my address.

Ruddy:

P.S.   It ought to be a first class book for the young men.[2] I wish you could send me *The Admiral*.[3]
P.P.S.   Gosse asked me to go to Hedda Gabler[4] last Monday. This is why my stile is curt and severe, at present date of writing.

Notes
1. See 15 August 1890.
2. Henley's anthology entitled *Lyra Heroica: A Book of Verse for Boys* (1891).
3. *Admiral Guinea*, a play by Henley and Robert Louis Stevenson, privately printed in 1884.
4. Ibsen's *Hedda Gabler* opened on Monday, 20 April, in London, and ran for six weeks. Gosse, who was the earliest of Ibsen's sponsors in England and who was partly responsible for the translation of *Hedda Gabler* used in this production, emphasises the play's "rapid and concise expression" in an article in the *Fortnightly*, XLIX (1891) 5.

To Macmillan and Company, 8 May 1891
ALS: British Library

101. Els Ct Rd. / May: 8th 91.

Gentlemen,

I have just made the unpleasant discovery that a female writer has written and published a book called "Mine Own People".[1]

Under these circumstances I imagine that I am compelled to alter the title of the book now with you. It must now be called "Life's Handicap" with subtitle "being stories of mine own people."[2] I believe there is no objection to keeping the sub-title as it is.

Sincerely
Rudyard Kipling

Notes
1. By Louisa M. Gray, 1883.
2. The book was published in August 1891.

To John Tyndall,[1] 17 May 1891
ALS: Cornell University

101. Earls Court Road

Dear Doctor Tyndale,

Some time ago Mrs Clifford told me how she found you at the end of an illness reading my Light that Failed and saying that it made you feel better. That pleased me. Will you think me impertinent if I take the liberty of sending you with this a small book of mine that has a tale in it called "The Drums of the Fore and Aft"[2] which may perhaps interest you for a little time. If it does I shall esteem myself almost as fortunate as when I first had the honour of seeing you at Hindhead. With sincerest good wishes for your health

believe me
Yours very faithfully
Rudyard Kipling

May. 17. 91

Notes
1. Tyndall (1820–93), a physicist, was Professor of Natural Philosophy in the Royal

Institution, 1853–87, an important populariser of science, and a notable Alpinist. A resident of Hindhead, Surrey, since 1885, he was thus part of the Pollock–Clifford circle that RK knew.
2. Part of the *Wee Willie Winkie* volume. Tyndall acknowledged RK's gift on 22 May, calling "The Drums of the Fore and Aft" "exquisite" (ALS, Sussex).

To A. P. Watt, [June? 1891]
ALS: University of Texas

101.E[arl's]. C[ourt]. R[oad].

Dear Alick,

If it's the sign of a genius not to know what he is about to bring forth then I am a Howling Swell. I've just done *the* very thing fitted for the *Atlantic* and within two or three thousand words of the length they want.[1] I'm sending it over to be typed herewith. Please put it through *quick* and let the *A.* know that they can't print it without a revise. The Finest Story in the World[2] would need revision which means a month's delay. I'm told that Knowles[3] of the XIX is on the track of that tale. Maybe he'll take it. In which case it would be dam effective to lead off the London season here.

        Thine:
        Rudyard.

Monday.

Notes
1. Probably "The Disturber of Traffic", *Atlantic*, September 1891 (*Many Inventions*).
2. *Contemporary Review*, July 1891 (*Many Inventions*).
3. (Sir) James Thomas Knowles (1831–1908), architect and editor; edited the *Contemporary Review* before founding the *Nineteenth Century* in 1877.

To Meta de Forest, [23 July 1891][1]

ALS: Harvard University

[London]

Dear Mrs DeForest,

Forgive what looks like inexcusable delay but my pesky old arm wouldn't work satisfactorily before, though I wanted so much to thank you for all your great kindness to me.[2] I'm here in the heart of an English summer – drenching rain and much mud. However I've been in the country and transferred my young affections to raspberries three helps a day with all the cream I could get. I've devastated one small village and half cleaned out another. They *will* send their berries to London and give one the remnants. The New Forest isn't as nice as Syosset[3] and I haven't been properly warm since I left. Never No never will I go on a German liner again – hot boiled pigs feet and saurkraut don't seem my ideal of grub when there is a loppy choppy sea on.[4] Now the brutes of doctors are trying to chase me out of England again on another sea voyage.[5] I wish to goodness they'd give a man a rest sometimes. Mother's out of town, the Father is going north and I am getting back to the country this afternoon to further educate my arm in the playing of golf. The trouble is that all work of any kind is forbidden; and so I can't tell quite what to do with myself or how to do it.

Will you please give my best love to Mrs DeForest and Miss Julia[6] – her story shall yet be done some day – and remember me to the children if they haven't forgotten.

I've taken the liberty of sending over a photo of a picture of myself – the one in the new gallery.[7] There is a sort of satisfied smirk on it that does not please me much; but it's the best there is. With renewed thanks and all manner of good wishes for yourself and Lock believe me

Yours sincerely
Ruddy

I suppose Rudyard Kipling looks better but it doesn't seem to fit somehow.

Notes

1. Dated from postmark.
2. In New York. In June RK had sailed to New York with his uncle Frederic Macdonald to visit Henry Macdonald. RK travelled as "J. Macdonald" in order to avoid publicity but was detected anyway by the New York reporters. Uncle and nephew found on their arrival that Henry Macdonald had just died; RK thereupon returned almost at once.
3. Near Cold Spring Harbor, on the north shore of Long Island, where de Forest had a house.
4. RK returned on the SS *Aller* of the North German Lloyd.

5. RK sailed on 22 August for the Cape, New Zealand, Australia and India. The trip was cut short by news of Wolcott Balestier's death in December.
6. Lockwood de Forest's mother and sister.
7. John Collier's portrait of RK was exhibited at the New Gallery in 1891; the portrait, showing RK at half length in full face, now hangs at Bateman's.

To William Ernest Henley, [c. July 1891?]
ALS: Morgan Library

[London]

Dear Henley,

Yes you've himitated with a Wannion[1] but some of it *I'd* like to imitate; so we'll call it square.[2] *Is* that thing W.W.? I like it but it's more like cowshit – I mean Cowper.

I can't quite understand the English ways yet. That Edinburgh man[3] calls me a pimp and seems to think there's nothing vulgar in accusing a man of loading up pathos to make a tale pay. I wonder if he knows that men in India do not hang with palpitating eyelids on the taste of the English public and that a man may honestly do his own work to please his own self. You're lucky. You never got pawed over by the wrong Public – the people who came in to the shop and cried "Law! You've been making these pretty things for *us* all the time." But the advice is darned good and the man himself is the very curious insolent brutality to which he objects.

Ruddy.

Keep your hands off this till I've done it. Yah!

The Ballad of the *Bolivar*[4]

We put out from Sunderland loaded down with rails –
We put back to Sunderland 'cause our cargo shifted –
We put out from Sunderland, met the winter gales
Seven days and seven nights to the Start we drifted.

Racketting her dunnage out, smoke-stack white as snow,
Half the raffle loose adeck, all the rails below
Leaking like a lobster pot, steering like a dray
Out we threshed the Bolivar – out across the Bay!

One by one the lights came out, winked and let us by

Running coastwise like a crab, coal and foc'sle short
Mile by mile we waddled on . . . .
Left the Wolf behind us with a two-foot list to port

and so on and so on all through the storm till they cross Bilbao bar and
conclude joyfully: –

Overloaded, undermanned, sent to founder, *WE*
Euchred God Almighty's Storm, bluffed the Eternal Sea!

Notes
1. I.e., with a vengeance.
2. Perhaps Henley's verses "In Praise of England", *National Observer*, 18 July 1891, p. 223, are meant: parts might be called "Kiplingesque". I do not know what the rest of the paragraph refers to.
3. Rowland Prothero, *Edinburgh Review*, July 1891, finds RK's writing full of vulgarity and scandal and speaks of the "intolerable nausea" produced by the "heavily loaded pathos" of "The Story of the Gadsbys".
4. Published in the *St James's Gazette*, 29 January 1892; the text finally collected (*Barrack-Room Ballads*) differs widely from that in this letter.

To William Ernest Henley, 3 August 1891

ALS: Morgan Library

101. / Earls Court Road / Aug: 3: 91.

Dear Henley,

The Pater has sent on your note. Continue with full steam ahead. My book is postponed for at least six months – possibly ten.[1] BUT I don't see that that need make any differ to your necrology.[2] Just you wait till I have been round 't other side of the world and done my Song of the Sword![3] Then you'll be sorry you didn't delay your book. When are your own verses coming on?

Ruddy.

P.S.

Howell's has made me angry.[4] What do you intend to do with him? I had a notion which ended thus: –

Forgive us the slap and the pinch, dear Lord
The whimper, the scuffle and squeal –
We are fighting over our dollies, dear Lord
For we think that our dollies are "reel."

We shall laugh at the things we have done, dear Lord
We shall cry at the things we have said
When the dear nurse Death, comes out of the sea
And bundles us off to bed!

Notes
1. *Barrack-Room Ballads*, published in March 1892.
2. Henley's anthology, *Lyra Heroica*, contains two poems later included in *Barrack-Room Ballads*.
3. Henley published a poem called "The Song of the Sword" in 1892, dedicated to RK.
4. Probably RK had been reading Howells's *Criticism and Fiction*, published in May 1891. Among other things, Howells remarks on the coarseness of the English novelists' sense of reality as compared to the American, and adds: "It is with reason, therefore, on the part of an Englishman, that Mr. Henley complains of our fiction as a shadow-land, though we find more and more in it the faithful report of our life" (*Criticism and Fiction*, ed. Clara and Rudolf Kirk, New York, 1959, pp. 60–1).

To William Ernest Henley, [*c.* 10? August 1891?][1]
ALS: Morgan Library

101. Earls Court Rd.

Dear Henley:
   All thanks for your kind note, but – Keep your hair on. I too saw the thing in the *Star*[2] and was rather amused. It's just another sample of the public whom the reviewer prays one to respect:
   (Here I stopped for a day to see if I couldn't get you a thank-offering ere my departure. I find that I *can* – but the stuff if done in a hurry won't be good so I'm going to let it stay over. It shall come along. You of all men ought to know that you can't hurry rhyme.)
   Touching the influences of men upon each other we two especially are bound up in the queerest chain of give and take and one that I feel sure will last long. At the worst, my very dear man, you can only call me a "bugger" for developing along strange lines, and I shall but love you the more for it.
   Now take these charges from me. Go slow, sleep much and often, and never vex your soul over the children of men. If their work is theirs it will perish. If it be of God it will go forward. Finish the Song of the Sword this autumn. Send the N[ational]. O[bserver]. anywhere that I shall indicate by wire or cable. (You'll get some sketches from the far seas if I live). Wear flannel next your skin; kick Whibley whom I love

and Vernon Blackburn[3] judiciously at intervals and on the bottom and let me find you if I return

Ruddy.

Notes
1. In a letter of 11 August 1891 Henley mentions having received a "charming letter from R.K." (John Connell, *W. E. Henley*, 1949, p. 223). Perhaps this is the letter meant.
2. An attack on Henley and the *National Observer* by Richard Le Gallienne had just appeared in the *Star*.
3. Blackburn (d. 1907) worked on the *Tablet*, and then for Henley on the *National Observer*; afterwards music critic of the *Pall Mall Gazette*.

To Elizabeth Bisland,[1] 13 August 1891
Text: Copy, Cornell University

London Aug. 13, 1891

Dear Miss Bisland,

If you love me with a love which is so rare among pens and ink – do me a favour, please. It's for one of your compatriots. She's a Miss Elizabeth Nourse[2] from Cinn. O. (I decline to spell the rest) and she's more than an average painter who has worked in Paris under pere Durand[3] (whom all good students love) and success has come to her in the shape of an invitation from the Continental Gallery 157 Bond Street, to show two pics. which were in the Champ de Mars Salon this year. Vendredi Saint and A la Fontaine are their names (the first is the better). Can you directly or indirectly give a lift to those pictures in quarters best known to you? If you can, and I feel sure you will, you [will] be helping where help is honourable and justifiable and – but this is a detail – to my large admiration for you will be added gratitude. I'll pay the debt some day if I live.

Sincerely yours,
Rudyard Kipling.

P.S.   Work the American side of the switch. That'll help her most. Hasn't Cincinatti a "Leader" or "Plain dealer" or is it Cleveland.

Notes
1. Miss Bisland (1861–1929), American writer, and co-editor of *Cosmopolitan Magazine*, married Charles Wetmore later in this year. She was the friend and biographer of Lafcadio Hearn.
2. Nourse (1860–1938) first exhibited in 1888; she remained in Paris and had some recognition as a genre painter.

3. Charles Durand, called Carolus-Duran (1838–1917), portrait artist, a founder of the Société des Beaux Arts.

To Wolcott Balestier, 20 August 1891
TLS: Princeton University

London, / August 20, 1891

My dear Balestier:

I hereby authorize you to deal with and for my share in "The Naulahka: a Story of West and East"[1] – a tale written by you and myself in common, and jointly owned by us – absolutely as if it were your own; and I hereby give you the exclusive right and power, so far as concerns my own share in the said story, to sell, convey, lease, or make such other disposition as seems good to you, and to contract for the sale, conveyance, lease, or any other disposition whatever, of any and every right, of any nature whatever, in the said, "The Naulakha: a Story of West and East."

And I hereby declare that your signature, attached to a grant or conveyance of any such rights, shall be equally binding on both of us; and that, without such signature, no grant or conveyance of any right in the story shall be of effect.

very truly yours,
Rudyard Kipling

To
  Wolcott Balestier Esq.
  2 Dean's Yard, S.W.

Note
1. This is the earliest reference to *The Naulahka* in RK's letters, but the story must have been well along by this point. Balestier refers to his collaboration with RK as early as July 1890 (Carrington, *Kipling*, p. 178), and the story began serial publication in November. RK was just on the point of departure for his tour around the world, and had presumably completed his part of the story. Something of Balestier's influence over RK is suggested by the fact that negotiations for the publication of *The Naulahka* were taken out of Watt's hands and left entirely to Balestier (A. P. Watt to JLK, 20 November 1891: ALS, Sussex; notes on RK by Howard Rice, Marlboro College).

To Olive Schreiner,[1] 23 September 1891

ALS: University of Sussex

Cogills Hotel / Wynberg:[2] / Sept: 23: 91.

Dear Miss Schreiner

Your yesterday note has just come in. All thanks for it but . . . what *can* you know? It's sweet of you to hold a good opinion. I wonder if you'll think very much the worse of me if and when I forfeit it.

I've taken the liberty of sending you a book that contains the whole of the verses you do me the honour to like.[3] You have the same creed as myself I know but look to it that the very vehemence of your own desire to help others does not lead you into sorrow.

Now I go very far away but when I return to England in February I shall feel indebted to you if you would let me help you in the putting out of any work you may have in hand. My agent – he who saves me all my troubles in fighting with publishers and wasting time in bargaining – is Mr A.P. Watt, 2 Paternoster Square E.C. I don't know of course what your views are about intermediaries but since I know the comfort of mind that Mr Watt has brought to me I don't think I can go wrong in recommending him to you. He is very kind and nice and does everything for you except – writing your book. That we have all to do by ourselves isn't it?

Sincerely
Rudyard Kipling

P.S. If all the girls in all the world sat quiet and still at the right moments by all the men in all the world when those were in trouble we should all be perfectly happy instead of being hurt and worried. I'll show you about this time next year why Maisie was made as she was.

Notes

1. Schreiner (1855–1920), South African writer, published her best-known work, *The Story of An African Farm*, in 1883.
2. This is the only letter I have found from the period of RK's long tour in 1891–2. He left Southampton on the SS *Mexican*, 22 August 1891, bound for the Cape via Madeira. He arrived in Cape Town on 10 September. On 25 September he left Cape Town on the SS *Doric* for Wellington, New Zealand, where he arrived on 18 October, after touching at Hobart, Tasmania. After travels in the North and South Islands of New Zealand, he sailed on 6 November from Bluff for Australia via Hobart, Tasmania, on the SS *Talune*. He arrived in Melbourne on 18 November, and, after visiting Sydney, took the SS *Valetta* from Adelaide for Colombo on 25 November. From Colombo he crossed to India at Tuticorin on 12 December, and reached Lahore about the 17th or 18th. On the news of Wolcott Balestier's death, RK left Lahore about Christmas eve and arrived in London on 10 January 1892. His trip was thus cut short by about a month.
3. Presumably *Departmental Ditties and Other Verses*, 6th edn, 1891.

To Louisa Baldwin, 17 January 1892
ALS: Library of Congress

Langham Hotel, / Portland Place, London. W. / 17/1/92

Dear Aunt Louie

By this light prepare yourself for that which is coming in your own family! I am, for rare and singular merits which I cannot at this present moment realize or detail, to be married tomorrow to the sister of the man with whom I wrote the *Naulakha*,[1] now running in the *Century*. The affair has been going on for rather more months than I care to think about in that they were sheer waste of God's good life but – unless Miss Balestier or myself go down with the influenza before tomorrow noon – we are launched on the threshold of things from All Soul's Church. That I am penetrated with the solemnity of things in general is true. That I am riotously happy is yet more true and I pray that out of your own great store of happiness you will bless us, because we have gone through deep waters together. At present *only* her mother and sister[2] are down with influenza: and as Aggie and Georgie, and Phil follow suit, only Ambo will be any sort of family man present at the wedding.[3] Afterwards we go away for a year's wandering round the world from Mexico and Texas to Honolulu, Japan and India unless anything happens.

Tell Stan with my best love that when and if his time comes he will learn a few more things than he fancies he knows at present. But you will give him a festive and white satin favour wedding. Mine is of even a quieter nature than my Father's was. Wish then that my life may be quiet.

> Your loving nephew
> Ruddy.

P.S.   Edie is acclimatized in Lahore[4] and amuses me immensely. She will become an Anglo Indian in time and I honestly believe that, after her first attacks of fever, she will be very well indeed. She seems quite a different person from the Edie of England.

Notes
1. Caroline Balestier (1862–1939), the elder of Wolcott Balestier's two sisters. RK had received news of Wolcott Balestier's death at the end of December and had at once broken off his world tour to hasten home from India. He reached London on 10 January and on 11 January took out a special licence to marry Caroline. Evidence about the relation of RK to Caroline before this time is exceedingly sketchy and indirect.
2. Mrs Anna Smith Balestier (1838–1919) and the younger of her two daughters, Josephine (1870–1939), afterwards Mrs Theodore Dunham.
3. The marriage, at All Soul's, Langham Place, across the street from RK's hotel, was attended by Ambrose Poynter, Henry James, William Heinemann, and Edmund Gosse,

his wife, daughter, and son.
4. Edith Macdonald had accompanied Alice Kipling back to India in September of 1891.

To Cormell Price, 17 January 1892
ALS: Library of Congress

Langham Hotel, / Portland Place, London. W. / Jan. 17 / 92

Dear Uncle Crom –
I am just returned from New Zealand with news that will turn Crofts' hair pink in streaks. It appears that after months of delay and tribulation I am being married tomorrow to the sister of the man with whom I wrote the *Naulakha* in the Century. This is inexpressibly awful and I ought to feel bad but I am in a state of sinful joy and so write to tell you of it. Wish me modified joy uncle mine. All the family save the bride are down with influenza and the Lord knows when we shall have it.

I've just come off a 30,000 mile trip and crossed the trails of many O.U.S.C.'s. Some Gordons[1] to wit in New Zealand, Kelsall[2] in West Australia. Saw old Dunsterville for a day at Lahore (he has been pasteurized. Lord help the dog that bit him!)[3] He is doing well. Tweedie[4] is P and O sub-agent at Port Said (£1000 a year and married) and we talked old times over only a fortnight syne. The old school is doing well all the world over and I am writing what is nothing less than a flagrant puff of it in an American youthful paper called *The Youth's Companion.*[5] Look out for that!

All love to the Common Room. Tell Pugh that Dunsterville and I forgive him and tell W. C. C[rofts]. that I laugh at his jibes beforehand. "When I said that I would die a bachelor etc."[6] Willes will laugh but I don't care.

Ever your loving nephew
Ruddy.

Notes
1. Three Gordon brothers – Charles, Edward, and Frank – from Clifton, Hawkes Bay, New Zealand, were at USC between 1876 and 1885.
2. Henry Truman Kelsall, at USC 1878–81, practised as a physician in Perth.
3. Dunsterville was bitten by a mad dog at Lahore in 1891 and was sent to Paris for treatment under Pasteur himself (Dunsterville, *Stalky's Reminiscences*, pp. 106–7).
4. Arthur John Tweedie, USC, 1877–9.
5. "An English School", *Youth's Companion*, 19 October 1893 (*Land and Sea Tales*).
6. *Much Ado About Nothing*, II.iii.251–2.

To Margaret Mackail, 18 January 1892
ALS: University of Sussex

[London] Jan/18/92.

Dear Margaret:
   Never was anything less like a wedding. All the household except the high contracting parties are down with influenza and I hae my doots about the bride. You're safe over the threshold long ago but pity me within three hours of it and more things to do than I could in three days. None the less I am idiotically happy and thank you for your cousinly blessing. We get out of this pea soup air as soon as we can but also we come back to all we knew.

Your loving cousin
Ruddy

To William Ernest Henley, 18 January 1892
Text: John Connell, *W. E. Henley*, p. 236; and Sotheby's Catalogue, 21–2 July 1983, item 263

[Brown's Hotel]

Dear Henley,
   Your note came in the midst of many things and – it is answered by a married man. I don't as a rule care to let men into any part of my life outside the working sections but in this case methinks you are entitled to know. I have married Miss Balestier the sister of the man with whom I wrote the yarn in the Century and as soon as may be we are going off to Mexico, Texas, Japan, Honolulu, Batavia and other interesting lands. There ought to be some good stories found on the way if I can judge by what I picked up in the past in N.Z. and elsewhere. Don't bother about the "Tomlinson"[1] proofs to me, but yes, *do* cut out the last six lines. They ain't wanted. You'll get one or two rather rummy poems from me later, please God. The *Lyra*[2] to hand – very lordly and sumshus. Saw Whibley and others of late but am too much up to my eyes in work of sorts to remember exactly what I have done and seen.
   I shan't touch the *Sword*.[3] And I don't see what the deuce my initials have to do with it. All the same, can't you work in "mistress of mysteries, sweet-spoken, soft-spoken, maker of honours, adored"? Something about the clean steel that carves writing on God's blank signet-ring which is the world and so forth? See if it welds in.[4]

                                                Thine ever
                                                Ruddy.

Notes
1. *National Observer*, 23 January 1892.
2. Henley's *Lyra Heroica*.
3. RK had been asked to write a companion piece to Henley's "Song of the Sword" (Connell, *Henley*, p. 235).
4. Some echo of these suggestions appears in *The Song of the Sword and Other Verses*, p. 11.

To [Mrs Edmund Gosse],[1] 2 February 1892
ALS: Library of Congress

North Western Hotel, / Liverpool[2] */* Feb: 2. 1892

and I said – "another parcel!" Please forgive me. We unwrapped that wonder of a shawl in the train and I've been sitting in cinders ever since. It's an Oriental Georgeousity and shall ever be valued as sich. I've seen it a matter of eight times already by candlelight and its beauty *and* its Fringe grows upon me. Thank you again and again. When I twine it round my alabaster shoulder blades – I mean when Carrie wraps up her dishevelled head in it, I shall think of you.

I've got an evil thing of doggerel (you can't make verse when you're fighting with trunks) for your husband's book.[3] Please give it him on trial with my apologies and my love to him and to you. I owe you much kindness to my Carry and I am slow to forget these things.

                                                Sincerely
                                                Ruddy.

P.S.   Whack Philip and the girls[4] from me.

                    Men say tis wondrous strange to see
                    Their children stand about their knee,
                    But stranger 'tis for such as rise
                    Uncomforted by baby-eyes
                    To see in stately order spread
                    The lawless offspring of their head.
                    Repented some for lack of worth
                    And some be Ishmails from their birth
                    But all a friend hath gathered in
                    And all – ah woe! – be mine own kin.

* * * * *

Say, was there ever mortal sire
Who wished his children to the fire?
Unfatherly I make reply
To this my comrade's courtesy: –
"Better it is, these weaklings die
"There shall be worthier by and bye."

Notes
1. The former Nellie Epps, whom Gosse married in 1875. The Kiplings had dined with the Gosses on 22 January, four days after the wedding (Ann Thwaite, *Edmund Gosse* [Chicago, 1984] p. 332).
2. Where RK and CK had gone that day before sailing on the *Teutonic*, 3 February.
3. Gosse was evidently preparing his privately printed *Catalogue of a Portion of the Library of Edmund Gosse*, edited by E. J. Lister (1893). One of the items in this is a "collection of magazine articles and poems published by R.K. in English periodicals from 1889 to 1891" (p. 92). RK's verses are printed as part of the catalogue entry and identified as the "prologue" to the collection of articles (uncollected).
4. The Gosses' son Philip (see 16–17 December 1897) and their daughters Emily Teresa ("Tessa") and Sylvia.

To John Hay,[1] 16 February 1892
ALS: Brown University

Brunswick.[2]/Feb 16/92

Dear Colonel Hay,
    Very many thanks for your kind invitation. I've been wanting to meet you for a matter of some several years and shall attend with joy. We don't come to Washington till you and Mr. Adams[3] are back from the South.
    I fear me that the dinner date however is impossible as we don't leave New York till the first week in March. Tell Mr. Adams that we haven't heard from him. I suppose the letter has, like Bludso's ghost, "gone up alone"[4] and our plans are changed on account [of] Miss Balestier's ill-health. He'll remember that she wasn't very bright aboardship.

                                    Sincerely
                                    Rudyard Kipling

Notes
1. Hay (1838–1905), writer and diplomat, secretary to Abraham Lincoln and afterwards his biographer; Ambassador to England and Secretary of State under McKinley and Roosevelt.

2. RK and his bride, together with her mother and her sister Josephine, had sailed from Liverpool on the SS *Teutonic* on 3 February and had arrived in New York on the 11th; they stayed at the Brunswick Hotel on Madison Square until the 16th, when they visited CK's family in Brattleboro, Vermont.
3. Henry Adams (1838–1918), the American historian and autobiographer, was a fellow passenger with RK and CK on the *Teutonic*. "My only social resource", Adams wrote, "was Rudyard Kipling and his wife and family. With his aid I worried my dinners successfully, and found my pint of champagne tolerable" (to C. M. Gaskell, 26 February 1892: Worthington Chauncey Ford, ed., *Letters of Henry Adams (1892–1918)*, 1938, p. 6). On arriving in the US, Adams had gone off on a visit to South Carolina with his friend Hay. RK and CK did not visit Washington until 1895.
4. "And Bludso's ghost went up alone": from Hay's "Jim Bludso of the Prairie Belle", in *Pike County Ballads* (1871), next to last stanza. RK quotes this stanza at the head of his "The Question of Givens", *Pioneer*, 18 January 1889 (Rutherford, *Early Verse*, pp. 447–50).

To Mary Mapes Dodge,[1] 21 February 1892
ALS: Princeton University

11. East 32nd[2] / Feb 21 / 92

Dear Mrs Dodge –

I hear and obey. *Be Chesm.*[3] On my head be it.

If I thought for a minute that it was a Wee Willie Winkie audience I'd wave a slick pen in the air and address it at once; but I know its a People a good deal more important and discriminating – a peculiar People with the strongest views on what they like and dislike and I shall probably have to make three or four false starts before I can even get the key I hope to start on. However I've one advantage. I've read St. Nicholas since I was a child.

All thanks for the honour.

Sincerely yours

Rudyard Kipling

Notes
1. The editor of *St Nicholas Magazine*: see 22 August 1879. RK contributed ten stories to *St Nicholas* between 1893 and 1898, mostly from *The Jungle Books* and *Just So Stories*.
2. RK and CK returned to New York from Brattleboro on 20 February and were now staying at a boarding house.
3. "By my eyes".

To Richard Watson Gilder,[1] 26 February 1892
ALS: Library of Congress

11. East 32nd Street. / Feb: 26: / 92

Dear Mr. Gilder

Here's the typed poem.[2] I don't want to put in any foot-notes or things or I'd 'splain the Hindustani and the word patteran.[3] By the way every gipsy in addition to his tribal patteran has his own particular one which his woman can follow. It's generally some variant of a cross long arm down [sketch of a patteran]. In regard to the question of price – anything that you think it worth above $100.[4] It appears of course only in the Century.

Sincerely
Rudyard Kipling.

Could you send me by hand a complete set of Naulakha proofs up to the end. Wonder if an initial letter on the notion of the patteran might be worth trying.

Notes
1. Gilder (1844–1909), poet and editor of the *Century Magazine*, in which *The Naulahka* was then appearing.
2. "The Gipsy Trail", *Century*, December 1892.
3. "Patteran" (usually spelled "patrin" and meaning a gypsy trail sign) recurs in the poem; I find nothing "Hindustani" in the poem as published in the *Century*.
4. Gilder paid $150 according to CK's diary.

To Richard Watson Gilder, [27 February 1892]
ALS: Cornell University

[New York] Saturday. We're going out of town till
tomorrow / R.K.

Dear Mr. Gilder,

Very many thanks for the alligator.[1] He shall guide us back to the States again. That story you talk about is – fine – very fine on the face – but what the dooce was it? I misremember the candle in the middle.

The Pater I know would decorate any poem of mine like fits. If you send him the Gipsy Trail he'll go out to the Ravee[2] and draw a camp of wandering gypsies their tent and their horses and bring in a letter piece which will not be so bad.

Let me know if you want it and I'll write him too.

Was it you who doctored the last verse heading for the Naulakha?[3] Some one has shifted a line in the first and last verse thereof and added ever so much to the effect. If it's the typewriter girl tell her I'm grateful as I should be to a Kaleidoscope.

If it's you I'm grateful to a poet. By the way I'm doing a few more lines to the *trail* giving the scenery and the like. I've got at an old caravan song in my papers which might bear working out.

> A boy will go where the maids are
>> When night on the camp descends –
> But a man will go where the blades are
>> For they are the truest friends
> Ashes of fire at even – grass where the red blood ran
>> And the *Kafila* moves with its trampling hooves
> From the camp where I killed my man.

And so on and so forth *with* pictures.[4]

Sincerely
Rudyard Kipling

Notes

1. Gilder gave RK a compass for his journey: "The case is a lizard skin lined with a piece of Jap silk with the Great Dragon on it" (*Letters of Richard Watson Gilder*, Boston and New York, 1916, p. 218).
2. The river flowing just outside the walls of Lahore.
3. "My Lady's Law".
4. Nothing like these lines appears in "The Gipsy Trail".

To William Heinemann,[1] 11 March 1892

ALS: Princeton University

11. East 32nd Street / New York / Mar: 11 / 92

Dear Heinemann,

Yours of the 2nd with dolorous news of the Flue and your troubles. I'm the more sorry for you since your sorrows are complicated by that awful climate. May you have leisure to escape it soon.

The Pacific Mail Co. in their wisdom have cancelled the sailing of our steamer to Honolulu. *Wherefore* we should leave Vancouver per *Empress of India* for Japan on the 6th April arriving Yokohama on the 20th April. Beyond that the cable will tell. I send herewith *all the Naulakha* as it is ordained to be printed in books, including the 22 versified chapter headings, all home made which have cost me not a little thought. It's in full and ample time for printing by July 1st or for matter of that by May. You'll have to see what Watt does. Many thanks for what you have done about Cowen[2] and his letter to you. I think there would be much fun and perhaps a few shekels in the notion. When I return, you'll see from the chapter headings that I've a rough notion of some songs for a libretto. The woman-book[3] can only be done on the spot and it's there that I mean to have a try.

My father is hard at work on the Naulakha illustrations and will go down to Rajputana anon to finish his studies from live [*sic*] there.[4] My wife joins me in all good wishes for you and yours.

Sincerely
Rudyard Kipling

Notes
1. Heinemann (1863–1920) had been Wolcott Balestier's partner in the publishing business and published *The Naulahka* in England. As head of his own firm he became one of the country's most successful publishers, with a list notable for fiction and translations.
2. Perhaps (Sir) Frederic Hymen Cowen (1852–1935), composer and conductor, who wrote much popular vocal music but nothing, so far as I know, based on RK's work.
3. Evidently a suggestion of Heinemann's, never carried out.
4. This project came to nothing.

To William Carey,[1] [26 March 1892][2]
ALS: Huntington Library

[New York]

Dear Carey
This with tears and lamentations from us both. In the first place bless your thoughtfulness in sending the books for the long trail. In the second good bye. We're off today but do thou stay here and presently we will be back again and have good times not as birds of passage but settled down citizens of the United States.[3] I owe you much good time and some day I'll return it if I can.

Goodbye.

Thine
Rudyard K.

Notes
1. Carey, Gilder's assistant on the *Century*, was the factotum and the wit of the office.

2. RK and CK left for Chicago on the 26th (CK diary).
3. They had already bought property and commissioned an architect for a house in Vermont.

To Frank I. Whitney,[1] 29 March 1892
ALS: Library of Congress

The Aberdeen St. Paul, Minn. Mar: 29 1892

To F. I. Whitney Esq.
Dear Sir

I am sorry to have missed you this afternoon at your offices as I should very much have liked your help in the management of a singularly insolent baggage man who contrived to waste between thirty seven and forty minutes of my time in the checking of my trunks from the C.B.Q.[2] to the Great Northern.

In the first place he allowed me to argue with two Swedes one of whom could not write and therefore could not copy the checks for the small matter of ten minutes. Then he explained *not* that he was a baggage official but (I quote his own words) "sort of interested in this business." His interest consisted in asking me a number of impertinent questions which had nothing whatever to do with the business in hand; in misreading my ticket through his own gross stupidity thereby entailing a double walk across the depôt to the ticket office where a clerk had to set him right, and in spending my time which at least was as valuable as his own in sparring with and poking other baggage men in the ribs.

I suppose of course that the matter does not in the least concern your department but there must be some department which it does concern. I do not write in any way in my own interests – the affair being over as far as regards myself – but surely it is trifles of this kind that most affect the comfort of the foreign traveller and which make or unmake the reputation of a road.

With renewed thanks for your courtesy in reserving a section for myself and my wife believe me

Sincerely yours
Rudyard Kipling

Notes
1. Passenger traffic manager of the Great Northern Railway, St Paul.
2. The Chicago, Burlington, and Quincy Railroad.

To Cecil Spring-Rice,[1] [May? 1892][2]
ALS: Churchill College, Cambridge

Imperial Hotel / Tokio

Dear Mr. Spring-Rice

We came over here between showers this afternoon on our way to Nikko[3] whither we go tomorrow morning: so you see we didn't like just to make a convenience of the Legation for one night. My wife sends regards.

Sincerely yours
Rudyard Kipling

P.S.   Get Mowbray Morris's *"Montrose"*[4] if you can. It's worth reading.

Notes
1. (Sir) Cecil Spring-Rice (1859–1918), diplomat, began his career in the Foreign Office in Washington; he was briefly in Japan; Minister to Persia, 1906–8; to Sweden, 1908–13; Ambassador at Washington, 1913–18.
2. RK and CK arrived in Japan on 20 April and remained until 27 June (CK diary). They seem to have spent most of their time in and around Yokohama.
3. Nikko, in central Honshu, is famous for its mountain scenery, forests, temples and shrines. It is now a national park. RK's visit to Nikko with the Hills in 1889 is described in Letter 19 of *From Sea to Sea*.
4. *Montrose* (1892), a biography of the 1st Marquis.

To Meta de Forest, 14 August 1892
ALS: McGill University

Brattleboro / Vermont / Aug. 14./92

Dear Mrs DeForest

We've been fighting with a new and raw and empty cottage[1] for the past four days and have at last managed to lick it into something like shape – to leave alone for a bit. It has been an awful job though amusing in places. I don't think Heaven made me to put up bedsteads.

However we hope – if you can take us in – to come to you for rest refreshment and repair and picking up the scattered ends of the last few months – on Friday. We've a whole host of things to get in New York and so shall encamp at our old boarding house on N.E. 32nd[2] till we've got 'em. We move for New York tomorrow Monday but you see for several days we shall be unfit to associate with. No man can serve down town shops and frolic at Long Isand at the same time. Marshall

Sahib[3] is coming to see us early in September I believe and if we do not poison him with mad Swede girls[4] or drive him into a brook he will sit on our site and tell us about the house.

Oh, by the way, the reason we were mixed up with the Oriental banking corporation was because it is – or rather was, worse luck – my bank in India and in London *and* it happens to have a branch in Yokohama at a meeting of which I assisted in the capacity of a depositor.[5]

Send us a line at 11. East 32nd. Carrie sends you her much love. She's taking an easy day today – hunting servants. Give my severe and respectful salaams to Judith and a hug for Alfred.[6] I gathered from your letter he's better. I suppose I shall see Lock in town. With love to yourself, and Miss Julia,[7] believe us

Yours collectively and exhaustedly
Carrie and Rud.

Notes
1. RK and CK had returned to Brattleboro from their aborted wedding tour on 26 July (see n. 5, below); on 10 August they moved into Bliss Cottage, a small house on a farm near the lot they had bought north of Brattleboro: the house, RK says, was "generally inhabited by a hired man" (*Something of Myself*, p. 109).
2. 11 East 32nd Street, where they stayed on their first arriving in New York.
3. Henry Rutgers Marshall (1852–1927), a New York architect and writer on aesthetics and psychology. He was an old friend of the Balestier family, which was no doubt a reason for his being commissioned to design RK's Brattleboro house.
4. They had a Swedish maid, "newly-landed", who has been identified as Anna Anderson, later Mrs Hammarlund (Brattleboro *Daily Reformer*, 8 July 1971).
5. The collapse of the New Oriental Bank Corporation on 9 June 1892 while RK was in Yokohama took most of his savings and compelled the end of the wedding tour (though there is some evidence that they had already made a decision not to carry it out as originally planned). At a meeting of creditors on 24 June RK had proposed to accept a 25 per cent repayment in preferred shares (CK diary). They left Japan on 27 June.
6. Alfred de Forest (1888–1945), second son of the de Forests.
7. Julia (d. 1910?), Lockwood de Forest's sister.

To Frederick W. Childs,[1] 30 August 1892
ALS: Library of Congress

[Brattleboro] Aug: 30. / 92

private
Dear Mr Childs

I'm sorry I'm not able to help you in the matter referred to in your note of yesterday's date but it is my rule never to supply newspapers with any information whatever. This saves my time, which is valuable to me, stimulates their imagination which is wonderful, and does no harm to anybody. I have not broken the rule yet and America is a bad place to begin in. Again, I am very sorry not to be able to meet you here, for it would have been of service to you – but business is business, and mine, you understand, is keeping still.

Sincerely yours

Rudyard Kipling.

Note

1. Childs (1849–1936), then the Brattleboro postmaster, was also special correspondent of the *Springfield Republican*. He did not persist in seeking to make copy of RK, and the two men remained on good terms.

To William Heinemann, 2 September 1892

ALS: Princeton University

Brattleboro / Vermont / U.S.A. / Sept: 2: '92

Dear Heinemann –

This is the nuisance of going to and fro about the earth – that your mails do follow you and you miss 'em. A much belated and very kind letter of yours has just strolled in from Singapore or Japan or the parts beyond Thule; and I daresay you are wondering the while why on earth I don't write. I'm settling down in a house and my soul is divided between painting floors and hunting for lost gimlets. It is an employment that leaves very little time for the fine arts or literature.

Yes, I've seen a few furious and festive reviews of the *Naulakha*. They give it snuff all along the line and, this side of the water, the book is selling gaily. Hope it's so your side. I can imagine the blind bewilderment of the Teuton translator trying to bewrap himself round Tarvin's slang.

All thanks for the books that have been to Japan and back. Yes, they're all they should be. I made one discovery in Japan that satisfied me. Jap designs must be done in Jap colours and Jap colours don't stay three months. The only thing would be to get samples of stamped cotton from India. That bad little nation over the water is being demoralized by English and American models and their designs are suffering.

Our flight from Japan was a swift one – but dramatic and amusing so far as it was a new experience. The bank *did* smash and took down all I had. The rest is in the air but I fancy we shall pull round. For details in Yokohama see letter in *Times* describing the smash. A year ago I should have worried my head off. Today, things being as they are, I seem not to mind much – and certainly not to fret about it. But it's a poor return for three years hard work.

In regard to your notion about the women – it is under advisement at the back of my head. Tisn't a thing that could be done unless it came and I make no doubt that some day it will come. I've given it a deal of thought and I think I see my way to doing it when it arrives.[1]

Queer news of yours about the N[ational].O[bserver].![2] I knew they would come to town some day but I didn't think they were in fettle to do it so soon. Never mind what Henley does. Words are things to that dear man and someday as he has lived by them so will he die by them. He's acutely sensitive or he wouldn't write the verse he does: and therefore much the more likely to resent the whip-lash across his own bottom. It's no business for a man in the business to criticize his fellow's output [   ][3] Thereupon I advanced an opinion which were better unwritten. If Wolcott had lived we would have seen what we would have seen, anyhow.

Carrie who is largely and imperially organizing the house stops for a moment to send you all manner of kind messages and to thank you for your many kindnesses. Let nothing, when you come over, prevent you from coming up here. We have a room for you and you will see new things and look into a new life.

No, I will not publish as a publish [   ][4] yet. I've a host of things to do and I must have time to write 'em in – time, light and quiet – three things that are hard to come by in London. If we have a confab when you get here I may be able to tell you things as to the American book market which may be of profit.

I've got two stunning Naulakha drawings out of Mary Hallock Foote[5] – Lord knows when the Father will do his share. He's busy over an exhibition in India where I gather that the weather is infernal.

With best regards from Carrie and myself believe me

Yours sincerely
Rudyard Kipling

Notes
1. See 11 March 1892.
2. It moved from Edinburgh to London in June.
3. Five lines deleted.
4. Word not wholly legible: "publishare"?
5. Mrs Foote (1847–1938), writer and illustrator, specialising in western American subjects. It was RK's idea that the western drawings for *The Naulahka* should be a "personal tribute" to Wolcott Balestier. JLK was to do the illustrations for the eastern parts of the story but failed to do his part and the project collapsed (Rodman Paul, ed., *A Victorian Gentlewoman in the Far West: The Reminiscences of Mary Hallock Foote* [San Marino, Calif., 1972] pp. 336–7).

To William Ernest Henley, [early September 1892]
ALS: Morgan Library

Brattleboro / Vermont / U.S.A.

Dear Henley –

After many wanderings your Book[1] has come in and it is a Book. What impresses me most is naturally the Voluntaries which are high water mark and over and above everything else. I love the way in which the music gives back the dull boom, pause, mutter and boom again of the London traffic as you hear it from the centre of the Parks.

My poem please you will write over again with rhymed endings. Swords sing, O Henley Sahib! And yet the way in which your blade comes out of the scabbard inch by inch till it drives back again with a clang on the last line is Good Enough. It is a "high irresistable song" – Most of the Book – but there are certain things, (groping round for some damned word fr'instance) for which I should in the quiet of the Savile like to heave brick-bats at you – exactly as you would like to persue me with javelins for some of my verses most like. Glory be, that we are not all of one mind! –

My time is divided among many things – stables and sewers and furniture and the settling down of a house. It's great fun and it keeps the mind off dwelling too much on words and their texture and composition.

I saw from a chance blown paper that you were whacking somebody over the head about something that somebody said or did not say about the Tendency of my Work – its Drift, Aims, Isms etc.[2] What a sinful waste of power it all is! We don't talk about Art here. We raise oats and colts and that gives me all the more time to work. You might recommend your friend the Reviewer to go an do likewise for a bit: it would open his bowels and keep his head cool.

I've bought back a deckload of notions from beyond sea and I'm busy putting 'em in order against the time that I can write 'em out. Mostly it's a bloody flux of verse which I'm anxious to see developed. The sun and the air and the light are good in this place and have made me healthy as I never was in my life. I wish you could see the place. It's three miles from anywhere and wondrous self-contained. No one can get at you and if you don't choose to call for your mail you don't get it.

Send me a line to tell me how you do; and what Whibley does and when you moved to London all of you and why, and who is dragging who round the walls of what at his chariot wheels and what particular Imp of the Perverse has possessed Barrie to pat James and Stevenson on the head – as I see that he has been doing.

Also, couldn't you persuade the office to send me a N.O. at intervals. Bread I have but the circus I wish to see. And with a Gladstonian Ministry you ought to be interesting.

He has been kicked over by a cow![3] Saw that yesterday. We ought to worship with the Brahmins henceforward, and that Inspired Beef should be bought by subscription and led about with gilded horns. It's a funny thing when you're out of England to watch an Empire between ministries, flapping about like a ship taken aback and to hear the groans of despair among the fellows in the outer port when she lies over on the other tack and all the colonies begin to say – "Now what particular brand of dirt are we going to eat." I saw it and it made me sick, sick, sick. Give my salaams to those who remember me, to Vernon Blackburn and the other. I've got to fly down to the village for paint for the stable and a hundred other things. Keep you well and remember (editorially) that if cholera were called influenza people wouldn't be half so scared. We shall have it here before long I fancy.

Ever yours
Ruddy

Notes

1. *The Song of the Sword and Other Verses*, containing the title poem dedicated to RK and the sequence called "London Voluntaries", published in mid-April.
2. RK is defended against the *Quarterly Review*'s attack on him as a mere "realist" in the *National Observer*, 23 July 1892, pp. 235–6.
3. Gladstone had been charged by a stray heifer in Hawarden Park on 29 August. He was shaken but unhurt; the animal was shot. Gladstone had returned to power following Lord Salisbury's resignation early in August.

To A. P. Watt, 13 September 1892
Text: Letters to A. P. Watt (London, 1894) p. 46

Brattleboro', / September 13, 1892

Dear Watt,

And now, having disposed of business in hand, let me thank you again for the skill, care, and foresight with which you have conducted my writing-affairs for the past three years. Large though the money value to me has been, that is the least part of it. It is the absence of friction and worry for which I am grateful; and mere cash cannot be counted against these things.

Sincerely,
Rudyard Kipling.

To Richard Watson Gilder, [26][1] September 1892
ALS: Syracuse University

Brattleboro'/Monday./25. 9. 92.

Dear Mr. Gilder

Yours of Friday received. The amended poem[2] should have been in your hands on Saturday at the latest.

I note what you say about a two or three number tale. It isn't my usual form of composition but I will consider of the matter and if I have anything that seems good enough for the Century I will send it along to you.

Very sincerely yours
Rudyard Kipling

P.S.   I have a short yarn by me – the outcome of much thought – which is called "The Legs of Sister Ursula." The only hint of impropriety lies in the title of which I am much enamoured. I fear though that no one will take it with such a name – in America![3]

Notes
1. Monday was the 26th in 1892.
2. "An Answer", *Century Magazine*, November 1892 (*The Seven Seas*).
3. The story first appeared in England, in *The Idler*, June 1893; it was not collected until the Sussex Edition.

To Lockwood de Forest, 1 October 1892
ALS: McGill University

Brattleboro/Oct 1./92.

Dear Lock,

I've kept this letter till the last moment so as to wait for things that turned up. Here's wishing you the best of good times in the Good East and the pleasantest of journeys both ways. The family out there have been in sore affliction through the illness of an Aunt[1] who came to stay with 'em for a year and then started to be violently ill (entre nous she rather cultivated her maladies) to the weariness and fatigue of my good Mother. Now Father and Mother both are heartily sick of India and by their letter dated the 30th Aug want to come away. I quote now from the Pater's letter: –

"I would throw up the Museum and India if I could get the maximum uncovenated service pension Rs 5000 which in fact I have earned excepting in the technical details, one that though my salary has been practically Rs 1000 per mensem for the last 15 years it has been technically below it by Rs 100 a local allowance for the Museum which does not count in the Accountant General's computations. Another is that I came out in 1865 under a covenant with the Bombay Government for three years, and it will take a petition and interest to get those three years counted in to my service under the Govt of India. I ought to memorialize on these two heads but I have a morbid horror of going abegging."

Neither of these things seems insuperable to me. Let the Pater only make up his mind to go and do. You stir him to memorialize and petition.

I have my own notions of what to do my side.[2] I wish to goodness tho' that there were a Conservative Government in power. Stir him up to get his pension question settled while you are with him.

Tell Meta, with many thanks for her note – yes we are heeled, well heeled in the matter of supplementary doctors in case any accident should arrive.

Enclosed I send letters to Aunt Georgie and Aunt Aggie – Mrs Burne-Jones and Mrs Poynter. You'll find Ambrose Mrs Poynter's son a delightful man.

Send us a line to let us know which your Indian boat is and when it sails. We desire much to keep track of you. Also tell us if you have an address in the Orient and if so where, or shall I write the Pater direct.

With much love from Carrie and me to you both

Yours
Rud.

Notes
1. Edith Macdonald.
2. RK was able to get high official support for his father's case: see 9 November 1892.

To Mary Mapes Dodge, 15 October 1892
ALS: Princeton University

Brattleboro / Vt. / Oct. 15: 92

Dear Mrs Dodge:

Many thanks for your kind letter with the news of Polly Cla.[1] Touching that joyous and dignified bird H.J.H. is no hog on dollars. He would be just as well pleased with $100 as $250 for he is a rich man. E'en send what you think fit and we'll not quarrel. I'm sorry about its unbookability.

I enclose herewith *The Potted Princess*[2] for your most stern inspection. My rates are $100 per 1000 words seeing this goes nowhere but to Saint Nicholas. I don't think it will run much over 2000 words. If it does the extras don't count. If it doesn't let them deduct $10 per 100 words shortage.[3] I hold the book rights of the tale. Perhaps we'll be able to do some more and make a little book some day; but it's a mighty difficult kind of composition; that public being particular to distraction. Therefore if it does not fit in your estimation, send him back and I'll do it again. There's only one man that could illustrate it and he's my father too far away for this present need. I'll return the proof within 48 hours of receipt, and I do most sincerely hope it will be an acceptable yarn.

Did you ever hear of the monkeys and the poison-stick with which they stirred the poisoned rice till it was fit to eat?[4] Or of the small boy who made himself a Noah's ark on an Indian tank and filled it with animals and how they wouldn't agree, and how the dove wouldn't fly for the olive branch and how Noah was ingloriously lugged to the bank with all his ark and spanked? Or of the small boy who got a blessing and a ghost-dagger from a Thibetan lama who came down from Thibet in search of a miraculous river that washed away all sin (the river that gushed out when the Bodhisat's arrow struck the ground) and how these two went hunting for it together – the old old priest with his priestly tam o'shanter hat [sketch of head with tam o'shanter] and the young English child?[5]

With kindest regards believe me

Yours sincerely
Rudyard Kipling.

P.S. Please return the M.S. of the Potted One: I send 'em to my Mother.

Hamti-Damti chargya chhutt!
Hamti-Damti girgya phut!
Rajah ki-pulton Ranee ki-ghoree
Hamti-Damti kubbee nahin joree!

That's how we sing Humpty-Dumpty in the East when we are small. Tell it to Jack-in-the-Pulpit and *please* put me down for a regular St Nicholas.[6]

R.K.

Notes
1. A ballad about a cockatoo written by H. J. Hunt, an Englishman whom RK had met on his voyage to Japan in April and with whom the Kiplings stayed in Yokohama. RK acted as intermediary between Hunt and *St Nicholas* in getting the ballad published. He also enquired about the possibility of having the verses printed as a book, without success.
2. *St Nicholas*, January 1893.
3. RK was paid $260 for the story (CK diary, 20 October 1892).
4. Written as "Collar-Wallah and the Poison Stick", *St Nicholas*, February 1893; not collected until the Sussex Edition.
5. The earliest known reference to what became *Kim*.
6. The Humpty-Dumpty verses appeared in the Jack-in-the-Pulpit section of *St Nicholas*, January 1893.

To Mary Mapes Dodge, [21 October 1892]
ALS: Princeton University

Brattleboro / Friday:

Dear Mrs Dodge:

I'm glad you like her and perhaps if the children think fit we'll try another – the tale of the Thibetan lama and Kim o' the Rishti for I would sooner make a fair book of stories *for* children than a new religion or a completely revised framework of our social and political life.

BUT – let her Pottedness remain for the very reason that you say. It is suggestive of canned meat. Children are pigs (little ones) in their insides. The title will stick in their tum – I mean their minds.

H.J.H. his money may be paid to me. I'm awfully pleased about Polly and I'll look the proofs over most careful. I made a blot on the next sheet so it came off.

Yours very sincerely
Rudyard Kipling

To William Ernest Henley, 26 October 1892

ALS: Morgan Library

Brattleboro. Vt. / Oct: 26: 92.

Dear Henley,

Of course if I'd had anything about Tennyson[1] you would have had it by this time but I hadn't. I didn't even for a minute try for the reason that the matter was too high for me.

But in regard to Sir Theodore Martin[2] – if he *is* to be the Successor – the chances for larks are lovely! Take thou a big new pen and say so. It's beyond me. As a Laureate he would be priceless. Again the reflections of Arnold,[3] Lewis Morris,[4] Gosse and the others in their own verses after the award would be fun. Couldn't you do that? Thus: –

> *Ôm arataya*! Lo the sage is bust!
> Tune us the zither neither low nor high,
> Saith Charan, nor in Princes put your trust
> ⸱ When Poet Laureates die

I could do better if I had some of E. Arnold at hand. Gosse and Lewis are intermediate colours: but Swinburne and Morris[5] would be fine. Nor would W.E.H. be out of place.

> The immitigable anti-macassar
> The bead-mat and the bible
> The flower glass glaucous and the flower
> Waxen, intolerable, stale,
> Relics of dead exhibitions
> Latent, miasmatic witheld
> Working in darkness forlorn
> Rise, a respectable mist   (damned if I *can* get
> Obese, flatulent jejune   the hang of your lilt.
> Irrepressibly British   This is Tupper)[6]
> Throning Vulgarity *here*.
> Here is the Master's chair and so forth.

Again a new notion has occurred to me. The P[all].M[all].G[azette]. wants to know why they don't write plays. S'pose you set all the fellows and fellaheen from Ouida up and down to say why the other fellows don't write plays. Mrs John Strange Winter[7] explaining why Oscar

W[ilde]. don't write would be beautiful. Commend this to Whibley, who could work it up. Wind it all up with a step-dance and song: –

> Have you got a yearning
>   Mission to instruct?
> Do you carry gall-stones in
>   Your biliary duct.
> Do you find your bladder
>   Or your genius burn?
> Was your wife a prostitute
>   How much did she earn?
>
>> Tell it to the papers
>> Tell it every day
>> But (en passant) let me ask
>> Why *don't* you write a play?
>
> *Why* don't you write a play?
>   Why don't you cut your hair
> Do you trim your toenails round?
>   Or do you trim 'em square?
> Are you sure to enter
>   Fame's immortal dome?
> Do you put your washing out
>   Or have it done at home?
>
>> Why don't etc.
>
> What's your last religion
>   Have you made a creed?
> Do you dress in jaeger wool
>   Sackcloth silk or tweed

You might go on for ever with this drivel. It goes more or less to the tune of *Where did you get that hat*?

I haven't thanked you yet for your long letter with the good news of your migration to London: nor for the N[ational].O[bserver]'s. Maude[8] is a good man, I think, but you are still lean as regards advts. I wish I had things for you but just now I'm busy with long work and shortlings are scarce. I'll see if there can't be something good before Christmas. Send me as it were a few ideas of what you'd like.[9]

The Pater writes me that he is elbow deep in his work t'other end of the world; but there is no other news. The days go peacefully, each with its stint and the Peace of God upon each. Now and again I have to explain the shortest way back again to a wandering reporter who tells me with tears in his eyes that he is a gentleman[10] and proceeds to prove it by trying to get the village cloth-smith I mean tailor to show him my clothes. Otherwise I am deliciously alone and am trying to master the science (*I* think it's a calling) of ox-driving. O Henley, papers are easier to edit than oxen, a yoke of 'em, are to drive.[11] They drained me dry of profanity yesterday in the woods, and as I danced undignifiedly about 'em among the dead leaves, there came unbidden a vision of Andrew Lang in frock-coat and tall hat set to the same work – what tongue *would* he swear in? Today I have a new ox-whip and tomorrow I will try 'em again. It's glorious work for the hinder muscles, and the chest. Winter is just coming on us but each day holds lovelier than the last. Presently we shall be under two feet of snow and if there is a long silence you will know that a new colt and an old sledge has been the death of me.

Never you mind about my living in America. If you saw this life of ours and didn't happen to know your geography, it would be Africa, or Australia or another planet. I have what I need. Sunshine and a mind at ease, peace and my own time for my own work and the real earth within the reach of my hand, whenever I tire of messing with ink. Good stuff will come out of this in God's time which is not my time; and if nothing comes then I shall have led a sane clean life at least, and found new experiences. Half my time in town was spent in hearing and telling how work was to be done, which is extremely interesting so long as you have not much to do. The farmers here do exactly what I did but their club is the lee side of a barn door, and their Art, the how and the why of farming. Therefore are their fences gapped and therefore do mortgages come upon them, and their young stock die. There's not so very great a difference between men after all. Give my love to the boys in town and don't forget the weekly N.O.

Ever yours
Ruddy.

Notes
1. Tennyson had died on 6 October, and there was much casual speculation about the successor to the laureateship. Henley himself hoped to get the appointment. In the interval between Tennyson's death and Alfred Austin's appointment in 1896, RK himself was "sounded" for the laureateship, at Arthur Balfour's instance, but was "not interested" (Ian Malcolm to Stanley Baldwin, 15 July 1943: ALS, Sussex).
2. Martin (1861–1909), drama critic, translator, and the official biographer of the Prince Consort.
3. Sir Edwin.
4. (Sir) Lewis Morris (1833–1907), a popular poet and the butt of the critics.
5. Not Lewis but William Morris, also frequently named on the lists of possible candidates.
6. Martin Tupper (1810–89), poetaster.
7. Pseudonym of Henrietta Eliza Vaughan Stannard (1856–1911), popular novelist.
8. Colonel Frederic Natusch Maude (1854–1933), author of a number of military treatises and studies, contributed three articles to the *National Observer* in September and October.

9. RK contributed only two more items to the *National Observer*: "The Dove of Dacca", 4 February 1893, and "The Lost Legion", 13 May 1893.
10. Two reporters from Boston appeared in Brattleboro on 14 October and "wrecked" the day (CK diary). RK wrote that "I told them I had nothing to say. 'If ye hevn't, guess we'll *make* ye say something.' So they went away and lied copiously" (*Something of Myself*, p. 113). The interviews appeared in the *Boston Herald* and *Boston Globe*, 23 October 1892.
11. These were used to clear the site for the house RK was building.

To Charles Warren Stoddard,[1] 30 October 1892
ALS: Bancroft Library, University of California

Brattleboro' Vt. / Oct: 30 / 92

Dear Mr. Stoddard

Your book[2] has come, been read and read aloud. I don't think it was quite kind of you to send it. I'm settled down for a New England winter, in a grey land among an austere people two hundred miles from blue water, and

"here you come with your old music"[3]

and give me as bad an attack of "go-fever" as I've had for a long time past. The mischief of it is that this time last year I was wandering round Auckland way and missed my steamer to those Islands of the Blessed.[4] I had got over the disappointment but you've stirred me up again. It's too bad. You should keep your Orient liquor for sober-headed folk instead of making a poor fellow who has "drunk delight of travel"[5] to the lees hanker after fresh draughts. Go to! Your book is highly improper, and I doubt not immoral. What has the *hula-hula* (or the John Kino[6] for the matter of that) to do with New England? There are no such things as cocoa-nut palms in the world, and the *lomi-lomi* (which we call *mālish* in India) is a pure invention.[7] A land where people do nothing, if such a land there be, is clearly a wicked land, and it is sinful beyond telling that a man should wear no clothes. *Therefore* you will see it follows that the South Seas never existed; and if they did or do exist I for one daren't believe in them just now. You've broken the peace of an ordered household and set two folks who are gipsies by birth and inheritance longing to take ship again and "get out." In return be pleased to accept as *an example* my sober and continent verses which have nothing to do with roving and roystering and racketting on far away beaches.

Yours hungrily, admiringly and upsettedly
Rudyard Kipling

Notes
1. Stoddard (1843–1909) began his career as a writer in California with Mark Twain and Bret Harte. He wrote poems, books of travel, and a novel that RK read in MS and made suggestions for: see 8 October 1895.
2. *South-Sea Idyls* (1873); republished by Scribners in 1892.
3. Browning, "A Toccata of Galuppi's", l. 4.
4. Years later RK wrote that he did not go to Samoa because the captain of the available boat was too 'devotedly drunk" to trust (*Something of Myself*, p. 101). But the real reason was that the steamship schedules were impossible for RK's purposes: see J. B. Primrose, "Kipling's Visit to Australia and New Zealand", *Kipling Journal* (March 1963) p. 13.
5. Cf. Tennyson, "Ulysses", l. 16.
6. Perhaps "John Canoe", masquerade dancers and their dance in a West Indian Christmas celebration; the term, of West African origin, has many variant spellings. It does not occur in Stoddard's book. RK uses "John Kino" in "Cities and Spaces" in *Letters to the Family*.
7. Stoddard describes the *lomi-lomi* and *hula-hula* in the chapter of his book called "The Night Dancers of Waipio".

To Lady Dufferin, 9 November 1892
ALS: Cornell University

Brattleboro / Vermont. / U.S.A. / Nov: 9th/92

Dear Lady Dufferin

Of course those verses[1] are all at your service. I only wish that they were better. The continuation of them perhaps might give you a line or two worth using. They go on to say (after the two verses in the *Naulahka*): –

These things ye know and more than these – foul secrets of the dead.
Black horror done in Ignorance, by Time on Folly bred –
The women have no voice to speak but none can stay your pen.
Turn for a moment from your strife and plead their cause Oh men!

Help now, and not to us the praise and not to us the gain,
Make room to save the child from death, the mother from her pain!
Is it so great a thing we ask? Is there no road to find
When women of our people seek to help your women kind?

No word to sap their faith, no talk of Christ or creed need be,
But woman's help in woman's need and woman's ministry.

Such healing as the West hath taught that healing may they win
Draw back the *purdah* for their sakes and let our women in.

I am very glad that you are writing about the Fund[2] and only wish I had new verses for it. They asked me on this side of the water to write about it; but I said "no" several times and very distinctly.

This week's mail from India brings me news that the Father has broken down at last (the heart has gone) and they are trying to patch him up for two years more of service by sending him round the coast in a steamer; while the Government sits down and calculates how much he may be entitled to in the way of pension. He thought that he had worked his term of 30 years; but there is a doubt as to whether a certain three years he served under the Bombay Government will count for service. If it does not count and he is kept to the mill, he will assuredly die. I wonder if Lord Dufferin could see his way to saying a word that might help in the matter. I wouldn't ask except that I am honestly afraid now for the father's life, and I want him to be released from his yoke. He is the dearest of all men in the world to me.[3]

Very sincerely yours,
Rudyard Kipling.

Notes
1. "For the Women", originally published in the *CMG*, 18 February 1887; RK used the fifth and six stanzas, revised, as the heading to chapter 10 of *The Naulahka*. The poem is not included in the collected verse, but a much revised text is in *Early Verse* (1900). The verses that RK quotes in this letter are the seventh, ninth and tenth stanzas, but differing in detail from both the *CMG* and *Early Verse* texts.
2. Lady Dufferin's Fund for the Medical Education of Indian Women: see [27] September 1885. RK wrote "The Song of the Women" in support of the Fund.
3. CK's diary for 27 February 1893 notes that Lord Lansdowne, Lord Dufferin's successor as Viceroy, will "use his influence" for JLK's pension. JLK left India for good on 17 April 1893.

To William Heinemann, 19 November 1892
ALS: Princeton University

Brattleboro. / Nov: 19: 92.

Dear Heinemann

Woe is me for a whorson procrastinator – a half finisher of jobs – a reproach among correspondents. On the arrival of a letter I set me down and half answer it with speed, vehemently and to the point. Next day the accumulation of leaves drives over that half letter and in a week I believe that it was taken down to the village and posted with the others. So it happened with your *last* letter. Comes now yours of the 9th and I abase myself in the dust. This shall really be answered and *sent*.

Somehow your casual allusion to those that tended you in your illness sounds like the ravings of delirium. Now I could conceive a fever patient *dreaming* that he was tended by Zola and Fronsiny[1] but the idea of it in cold blood – well, no man could have invented it. You pique my curiosity sore. What did they say and do; and so on? What sort of nurses were they? 'Tis a fascinating vista.

Touching that "Kipling book" I will basely betray to you what it is.[2] A collection of twelve tales such as "The Finest Story in the World," The Disturber of Traffic, The Children of the Zodiac and so forth ornamented and embellished with two new tales of about 30,000 words together. *But* one of the two new tales is strange and quaint being in the nature of . . . well, anyhow *if* you say anything to any one about the new tales I myself will presently take ship and murder you. I'll tip a line and a hint to Watt on the matter and you shall not be ruined but established. You have a lovely list of your own as I see it in the ads. but I think Le Caron[3] is the big coup. I have only seen bits from that book so far and I yearn for the rest. Aha! And they said my *Mutiny of the Mavericks* was improbable! It might have been a page out of Le Caron's book. Read it and judge. The Irish talk much of their honour but do not sweat to vindicate it.

Let us know as soon as may be how the Naulakha receipts are likely to run and what the expenses have been in getting it out.[4] I want to know where I stand before the year is ended. We hear of dire and awful fogs in town, of omnibusses nearly killing Gladstone and we chuckle. You, unluckily, have delayed coming over here till too late in the year so now the North Atlantic is very angry and the snow is beginning to fall in Vermont. However we look forward to your coming in the spring. I don't think this getting of colds in England is a good sign. What you need is light and dry air.

With all regards from my wife and myself

Yours ever
Rudyard Kipling

Notes
1. Name not clearly legible.
2. *Many Inventions* (1893) contained fourteen stories, four of them new: "A Matter of Fact", "In the Rukh", "Love o' Women", and "Judson and the Empire". Which of these is the one that RK calls "strange and quaint" is anyone's guess.
3. Major Henri Le Caron (pseudonym of Thomas Miller Beach), *Twenty Five Years in the Secret Service* (1892), an exposé of Irish-American Fenian activity, was one of Heinemann's biggest early successes.
4. On 2 March 1893 RK received £296.3.11 from Heinemann as his half-share in *The Naulahka* (CK diary).

To Mary Mapes Dodge, [24 November] 1892
ALS: Princeton University

Brattleboro. / Thanksgiving. / '92

Dear Mrs Dodge,

Your note and the monkey tails[1] have come.

The elephant tale did not come out in verse. At least I lathered away at it ballad fashion and it carried me out ever so far beyond child's depth. However I bethought me of some notes that were by me on elephant capturing (the which is a great science) and putting the surroundings into a Keddah camp made that which I send you now.[2] I think it will illustrate not so badly. It's long but I fear me I can't cut much more but if you like it I will try. Perhaps the little verse and the descent of the elephants to the plains is not needed but I got so interested I forgot brevity.

Now if that tale please you I will do "Tiger-Tiger"[3] – the tale of the man eater who was ignominiously squelched in his lair by the charge of the village buffaloes under the command of the little boy herd. That's a true tale.

Also, there will be (D.V.) a wolf tale, "Mowgli's Brothers."[4] *He* was a wolf boy (we have them in India) but being caught early was civilized. His brothers the wolves followed his career respectfully and afar (but they wanted food and were used to three meals a day) from village to village till at last Mowgli's too faithful retainers became a nuisance and he took council with a holy man in a grove and the upshot was that he went out in the moonlight and explained things to those four grey wolves of Oudh and they saw the justice of his demands and left him in peace.

Then after that (if you care to have the set of six finished) we'll do a camel tale.[5] I haven't looked up my notes for that but it should come. Altogether the six ought to make a little book. The question is won't they be rather too much of a load for St Nick? Consider the invoice.

The Potted Princess
Collar Wallah and the Poison Stick
Toomai of the Elephants
"Tiger-tiger"
Mowgli's Brothers.

And the Camel. It will be a regular Zoo. I'm interested in them and

want to finish them off before my spring work sets in.* Here with I
return *Collar Wallah* for proofing.

Very sincerely yours
Rudyard Kipling

*there ought to be a regular title for all six. Noah's Ark tales? or how.

Notes
1. "Collar-Wallah and the Poison Stick".
2. "Toomai of the Elephants", *St Nicholas*, December 1893. This and the next two titles
   are all part of *The Jungle Book*. A *keddah* is an elephant corral. RK finished the story on
   16 November (CK diary).
3. *St Nicholas*, February 1894.
4. *St Nicholas*, January 1894. Finished on 29 December (CK diary).
5. Never written, so far as I know.

To Louisa Baldwin, 29 November 1892
ALS: Dalhousie University

Brattleboro / Nov: 29: 92.

Dear Aunt Louie
Yours of the 10th enclosing letter from Louise Rebentisch in regard to
German translations of my books has stayed by me until I could find
out how matters stood on the continent.

To the best of my belief most of my books are translated already but I
have written to Watt and asked him to let me know which remain
untouched.

I get so many demands for translations that it is hard for me to
remember what has been done and what undone.

However there will be a new book of mine coming out in a few
months. Shall I make over the German translation to your friend?[1] I
don't want to write to her myself because it would look as tho' I were
doing her a favour, or she might think so. Best have it done through
my agent; but please let me know. I'm very busy and very happy up
here among the hills. The winter snows have not come yet but we
expect them so to speak every minute and sleighs and snow shoes are
being got ready with the fur coats and rugs. We two are also waiting
for another arrival. He is expected late next month or early in January
and very many things have to be got ready against his coming. He'll be
a snow baby but I hope none the worse on that account. I hear great

and glorious things of Stan his marriage.[2] Give him all my best wishes and tell him if he really wants excitement he should turn to and build a house. We've just got our stone foundation in – it was a race against the snow – and we feel vastly rich and settled by consequence.

Next summer may be we shall have to cross the water and look at London again. At present when I read of the week of black fog I rejoice in our diamond clear weather and sunshine up here. Edie should be with you by this time almost. I'd give a good deal to hear her experiences of a year in the Gilded Orient.

All love to Uncle Alfred and yourself and to the dear ones in England.

> Ever your nephew
> Ruddy.

Notes
1. I cannot find that she published any translation of RK.
2. Stanley Baldwin married Lucy Ridsdale on 12 September.

To William Heinemann, 6 December 1892
ALS: Princeton University

[Brattleboro] Dec/6/92.

Dear Heinemann –

All of which is interesting but superfluous. I send you Smalley[1] of the *Tribune* on the same head.

Your letter says everything that a man could say to carry conviction: *but* you omit to state that Ouida threshed this thing out personally with *Wolcott* about a year and a half ago as the files in Waugh's office ought to show.[2] She has therefore no reason (save to defile the graves of the dead) to bring the matter to light again.

'Tis a stale old whore any way and I suppose her book sales are running down and she wants to lift 'em. Ask McClure how he got on with her – whether she didn't make him weep and tear his hair.[3] It's a sweet sight to see a woman doing business as a man and *then* claiming all the advantages of the sex.

Carrie is not a little amused over the correspondence. She knows the thing from the inside and heard Wolcott tell of his interviews with the bitch.

All this rowing, seems to me, isn't bad for Heinemann his firm.

> Thine
> R Kipling

Notes

1. George W. Smalley (1833–1916), London correspondent for the New York *Tribune*.
2. Ouida (Marie Louise de la Ramée, 1839–1908), popular novelist; she had written a letter to *The Times*, 22 November, to protest the forthcoming publication of her *Tower of Taddeo* by the firm of Heinemann and Balestier in a European edition that would compete with her old publisher Baron Tauchnitz's English list. She called Heinemann "treacherous, mean, and unjust", and said of Balestier, to whom she had sold the rights in the book, that he was "a singularly sharp Yankee". Heinemann replied merely by quoting the terms of the contract that Ouida had signed, which made no reservations and gave full rights to Balestier and his firm without further stipulation of any kind. Arthur Waugh had been Balestier's assistant in the London office of John W. Lovell.
3. Having failed to sell a romance to McClure, Ouida published a letter in *The Times* calling him a pig-dealer, a maggot, and a toadstool. RK, she said incidentally, "has neither knowledge of style nor common acquaintance with grammar, and should be whipped and put in a corner like a naughty child, for his impudence in touching pen and ink without knowing how to use them" (see Peter Lyon, *Success Story: The Life and Times of S. S. McClure* (New York, 1963) pp. 108–9).

To Henry James, [19 December 1892]
ALS: Harvard University

Brattleboro' / Vermont. / U.S.A.

Dear Mr James:

In the first place our salutations after long silence. In the second a Merry Christmas – if the London sun allows.

I've just been down to New York on a shopping expedition; and met there Mr Adams[1] your friend who, off steamers where he is adorable, is painfully civilized and wears a tall silk hat – a thing I have not seen since June.[2]

Late enough – but I couldn't get a decent copy before – we are sending you a copy of the Barrack Room songs[3] not to be read necessarily but in proof of our regard. Mother and Josephine[4] are here in our wee house for Christmas (no snow yet but we expect sleighing every day) and after Christmas there should be yet Another in the house whose arrival will be dearly welcome. When that International Episode[5] is over we hope to be coming over to see you when there is a reasonable certainty of sunshine in town. Here we become angry at an overcast day and accept God's light as though it were in the nature of things – as indeed I am beginning to believe that it is. The special beauty of the weather is that one can work largely, longly and continuously and the burden of the work evaporates in the sunshine so that a man can do much and yet not feel that he is doing anything. I wish to goodness that you could come over and be driven over stone walls in an ox cart. That is Life.

We all send you our loves – Josephine upstairs; Mother flitting generally through the house; Carrie at the table here and I also. Josephine is much better in health and has followed the Inky Way (only a child's tale but still it is printed).[6] I do not see therefore what right she has to send messages. Once again, a good new year to you and all happiness.

Affectionately yours
Rudyard Kipling.

Notes
1. Henry Adams.
2. That is, since leaving Japan.
3. *Barrack Room Ballads and Other Verses* (1892).
4. Mrs and Miss Balestier.
5. The title of a Henry James story (1879).
6. *Life and Sylvia: A Christmas Journey* (New York, 1892).

To Lady Dufferin, 21 December 1892
ALS: Public Record Office of Northern Ireland

Brattleboro / Vermont. / Dec: 21. 92

Dear Lady Dufferin,

Very many thanks for your letter of the 6th and what you say about the Father's three years' service. It means a good deal to us if the government sees it in a decent light.

Your "press" enemies will find out one of these days that your lines were in the *Pioneer* (most of them) not more than five years ago:[1] but it is never good to interfere with that thing called the public. It knows so much more of everybody's business than everybody does. I should very much like to see your article when it comes out – the more since the Missionary does not (I speak of him in bulk) quite understand why you should save bodies and leave souls alone. It is cheaper and much prettier on paper to save souls. If at any time you should need some verses at the head of chapters or anything, I would do my best to try to make something good and new for you. I've seen one side of your big work in India that is not the side generally seen: and I don't think that even you realize the blessings that it has brought.

Again with many thanks for Lord Dufferin's kindness believe me

Very sincerely yours
Rudyard Kipling.

Note
1. "The Song of the Women": see [*c.* 25 April 1888].

To William Ernest Henley, 3 January [1893]
ALS: Berg Collection, New York Public Library

Brattleboro / Vt. / Jan: 3:

Dear Henley,

So the Florio was you.[1] I might have known it. Indeed I was sure but I wanted to send you the story and the story wasn't good enough. Then I hove it into the waste; and after that I've been busy with domesticities that stopped work for a while. Now everything is happily over – but I *do* wish she hadn't had the bad taste to be born on Gladstone's birthday.[2] That reconciles me to her being a girl. If she had been a boy 'twould have been my duty to stand her on her head in a drift lest she also should disgrace the Empire.

You can guess how happy we are: all things going so excellently. Her chin is mine and the rest is dough but there's no doubt about the chin. Nor unluckily about the temper which is anything but civilized. I've been neglecting prose for verse and besides I've struck a vein of animal yarns that is leading me further afield than I thought. Only give us time and your tale shall be done. Thou knowest that I cannot do things to order without spoiling 'em

Your lament over the weather makes me weep. I've got to take the sun as a right and only your lament reminds me that the past weeks have been clear blue from day's end to day's end. 40° in the sun at midday and −30° at night. Yesterday we had our first sleighing snow – and a thaw and a frost again. The result is a glair which we call the crust and all the horses are out of their skins and all our sleigh-bells are on, and before tonight some of us will be tipped out. I'm extemporizing a sledge to slide down the hills with – a box on a board and perhaps the most dangerous business you could well get into. There is absolutely no finality to a slide down hill until you hit a stone wall.

Your note is scrappy and shows the influence of the weather sorely but what you say about advertisements is cheering. That means the paper is making headway.

Your plays with R.L.S.[3] haven't come in yet but I wait patiently – the steamers are badly demoralized by weather. Only Moody's prayers to his fetisch keep 'em afloat some of them.[4]

God send you a good new year and the half of all you desire. Give my love to the boys.

Ever
Ruddy.

Notes
1. The first volume in the series of "Tudor Translations" edited by Henley, the John

Florio translation of Montaigne, with introduction by Saintsbury (1892).
2. Josephine Kipling (1892–9) was born on 29 December.
3. Henley and Stevenson, *Three Plays* (1892).
4. The American evangelist Dwight L. Moody was a passenger on the German liner *Spree* when it was disabled in the Atlantic *en route* to the United States in December. Moody led the passengers in prayer before their rescue.

To Edward Lucas White,[1] 3 January 1893

ALS: University of Texas

Brattleboro. / Vt. / Jan: 3: 1893.

Esteemed Younger Brother in the Craft

I am as you say a very busy man just now, or I should very much like to sit down and answer your communication at fitting length. However I'll e'en answer your questions for I know that when I come across a thing in a book that I can't see the drift of I sit on thorns till it is explained.

(1) So far as I remember Mrs Herriott was considerably upset.[2] She had guarded her low cut dinner dress once before with a fan to hide the heave of the bust. What Gadsby meant, in his dread of a scene, was that she was beginning to pant and gasp again. Properly speaking that should be acted to make it clear.

(2) It took me three weeks to work out the way from the trap across the quicksand[3] – and I'm through with it. I don't know anything about Lovell's printing but I *do* know that I'll be peculiarly blowed if I go through the explanation of that miz-maze again for anyone. So there!

3. I know Plato as a man knows fossils – from the Bohns:[4] but your two friends I know not.[5] The tale is older than Plato by a few thousand years, at any rate; but men even lower than Peachey and Carnehan made themselves kings (and kept their kingdoms too) in India not 150 years ago. All "king" tales of that kind date back from the Tower of Babel.

4. In regard to the verses.[6] Get a friend to find the tune that fits "Trouble in the North etc." and I think you'll find it's Marching Through Georgia. We sang a version of that song going up to Afghanistan in 1880. Our men said: –

> "So we'll sing the chorus from Jagdullak to the sea
> As we go marching to Kābul.

There's some more to it which I've added and doctored and done up in various ways but it's of no account. I will however remember your bequest.

If you're interested in metres of course you know Lanier's work.[7] There's some most excellent suggestion there for a man anxious to experiment in new forms. The Galley Slave[8] is no new thing – on the serious side. There's an old ballad called "The Captain" that uses the same metre and I daresay if we looked we should find it had been used a dozen times in the last few years. New metres are mighty scarce.

And now may providence send you a very good and happy year that is coming. Don't worry about your nerves. Half the nerve trouble lies in thinking about 'em. Remember above all things that [it] is the bounden duty of a man to loaf as much as he decently can. If it is written that you will do good work the good work will be done without your frazzling yourself to pieces on it: and the best work is likely to arrive after what a disgustingly energetic world calls idleness. I had to work for my bread and for matter of that have still but I'm breaking myself slowly of the bad habit of petty industry that my training taught me. Nothing is gained by sweating and fidgetting. Lie low: go slow and keep cool and good luck be with you.

Very sincerely yours
Rudyard Kipling.

Yes, the trolley is another Institution. We've got about 6000 folk in the village and – God knows why – they are yearning to defile their pretty town with a trolley.[9] Not street cars – that would make them a "back number" but a sizzling electric outfit in order that they may keep up with the procession. These things make me a Dynamitard.

RK.

Notes

1. White (1866–1934) taught Greek and Latin in Baltimore schools, 1892–1930; he published poems, stories, and historical romances. He and RK never met. RK's calling White "younger brother in the craft" apparently has nothing Masonic about it but alludes only to their common labour as writers.
2. In "The Tents of Kedar", *The Story of the Gadsbys*.
3. "The Strange Ride of Morrowbie Jukes".
4. The "Classical Library" translations published from 1848 by the English publisher Henry George Bohn.
5. White thought that "The Man Who Would Be King" might have been suggested to RK by the brothers Euthydemus and Dionysodorus in Plato's "Euthydemus".
6. Probably the verses in "The Mutiny of the Mavericks" beginning "Listen in the north, my boys, there's trouble on the wind": there are only eight lines, which have not been collected apart from the story itself.
7. Sidney Lanier, *The Science of English Verse* (New York, 1880).
8. *Departmental Ditties and Other Verses* (London, 1890).
9. They did, over RK's protest: see [21 February 1895].

To Mary Mapes Dodge, 11 January 1893
ALS: Princeton University

Brattleboro: / Jan:11:93.

Dear Mrs Dodge:

Many thanks for your kind little note of welcome to the Young Person. I haven't been able to acknowledge it for the reason that I've been very busy these few days gone. However now I'm back to the desk and getting through with my duties. Oliver who is called Herford[1] has just strolled in from the other side of the Atlantic. He broke the Umbria's screw shaft en route[2] (probably tried to draw the poor thing) but don't you think that he'd be the man to illustrate *"Toomai of the Elephants"*? He knows Beasts intimately and he knows me and I know him and perhaps by the Grace of Heaven we could get him to work on it. He's not exactly a hog (in a manner of speaking) on swift enterprizes but if his Dæmon interests him in *Toomai* and the weather is fine and he feels happy in his inside he might do lovely drawings. Do you think it could be arranged?

I have another beast tale finished[3] but it doesn't look very nice and I have to do it again from the beginning.

Sincerely yours
Rudyard Kipling

Notes
1. Herford (1863–1935), English-born illustrator, caricaturist, and writer. He did not illustrate the *Jungle Book* stories but did illustrate the first three of the *Just So Stories* in *St Nicholas*.
2. The Cunard liner *Umbria* arrived 31 December in New York long overdue owing to a broken shaft.
3. Probably "Tiger! Tiger!". RK was working on this and "Mowgli's Brothers" at the same time.

To Cormell Price, 14 January 1893
ALS: Library of Congress

Brattleboro' / Vermont / U.S.A. / Jan. 14. 1893

Dear Uncle Crom,

Here's looking to you from under a foot of snow in the Vermont hills. There is a business on hand in which I want your help.

The "Youths Companion," a young man's paper with about 1,000,000 readers has got from me an article on my school.[1] You can guess that I have just done my best to describe the old Coll. Indeed, I wouldn't have taken the work except for the sake of the school. Now they are clamouring for illustrations and it seems to me that W.C.C[rofts]. can be drawn upon to great advantage here. I know he has a splendid collection of photoes.

What I want are.

(1) The school crest from the Chronicle
(2) A general view looking out to sea.
(3) The line of the buildings
(4) A First fifteen
(5) Bathing on the pebble ridge.
(6) A view of the gym if possible and anything else that may give a good view of things about the college. The more the better.[2]

Could you ask Crofts to make up a parcel for me and send 'em along as soon as possible? We shall have the thing read in every country in the world and I want to make a good clean job of it.

Please *don't* forget.

I'm exceeding busy in these days and the arrival of the little daughter naturally fills all my spare time. You *might* give the boys a half for that interesting event.

Remember me to all the Common-room with great affection, and send the photoes.

Ever yours
Ruddy.

Notes
1. "An English School", *Youth's Companion*, 19 October 1893 (*Land and Sea Tales for Scouts and Guides*).
2. The article has three illustrations in pen and ink: the school crest, a view of the buildings from the pebble ridge, and a view from above looking out to sea.

To Margaret Mackail, [18 January 1893][1]
ALS: University of Sussex

Brattleboro: / Vt:

Dear Margot,

This week's mail brings in a small bagful of letters – the first I opened was yours – about that baby.[2] And today too just before I went down to the village I took Carrie for her first drive in twenty days. We've got a great roomy wicker Maryland sleigh something like a washing-basket on runners (Here's the picture) which we fill with robes [sketch of sleigh] and furs and things. It's a perfect conveyance for feeble folk and I think our horse knew what was expected of him. Carrie has been up and about the house this week past, very angry at being kept back from things that she says she is equal to doing; and this first breath of fresh air made her happy.

The Baby (whom for the sake of brevity we call the Joss) flourishes mightily, and has gained half a pound each little week since the beginning of her life. She eats and sleeps and I am told makes but little noise about it, compared with other babies.

She has a chin ear and nose which is a ridiculous plagiarism from her father – specially the chin but I can't understand how her hair comes to be downy fluff. She's to be called Josephine but Joss suits her better now seeing as she is the image of a Burmese idol and I'm afraid The Joss she'll remain till late in life. Carrie is walking through new worlds, wild with happiness and though I can't pretend to know The Joss intimately or to talk to her she is more than very dear to me. We can be very hoity-toity before a babe comes but once there, boy or girl, we're all too glad for what we've got to discuss it. Also you're right about boys being a little more difficult. She thrives and we are well content. In a few weeks now we shall take her out into the open. I wonder if you can realize weather that only goes above freezing for half an hour at midday sometimes: and yet is dancing, clear, dry buoyant weather. Last night the glass outside marked *15 below Zero* and 22° in some of the river valley farms but the air was dead still with a sparkle in it. Day after day the sun comes up in a cloudless sky burns across the snow and goes out, clear to the last glitter. There is neither dust nor smoke nor defilement of any kind. Even the snow does not cling to the boot but kicks up like fine sugar so frozen it is. The trees are Emperors with their crowns on and icicles five and six feet long hang from our eaves. It's all like life in a fairy-tale – life when one sings and shouts for joy of being alive. I had to go out the other day with a hand-sleigh [sketch of sleigh] ("coasters" they are called) and slide down the snow-

swathed side of a pasture many times because the motion was good and the air was making me drunk. Then evil little rocks stuck out from under the snow and caught my coaster and spilled me out in a three foot drift. Also I've been out on snow shoes which are as though you put a semi-detached villa on each hoof and then quarrelled with either landlord for rent. One has to use them after a fresh snow fall and until the oxen have broken out the roads: we're behind our average so far – only six inches at most down – but the Lord is just and our winter allowance is six feet. We shall get it anon. Can you imagine life running on sleighs – calculated, arranged and controlled for and by the snow, for four months of the year? Life when the autumn brings huge stacks of cut four foot logs of cherry, birch, spruce, hemlock and red oak – piles almost as big as the house – for the winter fires and every one asks everyone else "Have you got your wood in yet?" Bulls of Bashan bring down the wood on sledges crashing through the undergrowth. I own four such monsters and in this weather icicles hang from their muzzles and their flanks are white with rime so that standing in the cloud of their own steam they look like cattle in Sagas.

Then there are times when the wind comes down from Canada with shoutings and all the pines begin to sing together and the snow rises in wisps and little billows and runs before it and when you drive you drive by the openings of the trees above the road for the line of the road is gone and the running brook is frozen and snowed over, and you hear the trees groan in the frost like oxen in the shambles.

If this sounds cheerless I can only say that I've never been cold yet as I've been cold in London and I have never had to put a wrap about my throat: neither have I had a cold or a cough since August last.

The village is three long miles from us and except to buy things we have no dealings with the aborigines. Nobody comes to interrupt; nobody wants to see me and I can work as long as ever I please and yet have time to be out for three and four hours a day. Till The Joss came the house would be as still as the grave for hours at a time. Now we cannot count on silence but it is good to hear her bellow. Tomorrow she'll be three weeks old and tonight she is having a musical evening to celebrate it. Yet it is true (don't laugh) that if I say: – "Joss, stop this nonsense" she is still for quite half a minute. She's wickedly and uncannily like me in profile but I wish I could understand her hair. It ought to be black, or potato brown at least.

Her coming ties and tames C's adventurous soul. She meditated a trip with me to Florida this spring – perhaps even the Bermudas but now she does not dance that dance any more. "We must stay with the Joss" says she. If the Mother and Father come to England this spring I shall come over and I fancy I must come for business anyhow, for a week or so.

There's a new book just done today[3] with some new tales in it and a verse beginning and end which has cost me a lot of trouble and I'm more full of tales than I can hope to be empty. They grow in this absence of distractions and utter happiness.

We've told The Joss that you are a brevet-Aunt so you must make us brevet-Uncle and Aunt to Denis and Angela.[4] Carrie sends you much love. May you have a good new year and all happiness that you may by chance have missed till now.

Ruddy.

Notes
1. Dated from postmark, 19 January 1893, and from internal evidence.
2. Margaret's second child, Denis Mackail (1892–1971), later a journalist and writer of fiction.
3. *Many Inventions* (1893).
4. Angela (1890–1961), Margaret's first child, afterwards the well-known novelist Angela Thirkell.

To William Ernest Henley, 18–19 January [1893]
ALS: Morgan Library

Brattleboro / Jan. 18.

Dear Henley,

Here comes old Pew and the Deacon and the Beau.[1] I've been revelling in the Montaigne for which I shall never be able to thank you properly and I've finished the Beau for the third time. Great God *how* they mangled it at that gaff in town where I saw it first![2] I don't know your estimates but it seems to me that the Beau is out and away and away the best of the three and a few thousand others. It's beautiful clean cut words such as I love, and all of a play too. The Deacon I like next. Pew I don't care for so much except in places. Now go you and write a play on your own bottom – a sumptuous play – an Elizabethan adventurer play. Here's a man this side the water (Weir Mitchell)[3] has been trying to handle Drake and Winter and so forth dramatically. It was a gorgeous opportunity but I don't think God made Americans for that time of history. As I read I thought what you could have done with it. The mischief is that the man is old enough to be my father and I'm blowed if I can see what to say that's decent.

The N[ational]O[bserver]'s come in refreshfully but you've been running at half speed for three or four weeks past. Those "middles" about dresses and such are getting a little too "precious" for the good of man.[4] How are the writer's bowels? It is sweet to sit at a distance and sling damnation from afar. All the same the N.O. is being more quoted here up and down the country. They hate it with a poisonous hatred and it is well that they should.

I've been very busy getting my new book of tales together. It's always the end part that takes up a lot of time. Here's the L'Envoi[5] for you to tell me what you think of it. The ship is getting out of harbour – head to wind.

Heh! Walk her round. Heave oh heave her short again.
   Over, snatch her over there and hold her on the pawl!
Loose all sail, and brace your yards aback and full
   Ready jib to pay her off; and heave short all!

Well ah fareyouwell – we can stay no more with you, my love!
   Down – set down your liquor and your girl from off your knee!
     For the wind has come to say
     "You must take [me] while you may
"if you'd go to Mother Carey when she feeds her chicks at sea"

Heh! Walk her round! Break, ah break it out o' that!
   Break our starboard bower out – apeak, awash – aclear.
Port – port she swings with the harbour mud beneath her foot –
   And that's the last o' bottom we shall see this year.

Well ah fare you well, for we've got to take her out again
   Take her out in ballast riding light and cargo free;
     For it's time to clear and quit
     When the hawser grips the bitt,
So we'll pay you with the foresheet and a promise from the sea.

Heh! Tally on. Aft and walk away with her
   Handsome to the cat head, now. O tally on the fall!
Stop, sieze and fish, and case her with davit-guy
   Up, well up the fluke of her and inboard haul!

Well ah fare you well for the channel winds took hold of us
   Choking down our voices as we snatch the gaskets free
     And it's blowing up for night
     And she's dropping light on light
And she's snorting under bonnets for a breath of open sea!

Wheel, full and by: but she'll smell her road alone tonight
   Sick she is and harbour-sick and glad to clear the land
Roll down to Brest with the old red ensign over us –
   Carry on and thresh her out with all she'll stand!

Well, ah fare you well for it's Ushant gives the door to us
   Whirling like a windmill on a dirty sand to lee
     Till the last, last flicker goes
     From the trembling water-rows
   And we're off to Mother Carey
     (Walk her down to Mother Carey)
Oh we're bound for Mother Carey where she feeds her chicks at
sea!

I rather like the metre of the thing. We've been sleighing for the past
fortnight and more and bright day follows bright day across the snow
till your eyes get dizzy.

The cradle is now as it should be; and what is better both mother and
child are exceedingly well. Have, in truth, not been otherwise since the
beginning. I take the wife out for her first drive this morning, so you
can see how quickly she is picking up.

If only I could share a little of the sunlight with you I'd be happier.
Some day write me a real letter and tell me what you do. All I've heard
is what I've seen – the Vanity Fair picture.[6] Bless you.

                                      Ruddy.

Jan. 19.
P.S. I finished this in the morning and in the afternoon your letter
about the child came: also one from Whibley. Bless you both in your
bogs and your darkness. Why don't you N.O. men start a small club of
your own somewhere. Call it the "Observatory" and to balance all the
writing part make only men who have built bridges and slain niggers
and administered countries members beside yourselves. I can see the
makings of a lively little informal cock-roost, if you find the Savile too
stuffy. Two or three rooms would do you to begin with. Gad, if I was
over I'd make a try at once.

This is written at the beginning of a snow storm – that is to say I
don't know when it will be posted: for the weather looks as if it means
steady business. New York has been frozen stiff and I'd have given a
month's pay to have gone down and seen the sea packed with ice as
far as the eye could reach. The night before last the glass outside my
door marked *15 below zero* and 22 in some of the river valley farms. Yet
I was driving all yesterday and in the sun it was hot. Queer land. You
can't get a cold and you can't feel cold here: the air's as dry as the very

best champagne. I scutter about on snow shoes and flop into drifts and rejoice in the snow. The other day, on what seemed a level road, our horses dropped away and were lost, all except the tops of their ears, their noses and the territs,[7] in the snow and it took a couple of hours to dig 'em out. Yet some men say life in the backwoods is not exciting. Old Du Chaillu[8] of all men under Heaven is lecturing this evening in this back of beyond and I'm going down to listen to him and see how the aborigines take it. Me and the aborigines are excellent friends but they can't understand why I don't come to chicken suppers and church sociables and turkey sprees. The farmers are delicious but there is a local society by the side of which Pogram, Scadder[9] and the others are pale and watery shadows. Dickens never did better work than his American Notes and the more I get to know the land, the more do I stand "astounded at my own moderation."[10] Zola could tackle the farm life that Mary Wilkins[11] touches so sweetly with her maiden knitting needles, and he'd have to work hard too. The moral dry rot of it all is having no law that need be obeyed: no line to toe: no trace to kick over and no compulsion to do anything. By consequence, a certain defect runs through everything – workmanship, roads, bridges, contracts, barter and sale and so forth – all inaccurate, all slovenly, all out of plumb and untrue. So far the immense natural wealth of the land holds this ineptitude up; and the slovenly plenty hides their sins unless you look for them. *Au fond* it's barbarism – barbarism plus telephone, electric light, rail and suffrage but all the more terrible for that very reason. I like it. When I have done with seeing what I want to see I shall be in possession of a few interesting facts. Then, O Henley, the band will begin to play. By the way, they are protesting feebly in New York against the Mayor appointing a gambler and a murderer to be a police justice.[12] Sweet isn't it? I am supposed to have overdrawn my little sketch of that city:[13] yet their own papers admit that not 50 per cent of the streets are adequately lighted: that the roads are barbarous: and that the clearning is early nomad. It's all immensely interesting as I watch it from my perch among the snows. T'other day I got a letter asking me for my views on an American Laureateship. Had I been in England I should have blossomed into verse but it's my rule to answer no letters and I mourn for that opportunity missed. They have been discussing it in Chicago. They are the most marvellous Papuans God ever made. Somehow they can, by merely writing about it, knock all the beauty, honour, wit, wisdom and reverence out of anything in the world and leave behind only the smell of an overheated hotel ante-room, or of a hollow tooth.

Yet individually heaps of them are fascinating. This spring I hope to get down for a trip to Florida and perhaps to the Bermudas to see what we have in the way of Forts there. 'Tis a grasping and annexatory land, eternally stirring Canada up to revolt and it will bear a lot of watching. Don't for a minute run away with the idea that a Democratic government means knocking down the tariff wall. I fancied you had a hint to that effect in the N.O. t'other day. They will at the most pull out a few bricks with vast clamour. Free trade won't come till the western farms are as much mortgaged as the New England ones. Then there will be trouble with the oligarchy that control the land. This last year being the most peaceful and prosperous in the history of these states there were only 14000 troops under arms at one time – to keep the prosperity going I suppose. Martial law (and Yank martial law is something) was proclaimed over territory about half the size of England.[14] Not bad.

Now I must go back to my book and give it another polishing. You seem to know a great deal over there. I haven't heard about my fifty pound poem but over the page as a stop gap till I can do something is a song for singing at your discretion.[15] I like the lilt but I can't say I am amazed with any amazement at the words. Do as thou thinkest best.

And now I'll really stop. Give my love to Whibley, Blackburn and the others good men all. Some day when you do not look for it I shall come over and get drunk in the nearest efficient substitute for the Solferino.[16] Send me a picture of your little maid,[17] *please*.

Ruddy.

P.S.   Did I tell you aught about my "Song of the Deep Sea Engines."[18] It's growing and that's to go instead of the song of the sword. *What* a song I could have done if you hadn't "come with your old music."[19] Hear my engines at *Half speed ahead* (Metre is copyrighted.)

> . . . . in the darkness we lay
> To the roar of earth's red pulses we dreamed of the day.
> From the mine head – from the well-mouth – to the try pit we rose
> Till a soul that was not man's soul was born of the blows.

RK

Why on earth not [a] scene from the Mutiny of the Bounty for a play. The time when they turned their first island into a hell. I've had a shot at that.

Notes

1. Henley and Stevenson's *Three Plays*: *Admiral Guinea* ("old Pew"), *Deacon Brodie*, and *Beau Austin*.
2. At the Haymarket, 3 November 1890, produced by Beerbohm Tree.
3. S. Weir Mitchell, *Sir Francis Drake, A Tragedy of the Sea* (1893). Mitchell (1829–1914), a Philadelphia physician specialising in nervous disorders, was also a successful writer of historical fiction. He had apparently sent RK a copy of *Sir Francis Drake*: the volume

is now in the library at Batemans.
4. "Evolution in Dress" ran in the *National Observer* from 20 August to 12 November 1892.
5. Collected as "An Anchor Song". The text in this letter is very slightly different from that printed as the "Envoy" to *Many Inventions*.
6. One of the long series of caricatures of notables published by *Vanity Fair* in London, that of Henley, by "Spy", appeared on 26 November. RK was added to the list on 7 June 1894.
7. Usually *terrets*, rings through which the reins pass.
8. Paul Belloni Du Chaillu (1835–1903), African explorer and writer.
9. The Hon. Elijah Pogram, congressman, and General Scudder, both from *Martin Chuzzlewit*.
10. As Lord Clive said when charged with illegally enriching himself in India (1773).
11. Mary Wilkins, later Mary Wilkins Freeman (1852–1930), New England local colourist. She had lived in Brattleboro and was well known there. RK met her in Brattleboro in October 1892 (Howard C. Rice, notes on Mary Cabot, "Kipling's Vermont Period", p. 24: Marlboro College.
12. The Tammany mayor had appointed Joseph Koch, who had once been indicted for failure to enforce the law as an excise commissioner, to a police justiceship. The murderer was a newly appointed fire commissioner named Scannell.
13. See the first paragraph of "In Sight of Monadnock" in *Letters of Travel*, first published in *The Times*, 13 April 1892: "the worst pavements in the world".
14. The National Guard was called out in July after riots growing out of the Homestead strike near Pittsburgh. A railroad strike in August at Buffalo also brought out the Guard.
15. No doubt "The Dove of Dacca", which appeared in the *National Observer*, 4 February 1893.
16. The Soho restaurant patronised by Henley and his group: the 'little restaurant off Leicester Square" where they gathered to "regulate all literature till all hours of the morning" (*Something of Myself*, p. 82).
17. Margaret (1888–94), Henley's only child.
18. Not published. It is perhaps the abandoned poem that RK describes to Henley in 2–3 December 1893. The last two of the lines that RK transcribes here are adapted in "McAndrew's Hymn", twenty lines from the end.
19. Browning, "A Toccata of Galuppi's", l. 4.

To Margaret Mackail, 29 January–1 February 1893

ALS: University of Sussex

Brattleboro. / Jan: 29 ⎱ 93
Feb: 1: ⎰

Dear Margaret:

You see, so far Josephine has not developed much but now she is coming on into the shape and likeness of a baby who is a baby. She has been putting fat on her small bones and it keeps her busy eating and sleeping. One fresh pound every seven days is her standard and now she is more than ten pounds. Speech she lacks though Carrie understands her: – with me she is reserved not to say stern, for the most part, but she admits by silence that I can handle her. The fair hair and the big blue eyes are getting more fair and more blue and that absurd chin (of mine) with the rolls of fat grows and becomes more fascinating. She is old enough now not to sleep every minute of her time and lies awake watching this new world with eyes that do not approve. Just now (I am writing in the afternoon) I was watching her long and it is my opinion (contested by C. who says that she wouldn't be so undignified) that she smiled when I dropped a tassel within her range of vision.

She certainly has smiled once or twice since she was a month old and I am sure it isn't wind – unless it be that from cherubs' wings. Also she has been out for a walk in the sunshine and that did not amuse her: she being persuaded that it was time for dinner. She lives on a pillow on a double chair this sort of thing [sketch of chair], in the living room and comes now and then to see me in my study. Her cradle is a clothes basket lined and fitted. When we go to the new house she will have a little brass crib and a day and a night nursery and everything handsome about her. Mercifully she won't be an only child because Babie Marjorie[1] my brother in law's child is here to take care of her or kill her. I don't know which. Her love for the Baby is very touching. She brings it every thing from old shoes to the waste paper basket, crooning with delight the while. Marjorie is really a radiantly beautiful baby and if she does not get kicked to death in the stables, or gored or stung or anything she will be a lovely woman. In the new house which will be about a long stone's throw from my brother in law's we're going to have a Baby-path set with hollyhocks and sunflowers for them to walk to and fro on. We've been seriously considering whether it would be better when they come to be able to run about

(a) to fasten a sheep bell round their necks

(b) to peg them down at the end of a forty foot rope in a meadow or

(c) to get a few score sheep hurdles and make a pen in the woods for them to play in.

You can't keep children indoors here for any day of the summer and for very few of the winter. Josephine will spend her summer to come I hope in a hammock in the covered verandah at the south end of the house. You will see from the picture that her nursery – the bay window in the second story and running back the whole depth of the house – gives onto a second piazza where she can nearly always get out. My work room is the room below; next on the right is Carrie's. Next (the big open window thing) is a loggia which can be entirely opened: next is the dining room, and then a little overhung verandah to play in.

The kitchen is the last room at the north. Above it are the servants' quarters: next going S. a guest room: then the bathroom (that is what I am most interested in. I never had a bathroom to meet my views yet) next our room and then the nursery. Overhead there will be a clear run of 70 feet of attic that we can use for the most delightful rooms as we want them. All the foundation is in place – grey stone with moss on it that you can't distinguish from the lichened rocks of the pasture behind. The four bulls of Bashan will draw up the timber as soon as we can get it but this winter has frozen running water *down to the bottom solid*, and the lumber mills have been shut down. Can you imagine eight feet of clear green ice? The lack of snow has caused the trouble (snow's a blanket to the cold earth) and everybody's water pipes have frozen. The next farm have theirs four feet underground and they are "friz" for two hundred yards. Two days ago there came a thaw – and a rain and the trees were a sight to see when the frost closed down again, and they all were turned to crystal. Underfoot it was pure ice and I had to manoevre our faithful Marcus[2] down to the village to be re roughened as to his feet. He went down hill sitting on his tail till the sparks flew. Carrie has been out driving herself today and very glad to get her hand on the reins again. I take her out sometimes in the morning on the little hand-sleigh, which is not an easy thing to control going down a slope. Then we forget for a while that we are parent-folk and frolic in the snow and scandalize the few squirrels who won't sleep for winter.

8: p.m.

How strange that you should talk about Sir Patrick Spens! Only the night before I was giving Carrie her regular massage (it's a beautiful thing for making tired folks untired) and the old song came back to me and I hummed it all through – (Enter at this present moment C. and Josephine (It's evening time). Her eyes are open and she is wondering whether her last meal agreed with her. She wears Aunt Aggie's little knitted garment and looks – there's no disguising it – the sweetest infant in all the world.) Do you think it is all good for Angela to learn ballads so soon? I have an extreme dread of Jo. learning *anything* for the first six or eight years of her life. I suppose though that she will develope some vile taste or other for something that is *not* done with the solid steady hands. But of course Angela, being so born, could be no more held back from that path of song than she could be beaten. I only wonder she didn't come into the world saying: –

> Mother doubtful, mother dread
> Dweller on the Fitful head.[3]

Rememberest thou? In the hall by the clock. Some day (it will be like walking in dreams) we must bring the children together at the Grange!

By the way we've got an English nurse for Jo. No good to defile her speech at the very outset with the Yank peacock cry! Now I must stop. Many days have gone since I began. It is morning now and Jo. is having her bath. Aren't they most amazingly frail to look at?

I told Aunt Aggie first about the child before Aunt Georgie because, with losing Hugh and all, Aggie was very poor just then[4] and I know Aunt Georgie is so rich and so dear that she will understand. All love to you all.

Ruddy.

Notes
1. Marjorie Balestier (1891–1921), Beatty Balestier's only child.
2. Marcus Aurelius, "a big philosophical black" (*Something of Myself*, p. 116).
3. From Scott, *The Pirate*. Describing how his uncle Burne-Jones played with them at the Grange, RK recalled that "we made a draped chair in the hall serve for the seat of 'Norna of the Fitful Head' and addressed her questions till the Uncle got inside the rugs and gave us answers which thrilled us with delightful shivers, in a voice deeper than all the boots in the world" (*Something of Myself*, p. 13).
4. When Hugh went to school his mother wrote that "the pain I feel is even worse than I foresaw . . . the happiest time of my life is gone irrevocably" (Baldwin, *The Macdonald Sisters*, p. 178).

To William Canton, 11 February 1893
ALS: Berg Collection, New York Public Library

Brattleboro / Vt. / Feb: 11. 93

Dear Mr Canton

Many thanks for your kind little note of last month in regard to the baby. Any man by the way who could talk of his own baby as being between "a fairy and an elephant" need not write about other folk being conceited.

I fear that "Pilate" – (what a splendid notion that was) would just flyte good words beyond expression.[1] You see from the way I tell it, the Scots missionary on the frontier goes mad and gives trouble masquerading as the Lord. Pilate, (the district magistrate of those parts) is naturally annoyed and after the tumult is over he sums up his opinion that Pilate was a shamefully ill-used man and that Living God or no living God the first business of an officer is to preserve order – yea, though the graves opened round him. *That* would never do and yon's the only way I see to do it.

When I'm free a little from my much work I'll try to send it on to you that you may judge.

Ever yours
Rudyard Kipling

Note
1. A "Pilate notion" was briefly discussed in a letter from RK to Canton on 3 February 1892 (ALS, Berg). The story was not published.

To Edward Lucas White, 25 February 1893
ALS: Ray Collection, Morgan Library

Brattleboro Vt / Feb: 25: 93.

Esteemed Younger Brother:

I've been busy experimenting along of those metres that you are so interested in; and now I'm through for a while. I had to hunt in the *Century* to find out what a Pæonic lilt was and it impressed me immensely. *I* do 'em on my ten fingers or shout them into the ear of a bullock (splendid public is a steer) and lo they have arsises and crisisses and pentabolic metronomes under the hypogastrium, all the time! Seriously there was a time when I read much about the nature and properties of verses:

> How the cothurns trod majestic
>   Down the deep iambic lines,
> And the rolling anapæstic
>   Curled like vapour over shrines[1]

but I have forgotten all that I read, and it comes back to one fresh. Remember me when your book is born.[2]

You are right about the old things being revived. Exempli gratia, all the French talk about the "colours of vowels" is not much older than original sin. The nigger knows it: the Afghan knows it in his love songs and if we could resurrect a mummy I daresay he'd tell us how the "Pyramids Pilot and Nile Review of Modern Literature" discussed it in his days. But mercifully, these things are hidden from us and we go on heaving our little packs of wares into the mud and the public tucks 'em away under its feet as an elephant in a quicksand tucks the straw bundles that you throw him but unlike the elephant the public never gets out. I've been working for a month on a nine storied pagoda of a song[3] when I ought to have been doing decent prose. So I have now the double satisfaction of doing verse and being bad. Also, we've had the father and mother of a blizzard and in the intervals of snow and song I've been out with a shovel or an ox-sled breaking roads. There are wonderful blue-and-green lights along the edges of the drifts that are worth being snowed in to see but I love not to stand on my head and shake the snow out of my collar. Can't you pull stakes for a while and get on the sea for awhile? She's the best doctor I know even if you try her as far as Bermuda only. And in this weather you'd have to devote all your soul to hanging on to the edge of your bunk, which would at first rack your body all to pieces and presently leave you with the appetite of a wolf and the inside of an ostrich; lying under wet clothes is not cheerful. I've done it with malarial fever (the cheerful thing that comes and shakes you once a week) but I don't care to hear of other men doing it.

To make a rough guess I should fancy that you took an exhausting interest in what folks said and did round you. Otherwise you wouldn't have taken the trouble to explain things to the Plato man. If you begin that way you lay up for yourself an ever increasing load of burden that plays the mischief with your work. I get about two hundred letters a week from them as wants to know things and read with their behinder hunkers – letters on every single thing that does *not* need writing about. I suppose it's just idleness and they very naturally conclude that I am all sizes and shapes of a brute because I keep their stamps and use 'em for my own mail. Let me recommend that process for the Plato man and those like him; and you'll find maybe that it will save you a day or two in bed. It isn't what we do that shucks us out. It's the worrying about what other people do, or don't do or think or might have thought or hadn't oughter think. I've seen it kill men dead, and they died saying it was "overwork." Now a pestilent thaw has begun and I must go out and shovel some more snow in spadyllic metre. Keep well.

Sincerely,
Rudyard Kipling.

P.S.   Here is a question for the schools? How far is a man justified in onoma – (I can't spell it) tapœic metres reproducing the beat of engines and so on? Where does legitimate Art end and sheer trick work begin?

Notes
1. Elizabeth Barrett Browning, "The Wine of Cyprus", stanza 10.
2. So far as I know, White published no book on metrics.
3. Perhaps "The Song of the Deep Sea Engines" (see 18–19 January 1893), or possibly "The Song of the Banjo", whose title is entered in CK's diary on 1 March 1893.

To Mary Mapes Dodge, 5 March 1893
ALS: Princeton University

Dear Mrs Dodge:

Herewith I am sending you two more of the Beast-tales – viz. the story of *Mowgli's Brothers* and *Tiger-Tiger* – its continuation. They have taken some time; and I think I've put into them pretty nearly everything that I know or have heard or dreamed about the Indian jungle. I only hope that you won't find them too long.

The last tale of the series should follow in a little time. Toomai is being unripped and stitched up the gores with some purfling on the bias and gigots to match.

Very sincerely yours
Rudyard Kipling.

Mar. 5/93.
Brattleboro.
P.S.   at the end of Tiger-Tiger (q.v.) I have made Mowgli sing a war-chant of victory but as that will make the tale too long for St Nick. I've left it out of the copy. If you see your way to enlarging the borders I'd be glad to send along the song: It's prose *not* rhyme.[1]

R.K.

Note
1. "Mowgli's Song at the Council Rock" did not appear in *St Nicholas*.

To James Whitcomb Riley,[1] 13 March 1893
ALS: Lilly Library, Indiana University

Brattleboro. / Mar: 13: 93.

Dear Mr. Riley:

They came in sooner than I thought for:[2] the Seven Brothers and I make haste to acknowledge them before I go to New York where there will be no time to do anything, except to explain you can't. It's not for the likes of me to criticize the merits of the same: for that would be an impertinence but

"I wish to remark and my language is plain"[3]

that I am very sick and tired of digging up radishes every twenty minutes to see how their poor little roots are getting on; and sweating and swearing and clucking in print over the nature and properties and possibilities of the American Literature that is to be

Therefore,

when I find a man sitting down and singing what his life is round him and his neighbours' lives, as a poet sees 'em with their ideas and their hopes and their fears all properly set out and plotted and calculated for his particular section of the country I rejoice with a great joy because half a dozen poems of that kind are worth as nearly as I can make it four and three quarter tons of the precious self conscious get-onto-my-curses stuff that is solemnly put forward as the Great American Exhibit. I suppose this is heresy but I don't care, because what you write incidentally of the Hoosier holds good for country life over a large area. That is why the farmer next door approves of "when the frost is on the punkin and the fodders in the shock" and I hug myself over "Coon dog Wess" and the hounds with the sorrowful eyes. Also I choke over "Mahala Ashcroft"[4] and because I don't know why I choke I am moderately sure that there is a poet at the keyboard.

I could say a good deal more but it wouldn't explain matters any further; Go on in Allah's name – the rest when we meet.

Sincerely
Rudyard Kipling.

Notes
1. Riley (1849–1916), Indiana journalist and poet, best known for his dialect verses. RK had admired Riley at least since 1890, when he wrote his verses "To James Whitcomb Riley" in praise of Riley's *Rhymes of Childhood*.
2. Probably Riley's *Green Fields and Running Brooks*, published in December 1892. I cannot explain the allusion to "the Seven Brothers".
3. Bret Harte, "Plain Language from Truthful James", ll. 1–2.
4. "When the Frost is on the Punkin" and "The Death of Little Mahala Ashcroft" are from *The Old Swimming Hole* (1883); "Coon Dog Wess", *Neghborly Poems* (1891).

To Ripley Hitchcock,[1] [*c.* 1 April 1893][2]

ALS: Berg Collection, New York Public Library

[New York]

Dear Mr Hitchcock

Very many thanks for proof and letters. By all means stick to the "so called English spelling." I have been Webstered by Lovell[3] and it hurt my emotions – badly.

I'll be writing to McClure myself, in a little while, but please let him know.

Sincerely
Rudyard Kipling.

Laid up with a cold or *I'd* have come to have talked over the cover. 230. W. 42.[4]

Notes

1. Hitchcock (1857–1918), writer and editor, the chief editor at Appleton's, 1890–1902, and later literary advisor to Harper and Brothers. He published works on the graphic arts and on American history.
2. CK's diary notes on 1 April that "Rud insists Appleton use English spelling" (for *Many Inventions*). They had gone to New York on 17 March and remained until 20 April (CK diary).
3. In the "authorized" editions brought out by Lovell of New York in 1890–1.
4. The address of the Dunmore Hotel, where they were staying.

To Mrs William Starr Dana,[1] 10 April 1893

ALS: Harvard University

230. W. 42. / "The Dunmore" / April: 10. 1893.

Dear Madam,

Will you permit a stranger to thank you very sincerely for the pleasure he has received from your book "How to Know the Wild Flowers."[2]

I live in Vermont a few miles from the nearest town and all last summer tramped about wondering what and which the flowers in our woods, swamps and pastures might be. The country-folk called them vaguely "weeds" or cheerfully misnamed them. This summer thanks to you, I hope to be wiser. Your book is exactly what I needed – not a botanical excursus but a volume for such beginners as I who may in time try to study botany.

When another edition comes out couldn't you write a small extra chapter on the keeping and pressing of specimens; how rough microscope work should be done; and how the tender flowers that go to pieces quickest can be doctored? Of course I mean nothing technical but something as simple and direct as the book as it stands now. Gray's manual has instructions but they are put together without enthusiasm – scholastically and austerely.[3]

Please don't be offended with my small demand and accept once more by best thanks.

Very sincerely yours
Rudyard Kipling.

Notes
1. Frances Theodora Dana (1861–1952), a widow, later Mrs James Parsons.
2. *How to Know the Wild Flowers*, first published in 1893, and in print for many years thereafter.
3. Mrs Dana did not adopt the suggestion. Asa Gray's *Manual of the Botany of the Northern United States*, first published in 1848, was the standard text.

To Mrs William Starr Dana, 8 May [1893]
ALS: Harvard University

Brattleboro' / May. 8.

Dear Mrs Dana,

A thousand thanks for your kind letter of directions and the enclosures. Collecting tins I used to know of old but I have discarded 'em in favour of a common fishing creel which is lighter, holds more and can be bodily ducked in a brook to freshen up the contents.

I've got a "Gray" and he makes me more bewildered than ever and the spring is pulling out plant upon plant and I feel hopelessly distanced in the race to keep up with things. We're so rich in swamp, swale, wood and dry pasture that in half a mile you can get most anything but as the things haven't flowered I am not very wise, and the local names for plants confuse me. They call everything "sourgrass" or "batseyes" or "pneumonia" or something equally helpful, and accurate.

I've tried to press some hepaticas – our woods are full of them – but it seems such a brutal job to ding the poor little beggars out of their homes and treat 'em as the court treated Giles Corey.[1] The roots squeak! I shall watch things as they grow and get seeds and husks to play with in the winter. I would give a good deal if there were some one within reach to point out the flowers to begin with.

They told me when I was in town that the Flowers had finished out its first edition and that was good hearing. When you revise I think you will find some misprints in the paging of the Index p. 126 for 120 and things of that kind that the base printer should have attended to. Also in Christina Rossetti's little book "Sing Song" there's a very pretty quotation for the wind-flowers

> Twine me a wreath of windflowers
> And I will fly away etc.[2]

I've forgotten exactly how it goes. I've lost my Culpepper's Herbal[3] too but *he* is full of the most fascinating astrological nonsense about the planet that each wild flower belongs to. Maybe he would be worth quoting. I hope the "Flowers" will sell out many and many times in the next few years.

Very sincerely yours
Rudyard Kipling.

Notes
1. Pressed to death in the New England witch trials, 1692.
2. "Twist me a crown of wind-flowers, / That I may fly away" (*Sing-Song*, 1872); Mrs Dana did not use the lines.
3. *The English Physitian, or an Astrologo-physical discourse of the Vulgar Herbs of this Nation* (1652), popularly known as Culpeper's Herbal. Nicholas Culpeper (1616–54), writer on astrology and medicine, is the hero of RK's "A Doctor of Medicine" (*Rewards and Fairies*).

To Alfred Baldwin, May 1893
Text: Copy, University of Sussex

Brattleboro. / May 1893

Dear Uncle Alfred,

I am in receipt of your note (of no date) in regard to the opium "traffic" in India.[1] All I can say would be of no good. Of course in my seven years in India I have had between forty and fifty servants under my observation one way and another. They are of the class most notoriously addicted to drugs. *One* man used to drug himself insensible at odd times. The "opium den" as described in the highly coloured fiction of the Cause does not exist. The native of India is by nature and environment temperate to an extent that the Englishman does not appreciate and his dealings with the drug (an excellent thing in itself and in moderation about as harmful as tobacco) are most strictly limited. In fever districts opium is much used as a guard against fever; also among coolies as a stimulus under heavy work. Why not call for the Govt. India birth and criminal statistics to see to what extent it affects (a) vitality and (b) the indictable offences? There's no good arguing with these idiots and the government of India will not of course defend itself. Last resort of the destitute why not press for a commission instead of taking action on ex-parte statements? I *know* that the opium habit in India is nothing as compared to the ordinary effects of liquor in a town full of white Christians but you see I can't prove it and my evidence wouldn't be worth a rap. Rivett-Carnac[2] of Shagipur[3] might supply you with some figures. Sir George Birdwood might know something about it. Sir Charles Aitchison[4] could answer for the Punjab I believe: but more than that I do not know.

I'm in the thick of house building which is an invention of the Devil for the destruction of time and temper but things are shaping themselves slowly. The Pater is coming over to see us I hope[5] and we ought to be across this autumn.

It's ghastly to see a baby and know that it's yours. I've gone up a whole generation and it makes me feel older than Cheops but the Babe is a fine, fair, flaxen haired infant with blue eyes and a turn for low comedy.

All love to aunt Louie and Stan. When does *he* follow suit?

Ever your loving nephew
Ruddy

Notes

1. Alfred Baldwin was now in Parliament, where the opium question was being agitated. The House of Commons had passed a resolution in 1891 condemning the cultivation of opium in India; in June of this year the Commons would defeat a resolution to appoint a royal commission to investigate the subject. For RK on opium see also Robert H. M. Dawbarn, "Opium in India – a Medical Interview with Rudyard Kipling", in Orel, *Rudyard Kipling: Interviews and Recollections*, I, 108–10.
2. Colonel John Henry Rivett-Carnac (1838–1923), at one time opium agent in India, and a friend of the Kipling family.
3. Thus in copy, for Ghazipur.
4. Sir Charles Aitchison (1832–96), Lieutenant-Governor of the Punjab, 1882–7.
5. JLK and his wife left India for good in April; she returned directly to England, while he went on to the United States, where he arrived in June.

To Ripley Hitchcock, 8 June 1893
ALS: Berg Collection, New York Public Library

[*Brattleboro*] / June: 8: 93

Dear Mr. Hitchcock

I have to acknowledge with many thanks receipt of 6 (six) copies of *Many Inventions*.[1] I fancied that the cover was to be a dull purple same as the sample. Do you think that that festive red is as good? It's more cheerful of course but I'd like to see some copies in the first purple – or maroon was it?

I cannot sufficiently admire Mr. Walker's[2] . . . enterprize. There is something truly "cosmopolitan" in trying to cut slices out of a book as you'd cut a ham at a lunch counter. If he sent the proposal in writing I'd love to have a copy of it as a human document. May I?

Many thanks for the information about the birds. They are bewilderingly many here. A blue bird has made her nest in a lard-pail in the wood shed; there's a robin under the eaves within touch of our window and an oriole is building in a cottonwood. I can hear them singing but the nest is hidden too well. Yesterday a man (I suppose he was concerned about chickens) shot an eagle (five feet from wing-tip to wing-tip) close to our new house and all he knew about the bird was just "eagle". I couldn't see the corpse so I couldn't fix it.

The locusts are out and the land is lovely from end to end. I hope to be down in New York in a week or ten days and then I will see you *and* make you restless more than usual for the country.

Yours very sincerely
Rudyard Kipling.

Notes
1. Published in June.
2. John B. Walker (1847–1931), owner and editor of the *Cosmopolitan Magazine* from 1889.

To Herbert Stephen,[1] 22 June 1893
ALS: Syracuse University

Brattleboro' / Vt. / June: 22: 93.

Dear Stephen

In the first place "Yah!" In the second "Go to!" In the third all thanks for your letter but in regard to "blasted suburbs" of "American

Manchesters" you err and are deceived. I am among hills three miles from anything like a town; in woods; on streams. This very afternoon I've been watching a fox who has been watching for my partridges. Does *that* convince you? "Suburbs" indeed! Do you shoot eagles five foot across the wings in suburbs. I'd drag you at the heels of my oxen if I could get you here but anon you shall learn for Walter Besant is coming up here. I went down to New York on Sunday to meet my Pater and found W.B. in the arms of reporters.[2] He will need cooling off in Vermont and he shall tell you that the countriest country in England would be suburbs alongside o' this ere.

Now to deal with your grosser follies – the geographical ones.

Mississippi Bay is at the back of Yokohama bay which is in *Japan*.[3] Japan is in the *East*. Thus, Q.E.D. and so forth.

The Golden Gate is reached for choice by rail *but* the sailing ship goes round the Horn, as a usual thing.

The two voyages are about the longest E. and W. runs you can make.

As you justly remark the eagle and the snake were both taken out under poetic license but what *can* a man do. Be thankful they weren't gryphons or narsinghas.[4]

I'm glad you like the new book a little.[5] The Hansom cab business[6] I couldn't get at or else I'd have used it somewhere for I look on that as the crowning flower of my Pen when it was at its best. Why can't a man do a good thing every other week?

I'm doing a lot more about the wolf man his early life and experiences, and some day they'll appear. Some day too when you aren't expecting it I shall turn up in that back den of the Savile and pick up our rows exactly where we left off for there is a deal that you've got to learn yet.

Besant's arrival brought with it a draught of hot London air and a rush of gossip and old news till I felt like a corpse that had been dead since the building of the Pyramids and couldn't quite catch up with things. I wonder how things really are across the water. From this distance it looks like civil war: but at close hand I suppose it's a highly respectable argument conducted in a highly respectable way. Give my love to all who remember me at the Club and believe me

Yours ever sincerely
Rudyard Kipling

P.S.   Whibley was Brugglesmith of course.[7]

Notes

1. Stephen (1857–1932), son of Sir James Fitzjames Stephen, whom he succeeded as 2nd Baronet, cousin of Virginia Woolf, was associated with Henley; he had known RK since early in 1890 (John Connell, *W. E. Henley*, pp. 174–5).
2. JLK arrived in New York on 18 June. The extant version of CK's diary does not mention a visit from Besant in Vermont, but he may well have paid one.

3. This and the next few statements refer to "The Long Trail" (afterwards called "L'Envoi") in *Barrack-Room Ballads*: "Or East all the way into Mississippi Bay, / Or West to the Golden Gate", and "There be triple ways to take, of the Eagle or the Snake, / Or the way of a Man with a Maid."
4. A *narasinha* is a man-lion, one of the avatars of Vishnu.
5. *Many Inventions.*
6. "The Battle of Rupert Square", *St James's Gazette*, 29 December 1889; not collected until the Sussex Edition. It describes a fight between a hansom cab driver and his fare.
7. As Carrington notes (*Kipling*, p. 156), Whibley and "Brugglesmith" (*Many Inventions*) shared an address at Brook Green, Hammersmith.

To Ambrose Poynter, 23 June 1893

ALS: Victoria and Albert Museum

Brattleboro' / June: 23: 1893.

Dear Ambo,

The Pater is here – whereof more anon.

Why are you not here?

Is it (*est-il*) that you have not the leisure of the fishmonger's aunt? Take (*prenez*) thought (*La pensee. f*). Afterwards write (écrire) me.

How are your engagements?

Arrange (*fixez*) a date.

Pack one trunk (*malle. m*).

(Venez) Come.

But say when you are coming and I will be on the pier.

We have food here.

Also (aussi) a bed.

I think the pater is pleased with this shanty (*content de ce shebang*).

He wants you to come.

I want you to come

Carrie wants you to come.

The baby (l'enfant) wants you to come.

You must (il faut-que) come.

In seriousness tell a lie – I mean make a date – and stick to it as near as can be and I'll bring you up from New York. Tell Aunt Aggie you will have at least a good holiday and the Pater will be here to play with.

All love but come along.

Best love to Aunt Aggie and Hugh from us all. The pater looks as large as life and twice as natural here.

Rud.

This letter requires an answer.
P.S.   The real reason is that you are wanted to work on the house.[1]

R.

To James Conland,[1] 3 July [1893]
ALS: Library of Congress

Brattleboro'. / Monday. July. 3.

Dear Dr. Conland

In sending you herewith cheque for your professional services from September to date may I take the liberty of thanking you for all your kindness and thoughtful care towards my wife and child this spring?

These matters do not appear on the bill but believe me we appreciate them most keenly.

With sincerest regards I am

Yours very sincerely
Rudyard Kipling.

Note
1. Dr Conland (1851–1903), the Kipling family doctor, RK's closest friend among his Vermont neighbours. As a young man Conland had been a sailor and fisherman; he then qualified as a doctor and practised in Brattleboro until his death.

To Frederick L. Cowles,[1] 19 July 1893
ALS: Berg Collection, New York Public Library

Brattleboro / Vt. / July: 19:93

Dear Sir

I am in receipt of your favour of the 17th instant with typed copy of short tale called "Jim."

I have gone over it with a pen and it seems to me that it is not bad enough to burn by a good deal but it will bear rewriting. It's too much in front, to my thinking – too heavy by the head and a few (not more than ten) lines should be given to the two years in Arizona where Jim in the nature of things must have fallen away from grace. On page 8 I have marked where some adjectives might with advantage come away and you will find all the copy will pay for a little cutting out in this direction. The dialect is unnecessarily misspelled. All you have to do is to give the reader a notion of the dialect. If he knows it he will read in the rest. If he does not no amount of commas and elisions will help him.

The title "Jim" besides being altogether colourless has been used probably not more than twenty times within the last year. I know myself of two tales called "Jim": besides one "My Friend Jim" and another tale called "Jimmy." It would be well to give a new title. I submit therefore these three as suggestions.

"The Female of his Species."
"A little Progress" or "Progressive Euchre"
"Ace Orson of Black Hawk."

None of these titles are good and the last is Bret Harte pure and simple but they are all better than "Jim."

There's much too much of newspaper phrase in the tale which I have over and underlined. The simplest and straightest words had better be substituted. The minor character called Green shows that the name has been given in a hurry because he is a minor character. It is just as well to get a good name for a minor character as for a leading man and it looks much better.

As the revision of stories is not my regular work I must inform you that my fee for a written opinion suggestions etc. is $5 (five dollars). I shall therefore be obliged if you will send this sum to The Tribune Fresh Air Fund[2] at your earliest convenience advising me by letter of the same.

Sincerely
Rudyard Kipling

Notes

1. This letter, when offered for sale at the American Art Association, New York, 20 April 1921, was accompanied by the MS of Cowles's "An Angel of Tenderfoot Hill", with corrections by RK. I have not found any futher information about Cowles or his story.
2. This was a favourite charity of RK's and served as his means for making the many people who asked favours from him to return some compensation.

To Margaret Mackail, [27][1] August 1893
ALS: University of Sussex

Sunday Aug: 24 93 / Naulakha. / Brattleboro. / Vt.

Sweet lady – ho! ho! You mustn't expect me to be rational just now because we've but a week since moved into our new house and it is as a toy and a delight.[2] None the less before I left for a visit into Canada with the Father I should have answered yours with Denis's picture but I didn't because I had twenty thousand things to attend to. He, (Denis with his clothes off) lives on the bedroom mantel piece where he can daily see Josephine with not much more on. Thus he is kept in countenance who is already "all face." You're lucky to have your boy and your girl behind you. After this there will be no more surprises. He looks well put together and deep in the chest. Now I want a photo of his head as it appears when he keeps it still.

Carrie wonders how in the world you stand up to the two of them but I suppose these things are given from on high at the proper time. Our Baby Jo though calm and not blackguardly as babies go seems to be all of a houseful in herself as is the custom of first babes. She keeps most beautifully well and to our thinking grows in grace daily. The little innocent is just beginning to creep and as she doesn't quite know "go ahead" from "go astern" she is just as apt as not to skitter backwards across the floor when she wants to grab a rattle a foot in front of her. Yes, she is masterful but we've had our first big row with her. 'Twas going to sleep by herself and not asking to be taken up. The war endured for twenty minutes but she has understood the situation ever since. I can hear her, arguing with her nurse as I write in her upstairs verandah where she sits and is wheeled when the sun is too hot. Otherwise she goes driving at least twice a day – with her mother and nurse for milk and eggs, or any other excuse – long drives of eight or ten miles when she sleeps and puts on a beautiful tan colour.

So long as she keeps well we're full happy. Carrie has been working like a demon to bring the new house into order and now it runs silently. You can't imagine the bliss of getting into a place where you can turn round, unless you've spent a twelvemonth in a shanty one atop of the other. And unless you have lived with the laborious and futile foot bath in your room for that time you can't realize the bliss of a decent, clean porcelain tub and hot and cold water in the taps. It sounds absurd but when I luxuriously parboiled myself in a hot bath knowing I was beholden to no man therefore and shouldn't be charged for it on any bill I felt that I was well paid for all my work and waitings. Your mind I perceive instantly leaps to one conclusion "Ruddy hasn't bathed for a year. How he must have enjoyed it!" That is untrue. I have; but it was with difficulty.

Then there is the delight of real doors that shut and cupboards where you want 'em; and built in bookcases and the like that make us very happy. So far we have found no mistake in our new dwelling and that is good because we made it for ourselves. The joy of the house is the loggia with the ten foot window that slides up bodily and lets all the woods and mountains in upon you in a flood. I left the Father avisiting at Long Island. He'll be up tomorrow and he hasn't seen the house lived in yet.

I took him to Montreal, Quebec, the Saguenay, Boston and New York and I fancy from a few things that he said as how he had rather enjoyed himself. He and Baby Jo are extreme friends and I think he'll be sorry to say goodby to her. We don't talk of going away yet but he's getting a little restless and I suppose the Mother's house at Tisbury[3] will really be finished one of these days. Never mind. Now he knows the way he'll come again. I want him to try a Southern California winter if he finds the English fog is too deadly. The Mother's letters incidentally bring us a lot of news about you all. I don't like the persistent way Aggie goes sick. It's bad for her and worse for Ambo who is a Gay Deceiver. He went to Naples instead of coming here for awhile and when I see him I'll tell him just what I think. I heard of Stan also and his wife and her prospects. Poor devil! Stan doesn't know what he's in for – mercifully – but there will be grief and weepings among the Baldwins if it isn't a boy![4] Please write me a letter and tell me things. I'm fearfully busy but the answer shall be sent.

All love to you and yours from us both

Your cousin (and which is more a householder)

Ruddy.

When I was in New York the other day I saw Ada Rehan *but* Malvolio was done with a strong Irish accent. I left before the end of the play. An Irish accent.[5]

Notes

1. Sunday was the 27th.
2. The move to the new house, called "Naulakha" (alluding to the collaboration of Wolcott Balestier and RK on *The Naulahka* but correcting the spelling) was made on 12 August, while RK and his father were on tour to Canada.
3. Tisbury, Wiltshire, twelve miles west of Salisbury, where the elder Kiplings spent the rest of their days.
4. The Baldwins' child, a boy, was still-born in 1894.
5. RK refers to his trip in the spring. The production of *Twelfth Night* with Ada Rehan at Daly's Theater opened in February with George H. Clarke as Malvolio.

To Charles Eliot Norton,[1] 2 September 1893

ALS: Harvard University

Brattleboro' / Vermont. / Sept: 2. 1893.

My dear Sir,

I have to thank you very sincerely for your kind letter and invitation of the 1st instant, and I should be delighted to come to you as you propose. Mrs Kipling is not able to leave home this summer on account of our baby. My father has been spending some months with us and when he and I were in Boston the other day we hoped to have seen you. Might I bring him with me, and is next Friday (Sept 8th) convenient for you to have us?

With renewed thanks I am

Very sincerely yours
Rudyard Kipling.

Note

1. Norton (1827–1908), Professor of the History of Art at Harvard and devoted Anglophile, had been part of the Pre-Raphaelite circle in London and shared many friendships and associations with the Kipling family. On his visit to Norton that followed this letter RK struck up a friendship that lasted to Norton's death. Norton was in many ways the last of the high brahminical tradition in Boston and gave RK a privileged idea of what that culture had been.

To Guy Boothby,[1] 5 October 1893

ALS: Syracuse University

Brattleboro / Oct. 5. 93

Dear Boothby

Give a man time to get his breath, will yer? Here's yours of the 26th announcing that you are going to get married. You'll have your hands full one way and the other but I shouldn't be surprised if matrimony didn't do you a heap of good. Tisn't a panacea that I recommend right and left by any means but it teaches a man to keep his temper and to remember that the earth does not revolve absolutely and eternally round his hat. It teaches the tougher virtues – such as humility, restraint, order and forethought and like literature is its own exceeding great reward. These things, though, you will have to learn painfully for yourself who are at present walking and smirking idiotically through Paradise – which well I knows it.

If you'll take my advice you will *not* start on a sea tour, of cabins and decks and the like, immediately after you are wed. Get to know each other a little ere you deliberately face the cooping up of shipboard and all the attendant evils. That is if She has not travelled much. It would be splendid if you could come to the States but you would *not* be wise to bring your wife across a November Atlantic into a snow bound land. Just remember that what is pie to a man who goes across Australia for fun[2] is not a joy to a girl ignorant of anything longer than a three hour trip to London. You'll be wiser in a year than you are now. I'd go East if I were you or Madeira or just the Gib, Malta, Port Said and round again – or there is a heavenly 16 day run to the Cape which is lovely. Show her heaths and lilies and Zulus and niggers and return.

Well, bless you both. My small daughter upstairs with her first tooth crows as I write this. Oh Lord what a lot you have to learn.

I was down in New York last week[3] and I murmured your name to Appletons* – the firm that are handling Many Inventions – and they took your address. I don't know if aught will come of it but you'll find them a pretty straight people to deal with – as the breed goes.[4] I fancy I saw your sweet Roman Hand in some articles on Perth etc. for the Nat. Observer. It's good practice but look out that you don't fall into the mannerisms of that journal. I'm glad to hear that you meditate a coastwise blow and have got rid of your Seccubus.[5] Were I with you I would talk to you like a Dutch uncle but since I am not I give you my blessing again and the old copy book heading: – Be good and you'll be happy.

Ever yours
Rudyard Kipling.

P.S.   Photo hasn't come to hand yet. I'd send one in return if I had such a thing but I haven't. Cautiously and discreetly – if young Love knows the meaning of these words – present my respectful salaams to Her and tell her if good wishes are any avail she has a shipload of 'em from across the water.

RK

* 1–3–5 Bond St / B'way / New York.

Notes
1. Boothby (1867–1905), novelist, was born in Australia. According to the *DNB* he did not settle in England until 1894 and did not marry until 1895, but this letter seems to call those dates in question. RK's letter is clearly dated, and the reference to a trip to New York a week before confirms that date.
2. Boothby had crossed Australia from north to south in 1891–2.
3. RK and CK went to New York on 23 September with JLK, who left for England on the 27th; they returned on the 29th (CK diary).
4. Appleton's published eight titles by Boothby between 1895 and 1901.
5. Thus in MS: if this alludes to anything by Boothby I cannot identify it.

To Charles Burr Todd,[1] 6 October 1893

ALS: Harvard University

Brattleboro: / Vt. / Oct 6. 93.

My dear Sir

Enclosed please find cheque for 5 (five dollars) in payment my dues for one year as member of the association of American authors: which kindly acknowledge at your convenience.

Sincerely
Rudyard Kipling

To
Charles Burr Tod Esq
Secretary
Ass. Am. Authors.

P.S.   I would point out that there is no official address on the association's note paper.

Note

1. Todd (1849–?), editor and historical writer, organised the Association of American Authors in 1892, on the model of Besant's Society of Authors in London. The Association included such names as Howells, George W. Cable, Julian Hawthorne, and Charles Dudley Warner, but it did not last long.

To James Whitcomb Riley, 13 October 1893

Text: James Whitcomb Riley, *Letters*, ed. William Lyon Phelps (Indianapolis, 1930), p. 333

Naulakha, / Brattleboro, Vermont, / Oct. 13, 1893.

Dear Mr. Riley:

It came in this morning – all gallant and gay in the beautiful green livery.[1] The *Century* folk certainly know how to turn out a book just so. I let the morning's work slide and went through it at once – which was weak of me. Squire Hawkins's tale of course I remember from that great night, and some of the others of course I have met in their first print dresses, but "Fessler's Bees" was teetotally new and I shook helplessly over it.

I can hear that tale being slowly drawled by the teller. Over some of the others, I won't say which, I choked and 'tis your blamed verses that are the only ones I know that can make me gulp. In revenge, I wish to state clearly that I don't like "Tradin' Joe." – It may be true to nature but it goes ag'in' my stomach. And that's all and a heap of thanks.

We've got a roof above our heads now, so if ever business brings you within ear-shot of this place you'll know where to "light an' hitch."

With kindest regards from my wife and myself.

Ever yours sincerely,
Rudyard Kipling.

Note

1. *Poems Here at Home*, published this month; RK and Riley had met in New York sometime during RK's stay there in March and April of this year.

To William Ernest Henley, [3–4]¹ December 1893

ALS: Morgan Library

Naulakha. / Brattleboro. / Vermont. / Dec: 2: 93.

Dear Henley –

Peccavi – but no sooner had I sent off the Sergeant's Wedding[2] (a singularly chaste and scholarly lyric) than your note came in. All the same I did acknowledge your little maiden's picture long ago – if that which I call my memory (no one else will trust it) serves me. Our bairn has got to great ages – teeth, four of 'em – and points with a lucid fore finger yearning and honing from her stomach upwards for things she can on no account be allowed to touch – pipes, knives and cates of that kind. She's crawling about my room now – a little ashputtel – prying into the wood basket and trying to get into the ashes and hauling down my books on her innocent head or stopping to sing runes in her own tongue. She has become very bonnie but with the deuce of a will of her own, and a chin to match.

You never talk seriously of your ails but I gather from this last that you had come within a little of going out altogether. For any sakes stick to the milk and ravalenta. It's the damned London drive that does it and men come to believing that they can't make a bolt because they are king-bolts in the machine (that'a a fine transatlantic jest) and – I wish you wouldn't, while there are so many men whose deaths I would hail with psalms. If you had six weeks and the will to it you might do worse than swiftly take a Liner from Southampton and come here for a month where we would give you great slabs of quiet. If I were the other side

I'd get you over on sick leave but I do wish you'd consider the matter. The voyage would be foul most like but one never knows the moods of the big water. Then we'd take you sleighing; give you your own table to mess at with pens and ink and if the stillness didn't benefit you you could stay till it did. Think now and consider. The first few days you'd hate it and would prance about waiting for things to happen but we'd tame you – This is a sabbath as it might have been early at the making of the world. The week's work has been carefully put away under a couple of feet of snow and lest that should drift rain has fallen on top of it, and frozen so that the whole is locked up under a two inch crust. You don't know how much this means. A high wind on the heels of a dry mealy snow quickly buries us up in snow drifts. Of course we are caught unprepared. That is the only news all over New England this time of year. We're building a stable and some of the drains have yet to be filled in – and they are but not by any workmen of ours and we've had a holy mess over a frozen pump which now stands like a ghost with a running cold – all covered with icicles. I could give you news of that cut for pages. How we are waiting for a windmill to pump water out of a 325 foot artesian well which we have been boring all summer; how the snowshoes after their long rest in the attic stretch and rack and twist; how the family sleigh is in the hands of the mender and God only knows when or how we are to get it up here and in use; how there is a female cow which will not calve though long overdue and how I waver between bringing a suit against the defaulting bull and sluicing her out with an enema; how we have made a mighty road with rocks and gravel and how the snow has wiped it out; how we rejoice in the new house which we can pat and play with and how because we pay no rent as we fondly remind each other we launch out into more books; how I have found Tonson's 1719 Donne with the portrait in crushed levant and how the ass that sold it knew not its worth: how I am in receipt of weekly catalogues from second hand book firms and find much that I never expected; how the generous days give me long times for reading and work: how I am consumed with an itch for verse which goes into the waste paper basket, most of it; and things and things and things all as small as this.

In good seriousness I am doing better than writing with my good right hand. I am throwing away what I have written with both as it used to be in the old days and it's grateful and comforting. Chiefly – and this I would impress upon you – I am sitting still and keeping quiet, for the good of my soul. T'other day, and it was like the skirl of a shell over a bomb-proof pit, there came to my address poor Adams's shrieking screed about "Mr Rudyard Kipling's verse."[3] Rummy thing to hear a dead man swearing at you as it might be before he got cold. Well he knows if the Ten Commandments rank with the Athanasian creed by this time.

For our Social Engagements – I quote from the engagement book – we went out to dinner for the first time in three months last Sunday – eight miles there and as many back – a blazing moon on white snow and the road dipping in and out of the pine hollows where the frozen brooks were. Other amusements did not take us so far. I've grubbed up a hundred and fifty yards of old stone wall with pick and spade; raked the leaves off slopes; lopped undergrowth and burned refuse and planted pines as long as the weather served and it's mighty consoling to look along a straight line that you have cleaned by your own lone self as the children say here. Later on we shall go to New York for a few weeks and there we join the Giddy Whirl and are no end fine and dissipated.[4] They have an intensely Literary society there – same old names cropping up week after week at the same old parties; same old gags; same old dishwater as it might be in any city we could name – allowing for local colour and the necessity of creating the Great American Literature. They count words and volumes here and I believe if a man of their breed could turn out sixty fat books with decent titles they'd hail him as one of the stablishers of the G.A.L. Don't spare the rod in your criticisms of anything. This 'ere is the land where "everything goes" and the lawlessness leaks into the books as it does into all the other things. Only, there's no force at the back of the incessant posing to be free – only common people doing common things in the cheapest and most effective way for immediate results. I believe in the critic, right or wrong so long as there is a critic and a canon. I believe in the *Saturday Review*, the *Spectator*, the *Athenæum* and *all* the Quarterlies. I believe in Mudie,[5] in the British Nation, in Mrs Grundy, in the Young Person, and in everything else that sits on the head of talent without form or rule. I believe in Torquemada and the Inquisition; in everything Doctor Johnson said about anybody and in all things that have authority and decency to back 'em. For they are necessary, and now I know why. I've come to the land where "everything goes" and don't you forget it. It's a colt training without bit, dumb jockey or lunging reins – chucking his feet and his head all over the place, wasting his power because he doesn't know how to carry himself.

Monday morning – All froze up deeper than ever and the trees done over with spun diamond. Now this is the kind of weather that would do you good. You see I could meet you at New York and bring you up – but what is the use of talking to a man set in his own street. Verily there is more hope for an obelisk than for him. The N.O. comes with a fair face and great punctuality – to my comfort, but I do not like your "middles" always and there are some yarns by a fellow called Murray Gilchrist[6] isn't it that turn me up – just on account of their style. Makes we want to pump on the writer with a large force-pump. I haven't seen

Gilbert Parker[7] but I was invited down to Boston to meet him and was sorry that I couldn't move. Who is this "Dodo" chap?[8] I haven't read Dodo but I hear it's mighty good and I see the young 'un has cut loose with a theory of composition.[9] Deja! If you can ever find anything decent to say about a book called "Steve Brown's Bunyip"[10] please do. I don't care about the author – don't know him – but I know that a word in his praise fills with joy two or three dear old ladies who were very sweet to me when I was a little fellow. And the book isn't bad either.

Now I must truthfully stop. The Pater is at Tisbury Wilts. He spent three summer months with us here and I fancy his marginal notes should be interesting.

Good new of old Whibley. Keep his hair cut and the front of his trousers buttoned and he may yet grow decent–ish and give him my much love. Vernon[11] I take it may have fallen in love. They do sometimes – some of 'em. Yes I saw about J. M. B[arrie].'s novel in *Scribner*[12] – more power to his elbow and from odd quarters I hear now and then of what the other chaps are doing. But Lord, Lord to think how far off it all seems. Yet some day when you do not expect you will see me; and if you have not the know-how to come and rest please keep well till I can overhaul you.

Ever yours
Ruddy

P.S.   The way collisions at sea come about is this way – and as I can't very well do it in a poem I send it to you without prejudice.

The iron in the mine and under the hammer; and in the plate and the engine room; has a sort of blind lust beaten into it, for to meet and I suppose nautically to copulate with, other iron and steel then being worked into the frame of another ship. All the seven seas over the ship yearns for its mate – tearing along under moon and cloud; sweating in oily tropic ports; resting in dock, and so forth. At last comes the bridal night – wind, current and set of the sea aiding while the eyes of men are held and steamer meets steamer in a big kiss and sink down to cool off in the water beds. What I want to get at is the steamer's unconcern about the men who happen to be crawling in her innards at the time. Now it seems to me that perhaps you might twist and turn these things to one of your unrhymed sheet lightning, orchid house, still and sweating poems. It's done gone broke in my hands for lack of sufficient study of metre.[13] Well, if Allah gives me another seven years we'll be able to handle a line better.

R.

Here's a picture of the pater and baby Josephine – domestic manufacture – that may amuse you. Much love.

Notes
1. The first part of the letter was evidently written on the Sunday which fell on 3 December in 1893.
2. If RK did send this to Henley it was not published until it appeared in the volume *The Seven Seas* (1896).
3. Francis Adams in the *Fortnightly Review*, LIV (November 1893). Adams (1862–93) had committed suicide in September. The review is filled with shrill insult, and apropos of a line in "Cleared" says "We shall have him vituperating somebody next for not accepting the Thirty-nine articles or the Athanasian Creed – this delightful 'illustrator' of Anglo-Indian social life, with five out of the six 'illustrations' based on breakage of the Seventh Commandment" (p. 600).
4. They did not go until 11 January 1894, and then stayed only until the 17th (CK diary).
5. Charles Edward Mudie (1818–90), as the owner of the largest circulating library in England, was able to exercise a *de facto* censorship on contemporary literature by refusing to stock books of which he disapproved.
6. Robert Murray Gilchrist (1868–1917), novelist, a regular contributor to the *National Observer*.
7. (Sir) Gilbert Parker (1862–1932), Canadian-born poet, travel writer, and novelist; MP, 1900–18.
8. E. F. Benson (1867–1940), son of the Archbishop of Canterbury and brother of A. C. Benson, made a precocious success with his first book, *Dodo* (1893).
9. "A Question of Taste", *Nineteenth Century*, XXXIV (September 1893).
10. By John Arthur Barry (1850–1911), a Sydney journalist born in England and for many years a sailor; RK contributed "The Sea-Wife" as a prefatory poem to *Steve Brown's Bunyip*, Barry's first book.
11. Vernon Blackburn married a woman strangely identified in *Who Was Who* simply as "a Jewess, tribe of Judah".
12. Perhaps an early reference to *Sentimental Tommy*, which appeared as a serial in *Scribner's* but not until 1896.
13. Perhaps this is "The Song of the Deep Sea Engines": see 18–19 January 1893.

To Edward Lucas White, 10–[17] December 1893

ALS: Syracuse University

> *Naulakha. / Brattleboro. / Vermont. / Dec: 10:93*
> (– and some days later)

Esteemed Younger Brother,

A scrupulously tidy soul (such as me) gets into trouble. I meant to have written you long before your last letter came; because I had a notion you weren't well but I'd filed your letter with that degree of care it could nowise be found. Then the Thanksgiving note came in and we recognized it from afar saying: – "It's the Baltimore man". Many thanks for it. What an augur-eye you keep on my output! But I'm glad "The Legs of Sister Ursula"[1] made you laugh, for it is meant to that end and now and again a laugh over a sheer absurdity is good for the liver and the stomach and the bile. That was what the mission of the "Legs" was. Brugglesmith is even as you say; needing explication and amplification.

Moreover the teller (who was indubitably loaded to the bung) speaks too rationally for a sober man amid those surroundings and too mixedly for a drunken one. When humour fails to come off it [sits] down more [flattings]² on its little behind than either pathos, sentiment or direct narrative. If you wish to show a friend exactly how a thing should *not* be done read him the tale in Longmans³ (Eheu! our sins pursue us. I thought *that* tale was dead and discreetly buried long since). No it was not the shape of the theatre that was wrong but something quite different, beginning with the inkpot. Let it and some of the others serve as awful warnings.

I've been scandalously neglecting my duties to follow – Euterpe, I think, but it is one anyway of the nine harlots – these few weeks past experimenting with divers metres and various rhymes. The results serve excellent well to light fires and the work amuses one while it goes on. There's a heap in verse though apt to get out of hand – some of it – very. Do you know to the extent you ought the poems of Donne who was Browning's great-great grandfather? I've been reading him again for the health of my spirit and – he is no small singer. Must have been a haughty and proud stomached individual in his life – with R.B.'s temperament for turning his mind clean upside down as it were a full bottle and letting the ideas get out as they best could. He is not very accessible – all of him – by reason of his statements which are occasionally free. There were giants in those days and it is profitable to read 'em – even Fletcher who sat down before the human carcass and hammered out God knows how many thousand lines of high and disposed allegory – or Drayton – or Drummond.⁴ These are not of the first ranks you say? No but they worked largely and gave all they had to their verses. Read 'em again and yet again.

Somewhere in the blue beyonds there's a big poem waiting for the man who can do it – The last supper at St. Julian's wasn't it – the sacrament supper when Drake got ready to slay his traitorous friend where Magellan had hanged certain of his mutineers – away down in the south, beyond the reach of God or man. The sailors of the *Pelican* looking on; Doughty cracking his very courteous jests; the crazy ships rocking at the world's end and the block and the headsman.⁵ Think of it! Why can't a man do everything he has a mind to by the mere wishing of it instead of having to dig like a badger before he can get out a decent couplet. I cannot work with ease or fluency worse luck: and the fluenter the thing looks from the outside the more worriment and sweat is it to me to evolve.

Don't you go a theorizing. Concreteness in expression is all very well if you happen to like it but consider how it may be a stumbling block to another make of mind. For myself I love not to hear a spade called a spade because there are so many varieties of spade; and so by preference

I say when writing of such: – a balance handle, cutting edge, Beaver Falls finishing or sod spade as the case may be but I can easily conceive how maddening that must be to a fellow who doesn't care two damns for anything except agricultural implements in the mass. Every man is too apt to make the law of his temperament the fly wheel of all creation. I confess I love accuracy of detail, inaccuracy being the besetting sin of a man I know pretty well; and since my life has been mainly spent among men who have to be accurate in describing the things with which they deal – guns, horses, machines, canals, roads and the steps of judicial procedure – I assume all the world is equally concerned. Which it isn't! There's room for all manner and kind of expression in this Wale but as things and lives and surroundings get more specialized I shouldn't wonder if there wasn't a drift towards saying things more clearly than the old laws allowed.

As for the Tory spirit – what would you have? It's a question of raising and training again. All I've been taught to see is that carelessness in administration, sloppiness of speech, vague appeals to the sentiments of great multitudes and tampering with the Decalogue, because a lot of people don't like to play consequences logically, ends in sending up the murder statistics and murder is no good thing. There's nothing in the People and the talk about the people a jot more to be reverenced than in Kings and the Divine right of the same. They are only men anyway – not gods above the law of wrong doing and, so it seems, much of the windy talk in England about the inherent rightness and righteousness of lots of folk in a lump is skittles – nothing more than the old bunkum about the Divine right of kings transferred to an ungetatable Fetish which isn't responsible for its own actions. You can't indict the People, and cut off their head for evil practices and for myself I like a responsible person whose head I can help to cut off if need be. I suppose all this is wildly out of date but I've had the honor of seeing the results of a few "popular" movements: when the regular administrators received a mandate to do certain things and "The People" lost interest in the show as they always do, and the luckless administrators were left alone to fight out all the sorrow and sin and dirt and filth and disease that "The People" (who are above the Law) so lightheartedly scattered for others to reap. There are in life such things as special knowledge, training, obedience, order, discipline and views that extend beyond the nose of the seer. How the deuce can you expect a million men keenly interested in their own domesticities to have those things?

Moreover (now this is worth millions tho' you'll laugh at it) "The People" is Mrs Harris.[6] *There ain't no such a person.* There are men, and women, and interests and communities but there's no clear-eyed, impeccable Overseer of all interests such as the papers pretend. If there were we should have no need of the almighty. "The People" is a

Brocken-spectre of man's own importance and if you walk up to it it disappears. It can only talk and throw its arms about exactly as you do but, so long as each man believes that somewhere round the corner lives this last of the Bogeys, the *maya* – the delusion, is as good as the reality. But I don't subscribe to that paper none the less. No profit is to be gained by insulting the God: for it is not good to interfere with any man's beliefs. Act only as though he were – just the least little bit in the world – to be laughed at and he will become a good servant. "The People" hates being made fun of – worse than ever kings did. I've tried and it called me awful names – on both sides the water – regular bone-breakers of names but the bones didn't break. And yet, remember, it is evil to do one's work baldheaded for the sake of a Purpose. Purposes are good things but they are apt to make writing stodgy – same as this last page and a quarter. Let the Purpose come in accidental like, obliquely, from afar, casually and do not drive it too hard –

Later. Much later. I've kept this letter an awful time on the stocks but every minute and thought has been taken up in fighting the weather which has suddenly gone mad – because I suppose it saw us trying to put up a windmill. Figure to yourself (eight or nine men trying to work in despite of it all) blinding wind and cold; followed by a heavy snow; then a day and a night and a day of 25 below zero, then an ice storm and then drenching rain and thaw and freeze coating everything half an inch deep. Oh, but I am almost out of patience. Yesterday I spent hauling on a rope to hoist an idiotic three legged thing like this [sketch of windmill on its side]. It looks awfully drunk still and a man is spending this sabbath puttering over its nuts and screws. Don't you never go for to dig a well and make towers and wind mills.[7]

And now, I must truly stop. It has been a long letter full of nonsense but it may fill up some of your time. Keep well and don't work too hard and have a merry Christmas and believe me

Ever yours sincerely
Rudyard Kipling.

Notes
1. Published in *The Idler*, June 1893; not collected by RK until the Sussex Edition.
2. "Sits" and "flattings" are my best guesses as to what RK wrote.
3. "For One Night Only", *Longmans*, April 1890; collected in Sussex Edition.
4. RK means Phineas Fletcher, Michael Drayton, and William Drummond of Hawthornden.
5. RK published no such poem, though Drake as hero is the subject of "With Drake in the Tropics" and "Frankie's Trade" and is alluded to in "The Song of the Dead".
6. The non-existent confidante of Mrs Gamp in *Martin Chuzzlewit*.
7. The water supply at "Naulakha" was a constant trouble. The windmill was later replaced by a motor-driven pump.

To Julie Lippman,[1] [21 December 1893][2]
ALS: Dalhousie University

Naulakha. / Brattleboro. / Vermont.

Madam,

I am officially insthructed – she bein' busy eatin' him tusks first an' a good deal incommoded by consequince – an' her father watchin' the same wid meltin' smiles shootably to acknowledge the same – manin' the stuffed elephint wid his *jool* and monogram as safely received an' right side up this mornin'. Barrin' that he will not wash in the way av her rubber doll that takes to ut like a duck bein' forced as ye might say an' hild under by her every mornin' he is a noble fat baste an' has tuk by this time more batin' an' scratchin' and whackin' than I iver dared give his god father, for I make bould that he was christened Malachi in memory av my doin's at Cawnpore. The beauty av his backview lookin' at him behind is such that she cannot express excipt by shoutin' at the same. He has been hild up by the tail an' waved generous to the breezes; his head has been grounded upon the flure an' chewed betunetimes an' if makin' a small child happy is wan av the things entered to credit that same is done an' double done by you my dear Madam.

My correspondence bein' mostly (up to this date) desultory an' onstamped I am not that manner av Roshus[3] in my complemints as I wud desire but I take my Pen which I do not understhand to report my large appreshiation on my own account av the Superior Baste an' hers singin' over it upstairs – she not knowin' any more than the angils that it is unwholesim to pull a elephint backwards by the scruff av his neck. Wid best regards an' wishes for the Coming seasons from me and Dinah Shadd
I am

My dear Madam
Yours respectfully to command
Terence Mulvaney

B. Company[4]

Notes

1. A note by Miss Lippman accompanying the letter explains that she made a stuffed elephant toy in allusion to "My Lord the Elephant" and sent it as a gift for Josephine Kipling.
2. Dated from postmark.
3. Roscius, the great Roman comic actor; Mulvaney refers to him in "With the Main Guard", but his relevance here is not clear.
4. Lined out in MS.

Part Two
At Home in Vermont
1894–96

INTRODUCTION

Kipling's American years were years of a great creative outburst, but his relation to America was very restricted and difficult; it ended, perhaps not surprisingly, in anger and deep resentment. Kipling's output included the two *Jungle Books*, *The Seven Seas*, *"Captains Courageous"*, and *The Day's Work*, an astonishing collection of distinctively original work that shows him recapitulating and transforming his Indian experience and striking out in new directions. Perhaps the isolation of his life in Vermont helped him to this achievement: Kipling himself thought that it did. He and his wife lived in, but were not at all of, the Brattleboro community. Carrie occupied herself with the management of the house, the care of her children (there were two by early 1896), and the defence of her husband against the intrusions of the world outside. Kipling had his work and his friendships, few of which had anything to do with Brattleboro. When he looked for amusement and diversion, he went to Boston or to New York or to Washington. Twice in their Brattleboro years he and Carrie travelled to England, where they could have as much attention as celebrities as either of them could wish.

Kipling made little effort to see much of the country in which he was living: perhaps he had seen more than enough in those weeks he had spent crossing the continent in the summer of 1889. At any rate, he never went west of Brattleboro once had had settled there. With his quick and imaginative apprehension of things he of course saw and learned much of American life, and it is clear that he hoped, after a time, to make extensive use of it in his work. He did not, however, treat America as he had treated India, seeking out as much of its variety as he could; he was, after all, no longer a working journalist, and he could pick his own occasions and follow his own purposes. He made several cordial acquaintances in Brattleboro, but his only real friend seems to have been Dr Conland, who, as a physician, was an observer of local life such as Kipling loved to consult. As a man without local connections and as a Democrat in Republican Vermont, Conland was doubly an outsider. For the rest, Kipling's American friends tended to be the rich, the well connected, the politically important, or the distinguished. The wealthy artist Lockwood de Forest in New York, the Catlin family of Morristown, New Jersey, the "little Washington gang" that included John Hay, Henry Adams, and William Hallett Phillips, and the Harvard professor Charles Eliot Norton were the sort of American to whom Kipling was drawn, and they certainly represented the highest level of privilege, cultivation, and accomplishment that the country had to show. It is interesting, but idle, to speculate about what Kipling's version of America would have become had he remained in the country among such people as these.

Kipling had always had a keen interest in American literature, an interest that continued during his American years. He knew and admired the work of, for example, Sarah Orne Jewettt, Hamlin Garland, James Whitcomb Riley, Joel Chandler Harris, William Dean Howells, Owen Wister, and Stephen Crane; he saw them as specifically American writers, rising out of local conditions and giving expression to particular times and places. Some of them he corresponded with, and some of them he took the trouble to meet. On the whole, he seems to have been less guarded towards American writers than he was towards the English. The conditions of American literary life worked against the formation of cliques, and Kipling had nothing to fear in America about being identified with the wrong sets or the wrong sorts. One should add that the only publishers with whom Kipling was ever on terms of friendship were his American publishers, S. S. McClure and, especially, F. N. Doubleday.

Even before he ever saw the country, Kipling was persuaded that the United States was a place of lawless violence; his American travels in 1899 did nothing to disabuse him of the notion, which is almost the central theme of the American letters that he wrote at the time and that were later republished in *From Sea to Sea*. Even after he had become a propertied man in long-settled Vermont, he never quite got over the conviction that, as one of his Vermont acquaintances put it, "every American citizen carried concealed weapons of war". Two episodes, one public and one private, confirmed Kipling in his view and ended by driving him away from the country. The first was a jingoistic episode at the end of 1895, when the United States grew concerned over a border dispute between British Guiana and Venezuela. President Cleveland invoked the Monroe Doctrine, and there was much sabre-rattling among the American press. The affair ended quietly many months later in arbitration that vindicated England, but the damage, as Kipling saw it, had been done: as a loyal English citizen – or rather, as an enthusiastic English imperialist – he could not accept a situation in which his daily experience on all sides was to hear his country reviled and his politics condemned, and that in a country whose leaders had, he thought, irresponsibly stirred up the conflict for their own ends. Perhaps he had never meant to be more than a sojourner in New England; at any rate, he seems to have made plans to leave the country indefinitely while the Venezuela crisis was still agitating the newspapers.

The second episode was all too personal. Kipling's nearest neighbour in Vermont was his brother-in-law, Beatty Balestier, from whom the

Kiplings had bought the land on which to build their house. Beatty had been employed by them to act as a sort of factotum during the construction of the house and afterwards, but conflict soon arose between him and his sister, Caroline Kipling. Beatty was loud, brash, impulsive, and irresponsible; his sister was strong-willed and self-righteous: it was inevitable that they should exasperate each other, as they speedily did. Quarrels arose on many questions, including money questions, and local gossip took it all in gratefully. One day in May 1896, Beatty encountered his brother-in-law Kipling on the road to Brattleboro, and, as Kipling understood him, threatened to kill him if Kipling did not retract certain stories about Beatty. Here was lawless violence again! The next day, after consultation with his wife, who doubtless confirmed him in his folly, Kipling had Beatty arrested on charges of assault and threatening murder. A public hearing was held, attracting national newspaper attention, and Kipling was humiliated in a circus atmosphere. Kipling held on for a few more weeks, not actually leaving Brattleboro until the end of August, but America, for the moment at least, had become impossible. Beatty Balestier, Kipling's idea of the archetypal American in his undisciplined, lawless energy, was left in possession of a field that Kipling seemed glad to abandon but that he could never quite forget.

To Brander Matthews,[1] 2 January 1894

ALS: Columbia University

[Naulakha] Jan. 2: 94

Dear Matthews

We have always been fouling each other's North East course with titles. That is because you and I invent the best in the market. By the way what an infamous sell *"The Frog that played the trombone"*[2] was! As soon as I saw the drawing of the ash-tray I saw how you had dragged in a really superb title by its hind legs.

In regard to the two other accidents I don't see why you need pull out for a *plain tale* anyway. They are pretty well extinct by this time and for the *Son of his Father*[3] if you'll only tell me where it's coming out (mine I mean for the tale was written two years ago and I've lost track of it) I'll change him to "Adam" an alternative title and you can go ahead for *The Son of his Father* is too good a name to spill on a 8,000 word tale. You can have it anyway. As I told the man who told me that *"Mine own people"* had been used before "Cant' help that. *I've* only just invented it and I'm mighty pleased."

I shall take *The Parrot that Talked in his sleep* for a child story. Make a note of it. It's the only inspiration-born title that ever was.

Why don't you do a dialogue called "Collusion" based on some vagary of mental telepathy between two writers living say in San Francisco and New York each desperately hunting for new titles and each foiling and fouling the other. They are introduced, not knowing the others nom de plume at a restaurant and each speaks of the hell-hound on the opposite coast who has pulled up the sprouts of his brain by stealth. Result a gaudy row neither listening to the explanation of the other till the electrics on the restaurant go out. There has been, as the waiter explains, a *Leak in the wires* which might be the sub-title. You could do that perfectly.

I see that you have been fed lately by public subscription. I knew times were hard in town but I didn't know they were as bad as that or I'd have sent down some pig and doughnuts and come to see that you ate 'em.

We hope to be in New York before long and then I will arrange a private copyright treaty between us for titles.

With every good wish for the new year believe me

Ever yours sincerely
Rudyard Kipling.

Titles for 1894
"Accent on the Penultimate" (yours)

"General Average" (yours)
"By Dead Reckoning" (mine)
"Paid to account" (mine)
"The Stevedores" (yours)
"Hot – with Sugar" (mine)
As per invoice (mine)
Overlooked (yours)
Storage Batteries. (yours)
His Shearing Strain. (mine).
The Obvious Inference. (yours)
Polly Andria. (yours).

Notes

1. (James) Brander Matthews (1852–1929), writer of fiction, playwright, critic, editor, theatre historian, professor at Columbia; prominent in literary New York. He was a notable clubman, a founder of both the Authors' Club and The Players. He was also a member of the Century, the Athenaeum, and the Savile. He probably first met RK through the last-named of these.
2. *Harper's*, LXXXVII (November 1893).
3. RK's "The Son of His Father" was published in the US in *Harper's Weekly*, 30 December 1893; Matthews's *His Father's Son, a Novel of New York*, appeared in 1894.

To Henry James, 7 January 1894
ALS: Harvard University

[Naulakha] Jan. 7. 94.

Dear Mr. James,

There is great joy in this house, for your letter of Christmas came up from town and was read four abreast so to speak with shouts and cheers and rejoicings. All the family are abiding with us. I believe from the envelope that the letter was addressed to Mrs Balestier but each of us took it to ourself and I am under severe orders immediately to write to you while the rest – Carrie, her mother and Josephine, tell me what to say.

They, the Mother and Josephine are well, to begin with. In a while they will return to New York which I am told is quite a large town and be gay for the rest of the season. Carrie and I have no clothes: so must go down to the sea and buy some. After that we two purpose raiding into London for a short time and have authority from the Mother and Josephine that we bring you back with us, whether you will or not. For this reason, were I you, I should make my summer engagements elastic – very. It is true that we worship a baby in a snow temple but that service does not run continuously and the idol has her shrine into which she is shut while the worshippers eat and drink and write. The very best bedroom shall be yours and you shall see *our* America which we have made and invented for ourselves. It is even the dear old shif[t]less, thriftless East; all huge promises and poor fulfilment wherein there is no time-sense and no sense of responsibility. It makes me weep to think how all these years gone the sober conscientious western powers have been treating this last of the Asiatic kingdoms as a grown-up person. *We* work it from the Oriental standpoint and it answers perfectly to that helm.

Our geography is simple. We are six hours from New York; eight from Montreal and in this weather the mails come in as Allah pleases. You shall come that way too and, so soon as you have made up your mind to the going, you will enjoy it. And this is written because it is not good to take a man unprepared without at the least leaving him time to pack. To our own vast amusement we two have stayed in one place now for more than a year – for nearly two – and a house has grown up with which we play like children; and a stable is all but done and our talk is of the planting of trees for we have digged a well and crowned it with a wind-pump (less fearsome than you would imagine) and things go well with us. I am over my ears in work that I want to do and the greatest worry that comes is the freezing of a pipe or a week's thaw. The land is like a cool grey studio to rest in and, thanks to its back of beyondity, one can chuck into waste paper baskets much that would otherwise and otherwhere come into print.

I've done a book of children's beast-tales and spent about a month finishing verses to adorn it fore and aft. At the last I was sorry to let it go from me. Decidedly the best fun would be not to publish, but chuckle over one's tales alone.

News comes fitfully up the valley from New York. Mr. Howells can't come up here because he is busy but we still lay traps in the hope. I am very much in love with him and want to know him more and more.[1] He's the gentlest of souls that go about the world cussing at it. They are giving dinners and talking about Literature and how to do it and if not why not and so forth and it is all very refreshing and quite new. We're no nearer America of the market place than we are to China up here.

The Christmas holidays, Christmas trees, sleighing-parties; suppers and a barn dance have left us flat and indigestible – full of turkey and good resolutions. I do not mind having to keep the good resolutions.

We all rejoiced at the news about Gosse: and prayed that he might be more so later on for he needs it. [Verily?] he was born a "laidy" but it slipped in the mould.[2]

Thank you for your kind word about the Seals. I had the poem copyrighted this side but the *New York Tribune* on the ground that there was an absence of copyright notification in the Pall Mall Gazette quoted it whole as "Kipling's poor ballad."[3] Whereby I lost my trouble and pains but even yet the *Tribune* may be led to think. We are putting machinery in motion and rejoice to think how much they may pay for the Ballad and how much for the adjective. You being an American and living in England are the only person it seems who ought to be able to protect himself against thefts this side.

I believe Josephine is writing you a letter. I believe they all are and they all say that they will tell you how fond they are of you. Observe, I spike their guns, and prick their compliments.

Carrie and I have a notion of going to Bermuda in a few weeks ere we go to England. Pray you do not leave town too soon in the spring or leave an address whereby we may catch you, and follow.

With much love from all

Yours ever sincerely
Rudyard.

Notes
1. RK had met Howells in New York in April 1893 (CK diary).
2. I cannot explain this reference.
3. "The Rhyme of the Three Sealers", *Pall Mall Budget* (not *Gazette*), 14 December 1893; reprinted by the *New York Tribune*, 27 December.

To May Catlin,[1] [16 April 1894][2]
ALS: Miss Matilda Tyler

[84 Ebury Street, London][3]

I do not like London. C and I have been wandering about and the only good thing we've got is an Indian necklace of raw amethyst strung with tiny turquoises and seed pearls. This is to console us on account of the greyness of the air. Now we have taken a large fat country house in Wiltshire[4] close to my people and I am promised all the fishing I like on Lord Arundel's[5] grounds. This consoles me a little more but we have still a week to put in in these pestiferous lodgings. I've been to the Club[6] – seen Lang and Besant; missed Haggard and got out of two literary dinners as well as an invitation to speak at the Booksellers dinner; and now I think it's high time to go fishing and get to work. I wish we were in Bermuda again. Pray give my best reverent greetings to your mother and remember me to your staid and sober sister. Anon I shall be writing on business to Raymond Hunt.[7]

RK.

Notes
1. May, Edith, and Julia Catlin and their mother, Mrs Julius Catlin, from Morristown, New Jersey, were at the same hotel with the Kiplings during their visit to Bermuda in late February and early March of this year; Catlins and Kiplings were quickly on friendly terms. May married Otto R. Hansen.
2. This note is written at the end of a letter from CK to Miss Catlin in which CK explains that RK is away in Wiltshire but will add a note on his return: that was, according to CK's diary, on the 16th.
3. Where RK and CK were from 10 to 25 April (CK diary).
4. Arundell House, Tisbury, Wiltshire, where they remained until early August.
5. The 12th Baron Arundell of Wardour, whose seat of Wardour Castle is two miles from Tisbury.
6. The Savile Club.
7. The pseudonym under which May Catlin published her setting of RK's "Shiv and the Grasshopper" (1896). Her mother was the daughter of Seth *Hunt* and Frances *Raymond*.

To May Catlin, 10 June [1894]
ALS: Miss Matilda Tyler

Arundel House / Tisbury:
The tenth of a fine old English June

Dear Miss Catlin:
    I am an unholily remiss person, or I should have written long ago and acknowledged your delightful settings. It seems to me they are exactly what the words need – and when you come to consider how much an author thinks his most casual words require (He never gets it!) you can see how much I mean. Only – forgive the criticism – they were not easy to read. In the language of some immortal bard or another "go ahead!" and take my very best thanks.
    We're wet and gloomy here beyond the power of any words fit for your eyes. An English June is not a thing to enter upon lightly. Since April 11th we have had I think two clear days of sunshine. Now it is N.E. wind with fifteen or sixteen showers of rain a day – raw, cold, gusty and above all dark. We come back – thank Heaven – early in August and I know one of us who'll be delighted. C. has improved her opportunities poor dear by a fine rich cold which skated generally all over her. Now it is going and she is sitting over a blazing fire reading Clark Russell. The wind is howling round the house. It is wet and soppy

twilight and the temperature is about 52°. I'm just down from town where I've been assisting at a regimental dinner of the London Scottish – huge men in kilts with claymores and dirks – old friends of mine.[1] The cab strike makes things pleasingly uncertain at the end of an entertainment and I had to career about for half an hour or so making shameless love to passing hansoms before a bloated cabby would condescend to drive me. A man I know had to pay £8 (eight honest golden sovereigns!!) the other night for what ought to have been a two shilling fare. To add insult to bankruptcy these pirates label 'emselves "Fair Price Cabs." News in town is small. Coming back as one does after two years absence, is like entering a theatre in the middle of the second act. You see all sorts of situations and hear a deal of vastly fine dialogue but not being privy to the events that led up to all the row, you are only a little amazed and more than a little bored.

Besant gave an "inky" dinner the other night on severe professional lines at the Club. Conan Doyle, and several reviewers (lambs among wolves) came and there was an interesting young American artist who is illustrating a new book of Besant's. We gathered in a corner and said really soul-satisfying things about the English climate. A year of it would slay C and me dead. Flat Curls is in enormous form; learning a new word every ten minutes; playing with the coal scuttle, eating pencils, smearing herself, bumping her head; singing, shouting and babbling from dawn till dark. I was very glad to hear you all liked the photoes of her but she changes very swiftly. We of course consider each change for the better: and she is adored by her grandfather. He was spreeing in town with me – Oh but I forgot you didn't know him. By the way at our hotel I saw an American (first trip – per *New York* – Wednesday night – devoting a fortnight to London and all the rest of it) tied up in unspeakable knots over an attempt to pay eighteen pence in the simple and uncomplicated coinage of this land. I picked him out of his difficulty and left him looking at a sixpence and saying: – "I *know* a shilling's a quarter but this thing is too small for a dime and it *can't* be a nickel." C. to whom I have read this has now picked herself out of a red shawl and Clark Russel and says: – "Go on. Tell them some more." So I await her dictation: Oh. You'll find *Shiv and the Grasshopper* (the lullaby) in the *Jungle Book*.[2] I can't get at an American edition and I wouldn't insult you by sending you an English copy for which you'd have to pay .50 duty. MacMillans do *not* shine in the manufacture of child books. The reviews are rather funny. They don't know how or at which end to pick the thing up. C. says I'm to tell (it's aggravating to hear a girl with her feet on the fender dictating) about our last new scheme. We've decided next year or later to put up a small bungalow on the South Coast here – just a sea side cottage and as my young cousin Ambrose Poynter who is [a] very clever architect came and stayed with us for a week we set him to make us plans. You'd think we would have had enough of building by this time but the old fascination came back and we spent the evenings fighting excitedly over details and doorways till Ambo entering into the spirit of our dreams gradually developed for us a young baronial castle. Then we squashed him and cut down the plans. It ought to be rather pretty: for he has new ideas in his head.[3] C. cuts in again and says you can each come over and spend your honeymoon in it. *I* say don't ruin your career at the outset by starting married life in this land. We two have been simply spoiling for a fight this week past (all on account of the weather) and the bungalow gives us a fine field [letter continued from this point by CK.]

Notes
1. 9 June; the dinner with Besant mentioned later was on the 8th (CK diary).
2. Published in England in May.
3. The plan came to nothing.

To Louisa Baldwin, 15 June 1894
ALS: Dalhousie University

Arundell House, / Tisbury: / Wilts: / June. 15: 94.

Dear Aunt Louie:
    The first thing I did after unpacking was to arrange them two by two in the proper way and then with paternal foresight I sucked a red and white moo-cow hard – after much sucking she turned slightly paler and so to make all certain the Pater varnished the whole hundred and twenty six of 'em and the Doctor looked in and he must needs play with them while they were lying all sticky on the window seat and then I arranged them scientifically once more and said how amusing a thing a Noah's Ark must be for such as cared for childish things.[1] It was decided in council that Baby Jo was too small, much too small, for so much natural history all of a heap and she probably wouldn't have had it for months but that she chose to come in and break up the council; and she gathered them to her heart as many as she could hold and put the cows to bed in a spare shoe and did her best to smite off legs and horns and so was removed calling Noah "boy" to the last. You should have seen her eyes open when she saw them first; and when you come to think of it, she *is* a good deal like Eve. I dare not promise the Ark shall be kept, but I know she will get deep joy from the last legless headless lump of all. Carrie bids me thank you greatly and Jo's thanks are beyond writing.

Only a phonograph would express them.

I've been reading *Richard Dare*[2] in the light of as much of your note to the Pater, as he chose to read me, and it seems, of course this sounds rather brutal, that you make a greater importance of the notices than is in any way necessary. I have the best of reasons to know that even a *Times* eulogy does not sell a shelf of books. A furious denunciation on the score of impropriety sometimes will but the public is a stale and jaded horse and you shall find no spur sharp enough to get through their hide. So we will put the reviews on one side. It seems to me that *R.D.* is essentially a book that will make its way in the best way – that is to say by being read through and then talked about from mouth to mouth and I am willing to stake a good deal that it will go more steadily than anything you have ever written. Criticism on my part would be rather like aunticide would it not? There's only one constructional fault that I've come across where you give away in ten lines the advance proofs, so to speak, of the drunkard's conversion. I haven't the book before me but it's about one third the way down on a right hand page in the first volume and it knocks the wind out of the next ten or fifteen pages. That is merely a question of workmanship. I don't want to read anything better than the scene between mother and son in the ward and the break down at the table after the operation or again the call of the would be suicide to the other man's folly. It's all good – as good as Mrs Oliphant[3] – but in the present state of things it is handicapped by being "good" in another sense; a clean and wholesome book, right-thinking and straight-minded in tone, has no chance for a big success now. The fathers have eaten sour grapes and the children are hungering for chalk and lead pencils. If you had painted Mrs Reveril penny plain and tuppence coloured: let R.D. pronounce death sentence on the Colonel: thrown in a few half hundred red hot kisses and described the cancer *au naturel* you might have "marked an epoch" or "exhibited a fearlessness" or "probed a social evil" for about twenty minutes or till the next book came along. As it is you'll be getting your reward (this is a prophecy) in notes from unknown correspondents whom the book has helped; and on the commercial side as I've said you'll find the book will stay. Were it mine I'd give it half a year or a year in 2 vol. form and then 1 vol at 6/- followed by a boarded 3/6 edition. *Then you will get your public.* Them as can afford to pay for a two volume novel they wants a ragout, mum. Better still would it have been to have run the tale serially week by week and made your public as you went along, you wouldn't have had to compete with three new novels a day then. I think I can get a man to say something about it but I'd rather not because the new animal on the papers is rather a godless young whelp and nothing would hold him from being smart if he thought he saw his chance. However if you say so I'll try – taking no responsibility. So in my zeal I have poured ink lavishly all over the page. But let not that or the reviews distress you, dear. I could tell you when we meet that they don't touch sales one way or the other and their only use is either to fill the heart with vain rage or the head with vainer wind. I've had to write 'em and read 'em.

Your loving nephew
Ruddy

Notes
1. The point of sucking the Noah's ark animal is explained in "Baa Baa, Black Sheep": "Aunty Rosa had told him, a year ago, that if he sucked paint he would die. He went into the nursery, unearthed the now disused Noah's Ark, and sucked the paint off as many animals as remained."
2. A novel, Louisa Baldwin's fourth, published in 1894.
3. Margaret Oliphant (1828–97), novelist and miscellaneous writer.

To the Editor, *York Monthly*, 15 June 1894
ALS: Mrs Lisa Lewis

Arundell House / Tisbury / 15. 6. 94.

Dear Sir

In reply to your very courteous note of the 11th inst. I can only say that I have just survived one interview[1] which leaves me faint and prostrate; and I would much rather be left severely alone.

I have no magazine and newspaper references to hand here but Elliott and Fry have the copyright of a remarkably beautiful photograph which is supposed to be me.[2] It was taken some four or five years ago and resembles no one with whom I am acquainted. I fear that that is all the help I can offer.

Very faithfully yours
Rudyard Kipling.

Notes
1. An interview with RK appears in the *Pall Mall Gazette*, 7 June 1894. The interviewer writes as an acquaintance of Kipling's, but I do not know his identity. Much of the interview is taken up with a sort of conspiracy between interviewer and subject not to ask and not to answer the usual questions: "I should write as much as I thought the public ought to know, and no more."
2. This picture by the London photographers Elliott and Fry, *c.* 1890, was the standard portrait of RK throughout the 1890s, reproduced either directly or in one of several engraved copies. It is the frontispiece, e.g., to G. F. Monkshood, *Rudyard Kipling* (1899) and to Will M. Clemens, *A Ken of Kipling* (New York, 1899).

To Robert Barr,[1] 17 June 1894
ALS: University of Sussex

Arundell House / Tisbury. / Wilts. / 17. 6. 94

Dear Barr –
    I have sent to *A. P. W*[att]. to be typed a tale which I have written with a single eye to the needs of the *Idler*, and I should be much pleased if you glanced over it – whether you bought it or not.[2]
    It is not for me to criticize a certain touch of frivolity which I notice from time to time in your magazine but rather, I conceive, by a well timed seriousness to hint that Life has something higher and holier in it than the making of a jest of all the misfortunes of our fellows. In that hope my little tale has been written: trusting you will not be displeased with my outspokenness I am

Yours very sincerely
Rudyard Kipling.

Notes
1. Barr (1850–1912), born in Scotland, educated in Canada, was a journalist in Detroit before going to England in 1881; he founded *The Idler* with Jerome K. Jerome in 1892 and was its editor.
2. Probably "My Sunday at Home", finished in June and published in *The Idler*, though not until April 1895.

To Eric Robertson, 17 June 1894
ALS: Robert H. Taylor Library, Princeton University

Arundel House / Tisbury. / June. 17. 94

Dear Robertson
    Curious thing. The Father and I both recognised your fist from afar while yet it was on the envelope and we said: – "Now where in the world is he?"[1] Yes, a very great deal of water has flowed under the bridge since the old days in Lahore Club (can't you smell the heat in those rooms yet) – with Harris[2] sick next door and Willy Egerton[3] fuming over the vittles, and your namesake "Rosalie the Prairie Flower" coming in all hot and sticky after Polo. It had its drawbacks but it was a good time in many ways. I'm glad, though, I took your many times proffered advice and got away. Luck has been very gentle with me and sometimes I hold my breath and wonder a good deal how it all came about.
    We're over here for a few months having hired a house close to the

Father and Mother who have by some waft of Kismet settled down here. It's a lovely land but an infamous climate. *You* must be nearly as wet as Mussoorie sometimes in your dales and scaurs.[4] I confess I like my weather drier and with more sunshine, as we get it across the water. Providence has sent me a small daughter with fair hair and blue eyes who is a wonder and a joy to us both. She's getting on for two and I feel unspeakably aged at times.

I'm glad you like the *Jungle Book*. I hoped it would go well for the reason that I got more pleasure out of writing it than anything I've done for a long time. Someday please the pigs I'll get a decent style all of my own.

Will you give my best salaams to your *memsahib*. The Pater sends you his and I am

Yours ever gratefully
Rudyard Kipling

P.S.   I am sorry for that Bishop.[5]

P.P.S.   I shall be more sorry for the parish when it has you for shepherd.

Notes
1. Robertson (see 28 February 1889) had returned from India to England to enter the Church. He was ordained in 1892, and from 1893 to 1896 was domestic chaplain to the Bishop of Carlisle. In 1896 he became Vicar of St John, Windermere, where he remained until his retirement in 1913.
2. Perhaps A. S. Harris, Superintendent, Accountant-General's Office, Lahore.
3. W. A. Egerton, Assistant Accountant-General, Lahore.
4. The letter is addressed to Robertson at Hawkshead, Cumberland.
5. Presumably the Bishop of Carlisle: see n. 1.

To Henry James, [mid-June 1894]
ALS: Harvard University

Arundel House / Tisbury / Wilts

Dear Mr James,

We want to know whether you received *the* copy of the *Jungle Book* sent you three weeks ago with Baby's photo on the page. We sent it to DeVere Gardens because we did not know whether you had changed your address but perhaps you warned your man strictly not to send on anything that looked like a book. A man we heard of had a letter from you only a few days ago so we feel sure you are somewhere. *Are* you coming home before we go away? This climate is only fit for marine monsters. C. has had a cold all over her for 8 days past. We abandon room after room in this hired girls school of ours and huddle over one fire like bears in a cave. The wind blows from the east except when it brings rain from the west: our roses are blighted: our sky is lead and ashes and we're going back on the 5th of August. There's no language I know to describe this thing that calls itself June. We are hopeless, impenitent, quarrelsome, damp and disgusted. London is worse for there it rains harder and the cabman argues ere he takes you up. Never was man so anxious to leave his all too native land behind him, as I am and I would I were Bryon that I might fitly curse it. *So* please come before August and cheer us a little. Our house is dry and we burn a ton of coal every ten days. More shall be added when you come and the garden walks shall be relaid with piping hot-water bottles. We will come down to breakfast with counterpanes and coverlets upon our shoulders and dine atop of the kitchen range. More we cannot do.

We both send our love and pray you by return of post to let us know where you are, how you are; and when we shall see you – for we did not come to England to enrheum ourselves behind a damp shrubbery. This goes to Venice.[1]

Very sincerely yours always
Rudyard

Note

1. James was then in Italy. He returned in July and stayed with the Kiplings at Arundell House at the end of the month (CK diary, 31 July). As for *The Jungle Book*, James found it "thrilling, but so bloody" (Leon Edel, *Henry James, The Middle Years* [Philadelphia, 1963] p. 380).

To Charles Warren Stoddard, [late June 1894]

ALS: Library of Congress

Arundel House / Tisbury / Wilts.

Dear Mr Stoddard

I rejoiced to see your handwriting again *but* the company that have disgraced and defiled the make up of the book[1] should be killed by slow fires and fish-bones and things. Knowing what manner of stuff would be inside it the flagrant binding made me very wrath. I have stripped off the hide and am sending the carcass into a man I know on the P[all].M[all].G[azette]. to see if he doesn't like it too. Yes, it's a very tropic of colour and fragrance.

Much do I wish too that you were here. Our wet and slobbering summer has sudden[ly] taken a brace and the last three whole days have been really warm – even hot in places; with a faint blue-grey sky and the hay smelling like all England since the conquest. My stays in England have been so short that I find I know very little of my own country outside London and it's very amusing to go about. We had an excursion the other day as wild as anything in a dream.[2] Went down seaward through a flat and fatted country and suddenly found ourselves in the middle of Macbeth's blasted heath – half heather half burned gorze – with a low mist rolling in from the sea and an enchanted castle – Lulworth Castle – bobbing in and out of the haze and somewhere out to the seaward – H.M.S. Thunderer creeping to and fro and firing Titanic guns. England's a fine land if she would only stop raining thrice a week. The wet and the damp make me want to be back in Vermont. When shall we see you in that place?

Always yours sincerely
Rudyard Kipling.

Notes
1. *Hawaiian Life: Being Lazy Letters from Low Latitudes* (Chicago and New York: F. T. Neeley, 1894).
2. To Lulworth Cove, 22 June (CK diary).

To Robert Barr, 1 July 1894
ALS: University of Sussex

Arundell House: / Tisbury: / July 1: 94

Dear Barr –

It's better to be shouted at in English (which is the effect a typed letter always has on me) than to be mumbled at in Chinese which is what some men write, when they take a pen in their hands. Now, how can a man give what he hasn't got? If a Mulvaney tale were written just for folk to read and not because I *had* to write it, it wouldn't be a Mulvaney tale anyway and I'd be deliberately firing at an old target for the sake of making bulls eyes. That way lies death. But the other business is purely delightful. With two whole years wherein to work your wicked will on the Idler and only a 50% raise to see, it ought to be as easy as falling off a log (though, at this point, I hear your swear aloud). I perceive I must pay good heed to my tales. Apropos, there's a thing on the market (about 5000) called "Leaves from a Winter Notebook"[1] which, mark you, is the *only* authentic account up to date of my surroundings in Brattleboro' – written by these lily fingers. It's all about the snow and the seasons and the choppers. A. P. W[att]. knows where the copy is. I took a deal of trouble over it; and if you can meet him I'll send our photoes of Brattleboro' for reproduction.

Then you will, of course, abandon the "Idlers Club" which has run itself out, and introduce Imaginary Interviews – W. D. Howells and Ouida; Henry James and Zola; Joaquin Miller[2] and LeGallienne;[3] W. W. Astor[4] (as an author) and Lewis Morris (as a poet). Others will suggest themselves and as no one need in the least be bound down to the truth you ought to get some startling developments. Equally, of course, you will cut down your illustrations with a sharp sickle, and spend the money thus gained on "dateful" articles which seem to be a necessity these days –

Now I was just sailing into a beautiful scheme for articles on lesser known trades and professions, when Burgin[5] sends me the copy of your tale. I'll attend to it on the spot.

A pleasant holiday to you. Why in the name of sense can't you get a man to interview Croker.[6] *He'd* send up your sales t'other side. He's somewhere in reach now.

Ever yours sincerely
Rudyard Kipling

Notions
(1) a workman's account of the building of the Tower Bridge,[7] *in dialect –* what he thought of it all: without any pretence of making fun of him.
(2) Moored hulks in the Strand. A harlot's view of traffic and life as she sees it.
(3) a Zolaesque account of a blank, foggy muddy day, in oilskins with the bobby who stops the unseen traffic of Piccadilly.
(4) *Why* men love their countries. Not patriotic rot but each nation giving its ideals of home and home vittles and society and what makes each man homesick. You'd get something very curious out of the Poles and the Swedes and the men on the Western plains.
(5) The history of a Noah's Ark. Do you know *how* the beasts are profiled and cut out of a revolving hollow disc of wood? One animal to each section without waste. I don't suppose many people have thought of that [sketch of wooden disc]. Little German kids shape the rough blocks with chisels. Might find out what a German kid thinks of it all.
(6) The lower decks of a man of war where the torpedoes and hammocks hang up together in the hot greasy air under the electrics. It's a picturesque submarine kingdom. Get a good man.
(7) Guy Boothby c/o A.P.W. has a tale of how he had a whole show of freaks, (Burmese hairy boys and cretins etc.) shoved on to him to take

care of by a man to whom he had once given a drink in S. Australia. He (B) took 'em out into the street and waited till they congested traffic and the police *had* to arrest them. Tell him I say he's got to write that tale for you.

(8) *"The Measured Mile"*. No one hardly knows where that is – on the Maplins. It's the straight stretch where all the navy is tried for speed, and a most historic mile of water. Send a man to describe that apropos of the *Daring's* last record.[8]

(10) Look up the Hong Kong plague[9] with photoes.

(11) Room for a timely article on Japan and Corea and China with a scare-head forecast how all Europe w'd be drawn into the war.

(12) The duties of a consul and how he does not perform 'em. There's a round dozen for you – one may be some use perhaps.[10]

Notes

1. Not published until May 1900, in *Harper's Magazine*.
2. Joaquin Miller (1839–1913), the California poet, parodied by RK in "Himalayan" (*Echoes*).
3. Richard Le Gallienne (1866–1947), poet, critic, and essayist associated with the literary movement of the 1890s. He published *Rudyard Kipling: A Criticism* (1900).
4. The American William Waldorf Astor (1848–1919), 1st Viscount Astor; he published several volumes of fiction. He was at this time owner of the *Pall Mall Gazette* and the *Pall Mall Budget*, in which RK was publishing.
5. George B. Burgin (1856–1944), journalist and novelist, at this time Barr's sub-editor on *The Idler*. He published over ninety novels.
6. Richard Croker (1841–1922), Irish-born politician, the head of the Tammany Hall machine in New York City; in 1894 he retired to England.
7. The formal opening of the bridge had just been held, on 30 June.
8. A torpedo boat destroyer, whose preliminary trials on the Maplin Sands were reported in *The Times*, 26 June.
9. Bubonic plague was then raging there.
10. None of these suggestions was used in *The Idler*.

To Cormell Price, 17 July 1894

ALS: Library of Congress

July. 17. 94

Dear Uncle Crom –

If I come down on the 24th; can you give me a bed or will I go to

Rowena? I must see the end of things at the old college, though it is pain and grief to me.[1]

Yours always
Ruddy

Arundel House, / Tisbury, Wilts.

Note
1. USC had long been in trouble for a variety of reasons – enrolment was down, competition up, and conflicts over what course to follow were persistent. Crofts had already quarrelled with Price over school policy and had resigned in 1892. Now Price was retiring. RK went down to Westward Ho! with JLK and made a speech at the retirement ceremonies, 25 July (*United Services College Chronicle*, December, 1894: uncollected).

To Brander Matthews, 19 July 1894
ALS: Dalhousie University

[Tisbury] July: 19. 94

Dear Matthews:
    The book is being returned. I like those pages in front immensely. Did you want me to fill 'em all?[1]
    As for the *Yellow book*,[2] let us remember what Pudd'nhead Wilson did *not* say:[3] – 'When you see a man standing on his head in the streets don't interfere with him. He won't walk far that way but the chances are he'll have learned a great deal about the centre of gravity by the time he is through." The thing's so mixed – any way.

Very sincerely
Rudyard Kipling.

Our next meeting will be in New York I suppose.

Notes
1. RK was returning a specially bound copy of *Many Inventions* that Matthews had asked him to inscribe; RK responded with three poems: a quatrain beginning "See My Literary Pants"; a parody of James Whitcomb Riley beginning "Hello, Brander! Lemme look"; and a parody of Browning beginning "Your trough first – *aqua pura: quantum suff'* (uncollected). The volume is now at Dalhousie University.
2. The illustrated quarterly magazine, whose first number appeared in April; it became synonymous with the artistic atmosphere of the 1890s.
3. Mark Twain's *Pudd'nhead Wilson* had just ended its serial run in the *Century Magazine* in June. Each chapter is headed with an extract, always cynical, from "Pudd'nhead Wilson's Notebook".

To Edmund Clarence Stedman,[1] 21 July 1894

Text: Laura Stedman and George Gould, *Life of E. C. Stedman* (New York, 1910) II, 189

[Tisbury] July 21, 1894

Very many thanks for your kind letter of the 13th inst. I did not know that you had done me the honour of proposing me at the Century[2] but I feel the more uplift in consequence.

As regards your "Victorian Anthology," of course all my verse is entirely at your disposal and, I would, equally of course, sooner trust your judgment, as to which should be taken than my own.[3] Most times I feel as though I would give a year's pay to have everything rhymed that I have written rubbed off the slate and start in fresh. And again, isn't it early to anthologize the likes of me? But it shall be as you please.

We're coming home on the 5th of next month and I think my father is coming over again with us.[4] England is a fine land when you can see it and have been born in it but I have a prejudice against fires in July or bitter east winds in June; and the sunny side of a piazza in Brattleboro is good enough for me.

Curiously enough, before your letter came, I was re-reading "Diversions of the Echo Club" (wasn't it Bayard Taylor?)[5] in the little limp paper-back pirated copy that I can remember led me to the joyful labour of writing parodies on every poet between Wordsworth and Whitman. I used to know whole pages of it by heart.

Notes

1. Stedman (1833–1908) was a New York poet, journalist, stockbroker, and editor.
2. See letter to R. U. Johnson, 4 November 1895.
3. Stedman's *A Victorian Anthology, 1837–1895* (Boston, 1895) contains six poems by RK.
4. He did not.
5. Bayard Taylor (1825–78), American journalist and traveller; his *The Echo Club, and Other Literary Diversions* (Boston, 1876) parodies all the standard nineteenth-century poets, English and American, including Stedman.

To [Dr George] Gore-Gillon,[1] [23 July 1894][2]
ALS: National Library of Australia

Arundel House / Tisbury / Wilts.

Dear Gillon:

Curiously enough I was asking after you the other day from a Lyttleton man I met out at dinner. It will be a very long time before I forget our breathless five minutes of silence when we were trying to wheel up the buggy behind your grey horse which the fool of a German had taken out against your orders. Do you remember?

I knew Mrs Gillon was in London but I didn't know you were coming – or on such an exceedingly ticklish errand. I only have known one case of floating kidney intimately and as it was a woman of course I couldn't ask questions. The intense nausea must be the awful part of it. We can stand anything almost sooner than being sick. There's a lack of originality about that which is soul-crushing.

You speak lightly, as becomes a professional man, of what must be a very interesting operation. Don't forget to write me *here* if you can write before the 5th of next month and to Brattleboro Vermont U.S.A. after that date, and tell me how you came through. Do you intend to start a fresh practice in London? Or do you go back in N.Z. as soon as you are refitted? Don't live in this infernal climate or you'll find your lungs will begin to do things. I have builded me a little house in Vermont among hills and woods on the Connecticut river which is not unlike the Waitaki[3] in places. My wife and I are still hoping to get to New Zealand again together – the last time we tried we got as far as Japan when our Bank broke and left us practically penniless at the back of beyond but we'll hope for better luck next time.

I never had a better time in my life than I had on my visit to N.Z: and it has given me a curious direct personal affection on the land – as though it were something alive and all you men were so good to me. Let me know how your health goes and if there is any way in which I could be useful to you in the line of introductions or anything of that kind let me know. With kindest regards to Mrs Gillon and yourself – not forgetting little Audrey (I've a two year old of my own).

Yours very sincerely
Rudyard Kipling

Notes
1. RK's letter is clearly addressed to Dr C. Gore-Gillon, but this must be the Dr George Gore-Gillon who was living in Wellington in the 1880s and 1890s (information from the Canterbury Public Library). A copy of *Departmental Ditties*, 6th ed, 1891, now at Columbia, contains a 6-line inscription by RK to Gore-Gillon, signed and dated Wellington, New Zealand, 22 October 1891.

2. Date added in another hand.
3. On the eastern slope of the South Island, between Christchurch and Dunedin.

To Henry James, [24 July 1894]
ALS: Harvard University

Arundel House / Tisbury. / Wilts

Dear Mr James –

At an unholy hour this morn Carrie went up to town to see a dressmaker[1] but before she left your letter came and I received instructions with the desperate gravity of a half-awakened man who is being shaken from time to time to keep his leaden attention fixed. These are my instructions.

You are to come down on Monday next by the 3.p.m. from Waterloo (No 2. platform) running direct to Salisbury without a halt. Arriving at Salisbury a few minutes before five you, waiting on the platform you came in at will, in five minutes, see a local backing in. That is your train which will land you at Tisbury at 5.35.p.m. where we will meet you with trumpets and shawms. Now for the reasons which make this a necessity. I go down to Westward Ho! today to my old school to see my head master retire – a doleful job made nothing better by the prospect of having to deliver a funeral speech. That keeps me till Thursday. On Friday, Mrs Poynter and her small son stay with us till Sunday. So you see why. We shan't be coming up to town any more by reason that I have a lot of work I want to get finished and your coming will make it light and easy unto me. But I can't work in London. And on Saturday week you see we march to S'hamptom where 'tis unseemly that you should stagger across the docks with our carpet-baggery.[2] So please come. I've a mass of verses I'm bursting to tell you;[3] you'll see Baby in her own home so to speak and you'll be quiet and much loved. C. comes down from town this afternoon. Will you write her here that I have delivered my message correctly (why do wives after a year of matrimony always assume their husbands are imbeciles in their absence?) and that you will come.

Yours ever
Rudyard.

Notes
1. CK's diary says she had lunch with James in London on this day; if so that would seem to make this letter unnecessary.
2. They left Southampton on the 5th on the *Kaiser Wilhelm II*.

3. One of them was "McAndrew's Hymn", when James came on the 31st (CK diary).

To Robert Barr, [28 July 1894][1]
ALS: University of Sussex

Arundell House / Tisbury.

Make a note. This is the *third* sunny day of this summer.

Dear Barr,

Thanks for your note. I'm glad you liked the tale[2] and will you please send me the typed copy of it? It hasn't been revised yet and the title is only a temporary soft-wood one. I must get a better one. I have beside me, apropos of your other tales, a sort of nest of notions in the complicated absurdity line: viz: an experiment made by four respectable English citizens to discover *what* connection might exist between the monkey and the monkey-puzzler (the prickly tree of that name). They seduced the ape of a wandering Italian organ grinder into the garden where it grew: but it wasn't their garden and the ape made things happy for many miles around:[3] 2 – the tale of a Japanese riddle which undermined the peace of two Clubs in Yokohama and Tokio:[4] 3 – the adventures of an American millionaire who bought an estate in England and one day when he was in a hurry to get to town flagged the York Express.[5] They are all full of the purely male horse-play and schoolboy rot that womenfolk bless 'em find it so hard to understand. I'll send 'em along as they transpire and eventuate: and they'll be written with a single eye to the Idler. *Only*: go slow on the illustrations – particularly in the case of the sick navvy. Leave a lot to the fancy![6] They'll all be short tales – not over 7,000 at the outmost.

A regular weather-breeder of a day to-day – real warmth at last and it waked in me a lively desire to be back in Main Street Brattleboro Vt. U.S.A. and hear the sody water fizzing in the drug-store and discuss the outlook for the Episcopalian Church with the clerk; and get a bottle of lager in the basement of the Brooks house and hear the doctor tell fish yarns and have the iron-headed old farmers loaf up and jerk out: – "'Bin in Yurope haint yer?" and then go home, an easy gait, through the deep white dust with the locust trees just stinking to heaven and the fire flies playing up and down the swamp road and the Katydids giving oratorios free-gratis and for nothing to the whip-poorwill and everybody sitting out in the verandah after dinner smoking Durham tobacco in a cob pipe with our feet on the verandah railings and the moon coming up behind Wantastiquet. There's one Britisher at least homesick for a section of your depraved old land and he's going, please Allah, the first week in August by the Kaiser Wilhelm and won't New York be hot just! There's a smell of horse-piss, Italian fruit-vendor, nickel-cigars; sour lager and warm car-conductor drifting down Carmine Street at this minute from Sixth Ave. which I can smell with the naked eye as I sit here. I shall go to Long Island to a friend's and eat new corn and visit 'em at the Senanhaka[7] the first thing and I wish you were coming too.

Doyle[8] tells me he'll be over in the fall to explain his burning love for the country and its Institutions at $1 a love – reserved loves $2 – and he'll try to repair a little of the epoch-marring mischief I've been doing. *This* isn't charged for. And the joy and the comfort of it is that, the whole of his tour, he won't see America any more than the dead: but don't you tell him I said so.

I hope to be up in town shortly and will try to come and see you. With best regards to Mrs Barr

Yours very sincerely
Rudyard Kipling.

Notes
1. Dated from postmark.
2. See 17 June 1894.
3. "The Puzzler", not published until 1906.
4. No published if written.
5. "An Error in the Fourth Dimension", *Cosmopolitan*, December 1894.
6. "My Sunday at Home" is not illustrated in *The Idler*.
7. Not identified.
8. (Sir) Arthur Conan Doyle (1859–1930), the creator of Sherlock Holmes. He came to America in September of 1894 to carry out an extended lecture tour and called on RK in Vermont in November.

To [Dr George] Gore-Gillon, 2 August 1894
ALS: Cornell University

Arundell House / Tisbury / Aug. 2. 94

Dear Gillon –

You've had a mighty hard row to hoe and it is you that are the plucky man: and more than all do I admire you for being able to keep your eyes open and see the humours of the hospital.

Doesn't it seem a piece of the most bitter irony that you should get your M.D. while your innards are being swabbed and sprayed and generally polished, in an operating ward? It is rather like giving a chronometer a Kew certificate just when it is being unscrewed. I don't know whether sympathy is much good in the face of a stomach-pump but at any rate it can't do you any harm to know that I'm sympathizing with you – with the trouble and the worry – and admiring the bravery with which it is met.

In regard to the other business I've got your second letter but the extent to which I do not meddle with a man's domestic concerns cannot be measured by mere degrees of latitude. It is my business to forget all those things or I'd be one walking museum of confidences. If I had a half a day to spare I'd come up for the purpose of looking at you but we – and that means the Missus and me and the baby and nurse and maid and 26 boxes – sail by the *Kaisar Wilhelm* for New York on Sunday and as I have faithfully neglected a lot of work till the last minute I am moving in a whirlwind of proofs and M.S.S. and when I am not doing that I am pretending to help pack and making more mess than two women can clear up behind me. However I've made a long arm and told my publishers to send you the last book I've done.[1] It's of a kind which I have heard profanely called "The Gordam lie" build but I can guarantee that it doesn't need any strain on the intellect and being purely meant for kids ought to amuse you for a while. I haven't a copy of it here or I'd send it along. When you've done with it you can lend it down the ward.

I confess I'm puzzled to think what you ought to do next. I've been talking to the local doctor[2] here and he's given me some figures of competition in the country which are not pleasant. The all round general practitioner seems to be worked like a bullock and paid like a ploughman. Have you any speciality – ear or nose or colon or whatever it is that is obscure and mysterious?

Even then a man wants a lot of "pull" in town and the only medico I know is Robson Rose[3] who is rather a kid glove swell. I think were I you I'd stick to New Zealand where you have made your mark at any rate and even if the worst came to the worst N.Z. is a better place to starve in than England.

I don't know whether through your windows you notice our infernal English climate. I am wearied of it and shall be more than glad to get away to where the sun does more than look like a badly poached egg at the bottom of a bowl of thick soup. Brattleboro Vermont U.S.A. will be my address after the 5th and if you care to send me a line there I'll be more than pleased to answer it. And, now, I needn't tell you to keep a stiff upper lip because you seem to do that without being helped. Lie low, go slow and keep cool and some day either here or in America or

in N Z – for I have by no means abandoned my resolution of making a
second trip to that lovely land – we'll meet again.

Ever yours sincerely
Rudyard Kipling

Notes
1. *The Jungle Book.*
2. He was Dr John Arthur Ensor.
3. This seems to be the name in the MS, but I can find no one of it in the medical
   directories.

To Charles Scribner's Sons, 17 August 1894
ALS: Syracuse University

Naulakha. / Brattleboro. / Vermont. / Aug: 17. 1894

To the Proprietors Scribners Magazine

Gentlemen:

Mr A. P. Watt, my literary agent, informs me that you have purchased
the serial use, for your magazine, of some verses of mine called
McAndrew's Hymn.

I do not know whether it is your intention to illustrate them but if
you should think illustrations necessary I should be much in your debt
if you could kindly place me in communication with your artist as it is
possible that he might see his way to using some of my suggestions.[1]

Very sincerely yours
Rudyard Kipling

Note
1. The poem was published in *Scribner's Magazine*, December 1894, with illustrations by
   Howard Pyle; see 21 August 1894 and 25 August 1894 (to Pyle).

To Edward Lucas White, 17 August 1894
ALS: Ray Collection, Morgan Library

Naulakha. / Brattleboro. / Vermont. / Aug. 17. 94

Esteemed Younger Brother

Curious, isn't it, that I should not know your "sweet Roman hand"
except through a typewriter. I wondered who it was that was writing at

me with a hatchet – a fine broad edged axe and then I found it was you. We're only just come home after surviving four months of an English summer. *Now* do I understand why my people go forth and colonize the earth. Nothing could amaze them in the way of temperatures, but I am a weakling. I

> "Will not walk in running brooks for choice
>   Nor with thee rejoice
> Knee deep in flooded meadows rank with weed,
>   Nor share the dreadful pleasures of my breed
> Plashed to dull eyes that wink away the rain"

and so on and so forth as Arnold did not write and a warm rock on these burned pastures is good enough for me. We are dusty and white with drouth. Ancient springs that never failed before have gone under and farmers are at their wits end to know how to water their stock.

Behold the reward of forethought! They laughed at me when I drove my 300 foot artesian. Now *I* laugh as I watch a lantern staggering across a meadow at midnight where a man goes to tickle up a moribund ram[1] which is being choked with leaves and mud. My well is pure and icy cold and unfailing. Also I have the joy of looking down on my neighbours – which alone is worth the price of admission.

As to your letter (did you know I was coming home?) I don't see any special points in the seal song.[2] But, in one point you are dead right. It *ought* to sing well for to the best of my knowledge and belief it goes to the noble tune of "*I met Moll Roe in the morning*". The original words thereof are long-shore bawd pure and simple but the air is a cyclone as I once heard it. There's a hymn tune that fits it as well, and there are about twenty tunes to Moll Roe. See that you get the right one for I am incompetent to advise you may ears being wavering. Let me know how you grow and prosper and how your health is. We're all well here thank God, and Heaven was kind to me in England where I was safely delivered of several poems, four new jungle tales and a piece of broad farce[3] – viler than Brugglesmith which made me laugh for three days.

> "I sometimes wonder what the vintners buy
>   One half so precious as the stuff they sell"[4]

By this I mean I wonder if people get a tithe of the fun out of my tales that I get in doing 'em.

Very sincerely always
Rudyard Kipling

You leave *Willow-Wood*[5] alone. It's bad and must be re-coppered; fresh engined; new decked and rigged all over. You know too much about my output. I'd forgotten that old failure.

Notes
1. That is, a pump.
2. "Lukannon", published with "The White Seal" in *The Jungle Book*.
3. "My Sunday at Home".
4. *The Rubaiyat of Omar Khayam*, xcv.
5. "The Lamentable Comedy of Willow Wood", *Fortnightly Review*, xlvii (1890); collected only in Sussex Edition, xxix.

To Edward L. Burlingame,[1] 21 August 1894
ALS: Syracuse University

Naulakha. / Brattleboro. / Vermont. / Aug. 21. 1894

Dear Sir

I am in receipt of your letter with galley proof of *McAndrews Hymn*. I have marked the more obvious corrections, as far as the margin allowed, and shall be much obliged by a revise as soon as possible. Dialect poems are always a little bit unhandy in proof. I confess I should like to have seen the illustrator before he went to work – more for the sake of an initial L – and of the piston, cylinder and crank of a l[ow].p[ressure]. engine – than to suggest pictures. I have never yet seen a really good foreshortening of a tandem triple-expansion that was not a mechanical drawing so I hope that Mr Pyle[2] will put a machinery background to his full length of McAndrew. An American artist is, naturally, very apt to draw the American type and a Scotch engineer is a type by himself altogether. Would it be too much to ask for early proofs of the illustrations.

Very sincerely
Rudyard Kipling.

Notes
1. Burlingame (1848–1922) was editor of *Scribner's Magazine* from its beginning in 1886 until 1914.
2. Howard Pyle (1853–1911), illustrator and writer; noted for his treatment of historical and adventurous subjects, Pyle was the leading American illustrator of his day.

To Mary Mapes Dodge, 24 August 1894
ALS: Syracuse University

Naulakha. / Brattleboro. / Vermont. / Aug. 24. 94

Dear Mrs Dodge –

I have obeyed your behest and duly warned the *Century* that I was to write a tale as ordered. Than an idea came to me which promised well and if you like I can get it ready for Christmas. It's a beast-tale of course but on altogether new lines – at least I fancy so.[1] Our weather's sizzling hot and every one is out of water except we 'uns and our big artesian keeps us supplied and happy. Please give my salaams to Mr Clarke.[2]

Yours very sincerely
Rudyard Kipling

Notes
1. "The King's Ankus", *St Nicholas*, March 1895 (*Second Jungle Book*).
2. William Fayal Clarke (1855–1937), one of the original staff of *St Nicholas Magazine*; he succeeded Mrs Dodge as its editor.

To Matthew Howard,[1] 25 August 1894
ALS: Marlboro College

Naulakha. / Brattleboro. / Vermont. / Aug. 25. 1894

I am in receipt of yours of the 23rd instant:

In reply I wish to know whether you could manage to get along for yourself so far as meals went, with us till you got your wife over. It is impossible for us to give you meals in the house.

I wish further to know your age: I presume you have no children but should like to be certain.

I have already told you the wages – $35 a month with furnished house – These will be your duties.

To take sole charge of three horses.

To attend to the furnace in winter.

To carry coals for the kitchen fire and wood for the open fire places

To wash two small verandahs once a week with a broom and to beat such small rugs as may be required once a month.

I shall be glad to hear from you at once, if you think the service would suit you.

Rudyard Kipling.

Note

1. Howard (1856–1929), an Englishman, had replied to RK's advertisement for a coachman, placed in the New York *Tribune*, 20 August 1894: RK hired him as of 1 September. Howard represented himself as childless, but was soon joined at Naulakha by his wife and eight children. After RK's departure in 1896 Howard remained as caretaker of the house until it was sold in 1903.

To Howard Pyle, 25 August 1894

ALS: Cornell University

Naulakha. / Brattleboro. / Vermont. / Aug. 25. 94

Dear Sir:

Scribners tells me that it is my great good fortune to have you for the illustrator of some verses of mine in the Christmas Number. Also they write that you have not yet begun on the sketches. Is it permitted to a man who knows less than nothing about art to plague you with suggestions? I haven't the shadow of a doubt you'll do the verses considerably more than justice but it may help you a little to know that the ship *McAndrew's Hymn* belongs to is the old *Doric*,[1] once an Atlantic White Star I think, and now an S[haw]. S[avill]. A[lbion]. boat running to New Zealand via the Cape of Good Hope and home round the horn. She'd be about the same type, in her engine fittings, as the *Germanic* or the *Brittanic*[2] I should say – i.e. in no sense a new boat with any special gear. When I was on her her l[low].p[ressure]. cylinder had a play of about an inch and a half on the columns and every piece of machinery had the muffled and protected look of a long-voyage boat. Not a bit like all the shiny stuff on a racing Atlantic hotel; but lapped and swathed and junked up and all white with salt-crust.

If you use American machinery for models you'll get things much too light and graceful, for one can tell the difference between American and English engines as far as one can see them – or hear them they say who know. McAndrew also is a Scot of the Scots – clean shaven or with a torpedo beard I should say and his uniform would be pretty dingy after a three month voyage.

In regard to the salient points for illustration of the verses I suspect you have already made your own choice. It seems to me that little line touches of hoisting the passengers' luggage – the tramp steamer off Sumbawa head – all nose and stern and funnel [sketch of tramp steamer] and the run of a liner through the misty, ice-strewn south bergs might be worth something.

Then there's a good wash picture perhaps (a little one) of the couples kissing in the dusk. But I perceive I could go on like this for many pages so I'll e'en come to an end and leave the matter trustfully in your hands.[3]

Very sincerely yours

Rudyard Kipling.

[sketches of low pressure cylinder and initial-letter L] This is an initial L. that could be humoured out of an l.p. cylinder and crosshead and connecting rod – I fancy. I don't know whether it would be worth the trouble. [Note added to drawing] here come the condensers and things crosshead of pump lever connecting with L.p. rod.

Notes

1. The ship on which RK crossed the Indian Ocean, from South Africa to New Zealand, in September–October 1891.
2. White Star liners built in 1874 and 1875: "among the most succesful transatlantic liners ever built" (C. R. Vernon Gibbs, *Passenger Liners of the Western Ocean*, 1952, p. 190).
3. Pyle's illustrations pay no heed to these suggestions.

To Mary Mapes Dodge, [c. 22 September 1894]

ALS: Syracuse University

Fairholme, / Morristown, N.J.[1]

Dear Mrs Dodge,

Yours of the 19th has been forwarded to me here.

There is a Mowgli tale[2] by me which was just going to sea to try to catch up with unfulfilled promises (too many of 'em) the other side. I will now unpack his trunk and send him to fulfill a promise here. He shall be typed and the Saint shall see what he thinks of him for Christmas.

Frankly, I am not enamoured of myself as a business man. My ledger bears in upon me the fact that here I've been selling tales to the Saint at rates which just cover my bare English rights – setting aside American, Indian and Australian rights.

So, if St Nick buys for the Earth (i.e. wants to cover those rights too) please tell him that the pay is $135 per thousand [–] anyway, to old friends.

I had a letter from Mr Johnson[3] about "In the Back pasture"[4] and am writing him.

Very sincerely yours

Rudyard Kipling

Notes
1. The home of the Catlin family; RK and CK went there on the 20th and returned on the 26th (CK diary).
2. Possibly "Letting in the Jungle" (*Second Jungle Book*).
3. Robert Underwood Johnson, of the *Century Magazine*.
4. The original title of "A Walking Delegate", *Century Magazine*, December 1894 (*The Day's Work*). RK had just sold it at $135 per thousand words, the same rate he quotes to Mrs Dodge (CK diary).

To Charles Eliot Norton, 27 September 1894

ALS: Harvard University

Urgent business

[Naulakha] Sept. 27. '94

Dear Mr Norton

We've just come back and the Lowell books[1] were waiting for us. On the strength of them I've put my rubbish heaps in order a little and given them an honoured place where I can most easily get at them. Thank you for your kindness.

And now, will you do me a favour. When you were here you said something about wanting a windmill for your barn. We've got our hot air engine on the ground and hope to get him fixed and going ere our storage of water runs dry. Meantime the Unnecessary Pillywinkie is a nightmare to us. No one wants him here – least of all this household. We want to pull him over but even then he'd have to be buried, and he is nearly sixty feet high. Would you care to pay the expense of having him taken down and sent to Ashfield by the company that supplied him? I don't know what it will cost but it can't cost as much as a new one from the factory. He is a kind and affectionate windmill, without any flaw to the best of my knowledge and in a 20 mile breeze is supposed to develop five horse power. Also, as you know, he is painted a tender sage-green. The trouble with him is that in his present position he doesn't get enough wind to keep him busy. Now on your grey hills he would entirely lose his present laziness and become an extremely valuable servant.

If you say yes I will send for the company's man and get him taken down and send you the vouchers and he shall be sent to Ashfield in lengths. One team should haul him to Ashfield from the depot.

If you say no I don't know what we'll do. I'll have him on my hands blasting the foreground for years and in the end may have to trade him to a farmer for pig's flesh that will never be delivered and wood that will never be drawn. Besides, he will rust. A windmill is the only thing lacking to round up the beauty of Ashfield. He will open up whole fields of new experiences and interest you day and night. No house can pretend to completeness without a windmill. At the outside it should not cost you more than $50 whereas if you buy a new (and untried) thing from the shops it will cost you thrice as much – and you'll have to paint it too.

Please let me know. I am sure that Miss Norton[2] would like a windmill to play with.

Very sincerely ever
Rudyard Kipling

Notes
1. *Letters of James Russell Lowell*, ed. C. E. Norton, 2 vols (1894).
2. Sara Norton (1864–1922), called Sally.

To Julia de Forest,[1] 18 October 1894
ALS: Harvard University

[Naulakha] Oct: 18: 1894.

Dear Miss Julia:

I have not been allowed to write before because my Father and Mother don't want to stimulate my brain but as I have just been spanked for throwing a brush into the fire after I was told to leave it alone they think it would be safer for me to take to pen and ink.

I want to thank you for my White Seal slippers. They are good to eat though hairy, but this I am told is not what they were meant for. I use them to walk in about my nur – bedroom and they become my complexion. But I am not allowed to lift my skirts up to my waist when I have them on so I am afraid no one has seen them properly yet though I have done my best – such as lying on the floor and kicking and offering them to visitors.

Two people, a man and a women, stayed here the other day.[2] They said they belonged your way but I was busy cutting some eye-teeth and did not notice them much. The woman is crazy about a game called golf and the man's beard tickled. I am still cutting my eye-teeth and they do not let me sing in the night as much as I should like. I am always being spanked these days for making noises and taking things that don't belong but I am always

Your most affectionate
Josephine Kipling

(dict)

Notes
1. Lockwood de Forest's sister; she lived in New York City.
2. Lockwood and Meta de Forest stayed with them in early October (CK diary, 3 October).

To Charles Eliot Norton [19 October 1894][1]
ALS: Harvard University

[Naulakha]

Dear Mr Norton –
   Another big package of books to thank you for. I've been wanting the Carlyle–Goethe correspondence. The Emerson letters I've read (some of them before) but had not my own copy and for that I owe you most thanks.[2] Golly, what a digestion it must have been! And what a warning for ever that a man should keep his bowels, liver etc. to himself. He could not have lived up to the tone of ten consecutive pages, in private life, without being slain by the nearest stranger. It shows Emerson's character more sweet and wholesome than ever by contrast.
   I'd give much to know what the good folk of Ashfield thought when you advised 'em to wash more and brush their teeth! I think the man who put together "Picturesque Franklin" means the like by the Brattleboro' neighbourhood. Anyway he's been at me for a photo of my house.[3] Which reminds me that the Infamous Pillywinky is (thank Heaven) dead. A gale (the only one for seven weeks) sprang up as he was being dismantled and the man who was bestraddling his vicious old head was all but slain by being whirled to death and guillotined at the same time. So we dug up his wicked thin legs and put a tackle on him and pulled him over bodily. It was a beautiful sight. He fell with his nose in the ground and looked like the Vendome Column. And now we have a clean and sweet hot air engine in a little brick and shingle house. I'm glad you didn't take him or maybe he'd have killed you.
   Work has become very urgent all of a sudden, and I'm trying to bring out New Editions of some books[4] as well and I begin to fear that our

chances of getting away before Christmas are small indeed.

With very best regards from us both to you and Miss Norton

> Always yours very sincerely
> Rudyard Kipling.

The Pater writes me that you've been writing to him and he's pleased.

Notes
1. Dated from postmark.
2. *Correspondence between Goethe and Carlyle* (1887) and *Correspondence of Thomas Carlyle and Ralph Waldo Emerson* (1883), both edited by Norton.
3. *Picturesque Brattleboro*, edited by the Revd Frank T. Pomeroy (Northampton, Mass., 1894), contains an abbreviated version of RK's "In Sight of Monadnock" and photographs of Naulakha. *Picturesque Franklin* (Mass.) (Northampton, Mass., 1891) was edited by Charles Forbes Warner.
4. In September RK had bought back the copyright in his Indian Railway Library books from Emile Moreau and had at once arranged with Macmillan to bring out American editions of those titles. They were published, "revised, with additions", in two volumes in New York early in 1895.

To William Henry Rideing,[1] 23 October 1894

ALS: Library of Congress

Naulakha. / Brattleboro. / Vermont. / Oct. 23: 94

Dear Mr Rideing:

Many thanks for the almanack. It's a genuinely pretty one.

As to a fresh paper – thought is needed. I'll try and do my best in the matter. The lives of English boys in India vary so tremendously that I could hardly describe one that would be accepted as at all accurate, all round. And I can't say I'm fond of the "personal experience" racket. The *Ladies Home Journal* is running *that* into the ground with an indecency that is almost as bad as exposure.

I might do a sketch of the work of a young man in the Woods and Forests Department of India and incidentally say something about the forestry management of India. It would be picturesque. But first I must know how long you would like the tale. Again there's the Hughli Pilot Service – the most specialized and best paid I believe in the world. One might describe that and how a boy works up in it.[2]

How soon do you want the tale? We have been spending a damp and dreary summer in Wiltshire and I must confess that I am glad to get away to sunshine and dry air. My affection for England is in large part for the Head Quarters of the Empire and I cannot say that the land itself fills me with comfort or joy.

Very sincerely
Rudyard Kipling

Notes
1. Rideing (1853–1918), English-born journalist and editor. He was an editor for both the *Youth's Companion* and the *North American Review* in Boston.
2. Perhaps the first suggestion for "An Unqualified Pilot": it did not appear in the *Youth's Companion* but in the *Windsor Magazine*, February 1895 (*Land and Sea Tales*).

To Louisa Baldwin, 29 October 1894
ALS: University of Sussex

Naulakha. / Brattleboro. / Vermont. / Oct. 29. 94

Dear Aunt Louie,
   Your cable came in this afternoon and was answered to the Father. I didn't think it would be sent across the water in that way and I don't know what account you got of it. The reality, though no one was even scratched, was bad enough.[1] Our near horse it seems got his leg over the pole and as the coachman was pulling them away from a hill the off hind wheel of the trap gave way – spilling C., Armstrong[2] and Baby. The latter had taken a pickle-bottle to play with and her only contribution to the seance as she sat on the bank was "Phemie lost bopple". She wasn't even embarrassed.
   Carrie behaved superbly. She wrapped up baby and put her in the bottom of the carriage and endured through the suspense before the smash came without a sound. Armstrong also sat dead still and came out with C – baby 'tween 'em – all unhurt. Howard, our coachman, told me (he's an Englishman new to the country) he'd "never seen hany lady be'ave like Mrs Kipling." She paid for it after poor darling for tho' she kept a dinner engagement she was much knocked up the next day and must go slow now for a week or two. You see it was baby that made the difference. Without her, Howard would have thrown the horses and taken greater risks. Altogether it was a thing to thank God for and I've made my little thank-offering to a children's home in New York.
   If our horses hadn't been trained as they were and Howard had lost his head instead of fighting 'em till he was pitched out there'd have been a big trouble. Rick (the horse that god his leg over the pole. It was pure play and might have happened twenty times before) had the

excitement of riding on the pole which didn't break for the matter of a mile. He is flayed raw just in the place where he ought to be well spanked and now eats bran and smells of carbolic. Oh but you should have seen the trap. It fetched up in a cemetery sorely battered – and only that very morn we were hugging each other on the daintiness of the turn out – the new harness, the new livery and the general sober splendour of our little toy. I'm more sorry for the coachman than any one. He was green with disgust and vexation but – here C. is witness – the horses were never absolutely out of control till the wheel broke and one can't do anything when the ship sinks under one. Now that C. has had proof of Howard's coolness she feels satisfied. Of course everyone is saying how they would have stopped the horses but I have yet to see the man who can hold one horse while he is being skinned and another while he is being kicked in the stomach. Little Rick knows what did him his injury and another time he wont "swing his rump around" so carelessly. He's a lighthearted little chap without an atom of vice in him and is now very penitent and hungry. I was at home when the news came to me but C. had driven up in a neighbor's trap and as soon as I took an inventory and found no one hurt I didn't care. We were going to get rid of the trap anyhow but I should scrcely have chosen this way. I hope this thing wont spoil C.'s driving hand for she gets much pleasure from her outings.

Every your loving nephew
Ruddy

Notes
1. The accident described in this letter took place on the 27th (CK diary).
2. The nurse.

To Robert Underwood Johnson, 11 November 1894
ALS: Dalhousie University

Naulakha. / Brattleboro. / Vermont. / Nov. 11. 94

Dear Johnson:

Many thanks for yours of the 8th. with enclosures.

It is excellent – as a means of bringing the matter before the people but – why the formal piece of experimental forestry near West Point when the actual Govt. reservations are in need of policing.[1] Let 'em begin the schools in the Yellowstone and the Adirondacks – tent and horses for each student – and make them patrol the reservation as they learned.

My own notion is that the service need not be more than 150 strong all told – and all the best men that the colleges can turn out. But how to put this idea into print, and a few others on the same head, that have occurred to me I do not know. I can't do it in any 500 words and it seems to me if I gave opinions in the *Century* I might do more harm than good. I don't know whether you realize the extent to which the average citizen who has heard my little name in the papers, objects to me.

I am going to write to the Professor[2] secretly and not for publication and when I get the material of a forestry article over from India I'll see if I can introduce into it a sort of rough scheme for a working dept.[3] I haven't seen Dearth[4] yet but hear he's painting with Hardie[5] and busy.

Very sincerely

Rudyard Kipling

Notes
1. The *Century Magazine* published an editorial on "Congress and the Forestry Question", November, 1894, pp. 150–1, supporting the plan of Professor Charles S. Sargent of Harvard to hand over the national forests to the Army, whose officers would be educated in forestry at West Point, where an experimental forest was to be established. In February 1895 the magazine published "A Plan to Save the Forests", with contributions from F. L. Olmsted, Theodore Roosevelt, Gifford Pinchot, and John Muir, among others. The subject was a favourite one with Johnson, one of the pioneers of the conservation movement.
2. Charles S. Sargent (1841–1927), Professor of Arboriculture at Harvard and director of the Arnold Arboretum.
3. Nothing like this by RK is known.
4. Henry Golden Dearth (1864–1918), landscape and genre painter.
5. Robert Gordon Hardie (1854–1904), born in Brattleboro, studied at the Art Students League and with Gérôme in Paris.

To Ripley Hitchcock, 13 November 1894
ALS: Berg Collection, New York Public Library

Naulakha. / Brattleboro. / Vermont. / Nov. 13. 94

My dear Mr. Hitchcock,

Let us now consider the largest "No" with which we can answer Mr. Lincoln.[1]

If he is the father of a family would you suggest that he sends up one of his children (any one will do) naked, by express, in order that I may exhibit him or her before a Brattleboro audience a little while before the Father appears. It is by diligent cultivation of a more or less uncultivated prose that I hoist myself to the dignity and ease of being able to sit upon my verses like a hen. And not till there are two mortgages on "Naulkakha" [*sic*] and a sale takes place in my back yard, are my verses to be Bob-o-Lincolned in the way the Uncut Leafer suggests.

Are not Shakespeare and Milton and Longfellow – excellent little poets I am told in their way – enough for him that he wishes to form an illicit connection with my muse *coram publico*, and for pence? Take him away. He has hit the largest and most outlying boulder of my not small vanity. Send him to Tammany – tell him to vote the Democratic ticket as his namesake did not do. Publish him in a paper back and nothing else and let him lie unbound on a bookstall through December. Seriously though, approach him with honied words and tell him there aren't any poems coming. I'll keep them up my sleeve till they are all good and ready. At the same time I confess I don't know when the book will appear.[2] There are times when it seems tomorrow and others when it seems next century. I don't suppose it will seriously agitate the centuries but it annoys me. You will also be annoyed when proof time comes. You don't know me yet as an unchained Poet. Which reminds me how much I am in your debt for the trouble you have taken over the music.[3]

Our weather has gone crazy mad after the Democratic defeat and we're in the middle of what looks like a December blockade. I fancy it's going to be a hard winter. Game lies close to the house; and there are more wild things about (and bolder) than I've seen before. Got a hawk 3' 9" across the wings the other day – such a beautiful beast – and have made allies of three fat grey squirrels who are established in a colony up the garden walk.

A skunk has discovered that the coal cellar is a good place to live in of nights, and the cats don't like him and he don't like them. Who says country life is unexciting. I wish we could see you up here for a space.

Ever yours sincerely
Rudyard Kipling

Notes

1. Luther Lincoln, a bibliophile: see 21 December 1894. I do not know what his proposal was.
2. *The Seven Seas*.
3. RK wrote to Hitchcock on 18 October that he had "accumulated" a musical setting of "A Song of the English" and wanted to have it reproduced to fit the pages of a book: "the poem on the right hand page and the score on the left" (ALS, Berg Collection, New York Public Library).

To Charles Eliot Norton, 23 November 1894
ALS: Harvard University

[Naulakha] Nov. 23. 1894

Dear Mr Norton

The whirl of Thanksgiving and Mai[1] being down in New York has carried us off our legs – and we are both desperately busy. It is very sweet of you to let us pick our own time within so wide a margin. Would Friday the 7th December (in time for the evening meal) to Monday the 10th discommode you?[2] We'll be through the heaviest of our work then and should love to come.

The Pater writes that "Phil[3] has heroically amputated the very loose leg he shook in London and gone to Brussels *in earnest*" to study from the life and paint pictures. Now I can't fit Phil and Brussels together somehow. Has there any news come to your folk *why* he has done this. The "Shakespeare once more"[4] has given me three joyous weeks – working like a nigger all day and re-eating [*sic*] Shakespeare of evenings. After all, there is no liquor like the very old brandy when one wants to get royally drunk.

Now I am waiting like a child for *McAndrews Hymn* to come along in *Scribners*.

Ever yours sincerely
Rudyard Kipling

Notes
1. The wife of CK's brother and Vermont neighbour, Beatty Balestier. In her absence the Kiplings took care of the Balestiers' child, Marjorie.
2. They went to Cambridge on the 6th and returned on the 10th (CK diary).
3. Burne-Jones.
4. Not identified.

To William Sayer,[1] [November? 1894]
ALS: Vermont Historical Society

Naulakha. / Brattleboro. / Vermont.

Dear Mr. Sayer.

Many thanks for your kind note. I'm just as sick about it as you are – possibly more so. What you say about breaking records only makes me groan. I've broken every record on earth since the house went up. I am the only living man who ever lost an eighty foot well and six weeks work because the well-sinker hadn't screwed home the drill. I am the sole human being that ever had a "Gem" windmill blow over in a gale: and only the other day when it was coming down I broke the record by having the windmill pulled over bodily before it killed a man. Earth is just crammed with records ready to give 'em to me as I go past.

This last business has cracked every record to flinders. I've got to pay the two men who helped your man for a week the little matter of
$50

And the livery-rig that brought them.	15
And the men who pumped water by hand into the house while the siege was on.	7.50.
And the carpenter who repairs the leak in the roof of the new engine house.	5.50
	$78.0

I don't know yet how much is to be paid for 400 feet of window-cord that we ruined in fishing for the pump with a grapnel. There are some minor expenses in the way of teams to haul water etc: but the total, setting aside the inconvenience, is about $100. I'll sell the record to you for $75 – cash. Seriously though, let's send that bill back to the office and tell them to pray for guidance.

Very sincerely yours
Rudyard Kipling

Note
1. Sayer represented the Rider Engine Co. of New York City, from whom RK had just bought an engine to pump his water supply at Naulakha, replacing an earlier and unsatisfactory windmill (see 27 September 1894).

To Brander Matthews, 13 December 1894
ALS: Columbia University

Naulakha. / Brattleboro. / Vermont. / Dec. 13. 1894

Dear Matthews:

Many thanks for the note and enclosures. I send back the Roosevelt[1] letter. 'Can't say that I was thinking about the populists when I wrote the W[alking] D[elegate] or if I was it's a kind of populist not confined to America. I'm glad it amuses him.

Beshrew your literary pedigrees. It opens up to me a noisome path of skit and parody – the poets arranged on the lines of the stud book. Thus,

> R. *Browning* (white poet: aged.) by *Temperament* out of *Dictionary* her sire *John Donne*

and so forth.

> A. *Swinburne.* by *Imagination* out of *Sherris Sack*; by *Dante Gabriel* out of *Versicles* by *Gallipots* out of *Spenser*; her dam *Troubadour*.

But your diction is unfortunate as regards me and my friend Geoffrey. Before your statement has gone west a thousand miles they'll make you say that I am the biggest liar since Ananias – all the same you *are* French.

Ever yours sincerely
Rudyard Kipling.

Note
1. Theodore Roosevelt, then a US Civil Service Commissioner: see 13 September 1898.

To James Conland, 14 December 1894
ALS: Library of Congress

[Naulakha] Dec. 14. 1894

Dear Dr Conland

Apropos of our talk in town this afternoon I hope you entirely understand that Dr Hamilton[1] was called in to see the baby in no sense as the family physician but as a concession to the homœopathic leanings of my wife's folks.

I ought to have sent you word at the time but when a man is busy writing tales on the etiquette of jungle life he is apt to forget the etiquette of every day human existence. I know you'll understand.

Very sincerely yours
Rudyard Kipling

Note
1. Dr Fremont Hamilton, who began a practice as a homœopathic physician in Brattleboro late in 1893. The Balestiers had been attracted to Brattleboro in the first place by the water cure operated there by the homœopathic doctor Robert Wesselhoeft.

To Henry James, 15 December 1894
ALS: Harvard University

Naulakha. / Brattleboro. / Vermont. / Dec. 15. 1894

Dear Mr. James –

This is to bring you Christmas messages from all three of us and to tell you that we've been seeing your folk at Cambridge.[1] Also it is our opinion that you are blessed with as fine upstanding a set of nephews (and Peggie) as any man could desire.[2] They received us with shouts of "Oh *you* know Uncle Harry don't you" and Peggie who had been spending a Sunday afternoon making pea-nut candy offered us a whole plateful and we became sticky and inarticulate. We were staying with the Nortons for a day or two and that was why we could not stay with your brother who asked us; but we went into his house for a few minutes on our way back from a lunch – just to envy him his work-room and discourse with Peggie who is a dear. It all seemed delightfully intimate and friendly and if you had come in just at that moment it would have been quite perfect. Carrie thinks and I am of her opinion that your brother is almost as nice as you are which is saying something. Altogether it was a beautiful time but too short. Why *can't* you come over for a flying visit sometime and come here and loaf and watch the weather and bring your writing and keep your own work hours?

The Father and Mother write enthusiastically of Florence where they have each an Intercontinental cold but they don't pretend to our clear blue skies.

McAndrew's Hymn has done its little work. Melville,[3] the Engineer in Chief of the U.S. Navy, writes to thank me for at last seeing the romance of the engineer and drawing attention to his good qualities. Also he gives his professional opinion that I have made no technical errors. There's richness for you! And now I'm at work on a companion set of verses.[4] When the new volume comes out you shall have your copy earliest.

Except that all papers are liars I would believe that there is a new play of yours coming out in a little while.[5] "I will now let loose my opinion" and prophecy. This year is going to bring you luck and you'll have a play that goes. We're both of us praying for it and when it comes off you'll hear us rejoice. With every possible good wish and much love from us both

Yours always sincerely
Rudyard Kipling

Notes
1. The family of Henry's brother William (1842–1910), the philosopher and psychologist,

Professor of Psychology at Harvard.
2. William James's three sons, Henry, William, and Alexander, and his daughter Margaret, afterwards Mrs Bruce Porter.
3. Admiral George Melville (1841–1912), Chief of the Navy Bureau of Steam Engineering, where he presided over the rebuilding of the United States Navy.
4. "The Mary Gloster". RK was working at it as early as 25 October, though it was not published until *The Seven Seas* (1896).
5. *Guy Domville*, first produced 5 January 1895: RK's prophecy was unlucky, for the play was a humiliating failure with the public.

To Luther Lincoln,[1] 21 December 1894

Text: The Critic, 12 January 1895, p. 32

I am in receipt of your very courteous communication of the 20th inst. and shall, of course, feel honoured if your committee sees fit to place my name on the list of Vice-Presidents for the meeting on the 4th proximo. I am hoping, however, that the suspiciously circumstantial report of Mr. Stevenson's death may turn out to be a piece of newspaper enterprise, and shall remain in that way of thinking till I hear from well-informed quarters.

Rudyard Kipling

Naulakha, Brattleboro. Vt.

Note
1. Lincoln, director of the Uncut Leaves Society, organised a Robert Louis Stevenson memorial meeting at Carnegie Hall on 4 January 1895. Stevenson's death on 3 December had been reported in the American papers on the 18th. According to CK's diary RK was so upset by the news of Stevenson's death that he did no work for a week (19 December 1894).

To Sarah Orne Jewett,[1] 24 December 1894

ALS: Harvard University

Naulakha. / Brattleboro. / Vermont. / Dec. 24. 94.

Dear Miss Jewett
    Very many thanks for the Xmas gift. Of course I knew one of the books thoroughly before – "serially and in book form" as the trade says and specially: "The Flight of Betsey Lane"[2] which seems to me to have been altered a little at the end. Is that so?

"Danvis folks"[3] as you justly say is a mine which I purpose to work. We've got such hunter-men round us and even as I was reading it, I heard a "hound-dog" baying back of our wood-lot. What a mass of material there is to work at in this land! But it must – woe is me – be done by an inhabitant and that makes me rage like the heathen.

I am just revising a new edition of my tales for England[4] and am deep in that depressed and pulpy mood, which we all have, when all the bad work gets up and grins at you. Therefore I feel much cheered by your pleasant words.

No snow – the roads like iron – and the thermometer nearly zero and tomorrow is Xmas day! I hope it will be pleasanter weather with you than promises for us.

With best wishes from my wife and myself for all that the new year brings believe me

Very sincerely yours
Rudyard Kipling.

Notes

1. Jewett (1849–1909), New England writer of local colour stories.
2. Collected in *A Native of Winby and Other Tales* (1893); first published in *Scribner's*, August 1893.
3. Rowland E. Robinson, *Danvis Folks* (Boston, 1894) is a collection of sketches in Vermont dialect; several of them are about hunting. Miss Jewett sent the book to RK thinking that "it might be of use to you – (you see that I am crying MORE! ever since I read The Walking Delegate!)" (to RK, 22 December [1894]: MS, Sussex).
4. *Soldiers Three, The Story of the Gadsbys, In Black and White* (London, 1895): a revised text.

To Robert Underwood Johnson, 27 December 1894

ALS: Dalhousie University

Naulakha. / Brattleboro. / Vermont. / Dec. 27. '94

Dear Johnson

This mail should bring you, under separate cover, Snow's article on Pelagic Seal-hunting.[1] Will you let me know as soon as may be what you think of it? It seems to me it might be cut a good deal.

The *Century* pays well for good work and that is why I do not sell the *Century* second-class work – as the novelette[2] would be if I sent it along. It reads all right but it's out of key and must be redone or thrown away. Another time I shan't count my chickens before they are galley-proofed.

We're two feet deep in snow here – the first sleighing for nearly a month – and send you a Happy New Year.

> Very sincerely
> Rudyard Kipling

I'd have given a month's pay to have seen *The Walking Delegate* breathed into Peffer's[3] whiskers.

Notes
1. No such article appears in the *Century Magazine*. Snow is Captain Henry James Snow (1848–?), author of *In Forbidden Seas: Recollections of Sea-Otter Hunting in the Kurils* (1910) and *Notes on the Kuril Islands* (1897). RK describes Snow as "a bit of a pirate" who "owns at least one schooner, is rather a rich man and when he is not careering about dodging Russian patrol boats or being lost at sea is one of the mildest and best dressed members of the Tokio Club" (to R. U. Johnson [December 1894]: ALS, Dalhousie).
2. Not identified.
3. William Alfred Peffer (1831–1912), Populist Senator from Kansas, 1891–7. The yellow horse who is the "walking delegate" of RK's story is a Populist from Kansas.

To Stanley Weyman,[1] 3 January 1895
ALS: Robert H. Taylor Library, Princeton University

Naulakha. / Brattleboro. / Vermont. / Jan: 3. 1895:

Dear Weyman

Christmas has knocked the postal arrangements galley-west and your kind gift[2] only came in through the snow a little time ago: Then I took an afternoon off and having read it in paper backs sat down to a decent volume and slowed not till teatime. As had happened in the first reading my feet got cold. Do you know what that means? One gets excited and the blood goes to the head. I don't believe in compliments between men in the same business but if I were to see you again I'd tell you some pretty ones – both of my own manufacture and others that I've heard. The thing that impressed me *not* because it showed in any way but on thinking it over, was the tremendous amount of work that must have gone to its make up – the loads on loads of lost and buried "dig" that you must have flung down to make the solid ground on which your solid hero walks so convincingly.

By the way has it occurred to you that gentlemen in the Intelligence Department in this present year are careering about the continent and elsewhere on behalf of their governments picking up information about insides of dockyards and armaments and the like in much the same way as your steadfast De Marsac, allowing for telegraphs and railroads. If they get caught they are of course disowned. If they succeed they get decorations and things for no conceivable reason that the public can fathom. There's something in that I should think if you could get at the proper men.

We are under two foot of snow here with the thermometer 25° below Zero and a blazing sun day after day and all the sleighing that a man could wish. Doyle[3] came up a little before the snow fell but he didn't see the land at its best. Wish you could come along some day. You'll probably be over here before long and then I will make a long arm and catch you.

With all good wishes for luck and good work this year

Ever yours sincerely
Rudyard Kipling.

These papers lie so that I can't get at the rights of R.L.S.'s death – if indeed he be dead. It doesn't seem to me possible. It must be one of his jests and he'll "come up with a song from the sea" while we are mourning over him.

Notes

1. Weyman (1855–1928) was a successful writer of historical romances.
2. *A Gentleman of France: Being the Memoirs of Gaston de Bonne, Sieur de Marsac*, new edn, 1894 (first edn, November 1893).
3. Conan Doyle, with his brother Innes, was at Naulakha 28–30 November 1894. He remembered RK reading "McAndrew's Hymn" to him. "I had brought up my golf clubs and gave him lessons in a field while the New England rustics watched us from afar" (*Memories and Adventures*, 1924, p. 246).

To Meta de Forest, 14 January 1895
ALS: Harvard University

Naulakha. / Brattleboro. / Vermont.

Dear Meta

I write at C's dictation: she has burned her face looking into a furnace and is swathed in bandages and oil in consequence.[1] 'Doing well but decidedly angry, and uncomfortable: The cook – *your* cook – therefore could not have arrived at a more appropriate moment. C. has hastily built a Presbyterian Church for her against next Sunday and the other servants are showing her the way about. C. would scare her into fits if she showed her swathed and cotton-battened head so she lies low and issues her orders from afar. Mrs Hodges is installed in the nursery. Things promise well and C. overflows with gratitude to you. She has cooked one meal for us already and may she cook many more. I am of opinion that you are an angel for you have come down and helped us in great need. May you never live to regret it.

We are both awfully sorry about poor Judith.[2] Please give her and Appie[3] our love and with much to you and Lock (his bell adorns my mantel) always yours sincerely

Ruddy.

Jan. 14. 1895.

Notes
1. This had happened on the 14th.
2. The de Forests' daughter, afterwards Mrs Soule.
3. Their son Alfred.

Edward Everett Hale,[1] 16 January 1895
ALS: Cornell University

Naulakha. / Brattleboro. / Vermont. / Jan. 16. 1895.

Dear Dr. Hale –

I can't tell you how much I appreciate and shall value your kind letter. Praise from you is praise to be proud of and henceforward I shall look upon the *Jungle Book* with respect. There is to be a companion collection[2] issued this fall if all goes well and I can only hope that it will please you.

The idea of beast-tales seems to me new in that it is a most ancient and long forgotten idea. The really fascinating tales are those that the Bodhisat tells of his previous incarnations ending always with the beautiful moral.[3] Most of the native hunters in India today think pretty much along the lines of an animal's brain and I have "cribbed" freely from their tales.

With sincerest respect and admiration and all good wishes for the New Year

Believe me dear Dr. Hale

Yours very faithfully
Rudyard Kipling

Notes
1. Hale (1822–1909), Unitarian minister in Boston and popular author, especially known for "The Man without a Country" (1863).
2. *The Second Jungle Book*, published in October of this year.
3. Stories collected as the *Jatakas*. See 1 March 1897.

To William Heinemann, 20 January 1895
ALS: Princeton University

[Naulakha]

Dear Heinemann

Of course you'll come up, for New York in April is greasy damnation besides being cold. We'll drive you out of your mind round Brattleboro in deep mud and what Limericks I have manufactured I will disgorge. An almanack is a fearful task for the reason that there are 365–6 days in the year, as your contributors will discover.[1] It sounds too nice to be possible and ought to be splendid fun. You're in luck about the *New Review*[2] for W.E.H. has *got* to be heard from and there will be knives and clubs in the air by the time he has settled into his stride.

I am working hard but shall experimentalize on Limericks. Don't forget to give us your steamer date.

Yours ever
Rudyard Kipling

Notes
1. Perhaps Heinemann had proposed an almanac of limericks to which RK should contribute. I do not know whether such a thing materialised. RK later did an *Almanac of Twelve Sports* (1898) for Heinemann.
2. Henley had taken over the editorship of the *New Review* in December 1894, under the proprietorship of Heinemann.

To Ripley Hitchcock, 22 January 1895
ALS: Berg Collection, New York Public Library

Naulakha. / Brattleboro. / Vermont. / Jan: 22. 1895

My dear Hitchcock,

Imprimis we are much in your debt for your kindness to Miss Holbrook[1] who we hope will profit thereby. *Secundo* we await with impatience any news from the Potomac[2] for Mrs. Kipling now that every thing is over is a good deal shaken by the shock of that burning and we want to get away: Where can we lay our weary heads in decency without bankruptcy: for we are brought low in the land.

There is no question of bringing out any volume of past soldier tales for the reason that the yarns which close that chapter – including the death of Mulvaney – are not yet written, but I have been able to buy back through the immense cleverness of Watt, my original six books in paper backs from the Indian publishers and his English minions.[3] They were in no sense cheap but Macmillan came in with a big offer of royalty and I've just got through the deal.[4] It means a good deal to me – even at long prices – to control my early books. Of course there can never be anything much from America in the way of a perfect edition but Macmillan is ready to balance the risk against English sales which are certain – apparently. You will understand of course that this is from me to you – not official:

We are drawing ice in a heavy thaw against time and the weather is purely awful – cloud and mist and rain, and the glass at 35° feeling like midsummer, but the lights on the hills a miracle of colour. I've been up to my knees in the swamps wondering whether a beaver would have anything to say to such a place.[5] I think he would if his tail were pruned – same as *you* do a bird's wings.

Mrs Kipling joins me in kind regards to you and I am

Very sincerely yours
Rudyard Kipling.

Notes
1. Emerline Holbrook (1863–1958), of a prominent Brattleboro family; she married Edward Cooke Armstrong. Miss Holbrook studied art in Boston and in Paris, and had just opened a studio in New York. She had just spent a week as a guest at Naulakha while making a portrait in pastels of Josephine; the portrait, which now hangs at Batemans, was exhibited at a private party in Brattleboro (*Vermont Phoenix*, 11 January 1895; *Windham County Reformer*, 18 January 1895).
2. They were planning to go to Washington: see 15 March 1895.
3. See [19 October 1894].
4. Macmillan brought out a volume containing revised texts of *Soldiers Three*, *The Story of the Gadsbys*, and *In Black and White* in March 1895. Macmillan, which had published Kipling from as early as 1890 (the first English edition of *Plain Tales from the Hills*) was the sole English publisher of RK's prose works after 1892.
5. RK thought about introducing beaver on his property but learned that it would be impracticable: see 18 May 1895.

To Hamlin Garland,[1] 24 January 1895
ALS: University of Southern California

Naulakha. / Brattleboro. / Vermont. / Jan. 24. 95

Dear Mr Garland

Many thanks for your kind letter. It seems a bit early to be lecturing about me;[2] but if it amused the audience I suppose it is all right. I'd like to see what in the world you found to say.

We hope one of these days to go out west for a while but my notion of the west begins at Denver and ends at Portland. Chicago is getting to be practically East for business purposes – twenty four hours by rail being nothing to your countrymen.

I met Zangwill[3] for a few minutes in town last summer and he interested me immensely. He seems to be a born critic of things and I should not be surprised if in the long run he found criticism his special gift. Doyle stayed with us here and [sic] couple of days which we spent for the most part in golfing. He's a first class player and so's his little brother. He seems to have all sorts of good ideas up his sleeve and I shall watch with both ears when he turns to and tackles Napoleon in fiction.[4] He is very full of him just now.

I'm glad to know you approve of some of the things I do, but, don't run away with the notion that they are unconventional. They are based on a very old convention – so old that most folk don't know about it – but they are as conventional as any other work really – as all work has to be. No man can jump out of his skin.

I'm busy with verses and things at present and intend going south for the spring thaw. Give my best salaams to Riley when you meet him wandering about and remember if you're within hail of here any time to come along.

Yours very sincerely
Rudyard Kipling

Notes

1. Garland (1860–1940), writer especially known for his stories and recollections of the midwest; he was living in Chicago at this time. According to Garland, he first met RK in New York in 1892 at RK's hotel, where he and James Whitcomb Riley were the only guests – both unknown to RK but invited to reveal American literature to him (Garland, *Roadside Meetings*, 1930, p. 169).
2. Lecturing was a large part of Garland's activity; I have not found anything of his on Kipling from 1895.
3. Israel Zangwill (1864–1926), novelist of Jewish life, beginning with *Children of the Ghetto* (1892). Garland did not meet him until 1898 (Garland, *Diary*, ed. Donald Pizer, 1968, p. 199).
4. *The Exploits of Brigadier Gerard* (1896).

To A. P. Watt, 31 January 1895

ALS: Cornell University

Naulakha. / Brattleboro. / Vermont.

Dear Watt:

I am sending by this mail, (a good deal ahead of time, but the notion came to me suddenly) No. 1. of the new series Jungle Tales in the P.M.G. – called *The Manx Cat*.[1]

Please tell them that I want a proof as soon as may be and that I will send the verse heading either then or before.

Very sincerely
Rudyard Kipling:

Jan. 31: 1895:

Note
1. Published as "The Maltese Cat", *Pall Mall Gazette*, 26 and 27 June 1895. RK evidently intended a *Third Jungle Book* but the idea was not carried far; no further animal stories appeared in the *Pall Mall Gazette*. "The Maltese Cat" is collected in *The Day's Work*.

To Charles Eliot Norton, [8] February [1895]
ALS: Harvard University

Naulakha. / Brattleboro. / Vermont. / Feb (the date
has drifted up but it is the 8th or 9th)

Dear Mr. Norton:

It's worth while to have a little weather when one gets so kindly a note as yours in the middle of it.

But we seem up here to have been touched but lightly. There were two days of knife edged cold, a cloudless sky, a sun grinning like a skull and a wind that ripped the bones off you. Today it is only blizzard and tho' I do not see when we shall be able to use the roads we are warm and of good heart. But our house has been singing like a ship brought up in the wind's eye and the old maple has been creaking and there are five or six feet of snow generally about the place and at least ten in the air. Barring two local stoppages in our pipes nothing much has happened. But I am learning how this weather produces these men – and women.

Beatty[1] has achieved a magnificent cold which after skirmishing all over his body has blossomed into a sharp touch of rheumatism and he now lies in his bed too stiff and sore to do justice to the situation. But he is on the mend – or was last night. I have not been able to get down to him by reason of the wind. Did you know that Carrie burned her face opening the furnace door, about three weeks ago. It was more in the nature of a scorch than a burn but it naturally upset her very much and since then we have been living small and going softly together seeing no company. She bids me say that this is her excuse for not writing a letter which she owed to Miss Norton. Her eyes pain her when she reads but otherwise she is now well. We talk of going to Washington to play for a month or six weeks sometime not very far off and I think that will make her happy. The baby (glory be) keeps her rude health and becomes to us daily more charming. We are sending the Pater (he is getting fat in Florence and sends me the most unprintable stories of contessas and contadinas and all the draggly out at elbows easy polyglot society that camps on the continent) we are sending him a small pastel study of Josephine, her head, reading a book.[2] But what can one do with a small impudence who stops the coachman and enquires magisterially after the health of each horse by name. She has most of the Heart of Oak songs[3] translated into her own dialect – that of a distinguished Portugese as far as I can follow it. We love her. *Apropos*, there is no difficulty about *East and West* (or for matter of that any other set of verses you honour by thinking good). Strictly there is no copyright on that piece but I will send a line to Brett[4] of MacMillans this side, it appears in a book they publish, and tell him that it will appear in Hearts of Oak: and 'tis me that am the proud man.

By the way they are using the Jungle book in raised letters for the Blind and if I'd only known that at the outset I'd have written specially touch-and-smell Jungle tales. It's not too late now.

Work has been going easily. I have a yearning upon me to tell tales of extended impropriety – not sexual or within hailing distance of it – but broad-bottomed unseemly yarns, and am now at work on the lamentable history of a very fat Indian administrator who was, in the course of a survey, shot in his ample backside by a poisoned arrow: and his devoted subordinate sucked the wound, to the destruction of his credit as an independent man for the rest of his days. The administrator always like being toadied to. That it is a true tale makes it only more difficult in the telling. I want to be a Gaul for a week. One can't be serious always.

I suppose selling chunks of dead friends is all right. T.[?]W.[5] isn't *the* offender by any means. Edmund Gosse with a piece of Carrion, flirting his tail and looking sideways as he hops along with it to the nearest bank, can give Watts any odds.[6] They are digging out all of R.L.S.'s letters and nailing every chance word to the public barn door and I am very sick of it.[7] But Symonds[8] was brought up with that crowd and didn't know any better. It's rather like the Pest-cart of old with the bell and candle and the cry: – "Bring out your dead". We have added the book but I think I should prefer being shot feet first out of the tumbril with half a pound of quicklime into the common ditch. All the same it is pleasant to think what a splendid time the historians of the 21st century will have when they take to writing monographs.

Affectionate greetings

RKs[9]

Notes
1. Beatty Balestier (1867–1936), youngest of the Balestier children, RK's brother-in-law. He and his wife and child lived only a few hundred yards from RK, at a farm called Maplewood. It was from Beatty that RK bought the property on which Naulakha was built. Boisterous and reckless, Beatty resented any attempt to check him. A quarrel between him and RK drove the latter away from Vermont, never to return.
2. A smaller version made by Miss Holbrook of her portrait of Josephine: see 22 January 1895, n. 1.
3. *The Heart of Oak Books*, edited by Norton and Kate Stephens, 7 vols (1893–1902); a series of children's readers containing verses, fables, fairy-tales, and adventure stories.
4. George Brett (1858–1936), the manager of Macmillan's American agency, under whom, in 1896, it became a separate American corporation with Brett as president.
5. Not clear: RK perhaps wrote T.W. or F.W. or I.W. One guess would be Theodore Watts (later Watts-Dunton), but if so I can find nothing of his that might qualify as "selling chunks of dead friends" at this time.
6. Gosse published "Personal Memories of Robert Louis Stevenson", *Century Magazine* (July 1895), 447–54.
7. Sidney Colvin was at work on Stevenson's *Letters to His Family and Friends*, 2 vols (1899). One of RLS's letters to RK appeared in the fourth edition of this in 1901.
8. The biography of Symonds by Horatio F. Brown, compiled "from his papers and correspondence", published in 1895, contained letters from and references to Stevenson.
9. The closing and signature added by CK.

To Edgar W. Stoddard,[1] [21 February 1895]

ALS: Photocopy, Vermont Historical Society

Naulakha. / Brattleboro. / Vermont.

Hon. E. W. Stoddard
Attorney at Law
Brattleboro

Dear Sir:

I understand that you are the legal representative of the opposition to the projected trolley-line in this town.[2]

May I, though not an American citizen, be permitted to enter a protest against the scheme? I have at some considerable expense during the past three years purchased and, as I believe, improved real estate lying within a few miles of Brattleboro, in the belief that access to the town for business or for pleasure would at all times be safe and possible.

Should the trolley-line be made through the steep narrow and tortuous streets of the town I should find myself entirely cut off from my present railway-station and base of supplies; for no man who has had experience of trollies and their working would willingly risk the lives of his family or his horses by exposing them to the daily chances of accident from direct collision with the cars, from fallen wires or from runaways.

As far as I am concerned getting supplies from a neighbouring town and using a station higher up the line would be a small price to pay for comparative safety but it occurs to me that something more than inconvenience would fall upon the large farming community among whom I live. They are compelled by the nature of their business to visit Brattleboro very frequently. In busy seasons their women folk must go in their place meeting daily and certain risk.

It is beyond doubt that the greatest good of the greatest number is the law of civic administration; but there is, possibly, some danger of overlooking the fact that *number* includes not only the town people but all the inhabitants of the large district hitherto dependent upon Brattleboro as a centre of distribution.

It seems also that the good [   ]³ most clearly shown to be indictable and overwhelming ere the town or any section of the town sanctions a course of action which permanently disfigures streets already proven to be inadequate to any extra strain of traffic; which wholly destroys the beauty for which Brattleboro is so justly famous; which enormously increases the risk of fires, at the same time adding to the perils of extinguishing them; and which in every city of the Union has invariably been followed by the violent death or mutilation of human beings.

Trusting that you will not find these remarks altogether impertinent to the matter and wishing you every success in your opposition to the road

I am

Yours very faithfully
Rudyard Kipling

Notes
1. Stoddard (1846–96) was a Brattleboro lawyer.
2. The trolley, though strongly opposed, was operating by the summer of 1895. No use was made of RK's letter in the opposition campaign. According to Mary Cabot, RK was provoked to write some verses calling Brattleboro "Crosby's Dump": Edward Crosby was president of the Brattleboro Street Railway Company ("Kipling's Vermont Period", p. 41: Rice Collection, Marlboro College).
3. Illegible phrase in photocopy.

To John B. Walker,[1] 15 March 1895
ALS: Cornell University

The Grafton / Connecticut Ave / Washington.
D.C.[2] / Mar. 15. 95

Dear Mr. Walker,

Many thanks for yours of the 6th which has been delayed in following me here.

This is my idea. According to my present plans I hope to go to India for the winter reaching Bombay late in September and revisiting the North where I belong. It occurs to me that, if you cared for them, I could do for you a set of twelve letters describing the land from the point of view of the man to whom it means "home". Those would be more "cosmopolitan" than anything I could do on other subjects and I think I could make a good series. I should be writing the articles under any circumstances and so I should not feel that I was taking contracts ahead for the sake of the money.

Will you let me know how this appears to you.

Very sincerely yours
Rudyard Kipling.

Notes
1. Editor of the *Cosmopolitan Magazine*.
2. RK and CK went to Washington about 6 March and remained until 6 April.

To Edward Bok,[1] 25 March 1895
ALS: Library of Congress

The Grafton: / Connecticut Ave / Mar: 25 / 95

Private
Dear Mr Bok:

Now I think I can talk. I have by me in the rough-draft very much the kind of tale you would be needing for Xmas.[2] It deals with a wooing in the thick of a Madras famine – man and girl together working hard among the starving and feeding the abandoned black babies and generally going through deep waters: and it ends with their joyful return to their home province, the Punjab, in time for the festivities of the "Christmas week." By present reckoning it ought to be between 7–9000 words but I want to cut it as short as possible.

The price for all serial rights the world over will be $140 (one hundred and forty dollars) per thousand on delivery of the copy on the understanding that if necessary I can have two revises. If you will let me know when the Christmas number of the L J goes to press I will send it as soon as I can. For myself I should prefer the tale unillustrated for I have suffered much at the hands of persons who have tried to draw Indian scenery.[3]

I think the story ought to give your women readers a little notion of a woman's life where life is rather trying. At all events I have written with an eye to this end.

Very sincerely
Rudyard Kipling

Notes
1. Bok (1863–1930) was editor of the *Ladies' Home Journal* from 1889 to 1919. He and RK met on the voyage to England from New York in the preceding summer.
2. "William the Conqueror", *Ladies' Home Journal*, December 1895 and January 1896. RK began it on 20 March (CK diary).
3. The story was illustrated by W. L. Taylor.

To Lady Marjorie Gordon,[1] 5 April 1895
ALS: Dalhousie University

The Grafton / Connecticut Ave: / Ap. 5: 1895.

My dear Lady Marjorie
    I write to tell you how pleased I was to receive from you a bound copy of "Wee Willie Winkie" – *your* Wee Willie Winkie – and the January number. Do you know that besides yours and mine there is a third Winkie. It is in a book by Mr. C. G. Leland, called "Johnnikin and the Goblins"[2] where all the Goblins go to a feast in some ruins and Friar Bacon, Marjorie Daw, Charlie Cake-and-Ale-and the Church Mouse and a lot of other fairy book characters come in with "Wee Willie Winkie." I haven't seen the book for some years but it is rather an interesting one. You must find editing a magazine, even once a month, is a great deal of work. When I was at school I edited a small paper that only came out three times a year so I feel as if I knew something of the duties of the position. Don't you have trouble with lazy contributors? I did. Would you care for this in your puzzle corner? Its an old friend in an East Indian dress:

Chota Jack Hornah

Baita men Kornah
Kartha tha Kissmiss Mithai.
Unglee bech dalkur
Aur Kissmiss Nikalkur,
Bola – "Kaisa Khub lurka hum hai!"

And here is something that you might get a picture made for. I can't draw or I'd try to illustrate it.

There was a small boy of Quebec
Who was buried in snow to the neck.
    When they asked: – "Are you friz?"
    He replied: – "Yes I is,
    "But we don't call this cold in Quebec."

Wishing you all success in the future issues of your magazine, believe me

Yours always sincerely
Rudyard Kipling.

Notes
1. Lady Marjorie (1880–1970), still a girl at the date of this letter, was the daughter of the 1st Marquess of Aberdeen; she married the 1st Lord Pentland in 1904. Since 1891 she had been producing a magazine for children called *Wee Willie Winkie* at Dingwall, in the Highlands.
2. 1877. Leland's *Breitmann Ballads* were a favourite of RK's.

To Margaret Mackail, 13–15 April 1895
ALS: University of Sussex

Naulakha. / Brattleboro. / Vermont. / Ap. 13. 1895:

Dear Margaret,
    That's a lovely photo – one of the best I've seen of you in a long day. Likewise you look fatter. I send on a page some signatures. God forbid that I should use so fine a fist in my daily life but they'll look lovely in an album and Angela can cut them out.
    We've had an exciting and joyous time for we've been wallowing in society at Washington – such palaces of houses such vittles and such horses and carriages! It was the World the Flesh and the Devil in a lump and we took it in gulps for the reason that our "town" is other folks' "country" and we wanted to get it over. Then Josephine started her first

sickness and kept us on the rack for three weeks but is now completely well with a new vocabulary and a set of city manners. It was her tummy that went wrong and we were lucky to have a good doctor close by. Altogether we had nearly six weeks of purple and fine linen (when the head of the Washington Zoo let me frolic in private enclosures where the beaver lived and postponed feeding the beasts till I found it convenient to come I felt that Notoriety was beginning to be worth something) but we were very glad to climb back to our own peace and pull up the ladder behind us. The last of the deep snow is still lying in shady places; there isn't a sign of a leaf and the brooks are brown and brimming and it has been raining tropically all day. The roads up here are hopeless and will be for another fortnight but we couldn't stay away any longer – there were so many things to do to the garden and the trees. Carrie as you know had been having a lively time of it – first a runaway and then a burning. However her eyebrows are thicker than ever and her hair is very pretty and she has given up having styes in her eye (which was one result of the burning) and I have given her a new pair of horses (angels they are) which she is to drive herself, and a phaeton not unworthy of their beauty and their manners. So we hope to have a good summer up here playing about in the open and building ourselves an ice house and such like trifles.

Ap. 15. Here comes a letter from the Pater telling me, incidental like, that your Angela had been troubled with some "derangement of the mucous membrane." Dear Wop, let me weep sympathetically on your neck. That was Baby's trouble – all her linings out of order and yet while I weep I can't help thinking of the rocking horse and the bread and dripping under the sofa and grinning at the wild incongruity of our each owning a mucous membraneous infant. T'wasn't eight and forty hours ago that I had croup at the Grange and slept in Aunt Georgy's room and woke up to find myself in a mustard bath and three weeks back we were hanging round Josephine wondering whether she'd develop croup on top of everything else. She's just gone out with her mother and the Sacred Pair to look at our floods – the biggest since 1862 I do assure you as I am frequently assured. It's a hill country – what you might call mountainous and the Connecticut, above the size of the Thames below London bridge, has gone clean mad with the melting snows of the North and there hasn't been a train through from the North for two days. Lines washed out everywhere; and the water within a foot of the only bridge that takes us to town and stray engines moving like cows cut off by deep water on all sides. I've just been down to look – about two miles down the valley. It's a grand sight. We've had it ceaseless rain for three days but our new built road has stood nobly and our English coachman, a man of his hands, has been as busy as a beaver after the winter's inaction planting trees and playing gardener because he hasn't been able to exercise the horses. Four days had the Sacred Pair been in stable and they went forth today like unto clockwork after one preliminary flourish on their hind legs. C. is lusting to drive 'em (she did in the winter; a bandage over her burned eye and the Luck of the Lord to guide us) but the More Sacred Phaeton (blood red dear Wop with basket sides and wings and *such* a rumble) does not arrive till the roads are a little drier. A road a mile down the hill collapsed yesterday – holes formed in it; and she and I went down to repair it in deep mud with sticks and boughs and unmitigated dirt. It's nice to make mud pies always but when you feel you are doing the community a service and can get filthy without any one to say "don't" you revel in it. Also – domestic details are all I have – we have a fat new cook who cooks well; also we have found the first flower of the year, a liver-wort; also the new maple sugar has been made. (You don't know maple sugar. It's the sap of the big maple boiled down tasting equally of all things sweet and all things springsome); also we have hot beds which won't hot; also we have our garden to make and the frogs have begun singing o' nights. We shall probably be over in England early this autumn on our way to India for the winter. Mother writes me that Trix is coming on the *Bengal* to Plymouth, May 4th, so *she's* happy. The Pater seems to have tied himself into a knot over his house renting arrangements in Tisbury; has a house on his hands he doesn't want and is very funny about it. I do not love Tisbury and shall not stay there. It's wet and smelly. If you meet Sallie Norton, as you have I suppose, by this time, give her our best love. She's a dear superior dear and we like her. I'm going down to Boston to be dined at on the 24th by a club of which Norton, whom I much reverence, is President.[1] If you want to know how we live in these wilds ask Sallie. We gave her three dread days of it and I don't think it amused her. Aunt Georgie sent me her Manifesto to the electors of Rottingdean:[2] whereupon I wrote her eight small pages about "practical politics" as they exist here: but it was all so disheartening I tore it up and thought better of it. You see men and women are only folks – and when an angel like your Mother sails into our little world she'll find herself disappointed and hurt. Bless her and give her my love. Embrace the Noble Dennis for me and convey my respectful salutations to Angela (she needs some one to play with sorely) and with love to you and Jack.

Ever your affectionate
Wop.

Bips[3] came and edited my correspondence. That is why I write on half leaves.

Notes
1. The Tavern Club. According to the journal kept by a member of the club, RK spoke there on the 24th and recited "The Song of the Banjo" (see Flora Livingston, *Bibliography of Rudyard Kipling* [New York, 1927] p. 162).
2. Lady Burne-Jones successfully ran for the Rottingdean parish council at the end of 1894; as part of her campaign she wrote and published "An Open Letter to the electors of Rottingdean" (Ina Taylor, *Victorian Sisters*, 1987, p. 157).
3. A pet name for Josephine.

To Stanley Baldwin, 17 April 1895

ALS: Dalhousie University

Naulakha. / Brattleboro. / Vermont. / Ap. 17. 1895

Dear Old Man,

Hurrah![1] Floreat Baldwina! All the same when Baby Josephine was born I confess I didn't care one little continental curse about the child till I was sure the mother was doing well. I hope earnestly all's serene in that direction. It's a great pull to have a girl first because they are tough little beggars and stand things much better than boys. Also in the latter end of things a girl can't break your heart more than once whereas a boy can continue consecutively going to the devil for ever so many years and turning your hair white every fine day.

What's her name? What's her weight? What's her colour and her hair and – but of course she has neither manners nor morals at this age. Were I near you I could overwhelm you with much unprofitable advice but here is one maxim worth gold. Don't believe a grandmother is infallible. It's generally so long a time since a grandmother has had a baby that they forget things or get 'em mixed up and the results are apt to be disastrous for the Kid. Josephine is much set up with her new "cou-sin Baby" and wants to know her name. She's at that age when she wants to know everything. Lord what a time you have in front of you, – angina pectoris when baby is hoarse, paralysis when she coughs more than once; and the baser forms of heart disease when she comes out in a rash – likewise yells; likewise broken nights and such. But you'll find it well and well worth anything.

They aren't much fun till they are six months old from the point of view of the male animal but after that they delight the eye, educate the mind, and fill a long felt want. It was sweet of you to think of sending me the news at first hand. Only the disgusting part, for me and Ambo[2] is, that after all we are only second cousins when by virtue of our years and sobriety we should be uncles.

Carrie and I both send you love and good wishes. Let us know how the wife does and (this is worth knowing) you must be more than gentle with her these next months to come. A woman isn't well before her child comes bodily but it's her spirits and mind that are all on edge afterwards.

Ever your loving cousin
Ruddy.

Notes
1. For the birth of Baldwin's first living child, Diana Lucy, 8 April 1895.
2. Ambrose Poynter.

To George Saintsbury,[1] 17 April 1895
ALS: University of Sussex

Naulakha. / Brattleboro. / Vermont. / Ap. 17. 1895

Dear Saintsbury,
  Its a six box[2] volume on the face of it; and a one volume story at that by the looks of it and it's too big for the likes of me. There's a perfectly splendid volume of tales to be done about the machinery (ships, railways, mines, electric lighting and so forth) of the Victorian age but it would take me about five years to do it, and I don't think the publishers would be pleased. So I'm afraid you'll have to count me out and I'm very sorry for it. The distance is beyond my legs. Anyhow, to make that series perfect, you want an assortment of Monumental Geniuses; and they're scarce. I don't see why, if a good set of verses happen to come along in the nature of rhymes about the work that has been turned out in the last forty years, it could not be put into some number of the series as an introduction or an interlude or a L'Envoi, or something.
  I was immensely pleased by your last letter. I don't suppose it will do more than make you laugh, but I've a very large and reverent admiration for you and what you write, as a Warden of the Ancient Landmarks – a sane big critic who has read whereof he writes. Your Hogg, Smith, Hunt, Lockhart etc. essays[3] I've had these five years reading and rereading them for the reason that I delight in that time and that set and also for the same reason that a man drinks soda water to take bad taste out of his mouth. When I heard the news of the sale of the *Saturday* and the dispersal of the staff[4] I wrote a whole long set of verses all about you and thought them deuced fine but presently remembering

that nothing is so terrible as inopportune and explosive admiration I burned 'em. For this at least you have good cause to be grateful. Won't you send me your "Corrected Impressions."[5] I've been chasing bits of it in the reviews and want the rest. We don't have bookshops up in these hills.

Very sincerely yours
Rudyard Kipling.

Notes

1. Saintsbury (see 3–25 December 1889) was now living as a freelance journalist; in September of this year he was appointed Regius Professor of Rhetoric and English Literature at Edinburgh. I do not know what project he had proposed to RK.
2. The word is not clear.
3. *Essays in English Literature, 1780–1860* (1890).
4. The *Saturday Review*, for which Saintsbury had worked since 1880, had been bought by Frank Harris in 1894 and completely remade. For Harris, see 16 September 1897. The style in which the old staff was dismissed is described by H. G. Wells, *Experiment in Autobiography* (New York, 1934) p. 438.
5. *Corrected Impressions: Essays on Victorian Writers* (1895).

To Charles Eliot Norton, 27 April 1895
ALS: Harvard University

Naulakha. / Brattleboro. / Vermont. / Ap: 27. '95

Dear Mr. Norton

After the Lord Mayor's show comes the donkey cart;[1] and I've been expiating too good fortune by sorrow in my system – they call it the liver, and it makes me sad and sick and sodden all down the right side. No, it is neither too much "Italian decadence" nor champagne but a genuine complaint of nature and that is why I did not write yesterday but sat huddled in a lump reading the *real* Florio. Carrie, I found on my return, had accomplished wonders within doors and without and Bips was rejoiced to see me again. Old man Nourse[2] who had built about a quarter of a mile of three foot stone wall in three days, actually blushed all through the outer dirt of him when I bore him your inquiries about his hand! His answer was for the most part a large grin of gratified vanity. Not that it is for *me* to talk! I've been smiling all over to myself with the same complaint ever since I came away from the Tavern – a most discerning Club, Sir, which I am rejoiced to learn holds precisely *my* views in the more important matters of Literature. It was a beautiful time – and another bead on the long string of my debts to you. 'Wish I could write well enough to pay them as you would like them. With love

from us both (C. is sorry now that she didn't come) to you and yours.
Yours affectionately always
Rudyard Kipling.

Notes
1. RK had just returned from a visit to Norton in Cambridge.
2. J. R. Nourse, who did gardening and handiwork at Naulakha.

Lucius Tuttle,[1] 30 April 1895

ALS: Photocopy, Brooks Memorial Library, Brattleboro, Vermont

[Naulakha]   Ap. 30. 1895

personal

Dear Sir

I shall be much obliged if you can spare a few minutes to read what follows.

The trains of the Boston and Maine cross an iron girder bridge over the mouth of the West River as it enters the Connecticut a very short distance north of Brattleboro.

The only method of reaching Brattleboro from the north (for wheeled traffic) is by means of a wooden covered bridge some fifty feet east of and parallel to this Boston and Maine bridge.

Owing to the nature of the country, trains from the North and South alike emerge suddenly from cuttings and can neither be seen nor heard till they are actually on the girder bridge. Thus, when one is surprised by a train while driving in the covered bridge the situation is trying to the nerves of even the steadiest horse, who is close to and a little below a deafening clamour, and is unable to see where it comes from.

A daily annoyance and anxiety could be removed from the lives of many people who are compelled to use the covered bridge daily if you could see your way to instructing your engineers to whistle as they approach this west river bridge. This would give warning to drivers to wait outside the covered bridge till the train had passed. I feel sure that unless there is some serious working objection my notion will commend itself to you.[2] I enclose a rough sketch of the bridge and its surroundings

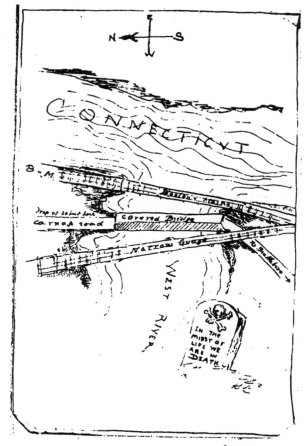

and am
Very sincerely
Rudyard Kipling.

Lucius Tuttle Esq/President/B M R R Co.

Notes
1. Tuttle (1846–1914) was President of the Boston and Maine Railroad, 1893–1911.
2. The arrangement was made: RK wrote to Tuttle on 14 May to "express my deep appreciation of your kindness" (photocopy, Brooks Memorial Library, Brattleboro).

To Edward Bok, 11 May 1895
ALS: Library of Congress

Naulakha. / Brattleboro. / Vermont. / May. 11. '95

My dear Mr Bok:
  I am in receipt of yours of the 10th instant with proofs of *"William the*

Conqueror" and very much regret that you did not open the question of a sub-title and the mention of intoxicating beverages before accepting the tale.[1] If you refer to my letter, you will see that I offered you the tale as it stood and on these terms did you accept it.

Had you hinted at the existence of office rules I should never have sent you a M.S. for inspection because, my one theory in regard to my work is that writing to order means loss of power, loss of belief in the actuality of the tale and ultimately loss of self-respect to the writer. If a man once deviates from this rule (I speak for myself alone) he mis-says himself at every turn and at the last ceases to be the author of what comes from his pen – I am sorry that the tale does not meet all the requirements of the LHJ. but you will see I trust that, *having offered you a full inspection*, the fault is none of mine.

Very sincerely yours
Rudyard Kipling.

Note
1. The *Ladies' Home Journal* had a rule against all scenes in which alcohol was drunk, and Bok had asked RK to "moderate some of these scenes" in "William the Conqueror". Bok says that he did not insist, and presumably RK made no changes (Bok, *The Americanization of Edward Bok* [New York, 1920] p. 220).

To William Hallett Phillips,[1] [c. 16 May 1895]
AL, Incomplete: Dalhousie University

Naulakha. / Brattleboro. / Vermont.

A.C.

To the luminous and law-expounding *Vakil*,[2] in the Sudder Dewany Adawlut in the City of the Feringhis who resemble the Feringhis and yet are not the Feringhis.

After Compliments.

My Brother:
The matter is comprehended through a wink no less than by a nod: and therefore I have written a short word of truth to the *Burra Lat Sahib Bahadur* – in the nature of an *urzee* – explaining the need of the *dâk*.[3] Allah knows what *bandabust* the Lord Sahib will make in the matter or what *hookum* he will be pleased to give but I shall not soon forget that thy hand showed me the short and expeditious way along the path of Enterprize. The event is behind the curtain of time which no man may lift. I have written to the *Lat Sahib* as one servant of Allah to his fellow.

1. Sir Walter Besant.

2. William Ernest Henley.

3. Kipling and his mother, *c.* 1890.

4. Caroline Kipling and her children, John, Elsie, and Josephine, 1898.

5. Charles Eliot Norton, Professor of the History of Art, Harvard University.

6. Dr James Conland: "the best friend I made in New England".

EMBANKMENT CHAMBERS,

VILLIERS STREET, STRAND.

Monday

Once upon a time there was a Coffee-pot and Allah-al-Bari' who is the greatest of all conjurors caused it to pour out sometimes coffee black as the Pit; sometimes milk white as the feet of little children and sometimes wine red as the blood of a strong man. And because Coffee-pots do not often pour after the usages of the trinity Those who should have Known Better surrounded that coffee pot as it went ahead on its occasions through the bazars thus:

And when it had poured wine they said "Pour milk" and when it had poured milk they said "pour coffee" and when it had done all these things they said "wah! wah! was there ever such a coffee pot."

7. Kipling's letter to William Canton (*c.* late June? 1890).

Dear Sir Walter —

— I saw the recent — & Co Day — Salisbury matter — and & Co will sent him a small cable of congratulations which I follow now with a letter. You are probably swearing at the mass of correspondence but it is nothing worse now. As it's only my tray and please I am, and also don't want to see that it was not a formality. This is my notion.

—— a lot bluff about it

—— gules. three bezants.

—— argent — a false prop. sable.

Now that if the Heralds Office do and I will not charge one scrap they will charge you for their charges.

. AUCTOR .

Frankly I could not be more delighted here if any one flatter. But the case of a person called Morris I am not so pleased. Indeed here is my notion for him —

—— argent a lock their liberty, beauty, and impartiality.

. HOTHELL! .

But they have a saying in the Trade that you can't begin to buy an honest man the first instalment of his deserts without having to subsidize mine forte, or was after at him.

Yours always sincerely
Rudyard Kipling.

At the most he can but make a refusal. Of a truth we most greatly need that *dâk* and I have so worded my letter to the Lat Sahib that that truth shines behind the letters after the manner of a firefly in a pomegranate tree.

But now O my Brother, *Vakil* among *Vakils* in whose head the entire course of all the Laws runs as a river through a pleasant land, the year passes. Jeth, the month of sowing is gone and we come near to the heat of Summer and ere long the *rabi* crops will be garnered and the dust will afflict the ways of man. In thy city men say it will soon be as Gehenna, and the tents of Eblis the Accursed. Remember, therefore, our doors stand open day and night for the coming of thy horses, the bubbling of thy camels down the pass and the creaking of the bullock wains. I have set aside certain drinks of Belait, water that smokes in the glass being poured, and arrack of the North together with *barf*, good ice white and clean.

Come and we will sit still, enjoying *Kif* together, – considering the ways of man and the land which Allah has made. When there is a need to speak we will speak together. When there is need to be silent we will cease speaking and lie upon our bellies upon the warm rocks. I have made me a place of peace – I and my house. Come thou when the hired talking in the Dewanny is done and we will remember that we be free men. My house sends greeting to thy house. Mayst thou never be tired. Remember what Hafiz has written: – They have made a God of little coins white and yellow and yoke themselves to great labours for their sakes. But there is a resting time provided and when friend meets friend we do not any longer vex our souls under the trees.[4]

Notes
1. Phillips (1853–97), Washington lawyer, specialist in American Indian lore, outdoorsman: RK's name for him was "Sitting Fox" (see [19 June 1895]). Phillips was a part of the circle made by Henry Adams, John Hay, and Henry Cabot Lodge – the "little Washington gang" to which RK was attracted (Henry Adams, *Letters, 1892–1918* [1938] p. 91). RK dedicated "The Feet of the Young Men" to the memory of Phillips, who drowned in a sailing accident.
2. The Indian (and other) terms in this letter may be roughly translated thus: *vakil*, attorney; *Sudder Dewany Adawlut*, chief court of appeal; *Feringhis*, Europeans; *Burra Lat Sahib Bahadur*, great governor-general; *urzee*, petition; *dâk*, postal arrangements; *bandabust*, arrangement, scheme; *hookum*, order; *Belait*, Europe; *rabi*, winter-sown crops; *barf*, ice; *kif*, the enjoyment of idleness.
3. RK was trying to get a post office established at the Waite farm, at the crossroads where the Brattleboro road and the road to Naulakha meet, and so free himself of the necessity of going into Brattleboro for his mail. He had written to President Cleveland (the *Burra Lat Sahib Bahadur*) on this day, asking the President, whom RK had met in April (CK diary, 5 April 1895), to authorise a post office at Waite (ALS, Dalhousie University). With the advice and influence of Phillips RK succeeded in his object. His petition for the post office was sent in to the Post Office Department on 3 June and was granted on the 13th (CK diary). "I have obtained for Kipling his *Dâk*", Phillips wrote to John Hay on 12 June 1985 (ALS, Brown University).
4. Possibly RK alludes to ghazal no. 376 of Hafiz, but if so, only very loosely.

To Ripley Hitchcock, 18 May 1895
ALS: Berg Collection, New York Public Library

Naulakha. / Brattleboro. / Vermont. / May: 18 '95

Dear Hitchcock

The ant was virtuous and he had his good time: but the grasshopper played about and he couldn't come. I've spent a whole solid month digging and delving in the dirt. The result is a brown hide and what promises to be, in time, a fairly decent garden: but there's no more holiday for me this month of Sundays. Last year's drouth has played the mischief with our waters, and there isn't one dirty little trout that doesn't shamelessly violate the six-inch law, within whipping distance of us. I've been out but I've given up in disgust and returned to my verses.

We weren't in New York[1] for longer than a man needs to shave but I much wanted to see you to tell me [*sic*] about my experiences with beaver in Washington. How I met Bill Hofer the trapper who trapped 'em; how I was introduced to the whole seven of 'em that made the dam in the Zoo (such a Zoo!); how I got photographs of the said dam in three lights and finally how I went into the fencing question with the head of the Zoo.

It's beyond my means because *unless* you sink sheet iron or concrete five feet below ground the beaver will burrow out. Everything else would be as easy as falling off a log but I can't fence ten acres in that way. I'm loaded up with facts about beaver.

A pleasant time to you in your excursions – good fish and fair fighting. I wish I could come but I must attend to some poems[2] that I am supposed to be getting ready for a firm of New York publishers called Appleton: Poems are four times harder to get ready than mere yarns.

With best regards from us all here

Yours ever sincerely
Rudyard Kipling

Notes
1. They were in New York on 6 and 7 April, on their return from Washington.
2. *The Seven Seas.*

To Sir Walter Besant, 27 May 1895

ALS: Dalhousie University

Naulakha. / Brattleboro. / Vermont. / May: 27 '95

Dear Sir Walter –

I saw the news yesterday[1] – Saturday rather – and forthwith sent you a small cable of congratulations which I follow now with a letter. You are possibly swearing at the mass of correspondence that is rolling round you: so I'll only try to say how pleased I am: and also how wrath to see that it was not a baronetcy. This is my notion.

[See Plate 8 ——a butterfly volant, *or*
in this volume] ——gules, three bezants or.
——argent – a palace flagged, sable.

Send that to the Heralds College and I will not charge 'em what they will charge you for these charges. Frankly I could not be more delighted were it my own father.

With the case of a person called Morris[2] I am not so pleased. Indeed here is my notion for *him*.

[See Plate 8 ——a Lewis[3] frappé
in this volume] ——argent: a back stairs
    bendy, wavy, and improper

But they have a saying in this land that you can't begin to pay an honest man the first instalment of his deserts without having to subsidize nine fools, or worse, to get at him.

Yours always sincerely
Rudyard Kipling.

Notes
1. Of Besant's knighthood, not officially conferred until 18 July 1895.
2. Lewis Morris (see 26 October 1892) was knighted at the same time as Besant.
3. An iron, dove-tailed tenon used for lifting large stones. RK's drawing shows a lewis mortised into a broken stone – a stone frappé rather than a lewis frappé.

To "The Lounger",[1] 31 May 1895
Text: *The Critic*, 15 June 1895, pp. 445–6

Dear Lounger:

It is not possible that some of your remarks, in *The Critic* of the 25th May, about literary agents would have been better for a little qualification? They give the impression that the agent sits at his ease drawing commissions from authors' sales year in and year out, for making bargains which the publisher would have made just as fairly had he dealt with the author direct.

We will leave the morality of publishers entirely out of the question. Literary agency is not by any means confined to drawing up contracts between authors of unsurpassed genius and publishers of embarrassing generosity. There is also the little matter, which most men in any profession hate, of collecting monies when they fall due. Looking at the literary agent merely as a collector, is he paid so very much more than other collectors, or are his difficulties less?

Again, with new magazines and syndicates rising almost weekly, it is his business to know which ventures are sound and which are likely to fail; because, though he "has no losses," as the writer you quote from says, he must look to it that his client suffers none. To this end he must, among many other things, control with accuracy the entire detail of simultaneous publication in three or four continents, as well as arrange for translations and Continental and Colonial issues. He must know when and where an unauthorized publication is secretly run into the market, and must stand ready to block its way at once. He must follow the exact rating of journals in England, America, Australasia and the East, their strength and their weakness financially and editorially, as well as he must "know his cables" and the difference in time between half a dozen of the leading cities of the world with which he may be in almost hourly communication. Incidentally, he must meet as they arise all possible complications of the musical and dramatic copyright law, and walk abreast of the thousand wheels within wheels of literary London where they touch his clients and the foreign markets.

His capital is experience and special knowledge of a highly specialized trade, gained by years of contact with a particular type of men and things; and it is this special training, this knowledge and this experience that save him from killing (as an amateur would assuredly try to do) your "goose that lays the golden eggs."

The reason of his being is not to grind the face of the publisher, but to meet him as one trained man of business meets another. At all times he saves the author the mass of profitless, temper-wearing detail that attaches itself to any extended market-work. Your statement that he declines to deal with the young author because "there is not money enough to be made out of the novice" is again very wide of the mark. To go back only a year or two, I know of several "novices" whose work has been introduced to the publisher by the literary agent. These men went to him without a shadow of prestige and he placed their work with success.

Finally, does it seem to you possible that nearly fifty well-known English writers of to-day would pay a man ten per cent, of their takings for doing nothing in their behalf? With apologies for trespassing on your time,

> Sincerely,
> Rudyard Kipling.

Brattleboro, Vt, May 31st, 1895.

Note
1. A column of this name ran regularly in *The Critic*. In the issue for 15 June it remarked on the hostile discussion of literary agency, then a new thing, in England and went on to doubt that the agent's contribution to an author was worth much.

To Mary Mapes Dodge, 18 June 1895
ALS: Princeton University

> *Naulakha. / Brattleboro. / Vermont. /* June. 18. '95.

Dear Mrs Dodge,

I have this week finished the last of the New Jungle book with the words "and this is the last of the Mowgli tales because there are no more to be told."[1] Now we must try new things. I do not go to India this year but abide so far as I know in Vermont through the winter and if I can think of a sufficiently good St Nick tale you shall have it either in time for September or the New Year as Providence sends it along.

With all regards to St Nick his staff

> Yours always sincerely
> Rudyard Kipling

Note
1. At the end of "The Spring Running".

To William Hallett Phillips, [19 June 1895][1]
ALS: Dalhousie University.

> *Naulakha.* – Wait's / via.[2] *Brattleboro. / Vermont.*

After this the name of Sitting Fox shall be entered among the Trues.[3] His Lodge shall be in the centre of the camp, painted and crowned with

feathers. I myself will make dances before it calling upon the name of
Sitting Fox burning tobacco and performing the ceremonies. My people
in my Lodge shall talk the name of Sitting Fox with honour, saying: –

> "Our Father came with a word to Sitting
> "Fox – a little word of no weight.
> "He said to Sitting Fox: – There is nothing I
> "need except to move a mountain and
> "make a road where none was before. This
> "is a little matter.
> "Sitting Fox said: – 'It is a little matter. I
> "Will make the medicine.'
> "*Ah! Yah! Yah ha! Haaah!* Sing to the honour
> "Of Sitting Fox.
> "He made a medicine and it turned the
> "hearts of the servants of the Great Father.
> "They hastened and they ran falling over
> "one another in their haste to obey the
> "orders of Sitting Fox.
> "Through the city of the Broad Blue Streets they
> "ran up and down.
> "Sitting Fox sat upon his tail making medicine.
> "In twelve days the mountain was moved and
> "The road ran where no road ran before.
> "Sitting Fox, carried them to our father, the
> "Mountain and the Road, saying: – 'This is a
> "little matter which has come about through
> "my medicine. Take it and see if it is good.'
> "Our Father beat his head upon the dirt
> "Crying 'Wah! Wah! He moves mountains.'
> "*Ahh! Yah! Ahai! Yah!* Sing to the Big Medicine of Sitting Fox."
> This is the song my people shall sing.

———————————————

I don't pretend to know how in the world, or in Washington, you
did it. Only I am quite sure that without your aid I might have asked
for Post Offices till Judgement day.

I have written sweetly, even as I feel, to Maxwell.[4] It's the first time
in my life that I ever felt dripping with the milk of human kindness to
all the members of a Government Department (as a journalist in India
of course I fought 'em on principle) and I like the experience.

You are a great man and I'll not forget it. As to my writings herewith
a song in an English magazine which may interest for awhile.[5] Keep it.

I wish we could get Adams[6] up here but we're chock-a-block till the

4th with folks coming and going or what is worse saying they'll come and light-heartedly postponing it. I find that I may have to go over the other side in July for a few weeks – four at the outside: but I'll be back ere mid-August.

We've a really serious job for you – *much* more important than P.O.'s. There's a long walk that leads to our woods on which baby plays and she wants a wigwam, wickyup, whairé[7] or whatever its name is and her father can't put two boughs together without their falling down. When you come – and you *must* now – we'll make one of proper design. By the way do you know that out of Langley's[8] books I have extracted an Esquimaux tale for the new Jungle book – it's called Quiquern[9] and is the history of a couple of sleigh-dogs. I told you that they'd be a mine of suggestion to me. That again is another debt I owe you.

Your letter of the 6th was held for insufficient postage. Hence the delay in answering it. It came with yours of the 12th: what do you mean about my petition? S'pose I forged 'em? You should have heard the farmers talk it over – you should have seen me getting solid with 'em on the lee side of barns. I find I have in me unsuspecting powers of softening the Vermonter and not suffering him to be ferocious. There be times when I think of running for the State Governorship and when you come up we will unfold to you the complete circle of our operations wherein the post-office is but the first step. *Now* I can tell chaps who want to build about here that there is good postal service. Anon we shall get a railway station for the Boston & Maine under whose heel we live are only waiting for the P.O. to give us a station. After which comes the telegraph freight and express agency. It is a beautiful little scheme; and the moral effect of our first victory (which is a victory for the whole of the township north of the West River – don't laugh at our local politics) will make things easier hereafter.

I believe the wife is writing you her thanks. I know Baby would if she could write, and I am

Yours always gratefully,
Rudyard Kipling

Notes
1. Dated from postmark.
2. This letter celebrates the success of RK's petition for a post office. RK has added the words "Wait's via" [Brattleboro] to the embossed letterhead. For the name "Waite" see 27 September 1895.
3. North American Indian gods; see [16 August 1897].
4. Robert A. Maxwell, Fourth Assistant Postmaster-General.
5. Probably "The Song of the Banjo", *New Review*, June 1895 (*The Seven Seas*).
6. Henry Adams.
7. Word illegible. Possibly "wharé", Maori for "house".
8. Samuel Pierpont Langley (1834–1906), Secretary of the Smithsonian Institution, astronomer, and pioneer of heavier-than-air flight. On 12 April 1895 RK wrote to thank

Langley for the gift of a number of Smithsonian publications, including the one mentioned in n. 9, below (ALS, Michigan Historical Collections).
9. *Pall Mall Gazette*, 24 and 25 October 1895. The source for this is H. W. Elliot, *The Seal-Islands of Alaska* (Washington, DC, 1881).

To John Hay,[1] 29 June 1895
ALS: Brown University

Naulakha. / Brattleboro. / Vermont. / June. 29. '95

Dear Mr Hay:

Your delightful note has just come in with the Poems[2] – most of which I "have the honour to point out" I know by heart. But here is a queer thing. I have been circulating up and down since I could read with the lively faith that "in day's of old when the Devil was loose" was Longfellow[3] – indeed have learned it in that belief and it clung as a mistaken notion will. I am now trying to find out how I made the error.

But when all is said and done – if this is not impertinent – "Israel" is good enough for me and that I read [it] as my memory serves me in India in the *Century* in 1887 or thereabouts.[4] As regards the invitation to come up to the Fells[5] I could swear at length. We are going to take the child down to East Gloucester on Monday, settle her there and depart for a few weeks to England on the worst cabin of the *Saale* on the 6th.[6]

A plain black damn is of no use because my work has held me back till over the 3rd. The date on which Mr Adams,[7] sailing in state, offered me the Lord knows how much of a deck-suite on the *New York*: and first I accepted with a shout and then I had to tell him I couldn't and atop of every thing comes your invitation when we shall be stewing opposite the boilers of the dirty little *Saale*.

We are both enraged over the matter. Almost beyond the point of declining decently. I want to say: – "Wah!" in the [   ][8] of the Bowery; but won't you be able to stop with us on your way down in the fall? We should be back in the end of August all being well. This seems a happy compromise. Please consider it. You see you must go south to get to Washington and Brattleboro is on the line of travel. But at present "as for me and my house we will serve the (N[orth].G[erman].) Lloyd."

With best regards from us both to Mrs Hay and yourself

Believe me yours ever sincerely
Rudyard Kipling.

There is a man called Phillips in Washington who when he dies will go straight to Heaven. I don't want him to die but I merely wish to put my opinion on record.

Notes

1. RK had met Hay (see 16 February 1892) this spring in Washington at the home of Hay's neighbour, Henry Adams.
2. *Poems by John Hay* (1890).
3. The line opens the second stanza of Hay's "The Monks of Basle".
4. Hay's "Israel" appeared in the *Century Magazine*, xxxiv (May 1887) 127–8.
5. The country home that Hay built in 1891 on Lake Sunapee, New Hampshire.
6. Josephine was left with Mrs Balestier at the Fairview Inn, East Gloucester; her parents sailed from Hoboken on the *Saale*, a German ship, on 6 July, arriving in Southampton on the 14th; they were in London until the 25th, when they went to Tisbury until 9 August. They then returned to London and sailed for the United States on the 14th; they were back in Brattleboro on the 22nd (CK diary).
7. Henry Adams.
8. One word illegible.

To Charles Eliot Norton, 5 August 1895

ALS: Harvard University

Tisbury / Wilts. / Aug. 5 '95

Dear Mr. Norton:

We only came away for a few weeks, secretly, in a great hurry, on a North German boat and we'll be coming back on Wednesday week, Aug 14. It wasn't worth mentioning or saying good bye for.

Aunt Georgie has gone abroad, Phil is somewhere in a Belgian bathing machine, Uncle Ned is at Rottingdean and Margaret is either back or just coming back from the Continent – and I haven't seen one of 'em.

We're just biding quietly here with the Father and mother in a house which backs into a wheatfield and the wheat is full of ticks and you *have* to scratch. But it's a lovely country on English lines – fat and fleecy and green. The Pater is doing pictures for the second jungle book[1] and I stand behind him and ask for more. We'll be back only a few days behind this letter and then maybe we'll see you and Miss Sally on your [way] back to Shady Hill. Carrie sends her love in which I join to you all. The little trip seems to have made her better and stronger.

Always your affectionately
Rudyard Kipling.

Note

1. *The Second Jungle Book* is extensively illustrated with line and wash drawings and decorative initials by JLK.

To William Colles,[1] [early August 1895][2]
ALS: Berg Collection, New York Public Library

Arundel House / Tisbury, Wilts

Dear Mr Colles,

Very many thanks for your interesting letter. It seems to me that America is too big a country to work under *one* copyright law – i.e. I can imagine circumstances under which it would pay a publisher, west of the Rockies let us say, to snap his fingers at the law and reprint cheap 25/c editions of a stolen book for his public. I am not sure that this has ever been actually done since the passing of the Act but I know cases where it has been threatened. This uncertainty perhaps to a small extent excuses the American publisher in cutting down his rates to the author.

But the real root of the trouble is that the average English Literary Agent does not *know* the American market. He says he does: he says he can manage business with America by letter; but the ins and outs of publishers' business in New York, Phila. or Chicago are altogether beyond him. What is needed is a first class English agency established in New York for the benefit first of the members of the Authors society[3] and secondly of the American author who also sells in England. I know no man whom I could recommend for the post but there must be such a man somewhere on the top of the earth. He ought to attend to the business of copyrighting books at Washington; he ought to know the relative position of all the American magazines from the Atlantic to the Pacific; he ought to be friendly but not too friendly with the literary syndicates that supply matter to the papers and he ought to know what publishers are "shysters" and what publishers are sound *and* he ought to speak with the whole weight of the Society of Authors behind him.

To that end, so it seems to me, the S.A. should invite a certain number of leading American authors to be members. Here are some names: – James Whitcomb Riley, c/o *Century* (He sells more than almost any other), Cable;[4] Stockton;[5] Page: all c/o *Century*: "Charles Egbert Craddock"[6] c/o *Atlantic Monthly*: Mary Wilkins (I'll speak to her if you give me leave) (Howells' principles I fancy might forbid his entrance). Twain does not care for the business so far as I could learn. Mrs. Burnett[7] of course; Sarah Orne Jewett; and so on and so forth. They ought to form a branch of the S.A. with a somewhat higher subscription than we charge this side.

As Conan Doyle is going over this fall, he ought to be the man to do the talking. He's great on binding America and England more closely together and this would be a practical step. If I were mixed up in the matter I should do no good because they don't exactly love me; and we'd have the papers crabbing the scheme at the outset. The question of the agent is the most difficult one, because, at first, he couldn't devote his time to the hob on the off chance of 10% commissions. Is the society rich enough to pay $2000 a year say (£400) for a year. It might be raised by a special call on the members. I'd cheerfully send a fiver for the experiment and at least thirty nine others I fancy would do the same.

There's not the least use in sitting here and expecting American trade to walk up three flights of stairs and ring at our doorbell. We must go over there and look round for it with a spade. Now, in regard to what you say about third-raters suffering. I hate to say "I told you so" but there's a ribald bit of verse in the *Author* written when the act was passed that prophesied as much.[8] When Wolcott Balestier was alive he said that the act cleared all but a dozen English authors out of the U.S. market. And the reason is this – Miss or Mrs Amelia Jigamerula (3rd class female novelist) at 1/- (pirated) is read at any idle minute – in the train; in the horse cars and elsewhere; without comment without criticism. She has the same sort of sale as chewing-gum. *But*, at 6/- (protected) is a very different matter. She is mentally compared with other six-bobbers – Bret Harte let us say and – she is eliminated. She isn't worth the extra five bob. The buyer thinks: – "well I know her scope pretty well. Let's try a new fellow or some one that really gives me fits." And so with all the others. It isn't fair to expect a six bob sale to go on as merrily as a shilling one and I fancy as the years pass, the thinning out of British authors will be more and more marked. You can't blame 'em. There will be big booms again and again – when an uncopyrighted book makes a hit in England and sells by tens of thousands in the States in paper back and again and again the British author will lift up his voice and wonder why this doesn't not [*sic*] continue for ever. It's the price that does it.

I should like to see the time when membership of the S.A. meant that a member's books were automatically copyrighted at Washington but I don't suppose the society will ever be strong or rich enough for that.

Your trouble about mutilated piracies – stolen ends and faked beginnings – can only be settled *by an agent on the spot*. Since I lived in the States I'm treated with much more consideration in that way, because they know I'm handy for a fight.

I've been some time answering this letter because I've tried to think over things a good deal. There's nothing new in it but I think there's a little truth. Please show it to Besant and see what he thinks.

Yours ever sincerely
Rudyard Kipling

Notes
1. Colles (1855–1926), a barrister and journalist, was a member of the council of the Society of Authors and in charge of the Authors' Syndicate; he later operated a literary

agency of his own.
2. This letter must have been written between 25 July and 9 August, when RK was in Tisbury.
3. The Society of Authors, founded by Walter Besant in 1884. RK joined the Society in 1890 and was elected a member of council in 1892.
4. George Washington Cable (1844–1925), author of stories and romances about the Creoles of Louisiana.
5. Frank R. Stockton (1834–1902), humorist and novelist.
6. Pseudonym of Mary Noailles Murfree (1850–1922), Southern local colourist.
7. Frances Hodgson Burnett (1849–1924), best known as the author of *Little Lord Fauntleroy*.
8. RK means his "Some Notes on a Bill", *The Author*, 1 July 1891 (uncollected).

To Richard Watson Gilder, 25 September 1895

ALS: Dalhousie University

Naulakha. / Waite / Windham Co. / *Vermont.*[1] / Sep. 25: 95

Dear Gilder:

I am glad to find The Brushwood Boy[2] interests you and I'm free to confess myself that I was not a little pleased with it when it was done.

As a matter of fact I've drawn the map of the dream-country several times but will make a clean copy for repro. in facsimile, as soon as I can. As to head and tail pieces why certainly *if* you can find any that will fit in any way from the Second Jungle Book: but why not a simple initial and tail piece from the office?

In regard to the boil[3] seeing as how the Century is a magazine and not a book; and somebody else's property and not mine, I will do what you suggest: to the extent of making the said boil, blain, pustule or tumour a cut hand or something similar. It grieves me much that you call my yarn a romance for what I prided myself on most was my grey and unflinching realism. Thus is a man misunderstood. Please send proof as soon as possible because I am sure to need a revise and certain to cut it down a little on re-reading.

Always sincerely yours
Rudyard Kipling.

P.S.   No – that price is by no means a record-breaker.[4] I haven't charged a cent for the following items: as under:

To writing one complete tale for Century last year: 10,000 words @ $100.	$1000
To finding said tale would not do.	.50
To putting said tale in w.p.b.	.25

To temper lost over discovery that said tale would not do.	1.39.
To meditating profoundly for seven months over another tale.	2.27.
To not writing second tale:	3.18.
To writing out The Brushwood Boy 5 times:	7.50.
To grief at being deprived of the boil incident in Brushwood Boy	*2350.*
	$3365.9

Total not charged for. $3365.9

Notes
1. RK's address now that the new post office was in operation, housed in the Waite family farm house and staffed by Mrs Anna F. Waite. It was closed less than a year following RK's departure from Vermont. To adapt his old letterhead to the new address RK has lined out *Brattleboro* and written "Waite / Windham Co."
2. *Century Magazine*, December 1895 (*The Day's Work*). The idea came to him on 23 August and he finished it on 8 September (CK diary).
3. In the published texts the Brushwood Boy has no boil but a cut on his thumb.
4. CK's diary reports on 6 December 1895 that RK got $170 from the *Century* for "The Brushwood Boy": presumably $170 per 1000 words is meant.

To William Hallett Phillips, 29 September 1895

Text: Extract, Alwin J. Scheurer Catalogue no. 6 (1931) item 2547: 2pp. 8vo.; dated Waite, Vermont, September 29, 1895

Great Sitting Fox! I think Tati's letter[1] is one of the most pathetic things I've read in a long time. Why in Hell does the white man, who is a pig – wander round the world bedevilling gentlemen of Tati's stamp with civilization? It makes one want to be a pirate and kill judges and lawyers and specially missionaries. . . . Do we NOT wish to know Smith of the Central Vermont?[2] What a world-encompassing mind is yours, O my Sitting Fox! Let us only get at him! He shall have his literary tastes fed full if he will but bring his influence to bear on Lucius Tuttle of the Boston & Maine who regrets at present he can't build us a station. Tell Smith he is a big chief with three tails and will infallibly be a second Shakespeare. . . . I had a grand time at the Hays.[3] They are all charming from one end to the other and Lord how curiously young is Miss Helen Hay.[4] Clarence[5] was my guide, philosopher and friend and Hay who is a golden talker told me tales with a finish that's rare in these degenerate days. And what a glorious wilderness he owns. If I had it with some dollars, me and you and Billy Hofer[6] would fill it up with beaver and bear and buffalo till never an excursionist should set foot on the further shore of Sunapee. I've been busy as usual – done, though I shouldn't own it, a really ripping good tale[7] which I took up and read to the Hays. . . . Westomannus on engendering of elephants is good but you ought to hear an old MAHOUT expatiate on the subject. . . .

Notes
1. Tati Salmon, of the Teva clan in Tahiti, whose story had been told by Henry Adams in his privately printed *Memoirs of Marua Taaroa, Last Queen of Tahiti* (1893).
2. Edward Curtis Smith (1854–1935), President of the Central Vermont Railway, 1891–1928; Governor of Vermont, 1898–1900.
3. RK spent 16–18 September with Hay at his summer home in Newbury, New Hampshire, on Lake Sunapee. Hay wrote of RK at the time, "how a man can keep up so intense an intellectual life without going to Bedlam is amazing. He rattled off the frame-work of about forty stories while he was with us" (W. R. Thayer, *The Life and Letters of John Hay* [1915] II, 126).
4. Hay's daughter Helen (1876–1944), afterwards Mrs Payne Whitney.
5. Clarence Hay (1884–1969), Hay's younger son.
6. See 18 May 1895. Hofer is mentioned in Henry Adams's account of a camping trip to Yellowstone made in company with Phillips in 1894 (*Education of Henry Adams* [1918] p. 350).
7. Probably "The Brushwood Boy".

To Louisa Baldwin, 29 September 1895

ALS: Dalhousie University

Naulakha. / Waite / Windham Co. / *Vermont.* / Sep. 29: '95

Dear Aunt Louie,

To be truly frank I don't think it is good for discipline or in line with the Catechism that aunts should dedicate books to nephews,[1] but setting that aside I am proud and happy. I know you used to tell most creepysome bogey tales and – well I shall see from the book which ones of my knowledge, you have included. Big sales and good reviews to you.

Life goes as quietly with us here as it does with Stan I hope. We dig and delve in the garden and blast out rocks to build ice-houses on, and try to put up a small greenhouse that shall endure the cold of the winter and small Josephine trots at our heels and gives orders. She is just now stuffing Bubble and Squeak the two pigs with acorns before she goes to the stable and gets her morning ride on the horses. I can hear her from time to time shouting: – "Tum along, Gwan muvver!" and I think it is true that Grandmothers are even more abject than immediate parents? How is it with you?

Business is lively with me – for the Christmas market. That is to say all the tales I've written this year are coming out apparently in Xmas mags. The *Graphic, Illustrated, Idler, Century*[2] and another magazine have each one a piece and in a few weeks the second Jungle book comes out. I want to spend the winter decently revising my verses. Do you remember the old copy book "To Ruddy from Godmother Louie 1881"? – I have it still.

We've had a host of "company" staying with us – among us [*sic*] Mrs Browning[3] – wife of the bad son of a good father – and you and she have met I think in Florence? Then we've had a young married couple and Sallie Norton and her beloved father and more folk are coming. One of the real joys of having a house and things is to take in people and I live in hopes some day when Hugo is bigger of catching my Aunt Aggie for three months which would do her more good than any three months she ever lived. Can't you help her to see this?

Now that the hand of the Lord has smitten the sons of Achan, I begin to be concerned for the conservative party.[4] The majority is too big, it looks from this distance; and every man is like to be lazy. *But*, I wish Uncle Alfred could realize the difference in tone and bearing that the big victory produced overseas. It was just the same as tho' he in the works had sacked some incompetent foreman: and the men with one accord and without saying anything, all took a little pull on themselves.

The Father and Mother write cheerily from their cabin in a garden and I'm glad to know that the Mother is taking more interest in the garden work.

Give my best love to Stan and his wife and bless the baby (she'll grow out of all knowledge in twenty minutes) and with love from us both to you and Uncle Alfred

Always your affectionate nephew
Ruddy.

Notes
1. Her *Shadow on the Blind, and Other Ghost Stories* (1895), dedicated "To My Friend and Kinsman Rudyard Kipling".
2. "The Devil and the Deep Sea", *Graphic*, Christmas number, 1895; "The Ship that Found Herself", *Idler*, December 1895; "The Brushwood Boy", *Century*, December 1895 (all in *The Day's Work*). Nothing of RK's appeared in the *Illustrated London News* after 1893.
3. Fannie Coddington, American wife of Robert Browning's son, Pen; they had separated in 1893.
4. Lord Rosebery's administration had been defeated in June and succeeded by Lord Salisbury's third administration.

To James Burton Pond,[1] 30 September 1895
Text: James Burton Pond, *Eccentricities of Genius* (New York, 1900) p. 526

Brattleboro, Vt., Sept. 30, 1895.

Dear Mr. Pond:
   I am much obliged to you for your letter, but I can't say that I see my way to the ententement you propose. There is such a thing as paying one hundred and twenty-five cents for a dollar, and though I suppose there is money in the lecturing business, it seems to me that the bother, the fuss, the being at everybody's beck and call, the night journeys, and so on, make it very dear. I've seen a few men who've lived through the fight, but they did not look happy. I might do it as soon as I had two mortgages on my house, a lien on the horses, and a bill of sale on the furniture, and writer's cramp in both hands; but at present I'm busy and contented to go on with the regular writing business. You forget that I have already wandered over most of the States, and there isn't enough money in sight to hire me to face again some of the hotels and some of the railway systems that I have met with. America is a great country, but she is not made for lecturing in. With renewed thanks for your very kind letter, believe me,

Yours sincerely,
Rudyard Kipling.

Note
1. Pond (1838–1903) was the leading lecture-manager of the day.

To Charles Warren Stoddard, 8 October 1895
ALS: Library of Congress

Naulakha. / Waite / Windham Co. / *Vermont.* / 8.10.95.

Dear Stoddard,
   Do not waste time in aniline hieroglyphics but send along the first chapter and we'll get to business.[1]
   There is nothing wrong with "Paul Westerly" but on the other hand there is nothing specially catching about it. Here are a few names that may come in handy some time while you are naming characters.

Wharton:	Eames:	Minicoy:	Blore
Hugonin	Mallaby	Los.	St John

Stratton	Mardall	Merriman	Napier
Willes	Longden	Laughton	Milne
Dunsterville.	Pyecroft.	Hinchcliffe.	Bray

All these are fairly good. They are all at your service.[2]

I do not like "So pleased to have met you" for the title of a whole novel. It's too long: but 't would do excellent well for a chapter heading: why not use it for that and stick (as far as the name of the novel goes) to "The Pleasure of your company."

Ever thine

Rudyard Kipling

Notes

1. RK was urging Stoddard to finish his novel, *For the Pleasure of His Company* (San Francisco, 1903); RK had already enlisted Watt to place the book, and he was now offering to Stoddard to read and criticise the MS. For RK's remarks and suggestions, see Stoddard, "Rudyard Kipling at Naulakha", *National Magazine*, xxII (June 1905) 263–7.
2. RK himself used the names of Eames, Blore, Hugonin, Merriman, Laughton, Pyecroft, and Hinchcliffe at various times; Willes and Dunsterville are, of course, from USC. Stoddard finally chose to name his hero "Paul Clitheroe".

To Edward Bok, 10 October 1895

ALS: Library of Congress

Naulakha. / Waite / Windham Co. / *Vermont.* / Oct. 10. 95.

Dear Mr. Bok,

The three proofs are indeed beautiful.[1] I've never seen anything better for a magazine in all my days – not even French work which is my highest notion of picture work. All this from the eye of art.

Regarded in the low light of natural fact (*don't* let the artist know this) they are, as one might say, a bit wide of things. William is a Baltimore girl and a very pretty one and the scene in Arizona where she watches the little Mexican babies curvetting round one of the men who surveyed the Southern Pacific is beautiful to behold. As a study of drapery the New England housewife, without corsets, welcoming the Chatauqua extension girl to board at $10 a week is very fine: but *the* most rampantly American study of all is William and the two men after dinner. The feet of Scott are American just as far as you can see 'em and so is the other chap's back and William might step from the block into "*Life*" without harm to any of the proprieties. Not one of your readers will notice this and I am frankly delighted that Taylor has come so near to things – but it made me chuckle to see how a man can't jump off his own shadow. My "American" stories when they come out will probably be just as English as the pictures are TransAtlantic.

Ever yours sincerely
Rudyard Kipling.

Note
1. The illustrations by William Ladd Taylor for "William the Conqueror". There were three of these in the *Ladies' Home Journal*; two are reproduced in the American trade edition of *The Day's Work* (1898).

To Sarah Orne Jewett, 16 October 1895
ALS: Colby College

Naulakha. / Waite / Windham Co. / *Vermont.* / Oct: 16. 1895

My dear Miss Jewett,
　The Life of Nancy[1] came yesterday and I read it then and there. I knew and had laughed over "Fame's Little Day": seen The War Debt in one of the magazines and read The Only Rose almost with tears but the others are new to me and altogether delightful – specially "All My Sad Captains": which is a perfect title. But who am I to send you compliments? I will for a change protest. *Did* you in the War Debt (serial form) put in those four lines italic at the end: because I don't remember having seen them and – I don't like them.[2] They explain things and I loathe an explanation. Please cut 'em out in the next edition and let people guess that he married Mrs Bellamy's grand daughter. I think the best of the lot in its manner (I wonder if you think this way) is "The Guests of Mrs Timms." To my thinking Miss Jewett can be when she thinks fit, masculine enough to equip three small average male story-tellers and in "The Guests of Mrs Timms" she gives proof of it. It's a kinder dry-point, firm handed work that pleases me all over. Then the Hiltons Holiday is another of the best in another manner. It's worthwhile spending three winters in New England to be able to draw the full flavour out of your stories: and when you come to think of it, I am about the only Englishman in the business who could turn in and review such a book from the more or less inside stand point. It makes me grin sometimes when I read of some man across the water laying down possibilities and impossibilities in American tales.
　We are preparing for the winter siege: digging and sodding and

hauling dirt and spreading phosphates and putting the garden to rights. I hope to get a copy of The Second Jungle book by the 10th of next month[3] when, if you will, I will send it you. With kindest regards from my wife and myself believe me

Yours always sincerely and admiringly
Rudyard Kipling.

Owen Wister[4] (whose Arizona and army-post tales you must know) has looked in on us for a day. He's a splendid young man and I think he has steam enough in him to carry him a long way. Have you ever met him. He's really and truly nice and a man.

Notes

1. *The Life of Nancy* (1895).
2. The book version adds these lines not in the magazine serial text (*Harper's,* January 1895): "*This was the way that, many years ago, a Northerner found his love, a poor but noble lady in the South, and Fortune smiled again upon the ruined house of Fairford.*"
3. American publication was on 9 November 1895.
4. Wister (1860–1938) is now best known for his classical story of cowboy life, *The Virginian* (1902); he had begun publishing stories of the West at the beginning of the 1890s but his first collection was not published until 1896. CK's diary for 8 October notes that "Owen Wister leaves".

To the Reverend John M. Gillespie,[1] 16 October 1895
ALS: Library of Congress

Naulakha. / Waite / Windham Co. / *Vermont.* / Oct: 16. 95

Dear Sir

I am in receipt of your very courteous favour of the 11th: inst:

To tell the honest truth, no letter that I could write would in any way assist your cause for my views on foreign missions are not such as would be accepted by any conference.

It is my fortune to have been born and to a large extent brought up among those whom white men call "heathen"; and while I recognize the paramount duty of every white man to follow the teachings of his creed and conscience as "a debtor to do the whole law,"[2] it seems to me cruel that white men, whose governments are armed with the most murderous weapons known to science, should amaze and confound their fellow creatures with a doctrine of salvation imperfectly understood by themselves and a code of ethics foreign to the climate and instincts of those races whose most cherished customs they outrage and whose gods they insult.

This is a matter that has been very near to my heart and I thank you for having afforded me an opportunity to testify.

Very sincerely yours
Rudyard Kipling.

Rev. Jno Gillespie

Notes
1. Gillespie was secretary of the Board of Foreign Missions of the Presbyterian Church in the US.
2. Galatians 5:3 "to do the whole law".

To Moberly Bell,[1] 26 October 1895
ALS: Library of Congress

Naulakha. / Waite / Windham Co. / *Vermont.* / Friday: Oct. 26.95

Dear Bell –

I am today a very proud man by reason of your letter[2] which however is open to objections as under: –

Beshrew your "hoofs" and "roofs." You try to sing that song which is written to be sung and you'll *have* to sing "hooves" and "rooves."[3]

But you saved me from an error in altering the ? which of course was a mistake of mine. I have not yet seen the *Times* with it in but I feel as excited as though it were my first proof.

You say the verses weren't written in relation to any definite event. This it is to be misunderstood! Doesn't C. E. Norton of Cambridge Mass send me the Weekly Mail and odd copies of the daily Times? Did I not see that colonial navy question coming up while yet it was afar off?[4] Didn't I bide my time with one eye on the cables and the song up my sleeve as your correspondents developed that question? And did I not throw in that set of verses at the precise time they were needed to counteract things which had been said in Australian papers and elsewhere. Do I not get Canada papers discussing the same thing? I may be a verse-writer by accident but I am a journalist by education. You will say the verses had nothing to do with colonial navies and such? They had – they have – heaps – and it is my great pride you published them.

What you say of the next "event" distresses me as a subject in every way – but it will be a glorious chance for someone. It's matter too high for me. I want to get things so that I can gently chaff the Australian about his views on federation which are queer. Some inspired idiot of a correspondent in your columns wrote some insanity about other nations at war with England keeping their hands off Australia for fear of "implanting hatred in the bosoms of a great and progressive nation" or some such skittles.[5] I wrote a set of rhymes about that which were teetotally unfit for publication. I think I shall now turn in and sing hymns about the Treasurer of Cape Colony, his notion of contributing war boats.[6]

Meantime you are the Manager of the Times and a busy man and I am

Yours always sincerely
Rudyard Kipling.

I hadn't time to turn round last time I came "home" – and I wasn't there three weeks.

Notes

1. Bell (1847–1911) had been manager of *The Times* since 1890. RK had known him from as early as 1892 (CK diary, 30–1 January 1892).
2. On RK's "The Native-Born". This was the first of RK's poems to be published in *The Times*, where it appeared on 14 October. Charles Eliot Norton had suggested to RK that he send the poem to *The Times*, and in writing Norton to thank him for the suggestion RK quotes from Bell's letter to him: "Let me thank you very heartily", Bell wrote, "on my own account and on behalf of the proprietors of the Times for the really beautiful poem you have allowed us to publish in the Times of this morning. It is I think the first time we have ever published a poem not written in relation to any one definite event and this caused us (as a good old conservative institution) to hesitate but as we read and re read your poem our scruples disappeared" (26 October 1895: ALS, Harvard).
3. In stanza five of "The Native-Born": all versions that I have seen print "roofs" and "hoofs".
4. The question of whether the colonies should help pay for the costs of the Royal Navy – as the supporters of colonial federation urged – was argued in the pages of *The Times* throughout September 1895. The Imperial Federation Defence Committee was the active propagandist in the matter: see, e.g. *The Times*, 6 September 1895, p. 3, and the correspondence following.
5. A Mr Armytage of Victoria wrote to doubt that possible enemies would attack Australia: "Are they going to plant seeds of hatred against themselves in our vigorous lands?" (*The Times*, 10 September 1895, p. 3).
6. *The Times*, 15 October 1895, p. 6, reported the Treasurer of Cape Colony as having said publicly that the Cape should help pay for the Navy: "It has been suggested at the Cape that the contribution should take the form of two men-of-war."

To Frank Hall Scott,[1] 3 November 1895
ALS: Library of Congress

Naulakha. / Waite / Windham Co / *Vermont.* / Nov: 3: 95

My dear Mr Scott,
    Many thanks for the "book."[2] It is as I suspected. The stuff is a hash-up of old newspaper articles written when I was twenty; and added to by some moral thief or other.[3] Of course I am as wild as I can be about it but – what can we do?

    I see it's marked "copyright" and "all rights reserved" on the title page. Can't we get at Dillingham here; because of course there's no copyright on the thing at all. The thief being barred from running slaves has taken to body-snatching and is peddling corpses – pretty stale ones too.

    (The particular mischief of the book is that it contains the bulk of my notes for the *Naulakha!*)[4]

    I am sending a short note to the *Nation, Critic* and *Tribune*[5] to say that I have nothing to do with the thing and I don't think that there is much more for me to do. It's the studied and elaborate un-morality of the wretched affair that makes me so sick at my stomach.

Very sincerely
Rudyard Kipling

Notes
1. Frank Hall Scott (1848–1912), formerly treasurer and now president of the Century Company.
2. *Out of India*, published in New York by G. W. Dillingham; it combines RK's "Letters of Marque", originally contributed to the *Pioneer* in 1887–8, the "City of Dreadful Night" sketches, contributed to the *Pioneer* in 1888, and some miscellaneous articles from the *Pioneer* and *CMG*, 1887–8. The source of the volume is evidently the two collections issued by A. H. Wheeler at Allahabad called *The City of Dreadful Night and Other Sketches* (1890) and *Letters of Marque* (1891). RK had had these titles "suppressed" as in violation of his copyright in India, but some copies went into circulation: see Stewart–Yeats, *Bibliographical Catalogue*, pp. 88–9, 94, 132.
3. New headings to the letters and sketches have been supplied in the Dillingham volume.
4. That is, the "Letters of Marque", describing the places that RK made use of in *The Naulahka*.
5. See the next letter: it appeared in all three of the publications named.

To the Editor, New York *Tribune*, 3 November 1895
ALS: Yale University

Naulakha. / Waite / Windham Co. / *Vermont.*

To the Editor
　Tribune:

Dear Sir
　Will you permit me through the medium of your columns to warn
the public against a book called "Out of India" published by a New
York firm? It is put forward, evidently, as a new book by Rudyard
Kipling. It is made up of a hash of old newspaper articles written nine
or ten years ago, to which are added moral reflections by some unknown
hand.
　It appears without my knowledge or sanction; is a common "fake"
and I must disclaim all connection with it.

Very sincerely
Rudyard Kipling.

3: 11: 95

To Unidentified Recipient,[1] 3 November 1895
Text: Kipling Journal, April 1946, pp. 5–6.

November 3rd, 1895. / Naulakha, Waite, Vermont, / Windham
Co., U.S.A.

Dear ———
　I am very much obliged to you for your long letter (of no date)
forwarded to me in America where I am at present living. Enthusiasm
like yours is a rare thing in this world – you'll grow out of it, worse
luck – but it is very delightful while it lasts. You seem to have gone
through everything that I have ever written and to like it. There are
times when I look over what I have done, and am anything but pleased
with the result.
　As to my female characters, I admit your charge, but I am doing my
best to remedy it. In either the Graphic or the Illustrated Christmas
number this year you'll find a tale that may perhaps interest your
brother, the engineer, (it's all about steam engines), and an attempt to
draw a rather nice woman.[2]
　But let me point out that you are a deal *too* young to bother your head
about womenfolk – in books or out of them. Your spelling for one thing
is nearly as bad as mine used to be when I was about your age and you
must get hold of it and repair it. I have a relation of my own in your
business,[3] so I know that there is heaps of leisure in an architect's office.

If you have found out from my tales that wickedness of any kind does not pay, you've learned something I have tried to teach very hard. Of course, I can't go about and cram a sermon into a tale, but I try to get at the same point obliquely – and so far no one has found me out. *The* point about all forms of grosser sin, such as women, drink, cards, lies and theft and bullying, is their essential *childishness* when the game is played out. Sooner or later there has to be a reckoning and the defaulter has to pay up with compound interest for every day that he has let his sin master him. You will probably fall into temptation of all kinds in your own way, but I beg you to try to remember that there's nothing fine, nothing impressive, nothing manly in giving way to one's impulses. Someone has got to pay for our misdeeds. When we are young it is generally our mother: when we grow older it is other people: but the net result is neither more decent or dignified than a baby making a mess in its clothes. Older men will tell you that this is nonsense, but it's the solemn truth, and you remember it. However I am not going to preach.

Yes, I like the Jungle-book like anything and I've just finished another which will be out by the time this reaches you – carrying on Mowgli's adventures: in fact it is a collection of the tales which have already appeared in the P[all].M[all].G[azette]. I hope you'll like them in book form as much as when you read them scattered. That ends up Mowgli and there is not going to be any more to him. After that I expect to try my hand at a series of engineer's tales – about marine engines and such like.

It is snowing hard in this part of the world (where our winters are long and cold) and if I wasn't eaten up by a cold in the head I'd write you a longer letter.

Again thanking you for your kind letter (I wonder what you'll think of things ten years hence).

Believe me,

Very sincerely yours,
Rudyard Kipling.

Notes

1. Said to have been a sixteen-year-old member of the Rose and Ring Club in East London, Cape Province (*Kipling Journal*, December 1943, p. 14).
2. RK must mean "The Devil and the Deep Sea" and "William the Conqueror"; the first appeared in the Christmas *Graphic*; the second in the *Gentlewoman*, December 1895: perhaps the passage has been confused in the copying.
3. Ambrose Poynter.

To Robert Underwood Johnson, 4 November 1895

Text: Facsimile in Robert Underwood Johnson, *Remembered Yesterdays* (Boston, 1923) p. 398

Naulakha. / Waite / Windham Co. / *Vermont*. 4: 11. 95

Dear Johnson,

Very many thanks. Now, as the private soldier said when they locked him up, "now, I have a place to get drunk in."[1] In all seriousness I am much indebted to you and Gilder and my many good friends. I hope to be down some day and explore my new possessions. Meantime I feel very gorgeous and grateful.

Very sincerely
Rudyard Kipling

P.S.   What the deuce is an "Imperial" photograph? The committee informs me I've got to be photoed that way and – I don't know how.[2] [sketch of RK wearing papal tiara and inscribed "Very sincerely yours / Rudyard Kipling. / Nov. 1895 Member of the Century Association."]

Something like this?

Notes
1. Johnson had just informed RK of his election to the Century Club of New York on 2 November.
2. The Century Club has no photograph of RK taken on this occasion.

To Edmund Clarence Stedman, 4 November 1895

ALS: Historical Society of Pennsylvania

Naulakha. / Waite / Windham Co. / *Vermont.* / 4: 11: 95

Dear Mr. Stedman,

Very many thanks for your kind letter of yesterday. It is a fine thing to be a centurion and when you come to think of it the original centurions marched under the Eagle.[1] I wait for the anthology and am proud to think my Last Chanty is in it.[2] Just now I am in extreme trouble over a new book of verses I want to get out in the spring.[3] I've held it back a year and cut it down a third and the longer I look at the remnant the badder and the balder it seems. Prose stays pretty much where it is put but verse is like an egg – it kinder addles, if you sit on it too long.

As to the long ago thing to which you refer so lightly,[4] I haven't known it, and a lot of it by heart much longer than – Oh "Tempus Edax" as the Ancient said to Galahad[5] eighteen good years – since the days when I first read the *Echo Club* and that set me to ravaging among American poets. But it is to be well preserved for the sake of the blue-pencil initials (you might have signed in full). It's curious how the unexpressed spirit of a poem sometimes drives out the words of the writer. *We* used to wind up Old Brown triumphantly with: –

> "May make it a damned sight hotter
> When you've nailed his coffin down."[6]

Ever yours sincerely and admiringly
Rudyard Kipling

Notes
1. An American eagle formerly stood in the basement of the old Century Club clubhouse (information from the Club librarian).
2. Stedman's *A Victorian Anthology* (see 21 July 1894) had just been published: it contains RK's "The Last Chantey", published in 1893 but not collected by RK until *The Seven Seas*.
3. *The Seven Seas*.
4. Stedman's "How Old Brown Took Harper's Ferry", originally published in 1859, between John Brown's raid on Harper's Ferry in October and Brown's execution in December 1859.
5. From the dialogue in Bayard Taylor's *The Echo Club* (see 21 July 1894) p. 45: "Thirty years ago, O Tempus Edax, must I say *thirty*?" This is just before Stedman's verse is taken up by the parodists. If RK's "eighteen good years" is correct, then he discovered *The Echo Club* in 1877, either just before or just after leaving Mrs Holloway's.
6. "How Old Brown Took Harper's Ferry" ends thus: "And Old Brown/Osawatomie Brown/May trouble you more than ever, when you've nailed his coffin down."

To Cormell Price, 5 November 1895
ALS: Library of Congress

Naulakha. / Brattleboro. / Vermont. / 5: 11: 95

Dear Mr Price
[. . .][1] And the truth is that we are both down with that most destroying sort of cold – a dull sobbled thing that is going the rounds. As neither of us look for this from years end to years end we are the more angry.

The Hans Andersen almost persuades me to let baby learn to read before she is ten – the age I have fixed upon for her soul's health – but perhaps I shall be content with reading them to her. She's had a small cold too but is now in great and riotous form – of that age which asks every conceivable sort of question all the while.

Life is busily monotonous with us here. We have put the garden to sleep for the winter and are now spreading dung and fattening swine and building stone walls. There comes a week or so in November – the Indian summer – as it were the middle of spring and it is the most perfect season of the year if the days were not shortened. I'm more or less busy over some new verses that may appear as a book next spring[2] and am waiting to see how "The Second Jungle Book" goes. I only hope things go serenely among your young men and you're getting 'em [in] shoals and passing into Sandhurst by battalions.[3] A propos there are some references in a yarn of mine that will appear in the Xmas *Century* which may possibly remind you of old days at Westward Ho![4] Some time I think I'll write a boys book and pitch the scene there.[5]

Would I could get you over now for a season to enjoy our perfect weather.

With best love from us both to you and Uncle Ned and all the Grange.

Ever yours
Ruddy.

Here's a mistranslation that beats even anything of Kipling's for a guess. I heard it the other day. Huc ubi discretas insula rumpet aquas. "Here where the discreet islander breaks horses."[6]

Notes

1. The first three paragraphs of this letter (omitted) are by CK thanking Price for a gift of books to Josephine; the rest is by RK.
2. *The Seven Seas.*
3. After leaving the United Services College Price supported himself as a tutor in London.
4. "The Brushwood Boy".
5. Perhaps the earliest reference to *Stalky & Co.*
6. Ovid, *Fasti*, II.194: "There where the island breaks the parted waters."

To Frederick D. Underwood,[1] 23 November 1895
Text: Copy, Dalhousie University

Naulakha. / Waite, / Windham Co. / Vermont. / Nov. 23: 95.

F. D. Underwood, Esq.,
  S[ault].S[ainte]. Marie. R.R.

Dear Sir:

My friend and onetime chief, Mr. E. Kay Robinson,[2] tells me that you would like to see a specimen of my handwriting. He has further shown me a folder of your R.R. in which appear the stations "Rudyard" and "Kipling".[3] He tells me too that "Kipling" may some day have a great future before it in the iron ore way. This immensely flatters my vanity: and I write to beg you to send me a photograph if possible, of either "Rudyard" or "Kipling" or preferentially both. I shall take a deep interest in their little welfares. "Rudyard" I gather is already a postoffice, but I have not heard of "Kipling."

Please encourage the development of "Kipling." Give him an express and telegraph office, and a new water-tank and if ever he has a restaurant let it be known for the best coffee on the line. Tell him – if he is big enough – to avoid strifes, and bloodshed: never to open the wrong switch and to be careful about his grade crossings. Some day I hope to be able to come out and see him and his brother. In the meantime and with many thanks for the splendid way in which you have given me a circulation, believe me

Very sincerely yours,
Rudyard Kipling.

Notes
1. Underwood (1852–1942), General Manager of the Minneapolis, St Paul and Sault Ste Marie Railway; he was afterwards President of the Erie Railroad.
2. Kay Robinson had been travelling in the United States and had come on from Minneapolis to visit RK in Vermont (CK diary, 10 and 18 November).
3. These towns, named by Underwood, lie in the upper peninsula of Michigan along the route of the Sault Ste Marie Railway, 100 miles apart from each other. Rudyard is just south of the straits of Sault Ste Marie; Kipling is at the head of Green Bay on Lake Michigan (and a suburb of a town called Gladstone!). RK later sent Underwood a set of verses on Rudyard and Kipling called "The Michigan Twins" (uncollected).

To William Hallett Phillips, 23 November 1895
Text: American Art Association Anderson Galleries Catalogue (9–11 May 1934) item 376: 2pp. 12mo; dated Naulakha, Waite, Vermont, Windham Co., Nov. 23, 1895

O Sitting Fox. I've just been down to Boston[1] where I've been having the hell of a time at receptions and tea fights and such like which are not good for my bile nor my bowels, and I am cheered to get your letter. I am horrid busy trying to get even with my mail. The weather is of a queer and dammable warmth with much rain so that we all feel unhappy and stale.

Mrs. Custer[2] is staying here for a day and a night preparatory to going on to public readings in Brattleboro, the mud is awful . . . John Hay has sent us half a dozen superb ducks which he has shot in Ohio, wish you could have tasted the one we had for lunch this noon. . . .

If England and America fight as indeed Dr. Chandler[3] of N.H. (I think) says is inevitable: you and I will take Lodge[4] and stick him into a conning tower and keep him there. Its the futilest piffle I've ever heard of and I wish to heaven I could write a set of verses chaffing the thing dead.[5]

By all means let's fight for good reason, fight like hell if necessary, not for dagoes, and Bolivars, and half-breeds in calico breeches. No, the plea is that in England they don't know a thing about it but I see the Daily Chronicle has been interviewing Lodge.

Notes
1. On 20–3 November, to visit Norton (CK diary). One of the things he did there was to see the Harvard–Penn football game (*Vermont Phoenix*, 29 November 1895).
2. Mrs Elizabeth Bacon Custer (1842–1933), widow of General Custer and an author and lecturer. According to the *Windham County Reformer*, 29 November 1895, she spent Sunday 24 November at Naulakha and gave her lecture on the 26th.
3. William E. Chandler (1835–1917), Senator from New Hampshire, 1887–1901.
4. Henry Cabot Lodge (1850–1924), pupil of Henry Adams, editor, historian, Congressman and Senator from Massachusetts for thirty-seven years. He was part of the Washington circle that RK met in the spring of this year. On the Venezuelan question (see next note) he was a vigorous supporter of Cleveland.
5. A dispute between England and Venezuela was in progress over the boundary of British Guiana, and talk of war was running high in the United States. In December President Cleveland sent a message to Congress declaring British action a breach of the Monroe Doctrine, but the matter ended in quiet arbitration. The episode was a main reason for RK's departure from the United States (Carrington, *Kipling*, pp. 227–8).

To Charles Scribner's Sons, 25 November 1895
ALS: Princeton University.

Naulakha. / Waite / Windham Co. / *Vermont.* / Nov. 25.95

Dear Sir,

I am in receipt of your letter of the 23rd inst.

I regret that there is no chance of my being in New York, as far as I can see, for the next few months and I have just returned from my winter trip to Boston. Should Mr Doubleday[1] however find it convenient to come up here I should be very glad to see him but sorry to give him the trouble. We are 4 miles from a telegraph office so I may say that telegraphic notice of his arrival would avail nothing. Could you not write me your scheme.

Very sincerely
Rudyard Kipling.

Charles Scribner Son

Note
1. Frank N. Doubleday (1862–1934), then in the employ of Scribner but soon to found his own publishing firm. This was to be a momentous occasion for both Doubleday and RK. The proposal was for Scribner to undertake a collected edition of RK's works, which, under the name of the Outward Bound Edition, commenced publication in 1897. Shortly thereafter, with RK's encouragement, Doubleday set up his own firm; RK was one of his original authors, and remained with him to the end.

To William Carey, [November 1895]
ALS: Huntington Library

Naulakha. / Waite / Windham Co. / Vermont.

Dear Carey –

A trip to Boston has left me with a mail standing in heaps around me. Hence this much delay.

As regards Out of India, it's old newspaper work ten years old with additions by some heavy-handed devil unknown to me. I never denied authorship. What *I* kick at is at getting behind a man's back and stabbing him with bad work ten years after he's done it. If it were merely some one else's stuff I shouldn't care a curse but – well how would you like a man selling your cast off breeches on Broadway?

The very sober and always cautious Macmillans write me that they have printed (25,000 + 10,000) thirty five thousand copies of the second jungle book *before the day of publication on the strength of advance orders!* Breathe this into the ear of the publishing department and see them smile.

With all regards from us both

Yours ever
Rudyard Kipling

To Joel Chandler Harris,[1] 6 December 1895
ALS: Emory University

Naulakha. / Waite / Windham Co: / *Vermont.* Dec. 6. 1895

Dear Mr. Harris:

I am taking the liberty of sending you with this a copy of the Second Jungle Book – which I see with delight you have been good enough to praise in the Christmas Book-buyer.[2] This makes me feel some inches taller in my boots: for my debt to you is of long standing. I wonder if you could realize how Uncle Remus his sayings and the sayings of the noble beasties ran like wild fire through an English public school when I was about fifteen.[3] We used to go to battle (with boots and bolsters and such like) against those whom we did not love, to the tune of *Hi! Yi!-tingalee: I eat um pea I pick um pea etc.* and I remember the bodily heaving into a furze-bush of a young fag solely because his nickname had been "Rabbit" before the tales invaded the school and – well, we assumed that he ought to have been "born an' bred in a briar-patch" and gorze was the most efficient substitute. And six years ago in India meeting an old schoolmate of those days we found ourselves quoting whole pages of Uncle Remus that had got mixed in with the fabric of the old school life. One thing I want to know badly (you must loathe the people who pester you with this kind of thing) but from what nature-myth or *what* come "Miss Meadows and the girls?"[4] Where did they begin – in whose mind? What do *you* think they are?

I hope you will not think yourself in any way bound to answer this note – except, please, about Miss Meadows and a post card would do for that. I know Christmas must be a busy season with you so I will not trespass on your patience.

With all respect and admiration

Believe me
Very sincerely yours
Rudyard Kipling

To
Joel Chandler Harris Esq.

Notes
1. Harris (1848–1908), author of the Uncle Remus stories, published from 1880 onwards.
2. Harris wrote that "now, as of old, the elemental in man rhymes with the elemental in all things else, and Mr. Kipling's genius touches the center of it all with a swing, a vigor, and a fearlessness that cannot be matched in modern literature".
3. Described in "The United Idolaters", 1924 (*Debits and Credits*).
4. Unexplained characters whose names recur in the Uncle Remus stories: "'Who was Miss Meadows, Uncle Remus?' inquired the little boy. 'Don't ax me, honey. She wuz

in de tale, Miss Meadows en de gals wuz, en de tale I give you like hit wer' gun ter me" ("Mr. Rabbit Grossly Deceives Mr. Fox"). Harris suggested in reply to RK that "Miss Meadows an de gals" may mean "nature and its forces" (14 December [1895]: ALS, Sussex).

To Louisa Baldwin, 14 December 1895

ALS: Dalhousie University

Naulakha. / Waite / Windham Co. / *Vermont.* / XII: 14: 1895:

Dear Aunt Louie:

There has been a good deal of rough weather on the North Atlantic and your "Shadow on the Blind" came in late by consequence. I fluffed with pride at the dedication which, however, still strikes me as unseemly between aunt and nephew – say almost aunticidal.[1] Out and away the best tale is the bairn with the second sight which is beyond all the others convincing and logical. The next to my mind is Sir Nigel's family ghosts in the courtyard: and the one that doesn't convince (where at least an opportunity to convince has been lost) is the tale of the empty picture frame and the ghostess who came visiting with her maid. Now, dropping the nephew, for a minute, will you let me say that what you want most is "heap plenty blue pencil?" The tales are good and more than good but you give the impression of wanting forty pages to turn in and there's an overlarge sprinkling of easy and accepted phrases that have been worn smooth by other pens. I don't mean journalese but more in the nature of padding stuff. It's like an etching where the central figure is bitten in clearly enough and the rest is a clutter of lines put in to make background.

The Lord he knoweth I would not council you to bring up your backgrounds too much (that's *my* besetting sin) but only to elaborate them cleanly and clearly in a few well chosen words that bring air and light and perspective into the show, and that, I take it, is only attained by considering every word of minor dialogue and description and most resolutely avoiding the set phrase. It's a mistake we are all of us most prone to in our business. I wish I could go through a page or two over your shoulder and show you what I mean. It wouldn't look so horribly impertinent as it does on paper.

The Pater sent me accounts of his Wilden and Burslem trip from which I gather that frolicking alone at the tables of the great his tummy fell out of order and you cured him lovingly. He told me too of his visit to Stan at Dunley Hall – "fine name that" – and I am beginning to wonder whether it will not soon be time for Stan and his wife to cross the water again and come to Naulakha for a while. Babies are great ties, as we know, but they thrive none the worse for a little letting alone.

Our baby is a voluble affable young lady who seems to know the nonsense-book by heart and the routine of the house by instinct. She is the joy of our souls and bids fair to grow into a clean and decent lassie. Her brother or sister should arrive some time in late January or early February and C's health and spirits and energy keep surprisingly good. But women are very marvellous creatures. I am not so busy as I have been. My prose work for the next few months is finished and I am revising my verses against next spring when I hope to make a book of them. Then I think I shall give myself a long holiday and go wandering.

This letter, with good weather, should come to you about Christmas and it brings our love and good wishes to you and Uncle Alfred. Give Aunt Edie my best love and a kiss.

Always your affectionate newphew
Ruddy

The handwriting of this is bad because Bips has been at my elbow wanting me to look at pictures.

Note
1. See letter to Louisa Baldwin, 29 September 1895.

To Robert Underwood Johnson, 14 December 1895
ALS: Dalhousie University

Naulakha. / Waite / Windham Co. / Vermont. / 14. XII. 95

Dear Johnson

Yours of the 12th. What you propose is an exceeding big job and one altogether beyond my scope.[1] I made a try at the same thing years ago in India and in turning over documents came across *one* file of John Lawrence's ordinary office letters for the month of June 1857.[2] That cured me. Besides '57 is the year we don't talk about and I know *I* can't. Again you overlook the little fact that it is much more difficult to catch the spirit, the hundred little shades, of society 40 years ago than of society of the middle ages or of the neolithic age for that matter. But it would be a great thing to have it properly done. Mrs. Flora Annie Steel[3] – she that wrote "From the Land of the Five Rivers;" "The Potters Thumb;" and so on, is I believe collecting material *in situ*, for a novel covering the same ground. Now I know that she has had at least 25 years' experience of India and knows more about certain twists of the native mind than any one I know. It seems to me that if you could get *her* novel you'd be likely to be buying something really good. She's a beautiful writer and she knows. Then again there is S. Levett Yeats – *The Honour of Savelli.*[4] When I knew him in the Punjab Club in the old days he was full of notions for a mutiny tale and he may have something up his sleeve that would be worth getting at. I throw out these here gratuitous suggestions because I very much want to see a good mutiny novel. I'd try in a minute if I felt I had a call that way but I'm rather convinced I have not.

Very sincerely always
Rudyard Kipling.

Notes
1. Johnson had suggested that RK try "a novel on the Sepoy Rebellion" (Johnson's note on MS of letter).
2. RK's attempt to write on the Mutiny of 1857 is "In the Year '57", *CMG*, 14 May 1887 and 23 May 1887 (uncollected). This is based on Lawrence's letters, preserved in Lahore. John Lawrence (1811–79), 1st Baron Lawrence, was Chief Commissioner for the Punjab at the time of the Mutiny and was credited with a large part in putting it down. He was later made Viceroy of India.
3. Mrs Steel (1847–1929) lived in India 1868–89 as the wife of a civil servant and produced a series of novels and stories on the country after she had left it, including *From the Five Rivers* (1893) and *The Potter's Thumb* (1894). She had long been known to the Kipling family, and served for several years with JLK on the Provincial Education Board. JLK, in 1881, told Lockwood de Forest that Mrs Steel knew more about India and the Punjab than anyone else (29 May 1881: ALS, Harvard); in 1894 he illustrated her *Tales of the Punjab.* Her Mutiny novel was *On the Face of the Waters* (1896).
4. Sidney Kilner Levett-Yeats, *The Honour of Savelli: a Romance* (1895). For Levett-Yeats, see [30 June 1889]. He was by this time already identified as one of the "imitators of Mr. Rudyard Kipling" (*Westminster Review*, January 1894).

To Robert Underwood Johnson, 20 December 1895
ALS: Dalhousie University

Naulakha. / Waite / Windham Co. *Vermont.* / XII. 20: 95

Dear Johnson –

Some one in the office has sent me the enclosed; and the wily Dillingham[1] sheltering himself behind a "person in England" has turned out a picturesque but malignant fiction. The books were published during my absence from England in '91: *without my knowledge or consent.*[2] I took steps under the law and the whole edition was ground into pulp. That was the long and the short of it: but I don't suppose there's any sense in taking any more notice of Dillingham. I don't mind theft but I do object to the receiver posing as a decent man.

If, as Mr. Cleveland seems to think, there is going to be war and you see me coming round the 14th street curve on a curvetting cable-car with a drawn sword in my hand you'll know that I'm looking for G. W. Dillingham.

Very sincerely
Rudyard Kipling.

Notes
1. George W. Dillingham, the publisher of the unauthorized *Out of India* (see letter to Frank Hall Scott, 3 November 1895).
2. RK means the "suppressed" editions of *The City of Dreadful Night and Other Sketches* and *Letters of Marque* (see letter to Frank Hall Scott, 3 November 1895).

To Charles Eliot Norton, [26 December] 1895
ALS: Harvard University

Naulakha. / Waite / Windham Co / *Vermont.* / Boxing-day. / '95

Dear Mr Norton:

The Donne[1] came yesterday with a batch of mail matter for which there was no accomodation – all the mails seem to be running late. I knew you wouldn't forget at Christmas, bless you: but the paper knife I was sending to you seemed in view of the present folly such a grisly gift that I forebore – even from good words.

I feel regularly upset and bewildered about it[2] – as if I had been aimed at with a decanter across a friendly dinner table. But I can only pray it will come out all right. Carrie who is sore pressed with Christmas doings bids me thank you both for the calendar and Baby's book (kittens in human clothes are new to Baby Josephine) and I am, as ever, with all good wishes for the new year on your house,

Affectionately yours
Ruddy.

Notes
1. Norton's edition of *The Poems of John Donne* (New York, 1895).
2. The anti-British outburst over Venezuela.

To Stanley Weyman, 30 December 1895
ALS: Library of Congress

Naulakha. / Waite / Windham Co. / *Vermont.* / Dec. 30. 95

Dear Weyman,

Here's a coincidence. I came up from a flying visit to New York yesterday[1] and the news-boy came through the train with all the latest books.

"Don't want the Jungle book" said he. "Well here's the Red Cockade[2] – sellin' like hot cakes. (I bought it – *not* allured by this recommendation – and he went on). There ain't nobody can't touch Wyman fer sales."

I curled up with the R.C. and put a six hour journey behind me in great comfort being in the middle of the Revolution for the most part and so lost my supper, on the way. I don't feel grateful for this last but I am pleased to find that you remember me. But first let me congratulate you on your marriage[3] – I saw some reference to it in a newspaper but knowing what newspapers are I held my peace. I believe it is good for all but a few men who are bachelors by instinct to be married after a decent and discreet age and in our business more than in any other who gets himself a good wife gets a good thing from the Lord. If marriage makes your life to you one half as good and wholesome as it has made mine to me, you'll be blessed: and I wish all good on you and yours and your house for many generations.

We expect to be over in late summer or early autumn for some long time[4] – so despair not if some day you see the wife and me coming over the hills very hungry with trunks in a cart.

I can't say I've been under any delusion as to the general American feeling about England (you can't use a common hate as a dogwhip to round up miscellaneous mobs of human beings without having to suffer for it in the long run) but I didn't expect 'em to show their hand so soon. However forewarned ought to be forearmed and if active trouble holds off for a while we ought not to slide back into our old easy credulity. It's a queer business and would make a good comic opera. But the land will have to sweat for it financially through years to come.

If you find yourself feeling repeating yourself why don't you lay off for a season. There's a heap of virtue in a voyage or a tour. I don't see any signs of it in anything you've turned out so I argue brutally that it is your liver. For myself I hope to go into dry-dock for a year or two after my verses come out: and to adjust my notions of things generally.

With all good wishes for the coming year for you and your wife believe me

Very sincerely always
Rudyard Kipling

Notes

1. According to CK's diary, RK left on the 26th and returned on the 28th.
2. Weyman's *The Red Cockade* (1895), a story of revolutionary France.
3. Weyman married Charlotte Panting in 1895.
4. This is the earliest reference I know of to RK's decision to leave the United States for an indefinite period: presumably he had already made arrangements for an extended absence, though he did not leave until 1 September 1896. CK was, however, already in advanced pregnancy, no doubt the main reason to delay their departure.

To Joel Chandler Harris, [early 1896]

ALS: Emory University

Naulakha, / Waite, / Vermont.

Dear Mr Harris:

And now there is a small maiden, just over three years old, who only knows enough to call the superb Uncle Remus "The Bunny Book" and this afternoon I have been unfolding to her the mysteries of the tar-baby. She realizes, acutely, that if once you hit a tar-baby you can't get away but for the life of her she can't see why. I've explained it's the same as the mucilage pot that she mustn't touch and she is awed. And it was only the day before yesterday I was lying on my stomach in front of a fire at school reading Uncle Remus on my own hook. So now my debt to you is two generations deep. May you live to see it four.

What a splendid job Frost[1] has made of the pictures. They fit, as Tenniel's did to Alice in Wonderland – and they will march down the ages as the signed and sealed pattern of Brer Rabbit and the others. So complete is their accuracy and inevitableness that I found myself saying with a snort: – "of course that's Brer Rabbit – any dam fool knows that. Now let's see what Frost has made out of it." That is good enough illusion. I have never come across any book yet till I opened your gift, where the beasts just naturally *had* to wear clothes. So natural is their unnaturalness that the picture of Brer Rabbit playing dead on the road to deceive Brer Fox struck me as indecent – and I don't think I'm a prudish soul – because he hadn't his trousers on.[2] The buck-jumping Fox is a beautiful little bit of action.[3] They are all good and I am a rich man. The baby would bless you if she knew how things are managed in this world but she has an iron belief that all the books that she knows were written by her father and illustrated by her grandfather. I heard her explain to the nurse serenely as if these things happened about every twenty minutes: "Father has made me another book!" If chance or fate ever bring me south be sure I shall avail me of your kind invitation. We were 28 below zero last night so I will not beg you to come up here yet awhile.

With renewed thanks

Yours sincerely
Rudyard Kipling.

Notes
1. Arthur Burdett Frost (1851–1928); he illustrated *Uncle Remus: His Songs and Sayings* (new and rev. edn, New York, 1895).
2. Illustration to "Mr. Fox Goes A-Hunting, but Mr. Rabbit Bags the Game", p. 74.
3. "Mr. Rabbit Nibbles Up the Butter", p. 85.

To Irving Bacheller,[1] 5 January 1896
ALS: Harvard University

Naulakha, / Waite, / Vermont. / Jan 5. 96.

Irving Bacheller Esq.

Dear Sir:

In reply to your very courteous letter of the 3rd instant I can only regret that it is impossible for me to see my way to any sort of interview. Of course anything that Mr Parker would do would be, I know, entirely dignified and inoffensive but the fact of my being once interviewed would lead to all sorts of complications from other quarters; and I could not in reason refuse after I had once broken the rule which I find secures my time to myself.

As to your other proposition it is very fascinating – especially the special car and the terms for the article. But I have crossed this continent three times in the ordinary way.[2] Once I nearly went through a trestle on the Siskiyou: once I was washed out in Colorado and once I lived on a drummer's samples of fancy confectionery when we were delayed by a burnt bridge.[3] The ordinary rate of travel is good enough for me but if you could fill up a special car with a few friends of mine carefully selected, I should be happy to give the enterprize my blessing. My own notions of suicide are cheap and inexpensive. Yours is a very good idea and I am sorry that it is not exactly in my line.

Very sincerely
Rudyard Kipling.

Notes
1. Bacheller (1859–1950) founded the New York Press Syndicate in 1884; beginning in 1890 he developed a successful career as a novelist and story writer. RK had contributed stories to Bacheller's syndicate in 1895, and some of the poems later collected in *The Seven Seas* were distributed in the United States by the Syndicate (Arthur Waugh, *One Man's Road* [1931] p. 230).
2. Once in 1889 and twice in 1892, on his wedding journey.
3. All of these things occurred in June and July 1889. RK crossed the Siskiyous on his way to Portland from San Francisco; he was delayed by a burned bridge en route from Yellowstone to Salt Lake City; and the washout in Colorado must have been at Gunnison, where he spent a day. See *From Sea to Sea*, ii, 23, 117, 143.

To Charles Eliot Norton, 8 January 1896
ALS: Harvard University

Naulakha, / Waite, / Vermont. / Jan. 8.96

Dear Mr. Norton:

That letter just shows what a fine thing it is to be reasonably sure of death in a little time – and a decent death in a really truly bed. For me it is otherwise for I seem to be between two barrels like a pheasant. If the American mine is sprung it means dirt and slush and ultimately death either across the Canada border or in some disembowelled gunboat off Cape Hatteras. If the German dynamite[1] is exploded equally it means slaughter and most probably on the high seas. In both cases I am armed with nothing more efficient than a note-book, a stylographic pen and a pair of opera-glasses. Whether or no, anyway and inevitably, C. will be confined within the next three or five weeks and till that time I am tied here by the leg. All things considered Godkin[2] has much to congratulate himself upon. I have arranged things so that C. ought not to starve: and she has the house and all my copyrights to boot. You see it is obviously absurd of me to sit still and go on singing from a safe place while the men I know are in the [   ][3] of it: and it may be that when I am closer to the scene of action I may be able to help with a little song or two in the intervals of special correspondence. But it is borne in upon me by the inner eye that *if* trouble comes I shan't live to see it out: unless I bolt and hide myself in the wilds of Patagonia or the Pole. Even in that resort I should be dead, and worse than dead.

All these things fill me with a deep love for Mr Cleveland who is responsible for the letting in of the waters. I permit myself however to cherish a hope that the row or rows may be delayed till May when I can hope to pick up C. and the children (D.V.) and take 'em to England. I shan't mind so much then: but whether it be peace or war, this folly puts an end to my good wholesome life here: and to me that is the saddest part of it. We must begin again from the beginning elsewhere and pretend that we are only anxious to let the house for a year or two. It's hard enough God knows but I should be a fool if after full warning I risked my own peoples' happiness and comfort in a hostile country. Godkin seems to me to be reasonably right. You can't teach hate for five generations and expect no harvest: and you can't debosh people's minds with light and easy talk of killing on slight provocation, and with the spectacle of private murder unavenged, without hurting their moral insides. All the same the American situation is intensely comic in a sombre and devilish sort of way. I have the melancholy satisfaction of saying to myself: – "I told you so" about a hundred times a day: but it seems to me best not to say or write or sing a word publicly – yet. As to the German business I don't care a continental. It will wake up the colonies I believe and teach us to keep our powder dry. But the American thing makes me sick and sore and sorry to my heart's core. People can say what they please. There was a much more genuine absence of hostility on the English side than there was on the American: and I do sincerely believe that the American interior press is responsible for the cherishing of that hostile feeling. But all this is a grossly personal view of the matter and a man with a wife and child and another baby expected may be excused for a certain amount of selfishness. Looking at it in other lights it seems to me that it will help the Empire enormously; will definitely shut out all notion of Canada's absorption into the States except by force and will teach us the beauties of an intercolonial tariff – may even send us to ally with France and Russia to rearrange the map of the world. But these are long long looks ahead and I can only say that whatever comes I and mine are always affectionately yours. No war or series of wars could make any difference in that, thank God. If Grover doesn't know when he has a good friend, I do.

Ever yours affectionately
Ruddy.

I have the Arnold letters.[4] Folks say they are dull but that's absurd. It's the fine quality of that expert razor never losing its edge as it goes through the board school grindstone that makes me take off my hat to it.
P.P.S.   But *why* Alfred Austin.[5] Pater told me he was living in Salisbury's pocket ever since Tennyson died: but I never expected he'd get it.

R.

Notes
1. Following the failure of Dr Jameson's raid in the Transvaal at the end of December the

German Emperor had sent a message to President Kruger seeming to recognise the independence of the Transvaal. This raised a storm in England, and troops were sent out to South Africa.
2. Edwin Lawrence Godkin (1831–1902), Irish-born journalist, founding editor of the *Nation* and editor of the New York *Evening Post*; an intimate friend of Norton. He opposed Cleveland on the Venezuelan question, a stand that drew praise from Norton (Rollo Ogden, *Life and Letters of Edwin Lawrence Godkin* [New York, 1907] ii, 188).
3. Word illegible.
4. G. W. E. Russell (ed.), *Letters of Matthew Arnold*, 2 vols (1895).
5. Austin had been appointed Poet Laureate on 1 January.

To William Hallett Phillips, 10 January 1896
ALS: Dalhousie University

Naulakha, / Waite, / Vermont. / 10. Jan. 96.

Dear Sitting Fox,

Then a letter of mine must have gone missing somewhere:[1] for I wrote straight off to thank you for the pouch and baccy and to scorn and repudiate your unnecessary arrows. All the same they are beautiful bits of work. I don't see where the letter could have slipped up – not in *our* post office I am sure.

The weather has been crazy mad and we have not been able to go on runners yet. Today looks more hopeful and I am going out on my *skis* (great things are *skis*) to investigate. Wish you were with me. There was a sober and godly N.Y. lawyer came up about a month ago when we had a little snow and I introduced him to them. Since that date he has been wildly trying to get a pair for himself.

I should like to come out for a spree, even as far as the Yellowstone with Hofer[2] and you but the Trues[3] will add a papoose to my lodge in a few weeks and therefore I cannot come. Didn't you know that?

I can't say I feel very festive. This damned Venzuelan rot has made me sick to my heart. It may be fine and picturesque and patriotic and all the rest of it but it has done America a damage it will take her fifty years to recover from, in the eyes of the civilized world.

Heaven send you a good and lucky new year – it's more than your red-Indian Sioux of a fatherland deserves – and remember me to all my friends in Washington. The wife is very truly well and Bips is as ever radiant.

Yours sincerely always
Rudyard Kipling.

P.S. I don't know where you can get settings of my songs. Sometimes a festive composer sends me a sample and it's generally Bad.

Notes
1. This letter has not been found.
2. Trapper and guide: see 18 May 1895.
3. Indian gods: see [16 August 1897].

To Frederick Norton Finney,[1] 23 January 1896
ALS: Dalhousie University

Naulakha, / Waite, / Vermont. / Jan. 23: 96.

My dear Mr. Finney:

Yours of the 17th shows me that there has been an Awful Error for which I am sure to suffer. One of the many correspondents who make home happy for me by sending me M.S.S. (priceless in their own eyes) to look over forwarded me that Primitive Man book and followed it up with a letter demanding its return. I thought the blessed thing was safely on its way back to New Jersey (I've mislaid his address now) but it would seem that my wife misunderstood my directions about my daily mail which is not a small one, and addressed the parcel to Michigan. For Heaven's sake send it back swiftly as per enclosed stamps. A she-bear robbed of her whelps is amiability itself beside a man whose pet notebook has gone astray. He'll be accusing me of wilfully stealing it next – and the Lord knows I never asked him to unload the stuff on me. It is one of the small tribulations of my trade and I suppose it answers, in your big business, to hunting a missing freight car. But I'm truly sorry to have given you this trouble.

Your guess at the Fourth Dimension[2] is nearly correct. There is, you will have observed, in every land a dimension in which no one except a lawful native of the land can move without violent collisions. Our friend in the tale knew his three dimensions perfectly. It was only when he tried to put a thing through in a hurry on hereditary lines that he came to grief. I am preparing a companion sketch to that tale.[3]

It grieves me that at present I have no photoes by me. The last went to Mr. Underwood – do find out whether he got it or not, but as soon as I come across another I'll send you one. I don't know the Kentucky horse as well as I ought to. Up here we need the little chunky Morgan to face our hills and sharp turns and to turn out up to his little belly in a snow drift when he is told. A down country animal may be perfect in summer and useless in winter up among these hills: and only a native beast understands how to flounder out of a six foot drift without cutting himself to pieces. How do your Kentuckians manage the snow?

The notion of a trip west in a private car is peculiarly fascinating – I've crossed that part of the world once as a loafer; once as a man [who] could just pay his way and once in a state-room with regular meals – the private car experience is the next step and I only hope that when the invitation comes I shall find my business will let me go.

Thanks for your kind words about this present dam-foolishness. It makes me plain sick at my stomach to hear the light hearted way the idiots about here explain that war is about as stimulating and amusing as a Turkish bath and ought to be taken for much the same reason. When one tries to explain it a bit (I have seen one or two ugly sights) they grin and say: – "Oh that's because you're afraid." Now it's just that kind of talk that lugs a nation bodily to the Devil. When the kids at the district school are filled with the same spirit, it only leads to a hair and nose pulling in the dirt. It's different with men. However, let's hope for the best.

Very sincerely yours
Rudyard Kipling.

Notes
1. Finney (1832–1916) had been President of the Soo Line, of which Underwood (see 23 November 1895) was General Manager. From 1893 to 1902 Finney was Superintendent of Construction on the Missouri, Kansas and Texas Railroad, and President of the line, 1904–6.
2. "An Error in the Fourth Dimension" (*The Day's Work*).
3. Perhaps "An Habitation Enforced", though that was not published until 1905.

To Frederick Norton Finney, 3 February 1896
ALS: Dalhousie University

Naulakha, / Waite, / Vermont. / Feb. 3. 96.

Dear Mr. Finney –

The "lone wandering but not lost" primitive man returned from Wisconsin today. Many thanks for him. As I have mislaid his author's address I shall have to sit still till a furious letter comes in and gives it to me – in each sense of the word. It's all very well for *you* to laugh:

you wouldn't if you were the butt of every misguided crank who ever slung ink between here and Los Angeles.

And I've had quite enough on my hands too. A small girl-baby was born to us yesterday[1] – both doing very well indeed – and now I feel so relieved that if that New Jersey primitive man would only give me an excuse for having a row with him I'd write him a letter on the impropriety of sending M.S.S. around that would astonish his poetic mind. Mr. Underwood got the photo all right for he sent me a note the other day: They were rather ornery doggerel I wrote on the back of the thing:[2] but he must remember that was the first time I ever had to acknowledge twins on the spur of the moment. Seems like as if I ought to christen the small kid upstairs Minnie Apaulina as a sort of return compliment?

This house seems overful of women. I don't know whether you have experienced the delights of the "Gander-month" as they call it in England, when the monthly nurse reigns supreme and a mere male man is allowed to exist in odd corners as he can. I gave the team twenty five miles yesterday on various errands and they are a bit leg-weary so I haven't even the consolation of going for a drive. Don't bother to answer this, which after all merely acknowledges that thrice-damned Primitive Man book.

Very sincerely yours
Rudyard Kipling.

Notes
1. Elsie Kipling (1896–1976), afterwards Mrs George Bambridge.
2. "The Michigan Twins": see letter to Underwood, 23 November 1895.

To William Hallett Phillips, 18 February 1896
ALS: Cornell University

Naulakha / Brattleboro' / Vermont. / 18: 2: 96

Dear Sitting Fox:

I am in need and want and to whom shall I go except you. It's a serious matter. Please can you lay your hand on a full set of charts or chart of the *Newfoundland fishing banks* together with any monograph on the cod-fisheries on the Grand banks as practised by the *American* fleet.[1] If you can, *and soon*, I shall be everlastingly your debtor. Rockhill[2] might know about it but I need it *urgently*.

Thine ever

Rudyard Kipling

Notes
1. RK had just begun work on *"Captains Courageous"*. The charts arrived on the 22nd: see the next letter.
2. William Woodville Rockhill (1854–1914), then Assistant Secretary of State; a noted Orientalist, he was later US Ambassador to Russia and to Turkey.

To William Hallett Phillips, 21–3 February [1896]
ALS: Cornell University

Naulakha, / Waite, / Vermont.

Feb. 21.

This is bad news indeed my brother. It grieves me to think of the Wise Sitting Fox wiping his nose with his brush at the door of his lair. I would I were with him to boil fire-water with lemons and make him sing. *Don't* I know what grip is? I had it in its youthful vigour, in London, '89 – six weeks alone in chambers: too weak to commit suicide and so angry I couldn't compass my ends that it cured me. Grip is a mixture of Bright's disease; a fall down five flights of stairs; the after effects of a prolonged debauch; and incipient typhoid fever. I feel for you with every muscle in my body. Now you *must* take care of yourself. Don't kite about to oyster suppers and such follies. Treat Washington's divine but treacherous spring with respect and wrap up. My note about the cod-fisheries crossed yours. If I'd known you were sick I wouldn't have bothered you. I'll dig 'em up in Boston. Congratulate Rockhill and tell him not to start a new war just now. My constitution can't stand more than one per six months and I've had my whack for a year in that line.

Feb. 23.

What a splendid brick you are! I was writing along yesterday morn, thinking of nothing at all, when they brought in a roll five feet long from the Post Office. Looked like a gun almost but it was a chart of the Grand Banks and I shouted with joy. Then came your note calmly announcing that you'd dug tons of state documents out of the Government, and I rejoiced afresh. *How* do you manage it Sitting Fox? Do you sing 'em songs or make 'em drunk or just hit 'em with a club? In a little while you'll see why I want the books and charts. In the meantime I send you a mean jungle book. Would you care for a full set of my works. There isn't a *uniform* one but I can make it very nearly so:

and the Lord knows I'd be proud and happy to send it along.

As to Washington it's very tempting but too far as things are now. One can't lug small babies up and down the land. We are splitting the difference and going to Lakewood[1] – a hell of a place I believe – for a month. Won't you be able to come up and look in on us there. It isn't far from Washington.

The ["Shangs"][2] haven't arrived yet but I am waiting with cocked ears. Blessings on you and yours.

> Ever sincerely
> Rudyard Kipling.

Give our love to Adams.[3] What does he purpose to do this summer?

Notes
1. They were at Lakewood, New Jersey, from 18 March to 8 April, staying at the Laurel House (CK diary).
2. Word illegible: "Shangs"? "Thargs"?
3. Henry Adams.

To Frederick Norton Finney, 2 March 1896
ALS: Dalhousie University

Naulakha, / Waite, / Vermont. / Mar. 2. 96

Dear Mr. Finney:

May I ask help from your office to enable me to clear up (on paper) the following situation which I am now dealing with in a story.

A millionaire (owner of two or three lines of railroads: lumber and shipping on the Pacific coast etc.) is at San Diego with his wife who has broken down in health because her son fell overboard from a liner while going to Europe. He receives a telegram from Gloucester Mass. saying that the boy was picked up at sea by a sailing ship and is now penniless at Gloucester. The millionaire with his wife then hitches up his private car and proceeds to whirl across the continent. What $\begin{cases} \text{routes} \\ \text{lines} \end{cases}$ would he use? What would be about the shortest time in which the distance would be covered? Which are the best types of racing locos? Would he gain by using a private car instead of the regularly ordained trains? How many engineers, approximately, would be called out for his special? And what particular type of frame and bogie are used under luxurious private cars? I assume the eastern end of his run would be Buffalo –

Albany – Hoosic – Fitchburg – Union Depot Boston. What I should like would be the western and central route. Time of year mid-August. Could you (it's taking your time I know) put yourself in that position and outline exactly what you, as a railroad man, would do?[1]

All goes well here and the new babe prospers.

With all sorts of apologies for bothering you and best regards to yourself and your wife from us both

Yours very sincerely
Rudyard Kipling

P.S.   If you have any special theory by which a private car could be shifted West to East, in record time, please let me hear it. I want the man's trip to be a "scorcher."

RK

Note
1. RK worked up the answers to these questions in ch. 9 of *"Captains Courageous"*.

To Moberly Bell, 3 March 1896

Text: Copy, Library of Congress

Naulakha, / Waite, / Vermont. / Mar. 3. 96

Dear Bell –

Thank you for your compliments. I had a notion five minutes after I had post[ed] the "Hymn"[1] that it would not be opposite till it was "damned opposite":[2] and I entirely agree it would be better for you to keep it up your sleeve till the time comes.[3]

The measured sanity and decency of the *Times* is a daily joy to me as I read it side by side with the hysterical underbred yacop[4] sheets here.

It is none of my business to estimate the chances of war. If things hold off till I can get over the water as I propose doing this summer, I shall be a blooming volunteer private again and then I can open my mouth and make other chaps join. For as the poet says: –

> 'Mid threat of war by land and sea
> Our duty plain appears –
> He must tell the truth under Schedule D
> And join the volunteers.

This year's naval estimates are a little cheering but – Lord! Lord! what a commentary on civilization! If I send you things in verse later on, it is always with the understanding you can hold them till the hour is fitting.

Very sincerely yours,
Rudyard Kipling

Some day I want that Hymn added to Hymns Ancient and Modern[5] for official use. Who had I better tackle – a bishop or a priest? They must have an editor of sorts.

Notes
1. "Hymn Before Action": RK's response to the furor created by the Venezuelan question and the Jameson raid. He sent the poem to *The Times* on 10 February (CK diary).
2. Thus in copy: "apposite"?
3. The poem did not appear in *The Times*. Part of it was published in *The* [New York] *Echo*, March 1896; it first appears complete in *The Seven Seas*.
4. Thus in copy: Perhaps RK wrote *yahoo*?
5. A collection first published in 1861.

To Harry Perry Robinson,[1] 7 March 1896
ALS: Miss Matilda Tyler

[Naulakha]

Dear Robinson –

I don't think you display much respect for my kids.[2] If you had to take 'em why didn't you wait till summer instead of showing them up to their poor little bare knees in snow. They look all froze up.

Yes, it occurred to me that Kay was ordained of God to tell the Century all about Indian forestry.[3] (He hasn't written me yet) but I am morally sure he won't do a line. He's a lazy chap and will delight them before he has done.

As to McClure he is running Mr Rudyard Kipling into the ground. He speaks to me of *two* articles[4] so I expect he is using both.

Ever yours sincerely
Rudyard Kipling

Where is your "pome"?
7. Mar. 96

Notes
1. Robinson (1859–1930), afterwards Sir Harry, was the younger brother of E. K. Robinson; he worked as a journalist and editor in the United States, 1883–1900. From 1887 to 1900

he was owner and editor of *The Railway Age*. Returning to England, he was a director of the publishing firm of Isbister and Co., 1901–4, and then joined the staff of *The Times*.
2. The towns named Rudyard and Kipling (see to Underwood, 23 November 1895). *The Railway Age*, 7 March 1896, p. 125, printed RK's verses on "The Michigan Twins", accompanied by four photographs of Rudyard and Kipling, Michigan. According to an editorial note, RK wrote in a letter to the editor of *The Railway Age* (that is, Robinson) that the towns as photographed looked "smallish and coldish at present" but he hoped that they would grow to be "good and lusty cities".
3. Forestry was a favourite subject of the *Century*: see 11 November 1894.
4. Kay Robinson's "Kipling in India" appeared in *McClure's* in July 1896, and W. D. Howell's "The Laureate of the Larger England" in March 1897. Meantime, *McClure's* was publishing "*Captains Courageous*" between November 1896–March 1897. *McClure's* appears to have published more of Kipling than any other magazine in England or America.

To Unidentified Recipient, 11 March 1896
ALS: Harvard University

Naulakha. / Waite / Windham Co. / Vt. / Mar. 11. 96

Dear Madam –

I am in receipt of your letter of the 9th instant. The question that you open is one that has puzzled the wisest heads in the world: and the answer, I fear, will never be found till the Judgment Day. The administration of 280,000,000 people cannot be settled off hand. All that the wisest can do is to give them good roads; justice and safety of life and property. Six months in India would show you how far this end has been obtained but not a library of books could give you any idea of the magnitude of the task. Naturally I believe there has been no civilizing experiment in the world's history, at all comparable to British rule in India. Thousands upon thousands of our best men have been used up in the toil and naturally many of them have held conflicting theories. It is out of the clash and compromise of warring opinions that the present system has been evolved. India has today a system of University education, post-offices; and law courts which I believe would compare favourably with those of this country; while in the matter of safety to life and property I think the comparison would be even more startling. I dare hardly recommend any book as a wholly trustworthy standard but I have no doubt you would derive much profit from Sir William Wilson Hunter's *Annals of Rural Bengal* and his last study *The Old*

Missionary.[1] Messrs MacMillan 66 Fifth Ave. should be able to procure you these.

I am, dear Madam

Very sincerely yours
Rudyard Kipling

You must remember that my little books only deal with a small section of a small province of only twenty five million people; and a province that has been barely fifty years under our control.

Note
1. *Annals of Rural Bengal*, 3 vols (1868–72); *The Old Missionary* (1890).

To Mrs Oliver Hoblitzel,[1] 12 March 1896
ALS: Maryland Historical Society

Naulakha, / Waite, / Vermont. / Mar: 12: 96.

Dear Madam,

I am in receipt of your letter of the 9th instant.

The tales to which you refer were written mainly because it amused and interested me to make them up: they were not manufactured with any special eye to children: and until I find myself as much interested in a new series as I was in the First and Second Jungle books, it is not likely that I shall turn out any more of that brand of tale. Mowgli's adventures, as I have said, are altogether come to an end.

In the matter of writing for children, my own belief is that stories deliberately designed to interest young folk are very often apt to fall flat: whereas tales told "for fun" as the children say, on the same principle that children make up tales for themselves, reach children and grown people alike.

I am dear Madam

Very sincerely yours
Rudyard Kipling

Note
1. Identified only from the envelope of the letter: she lived at 111 E. Lafayette Avenue, Baltimore.

To Robert Barr, 2 May 1896
ALS: University of Sussex

Naulakha, / Waite, / Vermont. / May: 2. 96.

Dear Barr:

Yourn of April: 22nd just in with all the compliments sticking out all over it and the blue-devil picture of the house enclosed. It's very pretty and I like your conservatory and your bays are fine and your chimneys ought to draw but . . . . you can't sit on your own piazza and cock your legs up on the railing and listen to the frogs hollerin' on a hot night. Piazzas don't grow in my native land which well I knows it.

You're dead wrong about my "sustained fiction." There ain't two cents' worth of plot in the blessed novel – it's all business – cod-fishing on the banks; and no love at all. 'Wish I hadn't told you now in such enthusiastic terms but I was bung full of it when I wrote. It's in the nature of a sketch for better work: and I've crept out of possible holes by labelling it a boy's story.

We've been down to Lakewood this spring where I met Pulitzer[1] of the *World* (rummy company but deuced interesting) and learned to bicycle and to despise New Jersey. Then in New York for three weeks[2] where I met Elihu Vedder[3] whom I much wanted to see and a whole raft of other folk. But I can't stand New York at any price and so we are all back here fixing up things for the spring. It's divine weather and we look forward to a peaceful summer and then, all being well, England. I don't want another Vermont winter just yet. As to the Ludgate hill article keep your hair on. Very probably I did tell the tale: very probably I didn't: but if it's a good tale I'll say I did and if it isn't I'll swear I didn't. Whatever it is I hope it's of a useful nature because, for all you've said, I have never "boosted" you up to date that I can remember. You riz on your own saleratus as you ought to have done about twenty years ago.

I'm supposed to be revising a book of verses but I'm chiefly playing in the garden and racing round with the daughter. The other daughter weighs about 17 lbs. and is a quiet judgmatic kid of a healthy build and an unbounded appetite. Please give my love to Alden[4] if you come across him and with best regards to Mrs Barr and yourself from both of us

Ever yours sincerely
Rudyard Kipling.

P.S.   There's a small boom in real estate up our way all on account of the P.O. I got out of Grover. Thus does England benefit even her enemies.

RK

Notes
1. Joseph Pulitzer (1847–1911), one of the founders of American sensational journalism; from 1883 he was publisher of the New York *World*. RK's meeting with Pulitzer is perhaps the reason why the verses about bicycling that he was then writing, "How Breitmann Became President on the Bicycle Ticket" (uncollected), appeared in the *World*, 26 April 1896.
2. They were in New York from 8 to 28 April (CK diary).
3. Vedder (1836–1923), American painter.
4. William Livingston Alden (1837–1908), American journalist and writer of fiction. He had been Consul General in Rome, 1885–9, and from 1892 until the year of his death he lived in London, where he was a regular contributor to the magazines.

To Cyril F. Herford,[1] 9 May 1896
ALS: Huntington Library

Naulakha, / Waite, / Vermont. / May: 9: 1896:

Dear Herford:

In the language of the lower Fourth at the old Coll "Do not be a dam' fool" – even tho' you are married and conduct a real estate business in the South. Your suggestion that I might have become too "great" to acknowledge an O.U.S.C.'s letter deserves to be treated by a dormitory courtmartial if such a thing were possible these days. I can at this moment recall your long nose and our battles: and curiously enough was thinking of you only the other day. When I read your letter-envelope it occured to me somehow that I had seen something like that fist on an exercise in the far away past. You have *not* improved in your handwriting. No more for that matter have I.

I was in England last year and went to the old coll to the last prize-giving under Price.[2] They've put in a fat and godly Parson man[3] and Price is cramming chaps for the army somewhere near Westbourne Grove. I made a speech and went over the old place with a lump in my throat. Met Savile[4] and Heastey ma.[5] at the cricket match there and generally had a splendid time. The judgment of God has befallen W.C. Crofts. *He's* assistant in a crammer's shop and the men make fun of him when he gets tight. Rather a downfall from the old days? I met little Saulez[6] running a real estate business in St Paul two or three years ago but most of the chaps are in India: I've met Dunsterville, Rimington, Young ma and mi (he died), Grant, Boileau and a lot of others. Berney ma: Berney mi. Stockwell: Armstrong: St John: Stratton and both [name illegible].[7] At one big camp at Rawal Pindi there were 17 of us O.U.S.C.s in 1885 and we met and drank some drinks.[8] Did you notice how Edwardes (Tuppeny) and Townsend III[9] (Poodle-dog) came out in that hill expedition in India the other day – a D.S.O. for Tuppeny and a brevet-majority for Poodle?[10] There are times when I could wish I had gone up for Sandhurst – and got it. But, more's the pity, I am fat and prosperous and a little bald but I still wear my giglamps and fear I am not much tidier than in the old days when "Belly"[11] used to make a butt of me. It pleases me to know that you are making a good thing of your business and here's wishing you luck in politics in England. Of course as an O.U.S.C. you'll be a conservative.

As things stand this summer it's impossible that I should get away to Tennessee but there's no reason why you and Mrs. Herford in New York shouldn't slip up here. Take the 12. noon Boston express from the 42nd Street Depot to Springfield: and you catch the 3.15 p.m. train which lands you with us at 5.45. Only write and let us know when you're coming, as we're four miles from a telegraph office. We've no fishing here worse luck but I'd like you to see what sort of diggings I've made for myself up among these Vermont hills. You can break yourself in three pieces on a bicycle if you like. I go about on the wheel in an old and greasy Campbell's house cap which I bought from the sergeant at the Coll last year. By the way it would break your heart to see the gaps and changes at Westward Ho! Little Evans[12] (do you remember "Bosser" as we called him) was the only one of the old lot and he had what used to be Campbell's house but he told me he was going away soon. That reminds me how when I was in New Zealand three years ago I met old Haslam[13] in charge of a University at Dunedin and he had clean forgotten how he used to lick us over Greek Testament on Monday mornings. But you *must* come up and we'll talk things all over and you shall give me all the news of our brotherhood by land and sea.

With every good wish for your luck prosperity and happiness

Yours ever

Rudyard Kipling

no. 264.

O.U.S.C.

Notes

1. Herford (1865–?) entered USC in the same term as RK, was given the school number of 265, just after RK's, and was assigned to the same house. He was in the school for the whole period of RK's residence. He emigrated to the US, and settled in south-eastern Tennessee.
2. In 1894, not "last year".
3. The Revd Percy Charles Harris (1859–1937) was head in succession to Price, 1894–9.
4. Name not legible; possibly Reginald Vernon Savile (1865–?); at USC 1877–81.
5. George Lewis Heastey (1863–1936); at USC 1876–82.
6. H. L. Saulez (1865–?); at USC 1881–2 in Pugh's house with RK.
7. All but four of these names have already been identified. The four are: Ian Hope

Grant (1866–1925), afterwards major in the Indian Army, at USC 1877–84 in Pugh's house; Richard William Berney (1867–?), at USC 1881–6; Captain Arthur St John (1862–?), at USC 1876–9; Major-General Joseph Cameron Rimington (1864–1942), RK's study-mate at USC, identified with Pussy Abanazar in "Slaves of the Lamp".

8. This was in March and April 1885, when Lord Dufferin as Viceroy met the Amir of Afghanistan in Durbar; it was RK's first important assignment as a reporter: see Pinney, *Kipling's India*, pp. 77–104.
9. No appropriate Townsend appears in the USC *Register*.
10. The affair was the siege and relief of Chitral.
11. The chaplain, E. J. Campbell: see 18–27 February 1886.
12. Herbert Arthur Evans (1846–1923) taught mathematics at USC; he is identified with Little Hartopp in *Stalky & Co*.
13. Francis William Chapman Haslam (1848–1924), classics master at USC, 1874–9; he went to New Zealand as Professor of Classics at Canterbury College where RK met him in 1891.

To Rudolph Block,[1] 16 May 1896
ALS: Cornell University

Naulakha, / Waite, / Vermont. / May. 16. 96

Dear Mr. Block:

Many thanks for your kind note. No – I don't remember anything about St. Louis as a political diversion.[2] One of these days if all goes well I purpose to attend a convention – for my own ends – but at present I don't know enough of politics in this land to make the inner meaning of things clear to me. I couldn't do the Journal any service and should only waste a heap of good material, that I might be able to handle to good advantage later. As to the "nightmare" it is behind me;[3] and I find myself slowly recovering. Do you know "apo-morphine?"[4] It's a drug, a subcutaneous injection of which makes you heave up your immortal soul. I feel as though about a gallon and a half has been injected into *my* soul but that too will pass away.

Thanks for your offer in other matters. I purpose to avail myself of it at once. What I urgently need at present is clippings of all the wild deep-sea yarns that the astute skipper tells the young marine reporter – such as running down whales, derelicts at sea, frozen compasses: and the like. I want picked and startling ones. So if you ever come across good samples would it be asking too much of you to send them along from time to time? This would really be a help to me.

Very sincerely yours
Rudyard Kipling

Notes

1. Block (1870–1940), editor and author, was on the staff of the New York *Journal,* just acquired by William Randolph Hearst.
2. The Republican National Convention was held at St Louis beginning on 18 July and nominated McKinley.
3. RK's fateful quarrel with his brother-in-law Beatty had occurred on 6 May, Beatty threatening to kill RK and RK having Beatty arrested (see Carrington, *Kipling,* pp. 232–9). The hearing on 12 May, heavily publicised and a humiliation to RK, left him, according to CK's diary, "a total wreck. Sleeps all the time. Dull, listless and weary."
4. A powerful emetic derived from morphine.

To Frederick Holbrook,[1] 18 May 1896

Text: Copy, Marlboro College

Naulakha, / Waite, / Vermont / May, 18, 1896

Dear Governor Holbrook,

I am just in receipt of your very kind letter: and if anything could make amends for such an atrocious affair as last Tuesday's[2] it would be such an expression of sympathy and friendship as you have written. – Am going away tomorrow for a little trip[3] and hope when I come back to feel less sore about the matter. In the meantime please accept my and Mrs. Kipling's best thanks and good wishes for you and yours and believe me

Very Sincerely yours
Rudyard Kipling

Notes

1. Holbrook (1813–1909), of Brattleboro, a farmer, banker, and writer for the agricultural press, had been Governor of Vermont, 1861–3.
2. Tuesday, 12 May, when the hearing in Brattleboro before a justice of the peace on RK's charge of assault against Beatty Balestier was held. The hearing was food for the newspapers for the rest of the week.
3. Conland took RK to Gloucester and Boston on the 19th; they returned on the 23rd, when RK was "much better" (CK diary).

To Elizabeth Stuart Phelps Ward,[1] 19 May 1896
ALS: Morgan Library

Naulakha, / Waite, / Vermont. / May: 19: 96.

Dear Mrs Ward –

Very many thanks for your kind note of the 16th: instant. But indeed, as you will see, my little tale is not of sufficient account to give you or your husband one moment's concern.[2] It is really a boy's story of some 50,000 words, and deals almost exclusively with life on the Grand Banks. The son of a western millionaire going to Europe with his mother, badly spoiled, falls overboard from a liner and is picked up by a dory of a Gloucester schooner. He is carried to the boat and his statements about his father's wealth and his own pocket-money are set down to the ravings of insanity. The schooner can't leave the banks in May, and so he is set to work as a second boy and goes through all the Bank experiences from trawling to witnessing a collision, and the gathering of the fleet round the Virgin. The three months experience makes a man of him or rather – he is only 15 years old – teaches him how to appreciate his father. He is landed at Gloucester, wires his father who comes across the continent in a private car and finds not only is his son returned to him but that he "has gotten a man from the Lord."[3] The tale ends with the memorial service to the drowned fishermen that they hold at Gloucester. As you will see there is no plot; no love making and no social problem. The boy works out his own salvation and learns discipline and duty. Gloucester is only the back-ground and I have never gone outside the purely fisherman's view of it. That is all my tale: I wrote it some months ago but I do not think there is any likelihood that the magazine which has bought it will publish before next year; so you see there will be ample time for your husband to get his tale or tales in first. I, as an outsider, am bound to make all sorts of slips and blunders – the scope of my story is very limited at the best – and it seems to me that your husband will have nothing whatever to change *his* course for. Let him go straight ahead and please tell him not to worry. Indeed it ought to be to his advantage because his special knowledge will enable him to steer clear of my errors and if the books parallel each other at all, why it is obviously the bounden duty of the impartial reader to buy both, and decide for himself. The title of my tale is "Captains Courageous" a Story of the Grand Banks: but it is possible that I may alter it. If there is any other point on which you or he need information I shall be most happy to send it. I would give a good deal if this fouling of hawses had not occurred; for over and above my great respect and admiration for you as a writer, no one realizes more keenly than myself the sickening sense of annoyance (and wrath) that rises even in the most philosophical bosom when it finds that another man has been poaching in private pastures. But the great thing is to prevent your husband from worrying. Tell him, once more, to go straight ahead and never mind the next man who in this case happens to [be] me, but truly he didn't mean to,

Yours very sincerely and a little penitently
Rudyard Kipling

If he'd care to look at the tale before hand it shall be at his service.

Notes
1. Mrs Ward (1844–1911), novelist and story writer, was best known for her theological fantasy, *The Gates Ajar* (1868).
2. Herbert Dickinson Ward (1861–1932), miscellaneous writer. The Wards had a summer home at Gloucester and had no doubt got wind of RK's researches for "*Captains Courageous*". Mrs Ward had earlier published some stories and a novel with Gloucester settings, but I do not find anything by her husband of that sort.
3. Genesis 4:1.

To Charles Eliot Norton, 24 May 1896
ALS: Harvard University

Naulakha, / Waite, / Vermont. / May. 24. 96:

Dear Mr. Norton:
    The reason that I haven't been to Shady Hill this journey was because I haven't been altogether well and have been playing about among the Boston tugs and the Gloucester fishing-craft with Dr. Conland who has been chaperoning me along those paths. It wasn't anything in any way serious only C. would have it that I needed a Doctor's overhaul and certificate and I have just got both and they are both satisfactory. I hope to be able to come down ere long on a visit if you will have me, as well as ever I was in my life, and in the meantime I am

Always yours affectionately
Ruddy.

To William Dean Howells, 4 June 1896
ALS: Harvard University

Naulakha. / Waite / Windham Co. / June. 4. 96.

Dear Mr Howells,

We are both of us sorry and disappointed that you can't come and more sorry that Mrs Howells is below herself. (Yes, I *do* understand). However one of these glorious summer days I despair not that we shall get you up here, for I don't think quite of quitting the land permanently.[1] It is hard to go from where one has raised one's kids and builded a wall and digged a well and planted a tree.

As regards the other matter I do remember that once in your official capacity you said something about a book by Mr Kipling which was salutary and chastening to that young man.[2] But as Boswell once remarked to Dr Johnson in the stately phrase of the eighteenth century: – "It would need a hell of a lot that I took unkindly from *you*, Sir" and I am cheered to think you like some of my yarns.

Affectionately always
Rudyard Kipling.

Notes
1. It is not clear when RK decided to leave Vermont or when he decided that the move should be permanent. The decision probably came about gradually, helped by many circumstances. See, e.g., 30 December 1895.
2. See [September? 1890].

To Butler Wood,[1] 10 June 1896
ALS: Dalhousie University

Naulakha. / Waite. / Vermont. / June 10. 96

Dear Sir –

I am in receipt of your very courteous note of the 29th May, in regard to Learoyd and Greenhow Hill.

If you were not yourself a Yorkshireman it is possible that I might use vigorous language when you suggest that I "may have Yorkshire blood in my veins." I have – a little. I am the grandson of Joseph Kipling, Wesleyan Methodist minister to Pately Brigg in 1857, and son of John Lockwood Kipling born in Skipton in Craven.[2] We used to be small Nidderdale yeomen and I believe that in a humble way few stocks carry back cleaner Yorkshire blood for a longer time. I think we are West Riding for a matter of two hundred year; a thing of which I am not a little proud. Yes, you may say fairly that I have good claim to be called a Yorkshireman, and as a fellow tyke I thank you once more for your kind expression of interest. If I could write dialect like "Ab o' th' Yate"[3]

I might try to tackle the Moorfolk and some day I think I shall come up north and see.

Yours very sincerely
Rudyard Kipling.

Notes
1. Wood (1854–1934), Librarian of the Bradford Public Library, was afterwards Librarian and Director of the Bradford City Art Gallery and Bolling Hall Museum.
2. JLK was in fact born at Pickering, Yorkshire.
3. Pen-name of Benjamin Brierley (1825–96), Lancashire dialect writer.

To William Alexander Fraser,[1] 2 July 1896
ALS: Dalhousie University

Naulakha, / Waite, / Vermont. / July. 2. 96

Dear Mr. Fraser,

Yours of June 16th waiting my return from a trip to Gaspé. Have you ever been to Gaspé?[2] It's a great land and I caught a 15lb salmon – my first on the fly; and have grown three inches in my boots since. The P[all].M[all].G[azette]. taking your tales is distinctly good business. Let's hope it will develop – I don't hanker after the "Strand" as a magazine. It's too snippety but it ought to be a service to begin with.

Once more let me advise you *not* to bother about the kind or quality of work any one else turns out – me or Quiller Couch[3] or any one. Your business is to proceed serenely along your own lines of develop. Say what you have to say – tell your own lie in your own way and all will be well: but if you bother about the shop next door it will only spoil your gait.

As to the Governor of the N[orth].W[est].T[erritory]. the case is thus. In this land one has either to run one's own business or be bossed by any son of Belial who has hired a printing press and got trusted for a fount of type. I prefer to run my own life and do not care for beats on ten dollars a week calling themselves brother-journalists and investigating my back yard and under clothing on the strength of it. I've stalled them off for four years; and now the dear boys are beginning to understand my attitude. It's only human nature that they should exaggerate it and as one irate person put it "make it d—d hot for me."[4] When your time comes to be similarly entreated you must take care to own yourself and your time. But if the Governor of the N.W.T. comes along that of course is entirely different and I should pursue the course

of the Governor of North Carolina.[5]
 I'll look out for your yarns in the P.M.G. With all wish for good luck

Yours always sincerely
Rudyard Kipling.

Notes
1. Fraser (1859–1933), Canadian journalist, novelist, and story writer, had prospected for oil in India and spent six years prospecting in the Canadian North-West. His fiction included stories about life in India, and he was sometimes called the "Canadian Kipling". His correspondence with RK began in this year.
2. RK had been there on a fishing expedition with Lockwood de Forest, 15 June–1 July.
3. (Sir) Arthur Quiller-Couch (1863–1944), novelist and editor, King Edward VII Professor of English Literature, Cambridge, 1912–44.
4. RK means the press treatment of his quarrel with his brother-in-law Beatty Balestier (see 18 May 1896).
5. "What did the Governor of North Carolina say to the Governor of South Carolina?" "Excellent notion. It *is* a long time between drinks" (*The Light That Failed*, ch. 8).

To Ripley Hitchcock, 29 July 1896
ALS: Berg Collection, New York Public Library

Naulakha, / Waite, / Vermont. / July. 29. 96.

Dear Hitchcock –
 At last the d—d thing is off my hands.[1] I send herewith p.p. 95–125 for revised page proofs: and also the balance of the book. *The Mary Gloster* has cost me much sweat and pains. It is to follow "An American" and will be followed by the "Sestina of the tramp royal." Then the new lot of Barrack room ballads come on: with a blank page or two and the introduction "When 'Omer smote 'is bloomin' lyre" to separate them from the poems. The L'Envoi concludes the book. I've done my level best with the thing: and that's about all a man can do. Now I suppose just as soon as the book is in type I shall be overtaken with a regular flux of verse. It's generally that way with me.

[signature cut away]

Note
1. *The Seven Seas*, published at the end of October 1896. It was the first publication of "The Mary Gloster".

To Frank N. Doubleday, 19 August 1896
ALS: Princeton University

[Naulakha] August 19th. 96

Dear Mr Doubleday –

Hurrah! I'm a desperately busy man these days, with getting out me book of verses and finishing a story in prose[1] but if you tell me *when* you intend getting out the "luxurious Kipling" I'll get to work.[2] I don't feel moved to write introductions however. Let the tales go on their own merits if they have any.

We are leaving for the other side on the Lahn,[3] 1st September, stateroom 193–197. Couldn't you send me a packet of reading matter for the voyage. Mixed novels if you have any old ones about and Mrs Burnett's last book.[4] I hope your child didn't have any trouble in this last heat wave. It must have been awful in New York!

Very sincerely
Rudyard Kipling.

Notes
1. *"Captains Courageous"*.
2. The Outward Bound Edition.
3. The SS *Lahn*, a North German Lloyd ship, sailing from Hoboken.
4. Frances Hodgson Burnett, *A Lady of Quality* (1896), published by Scribner's.

To Frank N. Doubleday, 28 August 1896
ALS: Princeton University

Naulakha, / Waite, / Vermont. / Aug. 28. 96

Dear Mr Doubleday,

Yours of the 25th demands vast and laborious consideration: and as I'm just off for the other side I shall take it along with me. But that is no reason why you should not take a MacMillan copy of *Plain Tales*[1] (which should be the first to lead the set) and set up from that. I have vowed a vow not to tinker with my old work any more and as Plain Tales (in many respects quite the worst of any thing I've done) has been before the public nearly ten years I purpose to let it go precisely as it stands in MacMillan. At all events that will give you something to go on with.

As to get-up, I like the Barrie[2] all except the colour and the gold-block thistle leaves at the back. I will, as soon as I get to England, ask my father to design some sort of little conventional totem to take the place of the thistle-leaves – perhaps a lotus or my old trademark the elephant's head with a lotus in the trunk.[3] And when I have got that settled I can fix upon a good name for the whole edition. At present I am frankly that [*sic*] I cannot think of one. This is the list of books

102[4] – Plain Tales.		1 vol
40 – Departmental Ditties.		1 vol
Soldiers Three.		
110 – The Story of the Gadsbys	}	1 vol
In Black and White		
Wee Willie Winkie		
113 – Under the Deodars	}	1 vol.
The Phantom Rickshaw		
128 – Life's Handicap.		1 vol.
98 – The Light that failed.		1 vol.
119 – Many Inventions.		1 vol.
60 – Ballads and Barrack Room ballads		1 vol.
106 – The Naulakha.		1 vol.
81　The Jungle book		1 vol.
78　The 2nd Jungle book		1 vol
The Seven Seas (verse)		1 vol
	(published this fall)	
Captains Courageous.		1 vol
	(to be published next fall)	

And by the time those are done there will be a new vol. of short-stories making 14 vols all told.[5] Probably you will have to print all the verse in one volume but that is a matter for the printing press. I will write you as to name and decoration from the other side. Meantime you can take Plain Tales and make 'em luxurious. If I can hack out a good set of introductory verses for the edition I'll try to do so.

> Ever yours sincerely
> Rudyard Kipling.

Notes

1. The first English edition (1890).
2. The Thistle Edition of J. M. Barrie then being published by Scribner's in a format closely resembling that chosen for the Outward Bound Edition.
3. The Outward Bound volumes have a gilt lotus on the spine and the elephant head, lotus, and swastika stamped in an ivory medallion on the front cover. The elephant head and lotus (but not the swastika) were used on the covers of the Indian Railway Library volumes.
4. This and the subsequent numbers on the left-hand side are apparently RK's statements of page lengths.

5. The first instalment of the Outward Bound Edition was in eleven volumes, containing all that RK lists here except for *"Captains Courageous"* but with the arrangement of stories considerably altered.

To William James, [31 August 1896]
ALS: Harvard University

Fairholme.[1] / *Morristown, N.J.*

Dear James –

It was just and luminous (but why, in God's name Bagg's Hotel[2] of all places?) and the thing that made it more impressive to me mineself was because I have just finished off a long tale wherein I have deliberately travelled on the lines you suggest – i.e. I have taken the detail of a laborious and dangerous trade (fishing on the Grand Banks) and used it for all the romance in sight. Also, I have thought along those lines – *and* also, I have been four days in Chatauqua seven years ago, when I thought unspeakable things.[3] *Half* your trouble is the curse of America – sheer, hopeless well-ordered boredom; and that is going some day to [be the] curse of the world. The other races are still scuffling for their three meals a day. America's got 'em and now she doesn't know what she wants but is dimly realizing that extension lectures, hardwood floors, natural gas and trolley-cars don't fill the bill. The Chatauquan "civilization" is to my mind precisely on the same plane as the laborious ordered ritual of drum, dance and sacred pollen that the Zuni (with other races) has evolved to fence off his bored soul from the solitude and loneliness of his own environments (I'm not a psychologist but you are and you'll see what I mean). Down below among the men of the trades you get, for proof that there is incident and colour in their lives, the melodramatic form of speech which is always resorted to in moments of stress or passion. We, the *bourgeosie*, became inarticulate or inept. It is a vast and fascinating subject and you'll see later how I purpose to use it. Your wail and "eructation" was delightful to my soul.

We sail tomorrow on the *Lahn* to be some time away. I saw the Nortons at Ashfield the other day. The wife and I send both our best regards to you and Mrs James and much love to Peggy.

Yours ever sincerely
Rudyard Kipling

The tale is called *Captains Courageous* and it comes out in McClure's in November.

Notes
1. The Catlin home, where RK and family went on 29 August before leaving on the SS *Lahn* from Hoboken, 1 September (CK diary).
2. James was on a lecture tour, which included a stop at Chautauqua.
3. See 9 August 1889.

Part Three
Return to England
1896–99

INTRODUCTION

Kipling slipped away from the United States at the end of August 1896 and went directly to a house on the Devonshire coast. We do not know why he chose this spot or when the arrangement was made. He remained there less than a year and left it without regret. The one lasting acquisition he owed to this period was his connection with the Navy; that began when he met the officers of the training ship *Britannia*, stationed not far away at Dartmouth, and soon grew into a continuing interest. He was invited to attend the trials of a torpedo boat destroyer off the mouth of the Thames in 1897; in the summer of that year he was a guest aboard a cruiser on manoeuvres with the Channel Fleet, and he sailed on manoeuvres again in the next summer. The immediate literary result of these new adventures was the series of sketches called *A Fleet in Being*.

From Devonshire Kipling migrated with his family to Rottingdean, on the Sussex coast, where his son John was born in the summer of 1897 and where they settled in a house called The Elms, on Rottingdean Common, across the road from the house of his uncle, Sir Edward Burne-Jones. It was here that most of the stories of *Stalky & Co.* were written, where the *Just So Stories* and *The Five Nations* were written, and where *Kim* was completed.

It was in Kipling's first year at Rottingdean that the Jubilee sentiment overwhelmed the country: Kipling pretended to be aloof from the public stir, though he made sure to attend the great naval review at Spithead, where the Queen saw displayed before her all the naval might of her Empire. He also contributed "Recessional" to the occasion.

Though Kipling was living a full and productive life following his flight from the United States, he had not recovered the high spirits he enjoyed in the euphoric Vermont years before the Beatty Balestier debacle. As his wife wrote at the end of 1897: "he has never been himself since that summer of bitter trial . . . and I sometimes feel sure he never will be" (to Meta de Forest, 5 December 1897: ALS, Harvard). It was partly in the hope of restoration, then, that Kipling took his family to South Africa at the beginning of 1898. He was immediately drawn to the country, partly, at least, because it could substitute for the United States as a place where a "new people" were "growing up" and allow him to participate in the process as poet and prophet. Kipling had already met Cecil Rhodes; he was now to fall under the spell of Rhodes and of the men associated with him, especially Jameson and Milner.

At the beginning of 1899 Kipling had been more than two years away from the United States; now, for no very clear practical purpose but evidently out of a strong wish to see old friends and revisit familiar places, Kipling took his family on a stormy crossing of the North Atlantic at the end of January. The children were all ill by the time they docked; they did not recover quickly in hotel accommodations in wintry New York, and towards the end of February Kipling himself fell ill. Pneumonia developed, and for some days the struggle of Kipling and the doctors against death was the front page material of the American press. Kipling recovered, though with his lungs permanently weakened; his first-born child, Josephine, did not. She died on 6 March, while her father lay in the crisis of his illness. The death of Josephine was also the end of Kipling's American life: he sailed for England in June, and, despite many opportunities and many invitations, would never return to the United States.

To James Conland, 8 September 1896
ALS: Library of Congress

Dampfer "Lahn" / Sept. 8. 96 / 65m. w.s.w. of the Scillies.

Dear Doctor –

It will be a long time ere the wife or I forgive you for slipping away as you did at the depot without saying a last good bye; and if you want to be forgiven you had better come over to England and we'll overlook it.

You were dead-right about the voyage. So far we have not had one whiff of fog! We ran the banks in brilliant sunshine, and passed within half a mile of the living image of the *We're Here*, slatting about under her riding sail and the dories bobbing on the swell round her. It made me think of old times with you. There has been no ice: but we have passed more ships than ever I remember, from the Thengralla line loaded down almost awash to a Nillen tramp last night who rolled so near to us that we thought she wanted to signal and burned rockets. She made no sign however. For the first time in my voyages, I saw a whale jumping clear. The boat is almost empty, and the crowd is a very quiet one.

Both children have stood the trip splendidly and I think the wife is much rested. Josephine has gone round among the men and had the best of good times. I've invented a benedictine cocktail which has opened the eyes of the smoking-room; and I'd give a [peck?] if you were here to taste it. Today we are running into the climate of my native land – a thick greasy sky, wind from the S.W. and a sullen, loppy sea. We ought to pick up the Scillies at noon and get in to S'hampton about midnight – an unwholesome hour for small kids to be awakened. Already I begin to think with sorrow of the fine clear September mornings on the hillside.

Please remember me to Mrs. Conland and Harry[1] (there is a boy aboard something like him, who goes about with a Kodak and his mouth full of crackers) and with our united best regards, believe me dear Conland,

Yours as ever
Rudyard Kipling.

Note
1. Henry H. Conland (1882–1944); he joined the Hartford *Courant* in 1904 and ultimately became the paper's publisher.

To Mrs Humphry Ward,[1] 27 September 1896

ALS: Library of Congress

Rock House, / Maidencombe, / Sep. 27. 96

Dear Mrs Ward,

I am delighted to have Sir George Tressady[2] from your hand. I have followed him from month to month with the liveliest wonder as to how the inevitable smash in his affairs was to fall and now that I have read the tale as a whole I see that of course there was but one way. Like all human books it has the unpleasant power of making you think and bother as one only bothers over real folk: but how splendidly you have done the lighter relief-work! "Fifteen out of a possible twelve"[3] has already been adopted as a household word by us who have two babies.

It will always be one of the darkest mysteries to me that any human being can make a beginning, end *and* middle to a really truly long story. I can think them by scores, but I have not the hand to work out the full frieze.

It is just the difference between the deep-sea steamer with twelve hundred people aboard, beside the poor beggars sweating and scorching in the stoke-hold, and the coastwise boat with a mixed cargo of "notions." And so when the liner sees fit to salute the coaster in passing that small boat is mightily encouraged.

Very sincerely yours
Rudyard Kipling.

Notes
1. Mary Augusta Ward (1851–1920), novelist and social worker.
2. Published in October 1896 after running as a serial in the *Century*, November 1895–October 1896.
3. "A good mother? I should think she is! That's the whole point against her. She always gives you the idea of having reared fifteen out of a possible twelve" (*Sir George Tressady*, ch. 21).

To James Conland, 1–6 October 1896

ALS: Library of Congress

Rock House,[1] / Maidencombe, / St. Marychurch. / October. 1. 96.

It says a great deal for the beauty of your handwriting, dear Doctor, that when your letter came in I didn't know who the deuce it was from. You see, I'd only met that calligraphy in the shape of notes for Captains

Courageous, when neither you nor I could make it out. But I was mighty glad to see it.

Now imagine to yourself, a big stone and stucco Naulakha, long, low with two stories, stuck on the side of a steep hill falling away almost as sharply as the lower slopes of Wantastiquet[2] to a hundred foot cliff of pure red soil. Below that is the sea, about two hundred yards from the window. The effect is a delightful mixture of land and sea views. I look straight from my work table on to the decks of the fishing craft who come in to look after their lobster pots. There isn't another house in sight; there is no harbour or landing place or any thing of the kind. We just sit like swallows on a telegraph wire and look across Torbay over to Portland Bill sixty miles away. Somewhere round the corner, four miles north, lies Teignmouth (which they naturally call Tin-muth) and three miles south the rocky nose that covers Torquay harbour. It is marked by a rocky island called – of all queer names under heaven – Thatcher Island![3] If you keep Thatcher Island two points clear of your port bow on coming out of the harbour you clear, say the sailing directions, all shoals along the west side of Torbay. The said "shoals" take the shape of peculiarly devilish half-tide rocks round which the whiting and pollack congregate. Our beach is a tiny cove reached by an almost perpendicular lane – just the place for smuggling in the old days – and a flight of rude steps. It isn't a wholesome place to look at because the cliffs have a knack of falling in huge boulders and there is no way of getting to the water except by crawling over them. I found out the peculiarity of the place by going down after a heavy gale: when I found that the heavy seas had cleaned out most of the sand between the boulders and utterly changed the lie of the land. No one seems to go there except myself and the fishers: for now and then I find footprints in the sand and the mark of a row boat's keel. Once down in the cove with the cliffs on either side it is as warm as a conservatory and as lonely as Land's End. The queerest thing about the place is its rich redness. The grass and trees come down literally to the water's edge but all the soil is pure red; and the mixture of red, green foliage and blue sea is splendid. I never saw such an unenglish place in my life: though almost our first introduction to it was a good old equinoctial – a sou'westerly buster that would have done credit to Vermont. The glass dropped about an inch and then began pumping up and down. The wind took about a day to get up and when it really took hold, it licked the channel up into lather. A big poplar on our lawn (it was a regular old cotton-wood just the same as if it had followed us) was the first to go. The wind twisted the top out of it. Then our back-gate was sent flying: and then a huge elm came over by the roots and nearly assassinated a hired yellow cow we keep in the meadow. About the beginning of the storm I saw a trawler blown out to sea – just a rag of brown sail in the smother; and once I heard the whistle of a steamer. But though it was clear overhead the scud was thick over the sea: and from a sheltered angle of the kitchen garden we looked down on a bath of lather. Then it rained and then it blew some more and then the glass went crazy. I was invited down to Dartmouth – half an hour down the line – to sleep in the Britannia – the old three decker training school for officers in our Navy. The train crawled round the line and as we passed Brixham I saw the fishing-fleet holding on under the lee of the land with everything down that could bite bottom and a brig loose down channel. I had a great time among the naval cadets in the Britannia while the wind whistled and tore down the Dart – the tiny little river where she is moored. All the instructors are naval officers – and their tales were beautiful. And it blew, and it blew; and it blew! Then a grey smudge shot up the river and moored. That was a torpedo-boat destroyer of 200 tons made to go 26 knots an hour, waiting till the weather cleared. The young chap commanding her had had a [   ]⁴ She just jumped her soul out and went under the water for the most part, and he said it was thick as soup in the channel. Meantime the Britannia's tender – the *Racer* – which goes out every week with a load of cadets for practical seamanship was about ten hours overdue somewhere up-channel. She turned up on Sunday – a steam sloop, barque-rigged and her Lieutenant arrived on the Britannia with the news that he had spent Sunday night in Portland harbour, both anchors down, *and* steaming to keep his place. All the cadets had been deadly sick but, he told me, his great secret was "never to let 'em get their heads down." "Once a boy's head goes under a blanket" said he "he's no good for the rest of the trip. So I kept 'em at it." They were very empty and very wet: and the *Racer* started next day into a good old channel swell with another batch – for the Channel Islands this time. They take out enough boys to man one mast and the boys like it. But I never saw such a gale. The torpedo boats were scuttling into port wherever they could find one. There were wrecks all along the coast and one of our cruisers stuck her nose into a big sea that smashed up a Lieutenant and three or four men. I was to have gone out on one of the destroyers. I'm thankful I didn't. Twenty knots is their easiest gait. You can guess how they bury themselves in every sea. Next week I go down to Plymouth to investigate men of war and see a steam trial – if it's fine. My father comes down today. I have already established friendly relations with the local pub, and a Sergeant Instructor of volunteers, as well as a volunteer Sergeant of Engineers and a R.C. priest. This is a very Roman Catholic part of the world. Devonshire always was. It will be a new world to you when you come over; and I think you will appreciate the beer. *The* local drink is sloe-gin i.e. good gin flavoured with sloe-berries. Rather like cherry-brandy but not sweet or sticky. Josephine after considering things in her little head has pronounced that "This Englandt is stuffy" but the moist climate agrees with her. Elsie eats and sleeps and sleeps and eats [   ] on [   ] I think the [   ] better but [   ] know, she wants to take hold of all the earth and shake it. As we have a conservatory and a gardener and his wife and a garden, and an orchard and about forty five acres of out houses to look after you can guess she has a large field to exercise her talents. [   ] I spend my time doing nothing very hard – chiefly on a wheel. There are times when I'd give a good deal for the keen sniff of an autumn morning up on the hillside, when the first frost has wilted things in the garden and the leaves are dropping of themselves. They tell me our new barn at Naulakha is rather a success. Have you seen it?

Tuesday, Oct. 6th. Raining like the deuce! But I have arranged things down at the quay where, yesterday, I found an able bodied ten-ton boat – a genuine old fishing boat of the model they build over at Brixham – cutter rigged, with small pole instead of top-mast for winter weather, fidded bowsprit running in and out, and a foc'sle about as big as a postage stamp. The Ancient Mariner who owns her is going to take the father and me out on the pollack and whiting grounds, and I foresee we shall have good fun this winter. It's only a three week sail from Torquay to the fishing – and now I'm happy. I want to astonish the natives with "nippers."⁵ Their fore fingers are all gashed and scored with the hand lines. Please mail me a pair of 'em – small size. They'll save me a good deal of discomfort. A few days ago down at the quay (all sorts o' queer craft come there) I stumbled on a thing I couldn't fix in my mind. It looked like this [sketch of two-masted boat] and somehow suggested smuggling. A blue jersey was smoking forward and her hatches were neatly battened down. Seen from above she was curiously narrow and fine in her lines. "What the deuce are you?" says I to the blue jersey. "No understand" says he. "Spik French."

"All right" sez I. "*D'ou venez vous?*"

Then he pattered a French I didn't savvy and I appealed to another aged salt.

Says he: – "That's a ketch – one of the smartest boats along the coast. She's come in with potatoes from Jersey – St Heliers."

"Oh" says I "and is it necessary to have so smart a boat to carry potatoes?"

The old fellow grinned all over. "She carries all sorts o'things sometimes" he said. If ever a boat was marked "smuggler" all over, it was this same little black ketch. I'd never seen the rig before. A light pole-mast aft, a huge main sail, and a top mast big enough for a racing yacht. Also, her bottom was as smooth as glass. You see there is still a duty on spirits, and I suppose she does a little quiet "running" now and then. Well, this scrawl has grown to an unholy length and I'll cut it short. I'm rearranging all my stories for the new Scribner Edition – getting 'em into groups according to their subjects, while my father is busy making pictures for them. The book of verses is all but finished and I've revised the proofs for *Captains Courageous*. Appleton's haven't yet sent me the sheet-edition of the verses and I'm sending them another reminder. All well here – specially baby Elsie who grows fatter and fatter. The wife and I send all kind regards in which the father joins to you and Mrs Conland and Harry, and I am as ever

Sincerely yours
Rudyard Kipling.

Notes
1. RK had rented this house before leaving Vermont, evidently on a year's lease; they moved in on 10 September (CK diary). The house stands a few miles north of Torquay, on Babbacome Bay; it produced in both RK and CK a "deep, deep Despondency" (*Something of Myself*, p. 134) and helped to inspire "The House Surgeon" (*Actions and Restrictions*).
2. The mountain towards which Naulakha looked, south-east across the Connecticut River in New Hampshire; "Our guardian mountain", RK called it (*Something of Myself*, p. 117).
3. Thacher Island, just outside of Gloucester harbor, is where the Cape Ann lighthouse stands. It is mentioned in ch. 8 of "*Captains Courageous*".
4. Passage erased; the other bracketed blanks in the text of this letter indicate the same thing. According to W. M. Carpenter, who bought the letters from Conland's son, the Conland family insisted on making these deletions of matter "purely professional" as a condition of selling the letters (printed note dated 28 March with Conland letters, Library of Congress).
5. "A band or mitten, knitted and stuffed, worn by New England fishermen to protect the hand in hauling fish-lines" (Funk and Wagnalls *Standard Dictionary*, 1895). Mentioned in ch. 3 of "*Captains Courageous*".

To Frank N. Doubleday, 6 October 1896
ALS: Princeton University

Rock House, / Maidencombe, / St. Marychurch. / October 6th. 96

Dear Doubleday –

Today's cable will have told you not to print the Plain Tales till you hear from me. The reason is this: *and it is very important*.

I have finally screwed myself up to re-grouping the whole kit and boodle of the books, i.e. am arranging the military; native; and fantastic tales in batches by themselves. Therefore I want you to take out from *Plain Tales* the four original Mulvaney tales –

The Three Musketeers.

The Taking of Lungtungpen
The Madness of Private Ortheris
The Daughter of the Regiment.

These four will go at the head of "Soldiers Three" which will contain *all* the Mulvaney tales collected and arranged in line; and after them all military tales. Index of these comes to you later.

To take the place of the four Plain Tales removed, I am sending you two of the old original brand which have never yet appeared in book form. The one called *"Bitters Neat"* is to follow *"Miss Youghal's Sais"* in Plain Tales and *"Haunted Subalterns"* will follow *"The Other Man"* in the same book.

I have no further directions in regard to *Plain Tales* except that I shall be sending a short preface explaining how I am grouping the tales – and if I possibly can, (but you needn't wait for them) a set of verses.[1]

With all regards

Yours very sincerely
Rudyard Kipling

P.S. You will readily see how this re-arrangement (which has long been demanded by the public) gives the edition a pull of its own. I want copy of *Bitters Neat* and *Haunted Subalterns* returned as they are the original newspaper cuttings.

Note
1. These changes were made, but RK did not, after all, provide any introductory verses.

To Frank N. Doubleday, 7 October 1896

ALS: Princeton University

Rock House, / Maidencombe, / St. Marychurch. / Oct. 7: '96

Dear Doubleday –

We have now advanced another step on our weary path. The work of putting the stories into groups has not been easy; but you will see from the enclosed indexes that I have managed it. They come – all my short stories – now under three heads – Soldiers Three – In Black and White – and the Phantom rickshaw——military – Asiatic and ghostly or ghastly. The order of their publication will be

(1st) Plain Tales (of course)

2nd Soldiers Three –
3rd In Black and White
4th The Phantom Rickshaw etc.

Fifth
{
  Under the Deodars
  The Story of the Gadsbys
  and
  The three child tales
  Wee Willie Winkie
  His Majesty the King
  Baba Black Sheep
}
one vol.

(Sixth) Jungle Book
(Seventh) 2nd Jungle Book
(Eighth) Light that failed
(Ninth) Naulakha
Tenth Verses. –

As to the Jungle books I have re-arranged them. The first contains all the stories of Mowgli concluding with In the Rukh: in one volume. The second has the scattered stories of beasts, seals, etc. by themselves – The Light and Naulakha are not changed at all but, under the new grouping, *Life's Handicap* and *Many Inventions* are wiped out of existence.

Now I have thought over the question of size and number of vols till I am tired: and have come to the conclusion that I don't know anything about it. Soldiers Three with all the military stories seems to me as if it were going to be a book of 500 pp. at the least. *You* can decide whether you will split it into two vols. Black and White will also be a fattish volume; and so will the Phantom Rickshaw. In setting up you will follow copy of the Macmillan Edition – the blue and gold one.[1]

I am adding as you will see two new pieces – The Enlightenments of Pagett M.P.[2] to Black and White and Mrs Hauksbee sits out[3] to "Under the Deodars." No other edition has these tales in 'em.

I am also writing a set of verses for the Edition as a whole and they ought to be pretty decent. But the less you give out about all these "dazzling attractions" the better for the present. I go into Torquay to be photographed in a low corsage with a bunch of pink rose buds on my bosom tomorrow.[4] No copies of that world-smiting countenance will be made public till your Edition bursts upon mankind.

It is raining and blowing hard and I almost forget what the sun looks like.

Yours ever sincerely
Rudyard Kipling.

I think that edition is going to be rather a neat one.

RK

The elephant-head medallion is to be photoed tomorrow and if you see fit, could be stamped in gold or otherwise on the back of each vol. It occurs inside in the title page of each vol also: but – with the exception of plain tales – each vol will have its own symbolical medallion as well.[5]

Notes
1. This is exactly the scheme of the first instalment of the Outward Bound Edition; *Soldiers Three* required two volumes, so that the total was eleven rather than ten.
2. Originally published in the *Contemporary Review*, September 1890.
3. Originally published in the *Illustrated London News*, Christmas number, 1890.
4. The photograph is the frontispiece to the first volume of the Outward Bound Edition.
5. They do not.

To John Hay, 8 October 1896
ALS: Brown University

Rock House, / Maidencombe, / St. Marychurch. / Oct. 8. 96.

Dear Hay –

Yours of the 26th must have had a devilish passage for we've enjoyed a succession of howling gales for the last week; and as we overhang the channel we see the "works of the Lord on the great deep."[1] Artistically, He is violent and monotonous but His cloud and spray effects are superb. Do you know the suburbs of Torquay at all? The town is smugly British – so that I want to dance naked through it with pink feathers in my stern – but the coast and cliffs and sea are lovely. If *only* we had a little sun! I am not grasping but Vermont has rather unfitted me for a succession of mildewed days with pale blobs of yellow wash on the ground, that they trustfully call sunlight. I am a sorrowful 'possum tell Phillips and my fur is wet and draggled. The father is staying with us, helping to decorate a new edition of Mr Rudyard Kipling's works which Scribner brings out shortly.[2] If there is one thing I hate it is ploughing through that man's stories and arranging them in groups. He is a diffuse writer and if I knew him better I'd edit him with a pair of shears. But the Father and the wife and I cheer ourselves with the hope of going off to Italy in the early spring where we shall probably be caught by vile cold weather.

Henry James made a promise (with the usual Jamesidian reservations) to come down and stay with us awhile. We are on the look out for him. I hear he has been staying with the Daudets[3] and expect his history of that visit will be fine. We haven't been to town yet so have seen nothing and no one; and Morris's death[4] touches us rather nearly for that [our] folks and his'n are so closely allied. I knew he was said to be failing but had no notion the end was so near.

I watch the tumult of elections from afar deeply thankful to be out of it for the present: but the news of the English here are killingly funny. It's no good trying to explain anything however.

Now I must go out, because there is a feeble glimpse of sun, and if I don't take it I mayn't see another till next month. Isn't it odd that a land with string-and-nail political institutions should enjoy a machine-cut, nickelled steel climate while a country with bevel-gear, bessemer fitted policies has the sort of weather that Bryan[5] might make before breakfast with one hand. These things are an allegory. I am writing to Sitting Fox but please send him my love and with all warmest regards (there is nothing else warm within three thousand mile of us; and the fireplaces are but inefficient chamber-pots) to Mrs Hay, your daughter and yourself from us both.

Ever yours sincerely
Rudyard Kipling.

Notes
1. Perhaps a recollection of Psalm 107:24: "These see the works of the Lord, and his wonders in the deep."
2. JLK's illustrations for the Outward Bound Edition appear in eighteen of the first twenty-one volumes. They are clay plaques moulded in relief; the plaques were photographed for reproduction.
3. James had entertained Daudet, the French novelist, in London the year before; he did not stay with the Daudets in France.
4. William Morris died on 3 October.
5. William Jennings Bryan (1860–1925), identified with the cause of free silver, ran unsuccessfully against McKinley as the Democratic candidate in 1896. He ran again unsuccessfully for President in 1900 and 1908. Bryan, a pacifist and a fundamentalist, was the antithesis of RK's friend Theodore Roosevelt, and a figure of burlesque to RK.

To William Hallett Phillips, [12 October 1896][1]
ALS: Ray Collection, Morgan Library

Rock House, / Maidencombe, / St. Marychurch.

Sitting Fox! I have been rained upon many devilish days and devilish nights for this is autumn in England which is also called "Merrie England" and my lodge is in the southern part which they call "The Riviera of England." May the Great Spirit forgive them! I am damp and cold: and my tobacco is like ox-dung newly dropped and I wrap my belly in furs and I swear till I have no more words left. Do not believe the medicine men who tell you that Hell is dry and hot. It is wet and cold and dark and mildew grows on your mocassins when you put them away.

My heart and my tongue were very full of you on the voyage to this country because there was a fat and delightful medicine man called Jones of Washington who was a friend of yours; and indeed I think he was good enough to be your friend. I made him (and some others) a cocktail which made their eyes bulge out and their hair turn blue: and we told more lies in one week than other people think of in all their lives.[2]

Now I was grieved (before I met the medicine-man Jones) because I was afraid you had shut your heart to me. Twice I wrote to you, Sitting Fox, from my own Lodge, and twice you did not answer. And I said to the medicine man Jones "What the deuce is the matter with Phillips?" and Jones said you were busy and had been cutting about the face of the country, on your own businesses. If I had know[n] what you tell me, that you had passed by us without coming in, I would have come back by next steamer to throw dirt at you. Take a steamer in the spring and come over and play with me. I can get fishing and show you beautiful things and take you sailing in a boat and give you flowers to smell and teach you how to dig in a garden and lead you into places that are more uninhabited than most parts of your own land. We sit on a great hill overlooking the sea; and the fishing boats seem to fish under our windows; and the beauty of the land (when the eternal rain dries up) is like no beauty on this earth. If I were dry I would be very happy: but sometimes I think of the autumn mornings when the first frost is in the air, and the grasshoppers are silent and the woodsmoke goes straight up from the chimney; and there is a smell of clean wood and dry grass. *Then* I feel sorry Sitting Fox for I think of my own lodge that I made with my own hands.

I have just finished my book of new verses;[3] and a copy comes to you so soon as it is in type. With that goes the full English set of my books, every one that I have ever done; as a love-gift from me to you. I do not know whether the customs will break them open with an axe; but that is not my concern. Your friend through whose hands it passes shall attend to the matter.

All is well in my lodge (which is a big stone house of the vilest sort of 1860 architecture). The babes eat and sleep and grow fat and the wife and I go about the lanes on bicycles. I don't mean to do any work for awhile but just to loaf and go fishing. Hay sent me a letter the other day on his return from "furrin parts." He seems to have had the best sort of a time. What a splendid chap he is!

I haven't seen any one but baggage-agents and livery stable men since I came over; but we plan going up to London anon to pick up the threads of things. Write me soon and tell me how things go with you; and whether we may expect to see you coming over some fortunate day. With all good wishes and blessings from us both.

Ever yours sincerely
Rudyard Kipling.

Notes
1. Dated from postmark.
2. See RK's verses dated 8 September 1896 beginning "There were five liars bold" (*Kipling Journal*, April 1944, pp. 9–11).
3. *The Seven Seas*. It was published on 30 October 1896.

To Charles Eliot Norton, 30 October 1896
ALS: Harvard University

Rock House / Maidencombe / St Marychurch / Oct 30. 96

Dear Mr Norton:

By reason of the distance I can't send you a Methuen copy of "The Seven Seas" in time: nor can I write what I should wish to on the title page. I have told Appleton to send you a copy which is a cold and sloppy way of doing things but you must know, as I think you do, that it comes to you with my best love and most sincere regard. I wish to goodness I could write poetry.

Mother and Father have been staying with us down here in our stone barrack of a house overlooking the sea. Our weather is and has been – British. "Bloody British" is the only word for it; and I have been studying my fellow countrymen from the outside. Those four years in America will be blessed unto me for all my life. We *are* a rummy breed – and O Lord the ponderous local society. Torquay is such a place as I do desire acutely to upset – by dancing through it with nothing on but my spectacles. Villas, clipped hedges and shaved lawns; fat old ladies with respirators and obese landaus – the Almighty is a discursive and frivolous trifler compared with some of 'em. But the land is undeniably lovely and I am making friends with the farmers.

We were sorry to hear that Sally goes to Cairo for the winter. It is a sorry occupation of Egypt. I suppose it's for the hay-fever. If Sally had told us where she was coming in we might have had sight of her for a little, and cheered ourselves. Margot thinks she can come down here as soon as she is through with nursing her baby.[1] I *won't* ask Jock McKail! They are in deep sorrow at the Grange over Morris's death which seems to have been unexpected at the last. Uncle Ned is naturally very broken up. He felt Millais' going[2] more than any one thought, the Father told me. Of course he won't leave London but we have hopes of getting Aunt Georgie down here. Aunt Aggie is coming for Christmas and we are in treaty with Henry James for a visit. But he is an evasive man and won't leave London either. By the same token he's seconded me for the Athenæum and I hope to be a Bishop before I die. There's some chance of the A's. electing me by committee – some day. Carrie takes well to our infernal climate but Josephine has a cold. This may sound like Ollendorf[3] but it's rather a nuisance. I long sometimes for a clean October morning with a touch of frost. We drip here except when we have hail.

Please try to look the verses into favour. I'm not pleased with them.

With best love from us all to you and Sally and Margaret – and "Aunt Theo" (I'm not sure how to spell Sidgwick).[4]

> Ever yours affectionately
> Ruddy.

P.S.   Carrie was blotting this and *she* smudged it with her usual American haste.

> RK.

It was the nasty British bolotter which never knew how to blot.

> C.K.

Notes
1. Clare Mackail (1896–1919), youngest of Margaret's three children.
2. Sir John Everett Millais died on 13 August.
3. See [17 September 1890].
4. Theodora Sedgwick was the youngest sister of the late Mrs Norton.

To Henry James, 30 October 1896
ALS: Harvard University

Rock House / Maidencombe / Oct. 30. 96

Dear Mr James,

Aunt Georgie writes me that you have seconded me at the Athenæum[1] and I might have known beforehand that was just the kindly thing you would have done. Ever so many thanks. I'll be a bishop and die in gaiters yet.

Norris[2] tells us you won't come down. At least he says you aren't coming. But why not visit us the same way you did in the Isle of Wight.[3] Come to your pet hotel so as to be free and come to us so as to be fed. We both want to see you ever so and there is no chance of our getting up to London yet awhile. Why not bring your work down? The sun shines a little here, in a gummy sort of way and at least we don't have fogs.

My new book of verses is by way of being out at last and this should bring you a copy with our love.

Please tell us you are coming down.

Ever yours affectionately
Rudyard.

Notes

1. RK was elected to membership on 2 April 1897, when he was the "youngest member by 20 years" (CK to F. N. Finney, 9 June 1897: Parke-Bernet catalogue, 10 December 1941). His election was under Rule 2, for "distinguished eminence in science, literature, or the arts, or for public services".
2. William Edward Norris (1847–1925), novelist and friend of James; he lived nearby in Torquay.
3. That must have been in the summer of 1890, when Wolcott Balestier had a house at Freshwater, Isle of Wight.

To Frank N. Doubleday, 1 November 1896
ALS: Princeton University

Rock House: / Maidencombe. / Nov. 1. 96.

Dear Doubleday –

Yours of the 22nd with enclosures just in this Sabbath morning: and I make haste to reply.

In the first place as to work and bother involved, I am pretty sure that *your* end of the stick has not been a light one; and as we are both keenly interested in the success of the thing *as a game*, quite apart from financial considerations, we will both pat ourselves upon the back.

Now, as to your circular, I don't think you make half enough of the curious way in which the edition will be illustrated. Of course you had not seen the photoes of the plaques when you wrote the ad: make more of it. Heaps of men can draw, but *very* few model with my father's skill and feeling. It seems to me that I don't remember any one who has ever had his illustrations done in the *solid*, before. *That* is the strong point of the edition.

And now, while I think of it, why can't DeVinne[1] cut characteristic black lotus flowers for his vine (or fig) leaf twiddles?[2] I have suggested this on proof of title page. It wouldn't cost seventy five cents, would it?

I have corrected the preface in which there was one big slip. Of course it is the Story of the Gadsbys and the Anglo Indian child-stories that stand as first issued.[3] In regard to "C[aptains]. C[ourageous]." you're welcome to it for all of me but my contracts don't include publishing it before Xmas '97. McClure will hardly be through with it before. *Better fight this out with Watt quick.* You will observe that under the new system of arrangement, three yarns: – *Badalia Herodsfoot: Brugglesmith* and *The Long Men o' Larut* are for the present not assignable to any pigeon-hole, but my notion is to get out next year a volume of new tales such as *William the Conqueror; the Brushwood boy;* An Error in the 4th Dimension, and so on: to which these three tales can be added.[4] They will make a volume of mixed matter, of rather wide range.

The mischief of completely publishing an author who is not completely dead is that the edition must necessarily be incomplete as long as the said author still owns an inkpot.

In regard to what you have written in the ad about facsimiling my verses of introduction. That is my fault. The notion of a set of verses has been set aside for the letter of instructions to the native captain: copy of which went to you last mail.[5] It's a heap too grubby to be facsimiled I think. But if in your judgment it would add materially to the attractions of the $100 edition (what a lot of fools with money must be knocking around America) put it in with all its imperfections on its head. I don't usually turn out copy in that style.

Of course, as Mrs K. has written you, I will sign any amount of editions.

I am sending with this a mounted copy of the photo:[6] signed. I do hope and pray I have kept this photo from leaking out but there is an evil-eyed Dutchman at Torquay who took it and I don't know whether he may not monkey with the negative. However, I have bought and paid for the proofs and if he doesn't keep his part of the bargain I'll sue him.

I hope very much Scribners will see their way to taking the whole batch of the father's illustrations. Pity to spoil a ship for a penn'orth of tar.

This, I think, covers your letter very completely. I don't know where you will put the introduction. My own notion would be to slip it in after the preface, belted with a blank page on either side. Only put it in to the first volume: Don't repeat it for each one.

God only knows what that Meriden-plated[7] ass Bryan may or may not do: but anyway even if the edition comes out a little late we shall gain in that people will have time to settle back to business and get a grip on themselves before we ask them for their money.

With best regards from us both.

Yours sincerely
Rudyard Kipling

Notes

1. Theodore De Vinne (1828–1914), distinguished New York printer and historian of printing. The first twenty-five volumes of the Outward Bound Edition were produced at the De Vinne Press.
2. Some of the edition's title-pages are ornamented with black lotus flowers.
3. " 'The Story of the Gadsbys' and the Anglo-Indian child-stories stand as first issued" (RK's "Preface" to the Outward Bound Edition, I, vii).
4. In the Outward Bound Edition all of these, except for "William the Conquerer", appear in volume 14, *The Day's Work, Part II.*
5. RK's Introduction to the edition is a letter "To the Nakhoda or Skipper of This Venture". He recopied it for Doubleday (to Doubleday [c. 23 November 1896]: ALS, Princeton), and a page of it appears in facsimile in the deluxe version of the Outward Bound Edition (see 14 March 189[7]).
6. For the first volume of the Outward Bound Edition: see 7 October 1896.
7. Meriden, Connecticut, is famous for silver plate; William Jennings Bryan was running on the free silver principle in the US presidential election.

To William Heinemann, 5 November 1896

ALS: Princeton University

Rock House, / Maidencombe, / St. Marychurch.

Dear Heinemann,

Many thanks for Mrs Steele's book[1] which is indeed a "topper" – in my opinion *the* mutiny novel for which we have waited so long. The best part is the description of the *pukka* Oriental slackness, vacillation and intrigue inside Delhi – no one has handled that side of the question before.

All the same I don't think I'll review it in the magazine because I've declined to review for so many men – and women – that if I broke my rule now I'd be making some twenty or thirty very angry people. It seems to me *if* you want knowledge of things and a word to carry weight you'd better get hold of my father, and see if he won't review it.[2]

The cover is the one weak thing in the book. It should have been bound in red and black instead of rooks and cranes and things that make it look like a society novel. Now run it out *quick* in a colonial edition at 2/6 to go side by side with a six-bob one.

Very sincerely ever

Rudyard Kipling.

5: 11: 96

Notes
1. Flora Annie Steel, *On the Face of the Waters* (1896).
2. He did: "The Novel of the Mutiny", *New Review*, xvi (1897) 78–83.

To Ripley Hitchcock, 8 November 1896
ALS: Berg Collection, New York Public Library

Rock House, / Maidencombe, / St. Marychurch. / Nov. 8. 96.

Dear Hitchcock

Many thanks for your two notes of the 30th Ult. and specially for the infant Ripley – regular young rip–ley he looks in his onteora[1] undress. I observe he has a satisfactory and well-filled stomach: whence I argue that he sleeps o' nights. We are just weaning our small Elsie: who is some six weeks younger than he. She protests and orates and swears through the night-watches. Kids are distinctly soul-chastening experiences as you know. The Seven Seas is going ahead cheerfully this side the water but being as it is rather pointedly British I don't expect it will do much with you. 22,000 (*sold before* publication) is rather a whack to lead off with.

I've bicycled myself into a go of tooth-ache and neuralgia which annoys me because, for a wonder, our weather has been nearly perfect. Only bright skies are bad for pike. I got two threes and one seven pounder out of a private water a few miles away. It's the most specialized form of fishing I've ever tackled and the beast takes hold of the bait rather more like a malignant minded demon than a cheery hungry fish. I was half an hour slaying my seven-pounder. No gaff, no net and he snapping like a dog when I got him to the bank. But it was royal fun.

Dry fly fishing is the kind of thing we may do when we go to Heaven if god gives us wisdom. It's a cross between scientific surveying and mounting objects for a microscope. If you doubt look at enclosed sample;[2] and imagine the tackle that goes with it. An eleven-ounce rod is about the *outside* limit of weight. The water is dead clear and the trout comes up and winks at you. I've seen men do it but I am not gifted in that direction. Salmon fishing closes on the northern rivers of the county the 14th of this month – record this season, I believe, 20 lb. Peal and grilse[3] up to 6 lb have been taking well on the minnow, prawn and fly but I've stuck to my pike with a Colorado spoon and a ten-foot bamboo pole. I'm going east – fifty miles by rail and the devil of a journey as they reckon distances here – for some more pike and coarse-fish as soon as they get my teeth fixed. The land is more full of beauty than ever I had imagined. England after all, *is* literature. One can't believe that the whole landscape hasn't come out of a novel – people houses and all.

Yes the boy's conversion was markedly sudden[4] but I didn't want to bother about his psychology till I tackle her in book-form. Reading serially people will have time to pause in. In the book, I'll explain for the benefit of the older people. I've just passed the proofs of the last part which have cost me more bother than all the rest put together. Now I'm going to be idle for awhile, and explore rivers ready for you when you come over.

With best regards from us both.

Ever yours
Rudyard Kipling

P.S.   Bryan will collapse as you say. They'll call it, nervous frustration. It's paresis.

Notes
1. In the Catskills of New York.
2. A dry fly has been pressed between the leaves of the letter.
3. Young salmon.
4. The "conversion" of Harvey Cheyne in "*Captains Courageous*".

To James M. Conland, 8–24 November [1896]
ALS: Library of Congress

Rock House, / Maidencombe, / St. Marychurch. / Nov:8–17.

Your letter and the news of the Republican landslide[1] came in together – so it's good news all round. From this distance it looks as though Bryan and his works were decently buried and now if the new men have the savvy to deal resolutely with the more openly burglarious forms of "high finance" such as trusts and the like McKinley's rule may be blessed in the long run. But if he makes the mistake of forgetting he has been sent to power by the country and *not* by the Republican party

there will yet be trouble. That's my prophecy. I can't help being sorry
for the poor windy devil out west who got hold of a half-truth and
didn't know what to do with it. I don't think he'll ever be heard of again
after the next six months. Hysteria is a background not to be depended
upon. [   ]² Robert Barr (of the Detroit Free Press that was)³ has got
hold of the proofs of Captains Courageous which is being published
here in Pearson's Magazine. It has knocked him galley-west and made
him homesick. I tell you that tale will be a snorter. I read it to my father
and he went to bed about as much impressed a man as you would hope
to see. 'Says it's a new world that we've opened. And that's what it is.
I told you, didn't I, that I bought blind for $150 the M.S. of that old
barnacle at Worcester Mass. I remember showing you his letter and you
advised the deal. Well, he has sent me 800 closely written pages. He
writes [   ]⁴ but it's a mine of valuable stuff. I shan't do anything to
it, till I see you again but there's the makings of a wondrous sea-yarn.
The nippers – both pairs – came in a day or two ago in the leisurely
style common to the parcel-posts between the two countries, and I am
ever so much obliged for them. They are of course utterly unknown
here and the fishermen's hands are cut and scored all over with the
friction of the hand-lines. They never seem to have heard of any sort of
protection, and I doubt whether any amount of persuasion would make
them take up a new-fangled notion. Fishermen are alike, you see, the
wide world over! I told Appletons to send you a copy as soon as might
be of The Seven Seas and Ripley Hitchcock writes me that they have
the [   ] – copy of the book by them. They haven't sent it over to me
yet. By the same token the "Seven Seas" sold mighty well this side the
water and seems to have made a small splash. But some of the critics
say that some of the verses might be called improper. Amazing, isn't
it? They are having no end of a discussion over it – a discussion in
which I absolutely refuse to take part.⁵ I shouldn't wonder if there were
rather a howl of outraged virtue on your side of the water too. This
mild damp climate (the fuschia bush is in full bloom in the open air
today) seems to be doing her well. It has played the cat and Banjo with
all my teeth: and for the past month I have been living in the embraces
of the local dentist who cheerfully jams in a wad of arsenic dressing to
kill a nerve and then says, while I am feeling like St Lawrence on a
gridiron; "Oh *that* can't hurt you."

　　We've got a governess to look after Josephine: only Josephine doesn't
exactly see it that way. She prefers looking after the governess and that
bewilders the governess. She is shooting up into a tall slim girl with a
most decided will of her own.

　　A fortnight of really decent weather has kept me out of doors all the
time on my wheel. I went out ten miles the other day, with my rod
strapped on the frame and my lunch on my back, for a day's Jack-

fishing:[6] but except a howling tooth-ache got no reward. I have discovered a perfectly lovely pub – six miles down the road – kept by a dear fat old woman and her two daughters. The private bar is also their parlor and you sit down on a sofa and they hand you hot whiskey and water with the air of duchesses. I stumbled on it by accident in one of my fishing excursions and it is the first pub I shall steer you to when you come over. The local volunteer company want me to give away their prizes at the yearly prize-giving and to make a speech as well. The captain of the company is a man who owns the fifty-acre farm next to me: and as he has given me free leave to slaughter rabbits – all the country is alive with small game – I suppose I shall have to accept.[7] I was out the other day with his son, a boy of seventeen, a shot gun and a ferret. Do you know anything of that kind of sport. The ferret is in the nature of a cream-coloured weasel with blood red eyes. You put him into the rabbit burrows, which he explores, and you pot the rabbits if you can, as they bolt. We worked half the afternoon in 3 rabbit warrens that backed on to an old abandoned smugglers cove – the genuine article, tell Harry. Just within gun shot the land went down to the sea in two hundred foot bluffs: and what with the screaming of the gulls, the echoes of the shot: and the sea booming and churning in the caves below as the twilight fell it was a curious experience. All the land here has been slowly bitten into by the sea, which covers a burnt forest, and after heavy gales blackened tree-stumps are thrown onto the beach.

Nov. 24! This letter has been a devil of a time on the stocks but I went off visiting my people near Salisbury: then I had a bad go of toothache: and *then* I read the first two dollops of Captains Courageous in McClure. I'm not as pleased with Taber's work[8] as I thought I should be but it *is* a good story and I crowed over it like a hen with one chick. How did it strike you in print? Now I'll hasten to shut up this rigamarole or I'll never keep up the connection. I wish you could have heard a man I met in the cars going from Torquay to Southampton. He was a bit of every thing – fisherman, coaster: and yachtsman: but his yacht had been laid up for the winter and he was hurrying to get a billet as a quartermaster on one of the Union liners running to the Cape. A cheerful liar and a most amusing one.

I send the autographs with this. If you want any more when those are done let me know, and give us all the news when next you write. I am sorry to hear [   ][9] is not well but hope his trouble is not more than temporary. Don't forget to write. With all regards.

> Ever yours sincerely
> Rudyard Kipling

Notes
1. McKinley defeated William Jennings Bryan in the November presidential election.

2. Passage erased here and in the other two bracketed blanks in this letter (see 1–6 October 1896).
3. An English weekly edition, published in London. Barr worked for it in the early 1890s, when the paper published RK's "The Record of Badalia Herodsfoot" (*Many Inventions*).
4. Indecipherable word here.
5. I can find no trace of this in the daily papers or in the literary weeklies, though the *Spectator*, 21 November 1896, deplored the "utterly squalid ballads" in *The Seven Seas*.
6. A jack is a pike.
7. I have found no report of the occasion.
8. Isaac W. Taber illustrated the story in *McClure's*.
9. Name erased.

To Edith Nesbit Bland,[1] 15 November 1896

ALS: Library of Congress

Rock House, / Maidencombe, / St. Marychurch. / Nov. 15. 96.

Dear Miss Nesbit

Many thanks for your note of the 10th. Honestly, if I could be sure of making something that would suit your magazine[2] I would do it but I haven't a thing by me. Won't you send me your prospectus and give me some sort of a lead? Is it a baby's magazine, a child's one or for young boys? There is a very wide difference in each of these directions. I have had some little sad experience in magazining and forgive me warning you that a list of "star" names is a snare unless and until you have 12 months good matter up your sleeve to carry on with. By this neglect have fallen many hundreds – and their money did follow them.

You must have the most extraordinary notion of the kind of person I am if you imagine I go to "smart" parties. I never go anywhere as a rule and I haven't been to London in a year. I shall hope however some day to have the pleasure of meeting you over a chafing-dish which I take it is the inner meaning of crabs with cream.[3]

Very sincerely yours
Rudyard Kipling

Notes
1. Mrs Bland (1858–1924), writer of children's books as E. Nesbit. She greatly admired RK's work, and her *The Butler in Bohemia*, 1894 (in collaboration with Oswald Barron) is dedicated to RK.
2. She was planning a children's magazine in 1896 that 'never got off the ground' (Julia Briggs, *A Woman of Passion: The Life of E. Nesbit 1858–1924* [1987] p. 254).
3. They never met (ibid.).

To Robert Barr, 25 November 1896
ALS: University of Sussex

Rock House, / Maidencombe, / St. Marychurch. / Nov. 25. 96

Dear Barr –

No, I don't take any New Vagabonds[1] in mine either – arrived at that conclusion by instinct but all the same am sorry to miss Bobs.[2] Just had to refuse (tho' I didn't want to) an invite from the American society for Thanksgiving. Golly! I could have described 'em a thanksgiving dinner from the oyster soup to the hickory nuts and the kids popping corn afterwards that would have made them weep. Indeed the invite stirred me up to Transatlantic yearnings. I want to sit over a register again instead of looking at a red doctor's lamp inside a damned iron grating. (We've three such futile appliances here and they don't warm us). Howbeit I couldn't get up in time.

I'm up for one night only for the Cecil Club dinner[3] and I'm lying low with relatives because I have a whole lot of them to see.

Things are looking up with my family. Got another Uncle with a handle to him[4] and shall have to wear a hardwood coronet of my own to keep abreast of the times if this goes on. But my two small girl babies (whom you must see) keep me humble. That story of Peter and God was new to me. That's what they think of Bryan out west as a matter of fact. In return here's a yarn I picked up from a mariner whom I met on the cars going to Salisbury: He'd been every where and had once sailed with a "gentle" Yankee skipper of a Glasgow sailing packet – "an' he was a very gentle man Sir. He used to creep up on deck when it was blowin' like Hell an' come right forward rubbin' his hands. An' then he'd say: – 'Boys it don't make no sort o' God-dam differ to *me* o' course: I'm old and I'm ready to meet my maker. But you're young an' if I was *you* I'd take in that top gallant sail pretty quick.'

We didn't understand it at first Sir till she'd nearly torn the sticks out of herself once or twice but by God Sir, after *that*, we'd just run to him an' wait with our tongues hangin' out till the old man had got off his little sermon about bein' prepared to die. He was a very "gentle" man Sir, but he made us more damned afraid than any other skipper I've sailed with. Rubbin' his hands Sir, this way" –

I present you with that character for your next short story.

Ever thine
Rudyard.

Notes

1. The New Vagabonds was a dining club organised by the journalist, Douglas Sladen, and the editor and novelist G. B. Burgin. RK had been a guest of honour at one of the

club's dinners (Coulson Kernahan, *"Nothing Quite Like Kipling Had Happened Before"*
[1944] p. 25).
2. Lord Roberts.
3. Probably the dinner at which Arthur Balfour presided: see 31 December 1896. I have
found no public notice of it. The Cecil was a conservative political club.
4. Edward Poynter was knighted in December on succeeding Millais as President of the
Royal Academy.

To Cormell Price, 18 December 1896

ALS: Library of Congress

Rock House, / Maidencombe, / St. Marychurch. / 18. Dec 96

Dear Uncle Crom,

If I'd known I was lunching at the Grange (but they told me Aunt
Georgie was sick – and she was) I'd have sent a cloud of telegrams to
you. I wanted to ask you to come down and rest a while here: and we'd
go and see Stevens[1] together at Plymouth. He was up here for the day
with his wife; and we mourned over the Old Coll. together. But I didn't
know whether things weren't busy with you. If you could only make
up some excuse for coming down here it would be a dear joy to both of
us. *Please* say you can see your way to it.

I got a letter the other day from Griffiths II.[2] Stanley Scott[3] is a parson
here at Cockington and I believe Plymouth is full of O.U.S.C.'s. I heard
indirectly that the ecclesiastic bounder in charge of the private school
near Bideford is by way of using my name [as] an O.U.S.C.[4] If his God
only puts it into his head to make the statement publicly, I shall arrange
such a disclaimer, also publicly, as will startle him. Stevens and I
meditated a trip down there but we felt it would be too ghastly. You
come down and I'll get Stevens up. Why shouldn't my name, and
Edwardes[5] who is a D.S.O. and the names of half a dozen boys come
in your list of references.[6] I'll swear we are quite as respectable as all
the blobby Colonels and Majors. Please let me have a place among
them – certainly you can put in the father and he is a C.I.E.[7]

Curiously enough, I am deep in a school tale, in which Dunsty,
Beresford, Crofts and all the rest of 'em come in. There's a lovely scene
with you in your study. It's for a Xmas number of the Graphic I think
or else for Cosmopolis.[8] I've never worked the mine of material I
accumulated at Westward Ho! But come down and you shall hear it
read.

Our smallest kiddy has been sick for some time but is now better.
Aunt Edie is staying with us; and we hope to have Aunt Aggie after
Xmas: but what we'd like best would be you. There isn't a thing to do

here and you can smoke and loaf and we'll think out new schemes.[9]
Your always loving nephew
Ruddy.

Notes
1. The Revd Henry Chicheley Stevens (1852–1922) taught mathematics at USC in RK's time at the school; he left in 1895, when he married, and was now curate of Stoke Demerel in the borough of Devonport.
2. Lieutenant-Colonel George Herbert Griffith, Royal Engineers (1870–1917), second of three brothers all at USC in RK's day.
3. The Reverend Hubert Guillum Stanley Scott (1866–1923), at USC 1878–83; curate of Cockington 1895–1901.
4. The "ecclesiastical bounder" is P. C. Harris (see 9 May 1896). RK evidently held that USC after Price's departure was no longer the school that he had attended: see, e.g., 17 February 1899.
5. Stanley Edwardes: see 31 January–1 February 1882.
6. For his business of tutoring.
7. Commander of the Indian Empire; JLK was granted this honour on his retirement.
8. "Slaves of the Lamp", Parts 1 and 2, appeared in *Cosmopolis*, April and May 1897 (*Stalky & Co.*).
9. Price stayed with them on 28–30 December (CK diary).

To Methuen and Company,[1] 24 December 1896

ALS: Library of Congress

Rock House, / Maidencombe, / St. Marychurch. / Dec. 24. '96.

Methuen and Co.

Gentlemen –

I am today returning your envelope full of notices of the Seven Seas: and have to express my thanks for your courtesy in sending to Mrs Kipling (who has a collection of my books bound in a style that *I* cannot afford) the sumptuous vellum copy.[2]

Could you kindly let me know how J. A. Barry's book "In the Great Deep"[3] is selling. I am very much interested in his work and should like also to know whether he has any new work in hand.

Very sincerely
Rudyard Kipling

Notes
1. The publishers of RK's verse in England since *Barrack-Room Ballads* in 1892.
2. One of thirty copies "on Japan paper, bound in white buckram with vellum backstrip lettered in gold" (Stewart–Yeats, *Bibliographical Catalogue*, p. 137). This copy is now in the British Library, part of RK's own collection of his writings.
3. John Arthur Barry, *In the Great Deep: Sea Stories* (Methuen, 1896). RK contributed introductory verses to Barry's *Steve Brown's Bunyip*: see [3–4] December 1893.

To Charles Eliot Norton, 31 December 1896
ALS: Harvard University

> *Rock House, / Maidencombe, / St. Marychurch. / Dec. 31. 96. / C's*
> Birthday.

Dear Mr. Norton –

"This comes hoping" it will catch your birthday[1] as it leaves on Carrie's, and you need not be assured how much love and how many good wishes it brings. We are both of us awed, and if the truth must be told a little scared at your article in the Atlantic Monthly[2] which came this evening. For it is one thing to have you say things at Shady Hill or Ashfield and quite another to have you write them. True it is, most sadly true, that I have not been true to my duties but I did not know that I had been so untrue.[3] As you know, I love the fun and the riot of writing (I am daily and nightly perplexed with my own private responsibilities before God) and there are times when it is just a comfort and a delight to let out with the pen and ink – so long as it doesn't do any one any moral harm. I don't believe very much in my genius, my own notion being rather than I am set to do Ferguson[4] for some yet-to-come-along Burns whose little finger will be thicker than my loins. At least I have shown him his lead. Then there is the danger it seems of a man running off into William Watson's[5] kind of wordy rot if he, at a comparatively tender age, considers himself a poet. But – you are the only man except my father and Uncle Ned whose disapproval or advice sways me; and I will say just as one says to one's father when one is little: – "I'll try to think and be better next time." But, even now, the notion that *you* should have reviewed me rather makes me gasp. I felt about eighteen inches high when I began to read; then eighteen feet at the end and ten minutes later, on mature reflection – excessively small. I don't think even you who know me, will ever know what that review means to me.

Crom Price, my old head master at Westward Ho! has been staying two days with us. We had a great time recalling the young dead all over the world. He knows Sally but never met you: for the which I pity him. Now young Hugh Poynter (Aunt Aggie's boy) is with us with a small arsenal of fire arms lusting for the blood of rabbits. Mother hasn't been very well and has gone up to town to see a doctor (she needed a tonic). Did I tell you of my run up to town to attend a dinner whereof A.J. Balfour[6] was chairman and I, vice?[7] It was rather a lark but *timeo Danaos et* etc. I mistrust politicians when they eat with literary men. But I had come to see Aunt Georgie (she of course bore the weight of Morris's death on Uncle Ned). She was in bed with reaction but an angel as ever; saw Margot talking socialism in a priceless irridescent corduroy velvet bodice, and Angela. But Lily is in Cairo so I won't tell you who Angela resembled. The new baby Clare is a darling and Margot seemed very sweet and dainty. A little too – dainty for this world, methinks; but she lives like the rest of us in one of her own. The Lord has hit Uncle Edward (Poynter) hard for his knighthood. He is ex-officio member of about every utterly uninteresting society in England, and spends his evenings eating with bores. I went over to Phil's studio. Phil is fat and forty (about) but as always, a mine of good things. He is working hard too. Norris (W.E.) sends us today an invite to lunch to meet Edmund Gosse. Now he is a dish I love not but I suppose we'll have to go. He has a mother in law in Torquay.[8]

We had a very nice American Christmas; and got some children from next door to come in and see Josephine's tree. Little Elsie turned up for the first time with a wreath of flowers on her fat head and was pleased to approve. She has been very ill – developed an abcess through excess of condition and was operated upon – 5 minutes under chloroform. Of course all the burden fell on C. Elsie rather seemed to enjoy being spoiled and is now as fat and phlegmatic as ever. But it is *not* nice to see your own kid cut into with a knife – specially if you have to hold the kid.

I get very little American news, except a line or two from Brattleboro. But among my letters I note with pain as they say, a cutting from the Evening *Post* in which Mr E.L. Godkin is pleased to turn up his nose at my "babel of Americanisms" in Captains Courageous.[9] Now I would be loath to destroy and abolish Godkin for that he is a friend of yours and a man who washes his literary hands to boot, but if he continues in this form of sin he will presently be annihilated by an avalanche from quarters that he would least suspect. I did not embark upon the dialect of *Captains Courageous* to be scoffed at by a New York mugwump.[10]

Now it is eleven and I must go to bed in the hope that this letter will catch the New York boat and come in on time. A happy new year for you and all your household, forgetting not my friend and ally the coachman. I wish I had had Lily's address in Cairo and I would have sent her a decisive telegram for the new year. I don't think we can stay out a whole year longer without coming over to have a look at things. It's an uncivilized land (I still maintain it) but how the deuce has it would itself round my heartstrings in the way it has? C and I sit over our inadequate English fire and grow – homesick.

Ever yours lovingly
Ruddy.

Notes
1. Norton's birthday was 16 November.
2. "The Poetry of Rudyard Kipling", *Atlantic Monthly*, January 1897.

3. "It is not strange that the insistence of his varied and vigorous talents should often, during youth, when the exercise of talents is so delightful and so delusive, have interfered with his perfect obedience to the higher law of his inward being" (p. 114).
4. Robert Fergusson (1750–74), Scottish poet.
5. (Sir) William Watson (1858–1935), poet, had been publishing since 1880.
6. Arthur James Balfour, 1st Earl of Balfour (1848–1930), Conservative statesman and philosophic writer, Prime Minister 1902–5; he was First Lord of the Treasury and Conservative leader in the Commons at this time.
7. Probably the Cecil Club dinner referred to in 25 November. I have found no record of the occasion.
8. Gosse's stepmother lived in St Marychurch, Torquay.
9. A review of *The Seven Seas* in the *New York Evening Post*, 11 December 1896, doubts the genuineness of RK's soldier-slang, and refers to the handling of American dialect in "*Captains Courageous*" as "a Babel of mixed Americanisms".
10. Godkin led the so-called Mugwump revolt in the Republican party, 1884.

To William Wilson Hunter, 15 January 1897

Text: Francis Henry Skrine, *The Life of Sir William Wilson-Hunter* (1901) p. 451

[Rock House] January 15, 1897.

It is curious, on looking back, to think how your essays, "Some Calcutta Graves," sent first myself and then my sister, Mrs. Fleming, over the same ground.[1] There is a marvellous fascination in that Park Street cemetery, where all the used-up machinery of the Empire is put away. And it comes out under your hand. I read the book through as soon as it came out; and once again, as many times before, I have sinfully envied you your pen. Do you remember how, in 1888, there came out in the *Academy* a review of a small book of verse called "Departmental Ditties,"[2] a long two-column review of kindness and charity that mightily encouraged me? I have a long memory, and I have not forgotten. It was the first English review that ever came to me.

Notes

1. Hunter had sent RK a reprint of his articles on "Some Calcutta Graves", originally published in 1887. RK's "Concerning Lucia" (*Pioneer*, 9 April 1888), describes a visit to the Park Street Cemetery, Calcutta (*From Sea to Sea*).
2. *Academy*, xxxiv (1 September 1888) 128–9, a review of the third edition. Hunter praised the truth of RK's view and hailed "a new literary star of no mean magnitude".

To Ripley Hitchcock, 17 January 1897
ALS: Berg Collection, New York Public Library

Rock House, / Maidencombe, / St. Marychurch / Jan. 17. 97

Dear Hitchcock:

I've been away from some days trying to fish in a howling fog and later a howling wind. Result, a most howling failure. Talk not to *me* of fly-fishing. I've been wrestling with baits and ligers[1] and snap-tackle and dead gorges[2] and now I don't think I shall fish any more – till next week. But I shall cherish your flies against the warm weather if that ever comes. I don't *know* for certain of any rod I should care to use for keeps, less than 9 oz: Don't see quite where you get casting power with a five-ouncer, but I'm willing to learn. My new St John's trout-rod weighs about 12 oz and I don't find that an ounce too heavy. But then I like a good spring under my hand and cast with the butt lying along my elbow, which is clumsy but effective.

The ccccccc's[3] goes on serenely here but you've unearthed a *very* queer thing in the *Bookman*. The long review[4] of course I had seen before this side the water but the references to the book in the library notes are (don't laugh) word for word a reprint of a leader in the British Weekly (a deeply religious paper) published in *1893* apropos of my Many Inventions.[5] They've cut out the tail part about my "not having found Christ" but the rest is the leading article itself. Now what is the *nexus* between a godly British journal of three years back and an American literary paper's notes supposed to be fresh? If I had my book of reviews with me I'd send you the article itself for comparison but it's lying up at Naulakha. It's rummy. It's very rummy and the godliness of the infernal thing makes me more suspicious than I'd be with a purely secular paper.

Our weather is more than usually atrocious just now – grey skies and a wind at freezing. What freezing means in England – cold that strikes to your very marrow – I pray you may never know. Added to all this my constant occupation is going to the dentist: for my teeth miss the dry air of Vermont and like cherubim and seraphin "continually do cry."[6] My pet lake where I hoped to get pike is frozen over. Otherwise, all well here.

With best wishes from us both to you and Mrs Hitchcock.

Ever yours sincerely
Rudyard Kipling

Notes
1. Usually *ligger*: a night-line with a float for pike fishing.
2. A method of baiting for pike fishing.

3. Seven *c* s = *The Seven Seas.*
4. *The Bookman* [New York], IV (1896–7) 443–5, signed "Y.Y."
5. Untitled note in "Chronicle and Comment", *The Bookman*, IV (1896—7) 413–14. RK is right: except for one brief transitional passage, the note in *The Bookman* is a verbatim transcript of parts of a leader in the *British Weekly*, 22 June 1893, p. 129, presumably by William Robertson Nicoll, the *Weekly's* distinguished editor.
6. "Cherubim and Seraphim continually do cry": Church of England's *Primer, Set Forth by the King's Majesty* (1546).

To Sarah Orne Jewett, [January? 1897]

ALS: Harvard University

Rock House, / Maidencombe, / St. Marychurch.

Dear Miss Jewett,

Mr. Norton, who knows what is good, sent the wife for Christmas your "Country of the Pointed Firs."[1] She read it first to herself: then I read it more or less to myself because she made me read a lot of it out aloud, and then we read it over each other's shoulders, saying the best things aloud together. Now I am writing to you to convey some small instalment of our great delight – our purring satisfaction in that perfect little tale. It's immense – it is the very life. It's out and away the loveliest thing of yours I've ever read. It – made me homesick! There's for you! So many of the people of lesser sympathy have missed the lovely New England landscape; and the genuine breadth of heart and fun that underlies the New England nature. I maintain (and will maintain with outcries if necessary) that that is the reallest New England book ever given us. I admit the Maine atmosphere. I don't know Maine but am prepared to make oath out of my own conviction that you have spoken the utter truth – but above and beyond all that you've got all New England. You should have heard Carrie and I reading and chortling and crying: – "That's Emma Scott. That's old man Nourse. That's Marm Bliss" – and so on. They're our neighbours on the farm up to Brattleboro. I've never been so quietly and thoroughly "shook up" in all my little days; and so says Carrie. The ass of a publisher has turned the thing out in blue and silver truck whereby it looks ephemeral and of no account but Joanna alone is an idyl worth fifty average pretentious books; and Mis' Blackett is worth another fifty. It's all a most perfect piece of art, truth, beauty and tenderness; and I'm as proud as a peacock to think I've met and known you.

Do let me hand the book over to my man of business (A.P. Watt) here with a view to getting it out on the London market if so be it's copyrighted in England. If it isn't, we'll still get it out.[2] I want my own people to understand the rarity and excellence of this kind of thing. I don't know whether your publishers will allow it but they ought to.

With all good wishes from Carrie and myself, and a bushel of thanks, believe me

Ever sincerely yours
Rudyard Kipling.

P.S. I don't believe even *you* know how good that book is.

Notes
1. New York, 1896.
2. The book had already been brought out in England by T. Fisher Unwin.

To Stephen Wheeler, 1 February 1897
ALS: Harvard University

Rock House, / Maidencombe, / St. Marychurch. / Feb. 1. '97

Dear Wheeler,
Yours of the 29th – but you haven't told me to whom I should confide my opinions. It must *not* be Birdwood because he doesn't love my Father I think. It seems to me that of all men I am peculiarly fitted to speak of your qualifications as a librarian; because I remember an awful siege when you put the old C[ivil]. & M[ilitary]. books in order; with me as a perspiring and inaccurate assistant. What I *do* know, and can swear to, is that you are ultra-rigidly accurate (as alas I am not) with a cast-steel memory, and a store of Oriental knowledge that most "Orientalists" haven't got. But to whom shall I testify on these matters? It seems to me that the billet of Assistant Librarian in that heavenly library from which I have occasionally borrowed a book,[1] would be the ideal one for you *and* for the library and I am willing to affidavit to that effect. Only give me a name or two, or let Sydney Colvin drop me a hint; and I'll take steps. But remember the frabjous Birdwood loves me not – I think. Would A.J. Balfour, or Eustace Balfour,[2] or any one of that kidney serve – or Lord Dufferin? If so I am all at your service.

Sidney Colvin is wrong. You gave me no need of a gruelling for four years but by the light of later knowledge I see it did me a heap of good.

I notice you say "locks" of Rose Aylmer's hair.[3] What is your price for one because Trix wrote some pretty verses about her and I should much like to send her a lock, if possible.

"Bobs" has sent me a copy of his Forty one years in India,[4] in which I

am amazed at the things he does *not* say and Sir G. Robertson[5] of Chitral
has been staying down here for two or three days telling us the history
of the siege.

Yours as always
Ruddy.

Notes
1. What library this may be is not clear. Wheeler was later librarian of the Oriental Club,
   but the present honorary librarian assures me that the Club never had a paid librarian,
   much less an assistant. Perhaps Wheeler was applying to the Royal Asiatic Society or
   to the India Office Library.
2. Colonel Eustace Balfour (1854–1911), a younger brother of Arthur Balfour and a member
   of the Savile Club. He practised as an architect. "One of the best of talkers, who died
   too soon" (*Something of Myself*, p. 85).
3. Landor's Rose Aylmer. Wheeler was a devoted scholar of Landor; he published two
   volumes of Landor's letters, 1897 and 1899, a bibliography of Landor in 1919, and
   assisted in the editing of Landor's *Complete Works* (1927–36).
4. Lord Roberts, *Forty-One Years in India* (1897).
5. Sir George Robertson (1852–1916), British Agent in Gilgit, in 1895 held out for six weeks
   in the fort at Chitral against an invading force of Pathans.

To Eric Robertson, 17 February 189[7]

ALS: Robert H. Taylor Library, Princeton University

Rock House, / Maidencombe, / St. Marychurch. / Feb: 17: 96

Dear Robertson:

I quite agree with you. It is indeed a "terrible" thing to say publicly
of one's "friend" that the two things beyond his pale are "God and
good women."[1] It is so terrible that I wonder you did not think what it
involved before saying it: because then you might have remembered
that you and I both knew my mother and sister and several other good
women in Lahore.

Ten years ago – and it must be some ten years since we last met –
your views on God and good women were not I fancy what they are
now. You have married and gone into the church – and I have at least
given you the benefit of the doubt.

Even had I chosen to dispense with "God and good women" in the
old days you might today have shown me the like forbearance.

I have had to take many misrepresentations from the worst of the
American newspapers during the past few years but it seems to me that
your little statement, in all the force of its "friendliness" and backed by
your position in the church, is, if it gains any notoriety, more subtly

than any other calculated to cripple any power for good that may lie in my work.

> Very sincerely
> Rudyard Kipling.

Note
1. I have not found where Robertson published this remark.

To William Alexander Fraser, 23 February 1897
ALS: Miss Matilda Tyler

> *Rock House, / Maidencombe, / St. Marychurch. /* Feb: 23. 97.

That was a great day yesterday. I took four and a half solid hours to the job and wiped off *every one* or my arrears of letters! Now a babe could kick my inkpot over and I should merely smile.

This morning at breakfast there walked into the house (you know the way a smell walks?) the well remembered scent of birch-oil or whatever it is that they dress mocassins with. It always brings back to me Medicine Hat[1] and the troopers of the Canada Police. You are indeed a generous giver. Our small Josephine is upstairs with a bit of a British cold so I haven't yet presented her with her pair: but the wife has borne off hers triumphantly and the parlormaid (whose education does not include mocassins) thinks *I* must be going in for gout. They are three pair of Genuine Stunners and we three of this household will frolic in them and as Baby Josephine says "play we are in America again."

But more than the mocassins did we value the family photo that Mrs. Fraser put in. May I – with bated breath – enquire if them two are Twins? If so, I am prepared to swear that the one on the left (on your wife's left arm) is the moral spit and image of her father. It's a lovely photo and shall be framed for the domestic hearth. You're a lucky man.

As to the two yarns. It seems to me you've gone a bit wide in the Indian one. 'Seems to me that you didn't quite believe hard enough in the truth of it when you were telling it: and that's a thing a reader spots very quickly. It's good enough for an ordinary man but it isn't good enough for *you*. It fails to come off somehow. I can't explain *where* exactly but if I could talk at you for twenty minutes I could make you see it. And again, you've got the vice I've hardly cleared myself of yet – *viz.* using auto-mechanically a whole raft of journalistic or semi-journalistic *cliches* which weaken the force of the tale and it's all too full of "it seemed" and "it appeared" and qualifications of that kind. Now you must *never* "seem" or "appear" to your reader. Just hint to him, as delicately as Chuck the Bo'sun did, that such and such things befell exactly so and in no other way and leave him to do the "seeming." Also you're mixed up in your Hindu, Sikh and Muhammedan names. I'd rewrite the whole yarn if I were you. I enclose a sample page for your perusal – and you can be as mad as you please.

The other yarn is distinctly good: but neither are first-chop. It's a bit too melodramatic.

Now having flourished the literary tomahawk I will return to my own inkpot. Don't be angry over what I've said but consider it quietly and do better next time. That is the utmost any one of us can hope to accomplish in this world.

Ever yours sincerely
Rudyard Kipling.

Note

1. In south eastern Alberta: RK wrote in "Across a Continent" (1892) that he had been in Medicine Hat "three years before when it was even smaller and was reached by me in a freight-car, ticket unpaid for" (*Letters of Travel*, p. 26). He therefore saw it on his American tour in 1889, though we have no other information about this detour. Medicine Hat lies far from what is known of his route in the summer of 1889. RK's letter on the name of the town was published as *Kipling's Advice to the Hat* (n.p., 1922).

To Frank N. Doubleday, [*c.* 25 February 1897][1]
ALS: Princeton University

Rock House, / Maidencombe, / St. Marychurch.

Dear Doubleday.

In the first place I've been away and in the second I've been thinking very hard over your letter of the 28th: and the net result is that I think you're too previous in cutting Scribner.[2] Not that I know anything of Scribner: but I do know something of the horror of sinking with capital borrowed from friends. To which you may with perfect justice reply: – "It's none of your g—— d—— business." And it isn't, but I take an interest in you because you're an immensely imaginative and fertile minded man who should go far if he doesn't start off on the wrong leg.

So far as I know you have practically a free hand in your dept. with Scribner where you can make yourself invaluable if you only hold on – so invaluable that you could get your partnership if not now at least a year or two later. It's all rot when a publisher talks of helping another man to set up publishing. You'd find them quietly putting spokes in your wheel in all sorts of ways and from all sorts of quarters that you never suspected. Again $50,000 isn't enough to start the kind of publishing business you want – at least not unless you paid $250,000 in mental anxiety and nervous frustration. *I* know what comes of pulling a business out of the road on faith. It's good for the business but it busts the man. However, New York, and for matter of that, Boston is paved with firms that put out dainty little 50 and 75¢ books (on which the profit may be large but the sales ain't certain and the discounts are awful) exactly on the lines which you propose to me. It isn't good enough, and if it was you couldn't at the outset afford me the profits I'd want from a richer firm. "Bread upon the Waters" comes into a new book of yarns I am hoping to publish in a year or so:[3] but God and A.P. Watt alone know (and I think Watt knows rather more than God) *who*, will have the publishing of that book. My own impression is that he has pledged it in advance to some one of the firms with whom he dealt when he was arranging for the complete Scribner edition. It is a part of some deal or other with Appleton, or Brett or perhaps the Century. So I couldn't guarantee anything in that line. Captains Courageous is equally pledged to the Century, I believe: so you see even with the best will in the world my hands aren't free.

If you dare to go in boldly for as near a substitute for Oxford paper as you can dig out of Japan or manufacture by your own genius: and if you start (what America hasn't got) a pocket edition of classics – *really* pocket – there might be money in it but I don't see exactly *what* line you intend to embark on.

Lie low for a bit – you're young – make yourself indispensable to Scribner and screw him down to the partnership on the subscription side. That's my impertinent word: but I don't think you'll be offended. The Outward Bound improves visibly at each volume. The second is glorious and I have to thank you much for the six copies of the first.

Ever yours sincerely
Rudyard Kipling.

Notes
1. "About Feby. 25. 1897" is written on the letter in another hand.
2. Doubleday had left Scribner to set up on his own and had consulted RK about the prospects. Obviously he wanted RK to publish with his projected new firm.
3. *The Day's Work*; it was in the event published by Doubleday's new firm, Doubleday and McClure Co., in 1898. "Bread Upon the Waters" first appeared in *McClure's Magazine*, December 1896.

To William Woodville Rockhill,[1] 1 March 1897
ALS: Harvard University

Rock House, / Maidencombe, / St. Marychurch. / Mar. 1. 97

Dear Rockhill –

Many thanks for the extra *jâtakas*[2] of which there is no end. The bear and the ungrateful hunter incarnation is new to me, but I suppose there must be a couple of thousand at least of them in various tongues. Some of the Ceylonese tales and legends are very curious; and I believe many are still unexploited.

We've been having Sir G. Robertson – the man who went into Kafiristan – staying with us; and he has been telling tales of the heathen of those parts which make my hair stand on end.

I can't get a letter out of Sitting Fox[3] (is he sick or gone west) but I'm looking forward to seeing Hay in his ambassadorial plumes.[4] He'll have his work cut out for him, for the virtuous Grover, Olney and Co have, in all good faith, done harm that it will take three generations to put straight – at a conservative estimate.[5]

With best regards to Mrs Rockhill and yourself believe me

Yours always sincerely
Rudyard Kipling.

Notes
1. An orientalist, one of RK's American acquaintances: see 18 February 1896.
2. Buddhist fables and parables.
3. W. Hallett Phillips.
4. Hay had just been appointed Ambassador to England by McKinley.
5. RK means the Venezuelan dispute of 1895–6. Richard Olney was Cleveland's Secretary of State.

To Samuel P. Langley, 8 March 1897
Text: Incomplete AL, Harvard University, and copy, University of Sussex

Rock House, / Maidencombe, / St. Marychurch. / Mar 8. 97.

Dear Mr. Langley –

I have to thank you very much for Mr. Wilson's monograph on the "Swastika"[1] which came to hand a few days ago. It is a matter in which I take a good deal of interest and after reading it I have sent it on to my father. My own heretical view is that the Swastika was almost the first pattern invented by primitive man on the first occasion on which he stepped on two twigs crossed in the mud and the buds at each end indicated the turn-over of the ends – [drawing of twigs in swastika pattern] something like this. But there are those who will see a mystic symbolism in every single chance found detail of design. Wilson I am thankful to see does not refer everything to Phallic symbolism[2] as some of our men this side do. I have read with vast interest an account of the success of your aero-motor in "Modern Machinery" and am looking for fuller details.[3] With renewed thanks and very best regards, Believe me dear Mr. Langley,

Very sincerely yours
Rudyard Kipling.

Notes
1. Thomas Wilson, *The Swastika* (Washington, DC, 1896). The swastika, a Hindu symbol of good luck, was used by RK as a sort of trade mark, in conjunction with an elephant's head and a lotus flower, beginning with the Outward Bound Edition of his works in 1896. It regularly appeared on the volumes of the English trade edition of his books, and on other editions. In May of 1933, after the rise to power in Germany of Hitler, who had appropriated the swastika as the emblem of his "Aryan" notions, RK instructed his publishers to cease to use the swastika on his books.
2. MS incomplete. The text from this point on is from a typescript copy at the University of Sussex.
3. Langley's unmanned, steam-powered, heavier-than-air aircraft made successful flights on the Potomac in May and November of 1896.

To Frank N. Doubleday, 14 March 189[7]
ALS: Princeton University

Rock House, / Maidencombe, / St. Marychurch. / Mar. 14. '95.

Dear Doubleday –

Yours of the 5th with Tribune scrap in corner. So it's S. S. McClure is it?[1] I thirst for further particulars; because I have a lively recollection of a winter day in Vermont when *McClure Magazine* was just being born: and for eight (or eighteen) consecutive hours that cyclone in a frock-coat whirled round our little shanty explaining, exhorting, [rating?] and prophesying. He is a great man but he'd kill me in a week with mere surplus of energy.

All I selfishly hope is that you aren't going to cut the painter till the Edition de luxe is through.[2] The first two vols are now in their box on the drawing-room table and each time that I look through them I feel as though I had just had a shave, and shampoo at the Hoffman House; a Turkish bath; a new suit of dress clothes; a Sherry's dinner, a green

mist *and* a cigar. Unless, the yellow silk (immense notion that silk!) is a
trifle too yellow there isn't a fault to be found with the get up, but I
wish I'd made that M.S. facsimile just the size of the page.[3] Doubled
insets are apt to tear.

I am rearranging the verses on the lines I indicated and want to know
when you purpose to publish 'em. With all good wishes.

Very sincerely
Rudyard Kipling.

Notes
1. The new publishing firm of Doubleday and McClure; in its various transformations it
   was RK's American publisher for the rest of his career.
2. That is, the Outward Bound Edition, begun by Scribner under Doubleday's direction.
   It was continued by Scribner down to 1937. Two hundred and four sets were printed
   on Japan vellum and bound in yellow raw silk with green spine.
3. The first volume of the deluxe set contains a facsimile of a page from the MS of RK's
   "Introduction" to the Outward Bound Edition.

To James M. Conland, 25–9 March 1897

ALS: Library of Congress

Rock House, / Maidencombe, / St. Marychurch. / Mar. 25–29th. 97.

I'm a busy man – I'm a very busy man. Indeed I may say that [   ][1]
but that is no reason why I should have shut my head and corked up
the ink-bottle for the past few months. But the real trouble was that
whenever it was fine (which wasn't often) I threw all my other work to
the winds and went out loafing: and when it wasn't fine I was so busy
swearing that I hadn't time for less serious occupations.

And after all there isn't very much to tell. You know how quietly and
evenly life goes with us, unless we are violently disturbed. The Father,
who is very pressed illustrating the Scribner Edition of my books, has
just run down from Salisbury for a few days. And that reminds me,
that he will have to illustrate Captains Courageous for Scribner's
"Outward Bound" in clay. His notion is to get a set of typical photoes
of New England faces and to make a set of medallions or busts of them –
not to try to illustrate the fishing scenes at all but to render Disko,
Salters and the rest enduringly in high-relief. Do you think you could
lay your hands on *typical* photoes of that kind. You of all men are the
one that would be most certain of the (ethnographical) features of the
individuals: and the father could as it were fuse two or three photoes
into one type. He bids me send you his best remembrances and to tell

you that if you could lay hold of photoes he'd be everlastingly obliged. We want a long lean N.E. type; a fattish ditto, an iron-lipped Irish type for Long Jack; a Cape-Cod type for Tom Platt; and – I don't know what the deuce and all we want for Penn's foolish face: but I 'spect you may be able to think one up. At any rate can't you raid into old photo albums for suitable heads, poses and such like? Many thanks for the cutting you sent me in your note to the wife. What does the son of a gun mean by saying that the Truro and Harwich fleets don't exist any longer? There must surely be one or two schooners – but if Truro, and Harwich are as dead as he makes out we'll have to alter it for book form.² I am very keen on looking out for mistakes and I'd give a good deal to be able to go through the tale all over again with you because one way and another a whole lot of small errors *must* have cropped up which you could point out easier by word of mouth than by writing. A man in New York has sent me a copy of "The Old Farmer's Almanac" with a serious note to tell me that it's name isn't the "Robert B. Thomas" almanack as I [   ].³ I knew that but some people are so [   ]⁴ particular. Another chap half way across the continent says I've got one of the grades wrong in that trans Continental run of Cheyne's special – and he hasn't the decency to tell me which one it is. *Those* are the little things I want to look out for and guard against. The tale isn't making much splash here but Pearson's Magazine in which it comes out isn't much of a thing anyway.

I've done a yarn about a locomotive for Scribners.⁵ Don't know when it comes out but they say they are going to illustrate it up to the nines. It may make you laugh when you see it. Doubleday of Scribners, and his wife, dropped in here to tea the other day and stayed to dinner and we heard a whole lot of news. It was very pleasant to listen to the energetic, New-York accent once more, and to learn who had been doing what and why, since we left. They said that Fifth Ave is being laid down in asphalte. I'll believe that when I see it. Also I had a note from Teddy Roosevelt who in the intervals of scrapping with the rest of the police board finds time to remember me.

So far as I have the means of judging the Senate has gone and done *rather* more harm to America in a few weeks than England ever put in in all the past hundred years. Their action in messing about with the arbitration treaty⁶ is – rightly or wrongly – supposed to be an outward and visible sign of the Union's hatred of England: and half the papers are saying: – "we never knew this was so. It's shocking" and the other half are saying: – "*We* knew it all along. We told you they weren't civilized." I have a notion that another eighteen months will see a smash compared to which the panic of '93 was a flea bite. And talking of smashes and their results reminds me that we are going up to London in a few days to meet Cecil Rhodes⁷ at dinner. I think it will be rather larks. March down here is the great spring month: things are as forward as they are in May in Brattleboro: and the white limestone roads fairly glare and shimmer under the sun. The hedges are out, and our spring flowers are almost over. You've no notion of the hot-house like nature of Southern England when the sun once gets at it. But in spite of the sun we continue to get our whack of rain.

I have at last found a captain of our navy, an old friend of mine,[8] who offers me a berth aboard of a new 20-knot cruiser for the naval Manoevres. Can you imagine me in oilskins chasing up and down the English channel playing at being a sailor. I rather look forward to the fun, which begins about the middle of June.

For the last two months we – and incidentally all Europe – have been living on the edge of a volcano[9] and even now the betting is about level as to whether the [   ][10] thing will blow up after all. I've got my billet in event of a big shindy: but it wasn't worth while going down to the Mediterranean and hanging about on a lee-shore (Crete has a *vile* coast) to see Turks and Cretans fighting.[11] One good result of the mess has been to show the continent that England has rather more of a navy than the rest of 'em put together. England has done her level best by hanging on to the European concert to make things smooth for the Greeks. If she had pulled out of the Syndicate, Germany, Austria and Russia (the three despotic powers) would have played hell with the Greeks all round.

[   ][12] we have another chance of a big row in South Africa in which Germany may or may not take a hand. It would be a good thing if she did: because England does not love Germany. Altogether, you see, life this side the water does not lack excitement. [   ][13] The children seem to be thriving. Young baby Elsie is wrestling madly with the English language and Josephine is deep in fairy-tales and kindergarten. We have a new and rather successful little governess who keeps her in better order than before. She really is growing into a very sweet-looking child – and now I've got to hustle out for a drive with my father who sends his best salaams to you. Write me a line when you can and with greetings to all your family believe me

As ever yours
Rudyard Kipling.

Notes

1. Passage erased.
2. In the book version of *"Captains Courageous"* ships from both Truro and Harwich are mentioned.
3. Illegible. A reference to "a 'Robert B. Thomas' almanac" in chapter 5 of *"Captains Courageous"* in *McClure's*, VIII (January 1897) 230, is altered to "'The Old Farmer's' almanac" in the book version.
4. Illegible.

5. "*.007*", *Scribner's*, August 1897 (*The Day's Work*).
6. On 23 March the Senate voted several crippling amendments to a general arbitration treaty between the US and Great Britain; later the treaty failed of ratification.
7. Cecil John Rhodes (1853–1902), English mining magnate in South Africa and ardent imperialist, founder of the British South Africa Company, through which Rhodesia was established; by his will set up the Rhodes Scholarships. RK had first met him in Cape Town in 1891. Rhodes had come to London to face a select committee of the House of Commons inquiring into the Jameson raid; he was now about to return to Africa.
8. Captain Edward Henry Bayly (1849–1904), whom RK met on his voyage to Cape Town in 1891, now commanded the small cruiser HMS *Pelorus*. RK sailed with him on manoeuvres in the first two weeks of July (see 21 July 1897).
9. Greeks and Turks were fighting over Crete; the Powers blockaded Crete but not, on England's objection, the Greek ports. Turkey declared war in April; the Greeks were beaten and accepted a treaty of peace by the end of the next year.
10. Word erased: "damned" seems most likely.
11. It was reported in the press that RK was to go to Crete as the correspondent of *The Times* at $5000 a month. Whether he had in fact considered such a thing is not known, but it seems at least possible.
12. Half a line erased.
13. Most of a page erased here.

To William Hallett Phillips, 29 March 1897

ALS: Photocopy, Harvard University

Rock House, / Maidencombe, / St. Marychurch. / Mar. 29. '97

Sitting Fox!

I am glad that at last I have found your trail, for it has been long hidden from me. I wrote to Rockhill and also, last week, to Teddy Roosevelt and him I told to send men and a gun to Washington to dig you up and make you speak. But now that you are digesting international law and etiquette I perceive you become proud and haughty. Seriously, something must have gone wrong with my letters to you and in future I'm going to send 'em to the Department of state direct. Naturally, if you haven't got any for *six* months you must have thought me all kinds of a pig – which indeed I am not.

Tiffany who lives in Regent Street is going to mount the totem for me in the similitude of a charm. The gut lashing of the white arrow is so delicate that the whole thing must be practically cased in gold because I want to carry it about with me wherever I go.

Now as to your books they will be the Scribner Edition with my Pater's illustrations and a new and bald-headed photo of me in front: but that edition is only coming along bit by bit. I've got three vols of 'em stacked away for you and if you like 'em in quarter-sections I'll send 'em over at once. I *never* forget my friend O Sitting Fox!

Just now I am in labour with a spring-poem[1] – not a Gordam ordinary spring-poem but how a man feels about April time when he remembers where he has caught salmon and watched moose the year before,[2] a poem describing the "hunting medicine" that the Red Gods made to drive men into the woods. Thus: –

"Do you know the blackened timber – do you know the racing stream
   With a raw right-angled log-jam at the end
And the bar of sun-warmed shingle where a man may bask and dream
   To the click of shod canoe-poles round the bend
Oh it's there that we are going with our rods and reels and traces
To a sullen grunting Red Man that I know
To a couch of a new-pulled hemlock with the star-light on our faces
For the Red Gods call us out and we must go!
   We must go – go – go away from here
   On the other side the world we're over due
(Pray your road is clear before when the old spring-fret comes o'er you
   And the Red Gods call for you!)"

I think if I ever get it finished I'll publish it in *Life* and I'll send you the M.S.[3] It will, if it comes out right, make you restless every time you read it.

As for "me and my house" we are in the thick of a South English Spring – primroses, violets, hyacinths, birds and butterflies abound already; and every sign of a warm summer. It's like a hot-house down by Torquay: I career all over the land on my wheel and Josephine is shooting up into a young woman of great fluency of speech and singular directness of manner.

And that reminds me that little Miss Hay will have a gay time of it this year.[4] A house in Carleton House Terrace is unmitigated lugs not to say guilty splendour. It will never do to send out a poor ambassador after Hay. I haven't bothered him with letters because I knew every dam phool this side Hell was pitching in letters to him but I hope to meet him ere long. American stock is way – way down just now – thanks to the [   ][5] incontinence of the Senate. You can't – but someday perhaps you will – realize the enormous harm that has been done not only in England but throughout the civilized world to America. It would be a tremendous amount of sunshine that would ever bring me back there for any length of time and the shame and the sorrow of it is that it was all so damned unnecessary.

But you come over and play with me. We don't talk about "hereditary foes" this side the water. There's a cliff-full of rabbits and a sea full of boats under my window. London won't be fit to live in this year. Prices are climbing up already on account of the Jubilee. But I'll tell you a secret Sitting Fox. I believe I'm the sole, solitary, single and only "poet" who isn't writing a Jubilee Ode this year. There will be a ghastly crop of 'em. Now I must go out and get my hair cut. With best wishes from my wife and baby Josephine

Yours as always
Rudyard Kipling.

Notes

1. "The Feet of the Young Men", *Scribner's*, December 1897 (*The Five Nations*). The passage that RK quotes in this letter is stanza three of the published version, from which it differs in detail.
2. RK has in mind his trip to the Gaspé with de Forest in June 1896.
3. Phillips drowned in May 1897; the poem as it appears in *Scribner's* is "Dedicated to the Memory of the Late W. Hallett-Phillips".
4. As the daughter of the new Ambassador in the year of Victoria's Diamond Jubilee.
5. Word illegible.

To Moberly Bell, 8 May 1897
ALS: Library of Congress

Rock House, / Maidencombe, / St. Marychurch. / May. 8. 97

Dear Bell –

All I need is the book rights of the Lady of the Snows.[1] I *want* papers to quote it like anything. The more the merrier. Please let 'em! I didn't know Wallace[2] was doing the Thessaly letter[3] but it caught my mind as a very good bit of work. Races who fire revolvers promiscuous are apt to go off at half-cock and incidentally to recoil, and blow off backwards.

As to the Jubilee, I loathe it. I've done a lot of costive disconnected bits of verse like macaroni, and I can't string 'em on one thread to save myself. After all, it's Austen's[4] job. Like a fool I've used up my best notions of a scheme in "a song of the English."[5] But I will try till the last minute.

Ever yours
Rudyard Kipling.

Notes

1. *The Times*, 27 April 1897 (*The Five Nations*); the poem salutes the establishment of a Canadian preferential tariff, favouring the British and colonial connection in trade.
2. Sir Donald Mackenzie Wallace: see 27 June 1888.
3. On the fighting in Thessaly, where the Greeks were being badly beaten by the Turks (see 25–9 March 1897).
4. Alfred Austin, the Poet Laureate.
5. *English Illustrated Magazine*, May 1893 (*The Seven Seas*).

To Stanley Weyman, 12 May 1897
ALS: Library of Congress

Rock House, / Maidencombe, / St. Marychurch. / May. 12. '97

Dear Weyman –

I've just come up from the wild and wet West, to find your outburst waiting me.

Well – you can say "Damn" and I can say "Damn" about the R.L.S. committee list[1] but – after all what's the use? They want the money. Dukes, Marquises etc. draw money at the head of *any* prospectus. Ergo: snaffle as many names for the list as you can.

Also you must remember that the Scots on account of their feudal training have even a keener scent for a titled Scot than the English. Any how (and be cheered by this thought) the committee list isn't Literature. It's plain business; with prospectus guinea pigs etc. all complete. I just grinned and sent in my contribution.[2] If Stevenson knows it must be priceless joy to him. But the other business – at the Academy Banquet[3] was unmitigated dirt. I sat next table to Austen, within four places of him and the little runt acted his piece – chucked out his skinny little arms à la "first lessons in elocution" and I felt hot and indignant all over. My only joy was that Irving[4] across the table was keeping up a gentle fire of contradictions ("But we don't do any such thing etc.") while Austen was babbling about the "Cinderella of the professions."[5] Yah! That made me much sicker than you were. And yet, after dinner Austen talked quite sanely about rose-growing.[6] There is only one moral to be drawn from these things. A man must go ahead with his own business, and honourably abstain from getting mixed up with Marchionesses and such like. There's a mildew in the air of England which is bad for the physical and mental liver if you aren't born to it, and I'm going to pull out again next winter. We've been rained on for eight [   ][7] months, and now I'm going to make love to Lang to see if he hasn't some titled territorial friend who can give me a little trout-fishing. There's consistency for you!

Glad you blew off steam in my direction – for I was of your mind. I've been married – lo! these five years and Allah has sent us two small maidens who are our joy and delight. Here's hoping you may be as happy in the venture as I have been.

Ever yours sincerely
Rudyard Kipling.

Notes
1. The committee formed to erect a memorial to Robert Louis Stevenson was headed by the Earl of Rosebery and included the Duke of Fife, the Earl of Kintire, and Lord

Balfour of Burleigh (*The Times*, 27 May 1897, p. 10).
2. The names of both RK and of Weyman appear on the first subscription list for the memorial (*The Times*, 27 May 1897, p. 10).
3. 1 May 1897: this was the first of the Royal Academy banquets presided over by RK's uncle, Sir Edward Poynter.
4. Sir Henry Irving (1838–1905), actor and producer.
5. In responding to the toast of "Literature" Austin called it, among other things, "the Cinderella of the arts" (*The Times*, 3 May 1897, p. 5).
6. Austin's work on gardening commanded much more respect than his poetry.
7. Word illegible.

To James M. Conland, 1 June 1897

ALS: Library of Congress

Royal Palace Hotel / Kensington High Street / London. W. / June
1. '97

I'm badly in your debt, Doctor dear, as the Irishman said when he had swallowed the carbolic acid by mistake for gin: but we've been living a chaotic and disorganized life for the last few weeks. You see we gave up the house in Devon – a lovely place but eight months damp, raw sea fog and mildew were rather more than we could stand. Then we decided to take a holiday from house keeping while we hunted for a new house: and to London (London in Jubilee year!) we came three weeks ago and have been living in a hotel overlooking the park: with children with us. The wife is hugely enjoying the rest from house keeping and the demoralizing comfort of not having to think about meals. Meantime a kindly relative has placed her house near Brighton at our disposal for as long as we want; and we go down on Wednesday next: to resume the dreary game of house hunting.[1] I feel like a houseless gipsy: and would almost be thankful for a hut and that – and the [   ][2] grind of society in London – is my excuse for silence. But my father is by no means silent. On the contrary he is jubilant over those splendidly typical heads that you've sent, and I think he is making some gorgeous medallions out of 'em. I also, sent over to the Mayor of Gloucester, for the city seal which he intends, somehow or other, to work into the illustrations. But the heads are superb. As usual, you've done the very right thing at the very right time. A "son of a monk" did write me a furious letter about the Portugee's absolution. I didn't answer it but all I meant to convey was Manuel's own way of looking at the business. Nothing would persuade an average Portugee mariner that one good turn didn't deserve another: and after all, it's Manuel's mind, and not the custom of the R.C. church that I'm dealing with. I've revised the tale from beginning to end and sent it off to the Century to publish in the early fall I think it is – about September. Don't be astonished at the dedication. I felt it only the barest form of justice to dedicate the book to you – on both sides of the water.[3] You can explain the connection to the public at your leisure. I don't know yet what the Century purpose to do about illustrations – can only hope they'll put in some really first class ones. We haven't any of that kind yet, goodness knows.

Life has been greatly mixed – not to say exciting for me lately. I went to the big banquet of the Royal Academy to begin with; and sat next to Irving and the Poet Laureate. Incidentally I met Hamo Thorneycroft the sculptor – brother to *the* Thorneycroft who builds the torpedo-boats.[4] Sez he to me "would you like to attend the steam-trials of a new thirty-knot destroyer." "Rather!" sez I: and about three days later I got a telegram advising me to come down to Chatham dockyard: so down I went[5] and on the way picked up the Thorneycroft crowd who represented the contractor's interests at the trial (She had to do her 30 knots an hour for three consecutive hours before the government would take her) and a most fascinating old navy engineer who represents the admiralty [sketch of a torpedo boat].[6] Well Sir. This is about all there was to the boat. She was 19.5 ft beam 7ft draft aft and 5 forward and 210 overall. She was filthy black – no bright work anywhere: and covered with oil and coal dust – a turtle back forward to turn the worst of the seas: a conning tower plated with $\frac{1}{2}$ inch steel to turn rifle-fire: but her skin was $\frac{3}{16}$ of an inch everywhere else! Her deck was covered with some sort of compo-like floorcloth but she tumbled home[7] so that her widest available beam wasn't over ten feet. We pulled out of the Medway into the mouth of the Thames at an easy twelve knots to get down to our course – from the Mouse light to the Lower Hope reach – a lumpy sea and a thirty-knot breeze. Then I was introduced to one George Brown – Thorneycroft's head man who had attended more than 2000 trials! He had a goatee beard and a head like a Yankee – was tremendously interesting: a born engineer. We talked about steam trials.

"Yes" said George Brown "we've had every damned thing happen to torpedo boats that could happen. We've shed our propeller blades, we've carried away every thing that could carry away: we've twisted our rudders off; and we've just waltzed the engines off the bed-plates. There's nothing that can surprise us now – unless some boat got out of the water and began to fly."

"Do you believe in ever reaching 40 knots" I said.

"Not at present" said George Brown. "I mean by that that if you were to come to us with a blank cheque and ask us to build you a 40-knot boat *now*, we couldn't guarantee her. We creep on knot by knot you see. Now this autumn (I hope you'll be present) we shall try a new 33-knot boat the *Express*. Next year perhaps we'll get to 35 knots and so on. 'Must go slow."

By that time we'd freshened up to 17 knots – jogging along easily. They wrapped my neck up in a comforter, gave me many oilskins: and tied a sou wester over my ears. The wind was pretty keen and now and then the top of a sea came aboard. She was steered from the bridge forward and we all huddled under the protection of the turtle-back – practically the break of the foc'sle. Then we struck a twenty-two knot gait – and very nice it was. They began to rig up the indicators, to show how many revolutions we were doing and I went down into the engine room. Two engines of 3,000 h.p. apiece were making about 230 to the minute – may be a trifle less. Our stoke-hold was open [   ]8 Then I heard some one say to the captain, – "we'll shut down as soon as you say sir" and they screwed down the stoke hold hatches and a fan (700 revolutions a minute!) began to pump forced draft into the fires. Then the captain said "Let go!" or words to that effect until – well do you know the feeling of standing up in a car when the thing starts up quick. I nearly fell down on the deck. The little bitch jumped from 22 to 30 like a whipped horse – and the three hours trial had begun!

It was like a nightmare. The vibration shook not only your body but your intestines and finally seemed to settle on your heart. The breeze along the deck made it difficult to walk. I staggered aft above the twin-screws and there saw a blue-jacket, vomiting like a girl; and in the ward-room which is right in the stern of her, I felt my false teeth shaking in my head! The pace was too good for her to roll. All we could do was to get under the lee of the conning tower and hang on while this devil's darning needle tore up and down coast. We passed 17 knot passenger boats, flew ten miles past 'em, turned and came back and overtook them. By the way when she turned she slung you to one side like a bicycle. The wake ran out behind us like white hot iron: the engine room was one lather of oil and water: the engines were running 400 to the minute: the guages: the main-steam pipes and everything that wasn't actually built into her were quivering and jumping: there was half an inch of oil and water on the floor and – you couldn't see the cranks in the crank pit. It was more like Hell, on a ten foot scale, than anything you ever dreamed – and through the infernal din of it George Brown shouted in my ear "Isn't she a darling!" Well, I climbed out of the engine-room rather thankfully and went up on the bridge by the captain. You never saw a boat steer as she did. One grey headed old quartermaster held her at the wheel; and her two heavy drop-rudders swung her over the face of the waters. We shaved a brig coming up the Thames just to show how near we could go: and our wash threw her up and down as though we had been a liner. We skimmed past buoys with about five yards to spare, running all along the edge of the Maplin sands. Just for fun – because she had been tested already on the measured mile – the skipper said: – "we'll take her over the mile." That is marked by two red admiralty buoys – and is the official testing mile for all ships of the navy. The first time we had the wind at our back going almost as fast as we were: so I wasn't blinded. Well, we all timed her and away we went! The buoys simply seemed to be flying to us and we covered the mile in 1.50½, or something over 32 knots to the hour. Just try to think of it. That's faster than any trotter or bicycle – and most trains. Then we turned her round (by this time the contractor's men were damning in heaps because they were out for the straight away trial and all these turns were knocking a little speed off her). We faced into that thirty knot gale and for the honour of the thing I *had* to stay up on the bridge. That was pure hell. The wind got under my sou'wester: and I was nearly choked by the string round my throat. But we did the mile in the face of wind and tide in 2.5–6 or 8 – the timings did not agree. Then we went on and on and on till we all turned white with fatigue. Up and down we flew and as it was impossible to sit down to a meal they gave us sandwiches (cut ashore: you don't cut meat on a destroyer) in a basket and some drinks. At last those awful three hours came to an end: but not before the speaking-tubes to the captain's bridge had been smashed off by the vibration. Then we drew breath: and every one said Thank God! She'd done ninety knots in those three hours: but if it had been straight away in deep sea, we'd have done 31. Everything was quite cool and nothing had smashed up and they all said I was the mascotte. Every engineer aboard knew McAndrew's Hymn by the way and enjoyed it. Well then we jogged back to Sheerness at 20 knots an hour. We were all as black as sweeps; and utterly played out. It took me two days to get the "jumps" out of my legs. But I wouldn't have missed the trip for any thing. Three days later[9] I went down to Oxford among the four hundred year old universities and dined with the tutors and so on at Balliol college. The boys cheered me so that the Master[10] couldn't say grace and altogether I had a most wonderful time. Since then I've been flourishing about in a frock-coat and top-hat when I wasn't dining out. Can you imagine me as a dude! But the wife and I thought we might as well play the game now that we were in for it. We went to the Lyceum the other night: Irving put a private box at our disposal; and after the play we went round and saw him and Miss Terry[11] in their war-paint on the stage. He's rather keen that I should write a play for him: and I should rather like it. But actors are rummy folk. Then Henry James came to dine with us and then I went out to a man's party of generals and military [   ][12] where I met George Curzon[13] – him that married old Leiter's daughter:[14] and is now a flourishing political person. Also we lunched with Hay who has a lovely home here – overlooking the line of the Jubilee procession. He has all his work cut out for him to manage his share of the Jubilee, and as if that wasn't enough McKinley has sent over a special batch of Jubilee ambassadors whom he wants to put under Hay's command. Poor Hay has been keeping the wires red-hot explaining that *he* doesn't hanker for the honour and that it would be better to let Whitelaw Reid[15] and General Miles[16] dig for themselves. All the Ambassadors are nearly worked off their legs this year and they will all thank God on all fours when this show is over. London is simply packed and double packed. There are stands and seats everywhere: and like the Embassies the Police are praying for the day to be over without accidents. Estimates say between 8, and 10,000,000 people will attend. There are 80,000 *extra* Americans in town: and Cook the tourist man has practically chartered all the suburb of Richmond for their accommodation.

We are going down to Brighton to be out of it all. There we have a house lent us by my Aunt, Lady Burne-Jones: and from there we hope to find a house for ourselves. [   ]17 Your news of [   ]18 is bad hearing. Failures are not wholesome for middle-aged men. I hope it hasn't hit the town hard. They suffered enough in the collapse of Kelly's mortgages. Fred Waite I hear is in jail and Mrs Waite is abandoning the post office so that also must go. Don't *you* go away but hang on till we come back if ever that joyful day arrives.

But here I am yarning over yards of paper and it's time for me to send this to the mail.

With all our best wishes to you and your household

Ever yours sincerely

Rudyard Kipling

P.S.   Eldridge of the *Nellie* might like to hear my account of the torpedo boat when next you meet. Anyway his engineer would.

RK

Notes

1. They left Rock House for the Royal Palace Hotel in London on 12 May, and went to North End House, the Burne-Joneses' house in Rottingdean, on 2 June (CK diary).
2. About two words deleted.
3. The American edition of "*Captains Courageous*" (but not the English) is dedicated to Conland.
4. For Hamo Thornycroft, see 3–25 December 1889. His brother Sir John Isaac Thornycroft (1843–1928), naval architect, was a pioneer in torpedo boats and destroyers.
5. On 18 May (CK diary).
6. The ship was the torpedo boat destroyer *Foam*; the engineer was William Joshua Harding, Chief Engineer, Royal Navy.
7. In a ship, the inward inclination of the upper part of the hull; the opposite of "flare".
8. Half a line erased.
9. 24 May (CK diary).
10. Edward Caird (1835–1908).
11. Ellen Terry (1847–1928), actress, long associated with Irving at the Lyceum.
12. Word erased.
13. George Nathaniel Curzon (1859–1925), 1st Marquess Curzon, Conservative statesman,

afterwards Viceroy of India; he was at this time Parliamentary Under-Secretary for Foreign Affairs in Lord Salisbury's administration.

14. Curzon married Mary Leiter, daughter of a Chicago millionaire, Levi Zeigler Leiter, the co-founder of Marshall Field's.

15 Reid (1837–1912), editor of the New York *Tribune*, was later Ambassador to Great Britain under Theodore Roosevelt.

16. Nelson Appleton Miles (1839–1925), Civil War general, now Commander-in-Chief of the US Army.

17. One line erased.

18. Name erased.

To William Joshua Harding[1] [25 June 1897][2]

ALS: Library of Congress

[Rottingdean] Friday:

Dear Mr. Harding:

If it hadn't been for Spithead[3] I should have come up to the *Mallard's* trials: but yesterday I got a chance to see the fleet and went off at once. 'Never dreamed that there was anything like it under Heaven. It was beyond words – beyond any description! Perhaps the most effective sight in its suggestion of deviltry was the line of t[orpe-do].b[oat].d[estroyer]'s. I spotted our old friend the "Foam" looking very spick and span and made the acquaintance of a Head Mechanician of sorts – don't know his precise rank – just in from 3½ years on the Australian station. What a splendid class these petty officers are. He was a Glasgow man: had served his time with Penn[4] and the Jubilee struck him as a damned nuisance. He wanted to get home.

All being well I'm off on the 1st for any manœvres[5] there may be going but keep me posted about trials. One never knows when one can get off. Just the merest official slip of intelligence will do.

Ever yours sincerely

Rudyard Kipling.

Notes

1. Chief Engineer, Royal Navy: see 1 June 1897, n. 5.
2. Dated from postmark and internal evidence.
3. The great Jubilee naval review, held from 23 June: RK went down to Spithead with his father on 24 June (CK diary).
4. The engineering firm of John Penn and Son, Greenwich, builders of ship's engines.
5. RK, on board the H.M.S. *Pelorus*, sailed with the Channel Fleet on manoeuvres off Ireland in the first two weeks of July.

To James Thursfield,[1] [June 1897]
ALS: Library of Congress

The Elms, / Rottingdean, / Sussex.

Dear Thursfield –

Ever so many thanks for the leader which I do now remember. It contains something that I rather want for quotation in a job I'm on.

As to manœvres I am your debtor and will make my own arrangements *privatim*. As I'm on my own lone pass book and not working for anyone nor intending to I'll be able to steal away a bit before to the West Country and watch the mobilizing. The verses shall follow. They are rather a hefty job to copy out. For 'Eavin's sake keep 'em quite till I use 'em. I don't want 'em to leak anywhere till the time is good and ripe.[2]

Have you by any chance seen the specification of the "Mujaboro Water tube boiler?" – It's a Jap. gadget done I believe by the *Engineering* Rear admiral of that navy. I don't know anything about bilers but it throws a new light on the Jap's methods. I don't think they are pleased to have followed our lead about bellevilles.[3]

Ever yours sincerely
Rudyard Kipling

Notes
1. (Sir) James Thursfield (1840–1923), leader-writer on *The Times* since 1881 and an expert on naval history and affairs; he was also the first editor of *The Times Literary Supplement*.
2. RK means "The Destroyers", on which he was working in June (CK diary, 3 June 1897); the poem was published in May 1898, in *McClure's Magazine* (*The Five Nations*).
3. A type of boiler, named after the French engineer Louis Delaunay-Belleville (1843–1912).

To Eustace Balfour, 9 July 1897
ALS: Dalhousie University

H.M.S. Pelorus / July. 9. '97

Off Ireland in a gale of wind.

Dear Balfour –

Many thanks for your invitation to the Regimental Dinner but – you see where it found me! I got it on the 6th in Lough Swilly where we were trying to coal out of three scandalously inadequate colliers. I've been away since the 30th with the Channel Fleet picking up tons of new notions and occasionally throwing up a meal or two. The new admiral[1] is a curious person of whom I hope to tell you more when we meet. He isn't Lord Walter Kerr[2] by a very large heap, and he handles his fleet rather like a new subaltern handles his company – any amount of orders and precious little order. But I've had a lovely time and am chock full of new tales.

Ever yours
Rudyard Kipling.

Notes
1. Admiral Sir Henry Frederick Stephenson (1842–1919) commanded the Channel Squadron, 1897–8.
2. Kerr (1839–1927) commanded the channel Squadron, 1895; he was First Sea Lord, 1899–1904, and Admiral of the Fleet, 1904: "a thorough seaman and wise administrator" according to the *DNB*.

To Moberly Bell, 21 July 1897
ALS: Library of Congress

[Rottingdean] July 21. '97

Dear Bell –

I entirely and absolutely agree with your Berlin ex-correspondent. By all means let us kick the Germans – "lest we forget." My fortnight with the channel Fleet makes me inclined to think that we could kick many more races than the Teuton and when I think of the pious hymn I am astounded at my own moderation.[1]

I suppose you've been on Fleet manœvres? It's amazing. All the same the New Channel Admiral is rather an ass. I notice your naval expert is down on Fellowes.[2] I hadn't been in the cruiser twelve hours before one of the *men* confided to me that the same Fellowes would walk round Stevenson. "E'll find an 'ole in the rules Sir, an' slip through it." Which seems to be precisely what he did; and Stevenson ought to have divined it.[3] At least he might have spent a cruiser or two on finding out. I'm mighty glad I went, as now I am sure of a ship in event of real bother, and have learned a few things about what they may be expected to do.

As to payment – be easy.[4] I'll turn out something some day not of a national character for which I will stick you as heavily as I can but you know my rule about this particular type of verse. And besides, the office gave me and the Queen a leader between us.[5] I've had any amount of letters about the thing. It *did* arrive just at the right time.

I may be in town for a volunteer dinner with Eustace Balfour on the 26th but otherwise I must stay down here and knock my naval notes into shape.[6] I should much like to have met Ian Maclaren.[7]

Ever yours
Rudyard Kipling.

Notes
1. RK means "Recessional", published in *The Times*, 17 July; cf. Lord Clive's "I stand astonished at my own moderation!"
2. Vice-Admiral Sir John Fellowes (1843–1912) succeeded Stephenson as commander of the Channel Squadron.
3. See *A Fleet in Being*, p. 8, where the rival admiral finds "a hole in the rules".
4. RK had refused any payment for "Recessional".
5. *The Times*, 17 July, devotes a leader to Victoria's letter of thanks to her people on the occasion of the Jubilee and to RK's "Recessional": poem and letter appear together in the same column of the paper. The note of "moral responsibility", *The Times* says, "rings out as clearly in the simple grandeur of the Queen's message as in Mr. Kipling's soul-stirring verses".
6. Incorporated in *A Fleet in Being* (1898).
7. Ian MacLaren was the pseudonym of John Watson (1850–1907), minister of the Presbyterian Church of England at Sefton Park, Liverpool, and author of successful fiction belonging to the "Kailyard School".

To J. W. Mackail, 21 July 1897
ALS: University of Sussex

[Rottingdean] July 21. '97

Dear Jack –

Thank you very much[1] but all the same seeing what manner of armed barbarians we are surrounded with, we're about the only power with a glimmer of civilization in us. I've been round with the channel fleet for a fortnight and any other breed of white man, with such a weapon to their hand, would have been captivating the round Earth in their own interests long ago. This is no ideal world but a nest of burglars, alas, and we must protect ourselves against being burgled. All the same, we have no need to shout and yell and ramp about our strength because that is waste of power, and because other nations can do the advertising better than we can.

The big smash is coming one of these day, sure enough, but I think we shall pull through not without credit. It will be the common people – the 3rd class carriages – that'll save us.

Ever yours
Ruddy.

Note

1. Mackail, a pacifist, had written on the publication of "Recessional" (17 July), "I cannot tell you how glad I am of it, or forbear writing to say so. There are all the signs of England saving up for the most tremendous smash ever recorded in history if she does not look to her goings" (Carrington, *Kipling*, p. 267).

To Moberly Bell, [22? July 1897]

ALS: Library of Congress

Royal Palace Hotel / Kensington / Thursday night.

Dear Bell –

That is a poor notion but if you hand over any money in *my* name, it simply means that all sorts of ancient sons of Belial will come down on me for subscriptions to their pet charity.[1] All I want to do is to get shut of the country parsons who want to know where Recessional can be procured. Any charity you choose will please me. As to the *Blind Readers*,[2] I confess the whole tone and scope of the poem is so altogether out of my beat that I'm all at sea about it. It looks to me as if it was bred by *The Two Voices*, out of the *Vision of Sin*[3] – her dam Blooming obvious. The latter is a well known mare and when bred to Pegasus had dropped some good colts but I do not see any trace, of Pegasus blood in this gelding. All of which simply means that as I said before I am not competent to criticize fairly. The stuff is smooth, facile, windy in spots but there is no reason why it should ever end. *Exempli gratia* – here is an extra last verse which I make bold to say is quite as valuable as any other: –

And soft beyond the shuddering hills –
Inexorable, iron-shod
Pursued of reboantic Norns
The spent day sighed her soul to God!

Moreover: – If you like it so
I hold it truth with him who sings
Lord Ronald brought a lilly white dove
With all the loveliness of wings!
etc. etc.[4]

But I never was cut out for a critic: so please don't be wrath with me.

I met Thursfield last night at the Athenæum and discussed naval manœuvres – and Admiral Stevenson whom I may some day respect but cannot love.

Thanks for the Hussar letter which looks very genuine.

Sincerely yours
Rudyard Kipling

Notes
1. After RK refused payment for "Recessional" Bell evidently offered to donate a sum equivalent to payment for the poem to a charity to be designated by RK.
2. Presumably Bell had written to RK telling him of some of the responses to "Recessional".
3. Among Tennyson's early poems, both published in 1842.
4. This burlesque pastiche contains scraps from Tennyson, Thomas Holley Chivers and traditional ballad as well as unidentifiable scraps from the general poetic stock. I do not know what RK is mocking, unless it is "Recessional".

To George F. Bearns,[1] [15 August 1897][2]
ALS: Library of Congress

North End House / Rottingdean.

Dear Sir:

What can I say in reply to your letter of the 13th, except that it is rather a large order to compress allusions to the whole of our Empire into two hundred lines of alleged verse.[3] And when it comes to my sins of omission – well, I ought to have included Perth, West Australia; Dunedin of the Southern Island, N.Z.; the West Indies, and a few other places.

But indeed I am not unmindful of Newfoundland. Perhaps I may know more about it than you think; and certainly no man in his senses ever doubted the loyalty of the senior colony. We can leave that, I think, to the Yankees, who seem to take comfort from inventing curious fictions of that nature.

However, when and if there is another edition of my verses, I will do my best to put in Newfoundland's voice also, but the task is not a pleasant one. If I leave out all reference I am taxed with "injustice." If I make a pointed reference, as I did in "Our Lady of the Snows,"[4] I am – to put it mildly – supposed to be scaring away immigrants by misrepresenting the climate of the Dominion.

But we will make a bargain. I will put in a four-line verse among "The

Song of the Cities,"[5] if you on your part will drop and influence other people to drop allusions to the "loyalty" of the "colonies." In the first place I dislike the word "colonies" and if you look through my verses you will find I very seldom use it. It is out of date and misleading, besides being provincial. In the second place there is no need to talk of "loyalty" among white men.* That is one of the things we all take for granted – because the Empire is Us – We ourselves; and for the White Man to explain that he is loyal is about as unnecessary as for a respectable woman to volunteer the fact that she is chaste.

Like yourself, I am a colonial in that I was born in Bombay but it has never occurred to me to say that I am "loyal," because, like you, I am a white man and – one can't step out of one's skin.

Very sincerely yours,
Rudyard Kipling.

* That is to say races speaking the English tongue, with a high birth rate and a low murder-rate, living quietly under Laws which are neither bought nor sold.

Notes
1. Bearns identifies himself only as "a Newfoundlander" in his letter to RK (ALS, Library of Congress).
2. Dated from postmark.
3. Bearns had written to complain that there is no reference to Newfoundland in "A Song of the English", which describes fifteen different colonial cities (*The Seven Seas*).
4. The poem set off a newspaper protest in Canada over the implication of its title.
5. He did not.

To Charles Eliot Norton, [16 August 1897][1]
ALS: Harvard University

North End House / Rottingdean.

Dear Mr Norton –

Your lovely letter to Carrie made me jealous: but I 'fess I deserve it. I ought to have written – not once but two or three times. But this England is an unholy place for small tuppeny-ha'penny notes which come in with our post and must be answered the next and day after day and month after month I've been trying to keep abreast of them instead of putting 'em where they belong and writing real letters.

I was away the first forty-eight hours of Sallie's visit to Carrie,[2] but from all I heard I gathered that they had not talked consecutively for more than 47 $\frac{1}{2}$. That cheered Carrie immensely but Sallie at Rottingdean; you at Ashfield and we away from Naulakha with bits of the downs for

Monadnock mixed things up. It would have been all right if you had come in from the garden with Taffy. We had one of your letters to Sallie read to us and got all the Ashfield news and the news of the family. Bless you and yours.

And now Sallie will be with you almost as soon as this letter. Did she tell you how we met up at the Humphfrey Wards'.[3] It nearly destroyed my gravity (I was in a frock-coat and a top-hat) and Sallie did quite when we escaped into Knightsbridge all three together. Curiously unreal and stuffy, somehow and H.W.'s keen businesslike face in all that gilded luxury the most unreal thing of all. (Now I will take a new pen).

The Trues[4] in the verses are – well the Trues – the old original four or five head-deities of the Red Man's mind – the old Beast Gods I think they were – Buffalo – Beaver – Elk $\left\{ \begin{matrix} \text{Fox} \\ \text{Coyote} \end{matrix} \right\}$ – or something of that nature. At any rate they are the Red Gods of the hunting-grounds – earth spirits waking man up in the spring. They live in the Reports of the Smithsonian Institute (Ethnological Bureau) these days but one can smell 'em of a fine morning sometimes. *You've* got some in your rock-pasture looking towards Monadnock.

But how can we ever come back? That's what I want to know. We're a slow moving people and it has just occurred to us that our concession over Venezuela didn't do us a bit of good. It isn't the upper crust who are saying this but the third-class carriages – people who get letters very occasionally from America. Their relatives have begun to tell 'em unpleasant things. So we are slowly – slowly warming up and one semi-imbecile politician goes around serenely your side of the water stoking the fire.[5] There is an article in the *Spectator* this week which is really interesting.[6] I don't see how Hutton[7] could have guessed the common-people's temper so closely. You see we are being girded at and goaded by Germany on the other side and there is an uneasy feeling that the continent is getting ready for the big Squeeze. We have only ourselves to trust to but the people won't move (you know our way) *en masse* till they consider it's a just war. For that war will be for the life. I don't know who'll pull the string first but at present it looks as if America were going to try. My memory is short but I don't remember anything that has made us more – polite than Sherman's statement that England quarrels oftener than she fights.

When Armageddon comes remember that whatever our sins may have been since America won her independence, we shall have been kicked into *this* war.

What has become of the "better people" one hears so much about? Our papers want to know where they are: or if they ever existed? Do they mean to save us the one insult or the one menace which will kick the beam? Because their time is *now*. In a little it will be too late. The wreck of the arbitration treaty has killed all confidence, though we are still saying polite things, and three generations will be needed to restore it. But, at least, the "better people" may help to stave off war. Ours have done their best.

Liberavi animam meam: and I feel all the better for it. I am preserving a discreet silence these days for which I pat myself on the back at all three meals. Golly! What couldn't I do with one set of verses? I feel like the quarter-million or so of veterans who personally saved the Union by advice to Lincoln at a critical moment only my merit is that I shut my head. Carrie who is reading beside me (no signs of that dilatory baby yet!) sends her best love to you all and so do I and I am

Ever yours most affectionately
Ruddy.

Notes
1. Dated from postmark.
2. Sarah Norton came to Rottingdean on 12 July while RK was with the fleet on manoeuvres.
3. (Thomas) Humphry Ward (1845–1926), journalist and editor, better known now as the husband of the novelist Mrs Humphry Ward (Mary Augusta Arnold): they acquired 25 Grosvenor Place in 1891. Ward, on the staff of *The Times* from 1881, was the author of the article on RK in *The Times*, 25 March 1890, that helped to establish RK's early reputation (Roger Lancelyn Green, *Kipling: The Critical Heritage* [New York, 1971] p. 50).
4. In line 3 of "The Feet of the Young Men", not published until December 1897 in *Scribner's*.
5. John Sherman, the American Secretary of State, had been reported in the New York *World* as saying, apropos of the current quarrel over seal-fishing rights, that England "quarrels oftener than she fights". RK's phrase "semi-imbecile" alludes to the fact that Sherman (1823–1900) was suffering from severe and increasing loss of memory.
6. "England and America", *Spectator*, 14 August 1897, pp. 200–1, saying that the American political leaders, not the American public, were distinctly hostile towards England, and accusing them of exploiting the ignorant patriotism of the country. The editorial quotes RK's "Et Dona Ferantes": "But, oh, beware my Country, when my Country grows polite?"
7. Richard Holt Hutton (1826–97), editor and proprietor of the *Spectator* since 1861.

To Lockwood de Forest, 17 August 1897
ALS: Harvard University

Rottingdean / Aug. 17. '97. / 11.a.m.

Dear Lock,

It's a sleepy frowzy-headed chap that writes for he has been more or less up all night assisting at a circus. It's a boy[1] – a black haired boy who howls like a month-old baby and, what is of much more importance Carrie is doing splendidly. Has an even pulse and a good colour and is sleeping. Nothing could be better say the Doctor and the nurse: but I shall believe 'em when the next three days are done. I've wired Brattleboro so I guess you'll see the news before I can catch you with a cable. Your salmon letter was a piece of cold-blooded villainy. You *knew*, jolly well, it would fill me with envy and all the baser passions and it did. But Lord! what a catch! The [   ]² day's record is a thing to write on one's tombstone. Carrie won't read me any of Meta's letters so I assume they are full of things not proper for me to know but I do hope Meta is doing well and the severe and haughty Loki³ also. Now we've a boy of our own this side we can confer with you as equals. I think our little rib is going to develope a temper of his own and all other vagaries you can imagine. Tell Appie that he snorts like a whale. This should impress Appie with the merits of his new cousin.

Now I'll go to bed and get some sleep. C. sends her love – was careful to do so ere she slept, and I am as ever

Yours affectionately
Rud.

Notes
1. John Kipling (1897–1915), born at 1.50 a.m. on the 17th.
2. Word illegible.
3. Lockwood de Forest, Jr (1896–1949), the younger of de Forest's two sons. He became a landscape architect in Santa Barbara, California.

To Sara Norton, 21 August 1897
ALS: Harvard University

[Rottingdean] Aug. 21. 97

Dear Sallie –

Thank you. Yours is the fine round rolling handwriting that can be read in sick-rooms without difficulty and Carrie shall be cheered with it after breakfast. Yes, she is coming on all right – better in fact than I've ever known her to do before and is just now starting the campaign of nursing John. Reserved young person John: but considerably better looking than he was two days ago. He lacks ideality but he has his mother's mouth, is a short square baby with a thick set look about him.

I am studying the English from an entirely new point of view – the Doctor and the Nurse being the glasses. They are amazing. C. is naturally langourous and does not demand novels or a skirt-dance on the third or fourth day; – and they don't understand it. She is "an 'ealthy little lady" says the nurse. "Why don't she pick up like the others." Rummy! But when you come to think of it they can't make any special fuss about birth in this land and "shock" they have heard of but do not understand. She is healthy – why should she feel it at all? I have explained that one of the many inexplicable peculiarities of the American woman is to feel that kind of thing: and that they the Doctor and the Nurse must allow for it. They are both very good and kind, and the nurse is splendid in her nursing.

The Doctor is only coming every other day now and C. is being stuffed with food. Mrs Shergold keeps a wary eye on her and cooks, I think, all the time. She is thoroughly enjoying herself and grieves audibly when C. doesn't demand a new dish every two hours.

This last gale ought to give you quiet weather across.[1] It's been a lovely summer and I fancy you got great fun out of it. 'Wish it were possible for us to come along too. Please carry our particular love to the Father and Lily[2] and Margaret[3] and Aunt Theo: and remembrances to the Jameses, and don't forget to send us letters now and again to keep in touch.

Carrie joins me in every good wish (she's an 'ealthy little lady. *Why* do she notice it so).

Yours ever
Ruddy.

Notes
1. Sara Norton was then in England, staying with the Burne-Joneses.
2. Elizabeth Gaskell Norton, called Lily, Norton's second daughter.
3. Margaret Norton (1870–1947), Norton's third daughter.

To Edmund Routledge,[1] 22 August 1897
ALS: Berg Collection, New York Public Library

North End House / Rottingdean / Aug. 22. '97

Dear Sir
I should be much in your debt if you could give me any information as to the authorship of a tale (presumably for boys) which appeared in a boy's annual between 1872–75 or thereabouts.

It concerned a man who wandered into the interior of Africa and there met a lion who (to the man's no small amazement gave him a Masonic sign. On the strength of this little variation from the normal he struck up a friendship with the lion, his family and the rest of the lion-people and discovered that their deadly enemies were some dog-headed (and entirely unmasonic) baboons with whom he and the lions fought a furious fight.²

There my memory of the tale, which has stuck in my memory for years, fails me. I dimly remember that the annual was a blue and gold one and in the same volume appeared Sheridan LeFanu's story of the bottleful of souls who escaped into the bodies of tin soldiers.³

Do you think that with so scanty information you would be able to fix the story of the Masonic Lions for me? If so, I should much like a copy of the annual. Apologizing for troubling you in this matter

believe me
Very sincerely yours
Rudyard Kipling

Edmund Routledge Esq.

Notes
1. Routledge (1843–99), partner in the publishing firm of Routledge, edited *Every Boy's Magazine* from 1862.
2. The story is *King Lion* by James Greenwood; it appeared in the half-yearly volumes of the *Boys' Own Magazine* for 1864. RK names it as among the memorable reading of his Southsea days in *Something of Myself*, p. 8: "I think that, too, lay dormant until the *Jungle Books* began to be born."
3. I can find no evidence that Lefanu ever contributed to *Every Boy's Magazine* or to the *Boys' Own*.

To Moberly Bell, 16 September 1897

Text: Copy, Library of Congress

Dear Bell –

The new paper¹ is badly needed now that the *Academy* is a variety-show; and the Athenaeum more than ever a museum of fossils; and the Saturday be-Harrised² and bedevilled generally, and Hulton³ dead. I hope it will be a big success.

I fancy I have something by me which I will try to finish and send in *via* Watt.⁴ How late do you suppose they can give me; supposing I can do it.

Yours ever
Rudyard Kipling

Rottingdean / Sept. 16/97

Notes
1. The weekly review called *Literature,* which began publication on 23 October 1897 and was the predecessor of *The Times Literary Supplement.*
2. Under the editorship of Frank Harris (1856–1931) since 1894. Harris, a successful editor but an unscrupulous and self-deluded adventurer and tale-teller, was, according to RK, "the one human being that I could on no terms get on with" (*Something of Myself,* p. 83).
3. Thus in copy, for Hutton. Richard Holt Hutton, editor of the *Spectator,* died on 9 September 1897.
4. "White Horses", *Literature,* 23 October 1897 (*The Five Nations*).

To William Ernest Henley, [*c.* September 1897]
ALS: Morgan Library

The Elms¹ / Rottingdean

Dear Henley –
    Words aren't in it to say how I feel about your gift to our Boy John, but I know you'll understand. Bless you both for it.
    I am a humiliated Pig – and I sit in ashes for the reason that I'm not sure that there is a spare copy of the R.K. *de luxe.*² I have supplicated MacM. with postcards but they haven't answered. Don't swear therefore if yours comes late.
    The Don Quixote³ I've been revelling in. Somehow they could write English in those days, on an empty stomach before breakfast which now we can't do – no not with straining nor enemas. As to Dumas, I am convinced God didn't intend me for a dramatist – and that's one point gained.
    There are some decentish reviews of your Burns,⁴ but (I don't know whether this strikes you as a compliment) no one seems to realize the enormous amount of common or back-coal-cellar *trouble* you've taken over the job; and that does not please me. Cope-Cornford⁵ has vanished from all horizons. I haven't seen him since you left but now that we have a hired house of our own I must get his Brighton address and ask him to tea. We live in a walled garden across the village green opposite North End House and there is everything in the place to make us happy except room for a bicycle. As we have two and a tandem we are just a little cramped.⁶ Tell Mrs Henley that I've been taking a girl out on the

tandem and that for sheer *pace* and excitement a tandem beats a bicycle to pieces. The wife is coming on greatly and the boy John is sinful fat and heavy.

Love to Tybalt the rat-catcher.[7] Send me a line just to tell me you've gone back to verse again.

Ever yours
Ruddy.

Notes
1. The house on the green in Rottingdean that RK leased at the end of September 1897 and where he remained until 1902.
2. The "Edition de Luxe", published by Macmillan; the first four volumes appeared in 1897; the thirty-eighth and last in 1938. It is the English equivalent of the American Outward Bound Edition.
3. Shelton's translation of *Don Quixote* appeared in Henley's Tudor Translations series (4 vols, 1896).
4. *Robert Burns, His Life, Genius, Achievement* (1897).
5. Leslie Cope Cornford (1867–1927), journalist, novelist, and miscellaneous writer, specializing in naval subjects. He wrote for Henley's *National Observer*, where his work attracted RK's attention. Afterwards correspondent for *The Standard* and then on the staff of the *Morning Post* as naval correspondent and leader writer.
6. The tandem was a gift from S. S. McClure in June (CK diary).
7. Henley's dog.

To Mrs Thomas Hardy,[1] 4 November 1897
ALS: Dalhousie University

The Elms / Rottingdean / Nov. 4. 97.

Dear Mrs. Hardy,

Many thanks for your kind little note. I've been rummaging all over the country in pursuit of agents and landlords and such like exasperating folk. My notion is to come down to Dorchester again[2] if I can see my way to a "roof" there, with my father whom I am going to pick up in Wiltshire. The Duke of Bedford's agent has suggested a place somewhere near Abbotsbury 8 miles from you which at least sounds attractive. But this house-hunting is a weary business.

I am glad to hear your ankle is better. One can get such very unpleasant accidents from and off and under a bicycle – as I have found out to my cost.

Our small son keeps Mrs Kipling at home but if I come down west I will surely let you know.

Please tell your husband that the other day, talking to an old man who remembered smuggling as a fine art in Rottingdean, I told him of the Dorsetshire folk who hid their plunder under a moveable apple tree in an orchard. "Ah" said my friend, "*we* used to scoop out the stuff from under the tombstone in the little church." Then, enviously, after a pause, "We've got no trees here. Tis a pity."

Very sincerely yours
Rudyard Kipling.

Notes
1. Emma Lavinia Gifford (1840–1912), first wife of Thomas Hardy, the novelist, whom she married in 1874. RK had gone to Dorchester in September of this year in order to house-hunt with Hardy's help (CK diary, 11–15 September 1897). Shortly thereafter RK and family moved in to The Elms, Rottingdean, but he continued to look for something more permanent. For an amusing anecdote of RK and Hardy house-hunting, see Carrington, *Kipling*, p. 269.
2. I have no evidence that he did.

To George Wyndham,[1] 12 November 1897
ALS: Public Record Office

The Elms / Rottingdean: / Nov. 12. 1897.

Dear Mr Wyndham –

Things seem to be in a bad way with Henley for the New Review is going to be discontinued and from what one knows of the man and his generosity it isn't likely that Henley will have saved much. What do you think of the enclosed draft of a memorial to Balfour asking him to put W.E.H. on the Civil List? It's merely a rough done by one of the many men who owe him much and being inexpert in this business what we want to know is if we have got the proper tone of a memorial, and if you will offer any suggestions on this head, we shall be very grateful.

If the notion strikes you as good will you please tell me so, and return with erasures, interlineations etc. the rough draft: at the same time putting in the fitting tail-piece of direct appeal to the authorities who look after the Civil List. Our notion was to get Blaikie[2] to print it, and to circulate it ourselves among the men named as per enclosed list. Again, if that strikes you as good, could you add to the list?

There will be a row if W.E.H. knows anything about what is going on and so we had better keep still. Please say frankly if you think the scheme is worth trying – it surely must be – and give us practical advice.

Very sincerely yours
Rudyard Kipling.

Notes
1. Wyndham (1863–1913) had been private secretary to Arthur Balfour and entered Parliament in 1889; he was later Chief Secretary for Ireland, 1900–5. He had contributed to both the *National Observer* and the *New Review* under Henley, and was one of the friends upon whom Henley regularly depended.
2. Walter Blaikie (1847–1928), after a career as an engineer in India, joined the Edinburgh printing firm of T. and A. Constable in 1879 and became its chairman. Blaikie was one of the founders of Henley's *Scot's Observer* and was its printer as well.

To Sidney Low, 24 November 1897
ALS: Dalhousie University

The Elms / Rottingdean / Nov: 24. 97.

Dear Low:

Of course I'm coming to the funeral,[1] if the Brighton cold which I have the beginnings of, doesn't develop into anything heavier than snuffles. But I am afraid that I can't lunch on Sunday by reason of people who are staying with us. What are you going to do? I heard you were going to India.[2] Is that true or is it only a newspaper "shave".[3]

I'll get you a photo – but it won't be pretty. Strang[4] has given me no end of an aquiline nose in his etching. Wouldn't you prefer one of them?

If I don't see you here's wishing you all the good luck in the world.

Ever yours
Rudyard Kipling.

Notes
1. Low, in conflict with his proprietor, had resigned the editorship of the *St James's Gazette* at the end of July 1897. Edmund Gosse organised a memorial dinner for Low, evidently the "funeral" that RK means. RK gave a speech on the occasion: see 16–17 December 1897.
2. He went to America: see 22 December 1897.
3. A false or unauthenticated report: military slang (Partridge, *Dictionary of Slang*).
4. William Strang (1859–1921), painter and etcher, made a portrait etching of RK early in May 1897; it is reproduced as the frontispiece to *Plain Tales from the Hills* (1899), the first volume of Macmillan's Uniform Edition of RK.

To William Alexander Fraser, 29 November 1897
ALS: Washington University

The Elms / Rottingdean – / Nov. 29.

I've been doing *much* worse things than shooting rapids or colloguing with half-breeds. I've been eating some dinners in town and, which is worse for the digestion, making speeches afterwards.[1] So I feel more "fed on soda-biscuit" to use your words than is good for me.

Bless you for the maple-leaves. They woke up many feelings. We're living in bare grass downs where one doesn't see the pheasant-breast monotony of ruined trees that people call "the turn of the leaf" in England.

Now listen. In January, all my camp goes down to Cape Town to escape the rigours of an English Spring.[2] Three months or four we shall be away so if there comes a long silence you will know why.

I am not doing much writing just now for the reason that I've taken the lease of this shanty for three years and I tell *you* Sir that English lawyers when they really get to work are more expert burglars than anything Chicago turns out. I told one of 'em that a brief-sheet of type-written paper with a stamp was good enough title for me. Whereat he looked upon me as an estrayed savage and went on babbling about "messuages and tenements as hereinbefore said."

No. I ain't writing a play about India – yet. Go ahead and see if you can interest folk in it. I have my doubts myself but that's because I've been talking to actor-managers whose notion of a play is like the law of the Medes and Persians.

Glad to hear that you are still coming on with your yarns. You'll do all right yet and when you arrive you'll hear me shouting.

I am busy. The weather is vile with a roaring northerly gale and sunshine like pale glue on the wall. I hope your household goes well. Write me a line anon. Don't swear if I take a few weeks to answer it and believe me.

Ever yours sincerely
Rudyard Kipling.

Notes
1. RK spoke on 25 November at a dinner at Limmer's Hotel in honour of Sir William Gowers, founder of the Society of Medical Phonographers. The speech is reported in the *Daily Mail*, 27 November, and in the *British Medical Journal*, 4 December 1897 (uncollected).
2. They left on 8 January: see 12 December 1897.

To Thomas Hardy, 30 November 1897
ALS: Dorset County Museum

The Elms / Rottingdean / Nov. 30. 97

Dear Hardy –

As usual one goes along the line of least resistance and because the owner offered to sell us his sticks of furniture too, thereby saving us the bother of immediately hunting for new things, we have taken for three years this ex-smuggling stronghold in Rottingdean. It's small, low and old and in time we hope to make it comfy. At present its interior is what you might call neolithic.

And what I wanted to write you about is this. A memorial is going round for signature on behalf of Henley – to get him put on the Civil List: and I am sending you a copy for perusal.[1]

I am not, in the language of America, a whale on Henley as a critic but he is distinctly a poet. Will you sign and return it in the envelope that accompanies it.

With all regards from us both to you and Mrs Hardy.

Ever sincerely yours
Rudyard Kipling.

Note
1. See 17 December 1897.

To George Earle Buckle,[1] 2 December 1897
ALS: Syracuse University

The Elms / Rottingdean. / Dec. 2. 97

Dear Buckle –

It isn't quite as easy as you'd think to catch one of Mason's boys. Forgetting my youth I asked him[2] on Monday (I've been fighting shy of the school by reason of measles which really existed at the other place) and that was of course "a whole day." However, I got him today for a short spell and write to you now that the visit is fresh upon me.

He is a most fascinating chap. I had no notion he was by way of being a "monitor" of sorts and as such concerned with the minor discipline of the school. But he explained to me in that sweetly grave schoolboy manner upon what lines *he* thought a fellow should look after the juniors when the juniors (and he's eleven or nearly twelve he says!) jump on an unpopular equal. It was the English Empire in miniature speaking and I took off my hat to him. Otherwise our talk was purely of school-life – and here I fear I told him some demoralizing anecdotes of my own career – till he launched out in all sincerity on his interest in Latin and "English" which "have some sense" – barring always (and herein I agreed entirely) Cæsar and Livy. And he told me of his notions of his future and his present surroundings with a beautiful courtesy and temper that I cannot sufficiently admire. Unluckily the shadow of Thursday's prep at 6.30 hung on him – as I remember it hung on me – so we didn't really have a good jaw. I went back to the school-gates with him and this visit isn't to count. He's coming again on Saturday when there is no prep: and I shall fire at his devoted head one of the series of school-boys tales I am writing.[3] He has freshened and delighted me immensely and I write to say that he seems very fit.[4]

Very sincerely yours
Rudyard Kipling

Notes
1. Buckle (1854–1935) was editor of *The Times*, 1884–1912, the biographer of Disraeli, and the editor of Queen Victoria's letters.
2. George Walter Buckle, then attending Mr Mason's Rottingdean School, one of the two boys' prep schools in Rottingdean. RK had earlier promised Mrs Buckle that he would see her son (22 August 1897: ALS, Syracuse).
3. *Stalky & Co.*
4. In a letter to RK thirty-three years later Buckle, speaking of his son, wrote that "You may have forgotten, but he never has, the kindness you showed my boy when he was at a private school at Rottingdean" (26 December 1930: ALS, Sussex).

To William Ernest Henley, 12 December 1897
ALS: National Library of Scotland

The Elms / Rottingdean / Dec. 12. '97

Dear Henley –

I haven't seen the *New Review* but I've seen the sonnet which shows you have taken no harm in the hand by lying by for the scandalous long time you have.[1] Now go on and get to work which is going to abide. New Reviews are deceitful: things made in Germany are vain but your poetry is your business. I'm more pleased that the gates have opened again than I can well say.

Talking of sonnets – you know the story of that Head Cashier of the Margate bank whose nightly dissipation was to go out with the surf-boat.[2] If he hadn't got drowned of course he'd be going out yet – "on the strict Q.T." and enjoying himself no end under pretext of giving first aid to the injured. That struck me as very fine stuff for – of all things – a sonnet. Well, of course I couldn't do it. I wonder if you could extract anything from the wreckage, which I send herewith: –

> Porter of dross, by day he dealt the spoil
> For which men die – all England's might to guard.
> (The money he dealt out and himself and his toil) . . . .
> Night and the $\left\{\begin{array}{l}\text{full}\\\text{new-roused}\end{array}\right.$ gale brought his reward.
>
> To sit with those that dog the something or other tide
> To cheat the lean shoal slavering o'er her prey
> $\left\{\begin{array}{l}\text{Between}\\\text{Out of the ribs of wreck to snatch away}\end{array}\right.$
> The all-but forfeit life, he chose and died.
> But for his death the world had never known (this is shit)
> By what quaint humour he was in the habit of dividing his days
> Between the bank counter and the tar barrel of a distressed
> ship – (*flame*).
>
> Errand of mercy. No, not that alone
> But rather $\left\{\begin{array}{l}\text{a lineal descendant of the}\\\text{instinctively true to the}\end{array}\right\}$ Blood that plays
> Plays evermore for its own sake the Game!

That's the abandoned scaffolding of my little plan, but *you* could make it splendid. If the lines or the notion of treatment suggest anything *please* do it.[3]

Yours ever
Ruddy.

I've got a hellish cold and yearn for a little sun light. If I come up to town before we sail I'll come to say goodbye to you of course.[4] We'll be back in May.

Notes
1. The December number of the *New Review* was the last edited by Henley: it contains a sonnet in memory of his old schoolmaster, Thomas Edward Brown.
2. Nine men had been drowned on 2 December when the Margate surf boat was swamped; among them was Charles Edward Troughton, cashier of Lloyd's Bank, Margate (*The Times*, 4 December).
3. Apparently he didn't.
4. RK and his family sailed for Cape Town on 8 January and remained there until 12 April.

To Charles Eliot Norton, 16–17 December 1897
ALS: Harvard University.

The Elms / Dec. 16. 97

Dear Mr. Norton:

I am in the deeps of an atrocious cold which I earned riding on a bicycle in a head-wind: and it has been blowing and galeing and hailing for the matter of ten days. So my spirit is brought very low and Macmillans have sent me the Atlantic Monthly's review of *Captains Courageous* which has made me lie down and cry salt tears.[1] Do you happen to know who wrote it. It's amazing in its coincidences for behold the writer misses in C.C. precisely and identically those very qualities I missed in his land. Had I gone about with a lantern to describe America I could not have hit on a more splendid description than "relief at the cost of life."[2] Relief from the material cares of the Elder Peoples at the cost of what the Elder Peoples mean by life! And again "There is an almost incredible insignificance in parts of it, *as if it were a steamer underengined on its length*". Why, hang it! that's his own very country and in half a dozen words he gets at the nub of the thing I was laboriously painting in C.C. Only he *will* apply it to the book and expects me to extract from a two hundred year old background all the tints of the gilded East. For this did I change my style; and allegorize and parable and metaphor; subduing my hand to the stuff I wrought in! I tried to get it thin, and tinny, and without passion. . . . and I've done it only too well. Even down to "every body being reasonably safe" does he parallel my concept of America. If you know him, I wish you'd breathe in his ear gently that he has paid me a gigantic compliment – the wrong way round. You see what I resent is a chap coming out of that *milieu* (He *must* because he accepts the note of the book as "healthy" "simple" and "vigorous" whereas – c.f. Harvey Cheyne's talk with his father and his father's talk with him – it is flagrantly un-moral not to say heathen) belonging to that life and serenely accepting its grubby ideals talking to me as though he didn't so accept 'em. But I won't bother you any more about it.

The rest of this letter is our answer to Sallie's delightful letter which cheered C. beyond telling. Firstly Mother's address[3] is *202. W. 79 St. New York* – a long and a windy way as I remember it. We have, secondly, taken the long lease of "The Elms" – the house opposite Uncle Ned's behind a wall, across the green. Sallie may know it by sight but perhaps she does not know its beautiful garden. It was an old depot for smugglers and its huge cellars attest this. It's old, red-tiled: stucco-fronted with worm-eaten stairs but low cieled and warm which in England is everything. We are puttering about putting up little things here and there and much enjoying our new "ploy". By the way we bought the out-going tenant's furniture and – Oh Lord! There is a blue lamp with a leperous distilment of white blobs over it which alone would curl the paper off the wall of any God-fearing shanty: and there are brackets and pictures of the '60's. They are now entombed in an attic.

We go – all of us, including Johannes Agricola in Meditation[4] (he meditates a good deal) to South Africa on the 8th Jan. by the *Dunvegan Castle.* This is to get away from the horrors of an English spring. We shall return all being well, in May; and the Pater himself and none other is going with us. He has had a cold most opportuntely, which has convinced him of the necessity of this. So we are well pleased. But two servants, 3 kids; two bicycles, unlimited "perambulators" and 2,000 ton of luggage are a rather large contract to move. The F. Marshall, and Commandress in Chief however continues serenely to face it and I as aide de camp run about and make myself useful. The Father, Mother and Trix arrive on the 21st for Christmas: Stanley and his wife – a daughter of Mrs Ridsdale across the Green – come to that house on the 27th: and Uncle Ned and Aunt Georgie come down I think on the 26th. So "the Green" will be very lively. Uncle Ned has been down here a good deal this autumn, and he and I have broused about in couples. It has been joyous and refreshing – a lift to me that I shall never forget. The things that that big man does not know, and cannot help in, might be written on a postage-stamp. Just now we are deep in the Roman occupation of Britain (this with an eye to stories) and he sends me volumes on volumes; but one talk is worth libraries. Phil appears occasionally to keep a strict eye on public rights. He is at issue now, legally, with a melon-headed landowner who *more Brittannico* has gone and flagrantly enclosed a bit of common land. Talk of Tammany! A small Parish council run by four Publicans and one sinner can give Tammany points any day! I believe I go on the register this spring as a householder, so please you, and for the first time in my little life may vote. Can you imagine me on a parish council agitating for drains!

The children mercifully keep well, Josephine getting older visibly: and Elsie, who tries her long-suffering sister to the bone, reaching the stage of adorable fatness when babies can do no wrong. This is good for our Josephine when she finds a headless toy or a legless Santa-Claus and forthwith in a loud voice proceeds to "forgive" the unreprehended Elsie. John is a broth of a boy and, for his gender, very fairly behaved. He smiles and eats and when we can do nothing with him, one or other of his sisters can generally keep him sober. Very good and pleasant is our family life these days: and if Brighton were not quite so handy for visitors and so unhandy for us shopping, we should be well content.

There is no work going on, other than bits of verse and an occasional shy at my new series of school-boy tales which I hope will make men laugh a little. Nothing has come to me and I am not bothering. Maybe South Africa will unlock something. Yet I forget. I *have* done something. Sir Walter Parratt[5] the Queen's head-fiddler I believe, wrote to me informing me that I was to contribute some verses to the Queen for some sort of musical "tribute." He quoted the "Tribute to Oriana"[6] and lest I should never have heard of it sent me an extract from the same. To which I, respectfully, pointed out that that sort of verse was a little bit beyond me and, please, I wasn't going to play. Now the Parrot is not pleased about it. Says it is "serious" for him; and generally makes me understand we have done evil in the sight of the King. I don't see that a man is justified in doing verses to order against his grain. Also, I've been making speeches – two of 'em – both bad. One at a short-hand doctors' meeting[7] (this means doctors who write down your symptoms in their short-hand so that it looks like prescriptions and no body can convict 'em of a wrong diagnosis) and one at a dinner to Low of the *St James's Gazette*.[8] Edmund Gosse was in the chair. I do not yet know the chair Edmund Gosse would not be in. But he was very human that night. His son Philip[9] has come back from helping to climb Aconcagua and is now a man – a keen naturalist who has also proved himself a leader of men, and the parent Gosse-bird is sincerely and genuinely proud of him.

Does Dingley[10] stand with a drawn sword at the customs gates. We sent you with our love early in November, hoping that it would reach you on your birthday, a set of the "Outward Bound" Edition and we can't make out yet whether it got in in time or indeed got in at all. It won't interest Dingley – unless he means to pawn it to repair the deficit he has so cleverly made. But politics are not pleasant things to talk of just now. England is still engaged in saving the peace of the world pretty much as the lady-passenger saved the Cunarder – by offering her virtue to the excited man who was about to sink the ship if he didn't get it and the common people are slowly growing wearied of it all. I wonder when the big break up will come.

This takes our very best love to you and your household and "Aunt Theo" – Christmas and New Year greetings. Carrie is going to write to Sallie if she has a minute to spare and I am

> Always your affectionate
> Ruddy

P.S. Our greetings to the James's across the road. Henry James is a householder too – has bought the lease of a house in Rye and talks – drains![11]

P.S. My nonsensical letter has called your sober and most comforting one out of the deep – and now we know that you have the books and that all goes well at Shady Hill. Once again, bless you all. As I wrote you some time ago, I will try to be good. But the standards are grievous high.

Ever yours lovingly
Ruddy

We will answer your letter later – *not* on little bits of paper but orderly. This is done in haste to catch the steamer and we beg pardon for the half sheet.
Dec. 17

C.R.K.

Notes

1. *Atlantic Monthly*, December 1897.
2. "Though it may bring relief from the go-fever and insistence of the earlier work, it is relief procured at the cost of life" (p. 856).
3. That is, Mrs Balestier's.
4. John Kipling, called here after Browning's poem.
5. Parratt (1841–1924), organist and composer, was made Master of the Queen's Music in 1893.
6. RK perhaps means the *Triumph of Oriana* (1601), a collection of madrigals edited by Thomas Morley.
7. To the Society of Medical Phonographers, 25 November 1897: see 29 November 1897.
8. I have not found any date for this affair, nor any report of RK's speech; the dinner (probably 27 November) is described in Desmond Chapman-Huston, *The Lost Historian: A Memoir of Sir Sidney Low* (1936) pp. 95–6.
9. Philip Gosse (1879–1959), only son of Edmund Gosse, accompanied a scientific expedition to the Andes, 1896–7; he became a well-known naturalist and author.
10. Nelson Dingley (1832–99), Congressman from Maine, author of the just-passed Dingley Tariff Act.
11. Lamb House, Rye, Sussex: see 19 September 1899.

To George Wyndham, 17 December 1897

ALS: Public Record Office

The Elms / Rottingdean: / Dec. 17. 97.

Dear Mr. Wyndham –

I am sending you with this the memorial which you so kindly said you would forward to Balfour.[1] It is all finished and done with now – except the pension-part and I hope and pray that A.J.B. will see his way to making it a fair-sized pension. I don't think many folk realize how hard up W.E.H. must be sometimes. He is not constructed to bow down in the house of Rimmon under any circumstances. He does very big work and gets no particular sort of prices. Moreover, all his life he has been supporting other people – sometimes of his own family and sometimes outside it. But these things and more too, you know far better than I and can put before Balfour with a force beyond me. I had some idea of writing a letter to Balfour myself, but now that I have seen the list of signatures it seems to me that it would be an impertinence – besides I have only met him two or three times and you know him personally. Isn't that right?

I can't tell you how grateful I am to you for taking charge of the thing. May it be fortunate.

Yours very sincerely
Rudyard Kipling.

Note

1. The memorial, signed by RK, Hardy, Barrie, Meredith, Henry James, Rider Haggard, Conan Doyle, and Yeats, among many others, was successful: Henley was granted a civil list pension of £225.

To James M. Conland, 17–18 December 1897

ALS: Library of Congress

The Elms / Rottingdean. / Dec. 17. 97

. . . . and, as I was about to observe, I fancied your wrist-trouble must have developed into paralysis or, perhaps, *Mischief* had at last succeeded in pulling your hands off and that you had given up writing for good. Then it occurred to me that perhaps I also might be in fault. Later I called myself evil names for a lazy scallawag and finally I come to cast myself on your mercy and beg you to take up your pen and sling a little ink at me for once in a way.

Among other things – such as a [genuine?] cold which I now am enjoying the end of – I've been rather out of sorts. Hipped and depressed from day to day and this climate does not help to put a man on his legs again when he once feels sorrowful. So I went up to see a doctor – same way that you and I went to Boston to see that very celebrated specialist whose name I have forgotten. He reduced me to a state of highly improper nudity and whacked and thumped and tested and did all the old old tricks, we know so well. "Liver" says I. "Liver and ghastly depression." "Liver be sugared" said he. "You haven't a trace of a liver but you've got a colon rather distended with wind. Also you smoke too much." Somehow it seemed to me I had heard that last remark before. Well the net result was that with a tonic, and knocking off tobacco, he pulled me out of the darkness and the gloom that had been enveloping me on and off since April of this year.

Being pretty much of the same dark temperament as I am you will understand what I suffered. Well now. I have felt serene – really at ease – for some weeks and the first use I make of my new lightness of soul is to write to you for I know that, dilatory as I have been about letters, you will sympathize with me. How long I shall stay "good" in this climate I don't know but we are all off to South Africa (Capetown) per Donald Curries's[1] Castle Line S.S. *Dunvegan Castle*, to play about in the sunshine of Cape Town till April: returning in May. We go from Southampton on the 8th Jan. Till Madeira (4 days) we may expect several kinds of unmitigated Hell but after that should have 14 days of level keel, double awnings, white decks and general laziness. It will be a rest for the wife: and Cape Town is the paradise for children. Little Josephine faces the prospect with great calm and serenity. She tells me that the best way of studying geography is "to go about in ships, Father, till you have seen them all" and frankly I am somewhat of her way of thinking. We take a nurse and a governess: two wheels, some baby carriages and about half a shipload of baggage. Pray for us *en route*: and send in a letter Poste Restante, Cape Town. We mean to invade a boarding-house down there and simply to do *no* house-keeping. Oh I nearly forgot. My father is coming down with us for the trip. It's a fair excuse to him to see a new country and a most opportune cold has confirmed him in his opinion that S. Africa is the *one* place he ought to go to. Which again reminds me that last Sunday, when I ought to have been in bed drinking ammoniated quinine out of a bucket [   ][2] to lunch at Gilbert Parker's who has taken a house in Brighton and there I met Poulteney Bigelow[3] – the man who wrote *"White Man's Africa"* that came out serially in Harpers. He had just come over and told me that ten days before he had dined with Henry Rutgers Marshall (who designed Naulakha) in New York. All this somehow seemed to bring the old life back with a rush and I found myself extra-double-friendly towards Poulteney Bigelow [   ][4] Mrs. Gilbert Parker (Miss Van Tine that was) is enjoying her first experience of an English winter. They are going to Cairo on the 28th of this month. So you can see for yourself what she thinks of it!

We've been having gale after gale – Roaring sou'westers chopping round to tearing North Easters (you can fancy the kind of sea that kicks up in the Channel). Day after day of wind that blows over naked grass as though it wanted to shift the very hills – day after day of flying scud and sheets of foam, shutting in the horizon a couple of miles off: and now and then a glimpse of a coaster fleeing for her life up channel. One day there was a lull and, watching from the beach, I saw about sixty ships that till then had been weatherbound in the Downs getting out to broad water as fast as they could. I hope they found searoom before the gale came on again. One night we were wakened by hail that seemed as if it would smash in the windows. Then there was a peal of thunder. Today is a mild, warm languid day in spring – and the land looks as green as though April were here. Sweet climate but a trifle mixed.

Saturday. 18th. Another heavenly day which we are going to use for Xmas shopping in Brighton. I've ordered a tree and greens and all sorts of Xmas things, but it is curious to find the season without trace of frost or snow. I rejoice to say that Carrie keeps well. You can guess with a new house to arrange, how pleased she is. She has a bit of a sore throat – caused by the incessant blowy weather.

I have been kicking myself for an ass these past few days. I had an offer to go down to Madeira and Spain in one of our men of war – same one I attended the manœuvres in – and I didn't go because I didn't know when she would come back. Now I find that she has had a simply lovely time – missed all our bad weather, and that the cruise was more like yachting than anything else! – I only hope our South African venture will turn out as well. The other day I went up to town and was roped in to two public dinners – one of them a doctor's entertainment to congratulate Sir William Gowers[5] (who is a crank on shorthand) upon his getting a knighthood. Gowers is the deuce and all of a specialist: but *I* believe he is simply a maniac on shorthand as a means to help Doctors put down their diagnoses. I [didn't] think much of the outfit till I was asked to get up and make a speech. I pulled through somehow and in the middle of this festive spread with electric lights and waiters and plush and flumdiddle, I suddenly had a vision of you with your nose inside your collar whipping along the Gulf road in half a blizzard [   ][6] out Chesterfield way. I [didn't] go out of my way to do it – for my speech was about doctors all the world over – but somehow or other I found myself describing a country doctor's life in America [   ][7] I wish you could have heard it.

Another – or rather the other dinner was to take farewell of the editor of one of our big evening papers – Sidney Low of the *St James's Gazette*. He is going out for a year's rest and is visiting America next spring. Says he "wants to see the politicians." I've told him that *that* isn't the way to find out anything about a country: and that his best chance to understand is just to go along quietly. I shall give him a letter of introduction to *you*, I think: for he is rather a nice chap and no end of a big-bug among editors. You can take him out for a drive and show him what a Vermont "thank-ye-marm" is like, and tell him something of the ethnology of one or two counties – as you used to tell me. It's that kind of thing that the visiting Englishman never learns.

We've an American or two in Brighton – notably one Winans[8] son of the American millionaire. *His* weakness is trotting-horses and he drives up and down the sea-front (it's a huge wide chalk-road cut out of the cliffs and crammed with traffic) behind first-class trotters. I passed him the other day on my wheel – he was jogging along in a pneumatic tyred four-wheel trotting cart and we had quite an interesting talk about gaits and gets and breeds and shoeing. He has one trotter with a 2.84 record – an ugly brute but a good one. Well. England isn't the place to trot horses in unless you get a track of your own. Winan's let the animal out to a four-minute clip and before he had gone a quarter of a mile the Police wanted him for furious driving. It was a dangerous thing to do because Brighton sea front is full of carriages. One of his training carts is a good old common piano-top buggy. We met it the other day in sunshine, hood up: horse with a breast-strap just like Marcus jogging along as easy as you please. Then we were quiet for about ten minutes. Then we began to talk about Naulakha – the wife and I. Josephine holds her tongue about it for weeks at a time. Then we hear her telling little Elsie about the summer-house under the trees and the fun of going bare footed. I wonder when we shall come back. There are times when I feel like taking the first boat and getting you up to dinner straight off. [   ][9]

Keep an eye on the place for our sakes. I tried to offer it for sale once but I took [   ][10] good care to put a prohibitive price on it. Howard[11] seems to be going ahead quietly. I fancy he'll be rather a wealthy citizen by the time we return.

There has been a rather interesting case of blood-poisoning in our village. Local liquor-dealer and strong politician got a cut on his hand and a scrape on his shin from the edge of a cask. You know how with that type of man recovery is slow in all cases. The local doctor is very young but very enthusiastic. I'm glad the patient got better because the doctor and I (I was egging on the doctor to it) wanted to try a new germ-killing remedy and oxygen gas (local) treatment. I went down and sat with the invalid once or twice; expecting erysipelas and all sorts of complications: but as I have said he pulled up. 'Curious how saloon-keepers' flesh is always unhealthy. There were blebs and pus and all sorts of larks on a merely abraded surface that, with normal health, a stick of plaister would have mended.

Well. I've gone on yarning about nothing for ever so long and you must forgive me. I'm afraid in the present weather on the Atlantic, this will miss Xmas in Brattleboro. If it does, it carries all good wishes for the forthcoming year, for you and yours. Now write me a letter because if we don't write the correspondence will peter out – *and that it must not do*. You've no notion, as they say in Vermont, what store I set by you.

Give my salutations to Padre Day;[12] and give him greetings for the new year. Tell us how Harry is coming on. Tell us all the news and tells us how Captains Courageous is going. It sold 16,000 in six weeks this side. Not bad for a book that they have given up trying to understand in England. (They wonder how I found it all out!)

The wife joins me in the best and warmest of wishes and I am as ever

Yours

Rudyard Kipling.

Notes
1. Currie was head of the Castle Line: see 7 May 1898.
2. Half a line erased.
3. Bigelow (1855–1954), American journalist and traveller, a friend of Kaiser Wilhelm II and a critic of American administration.
4. One line erased.
5. Gowers (1845–1915), physician, was particularly known for his work on diseases of the nervous system; he founded the Society of Medical Phonographers.
6. Half a line erased.
7. About two and a half lines erased.
8. Probably son of Thomas DeKay Winans (1820–78), an engineer and inventor, made wealthy through railroad-building contracts in Russia.
9. Several lines erased.
10. Word erased.
11. Matthew Howard, the coachman.
12. The Revd Charles Orrin Day (1851–1909), minister of the Centre Congregational Church in Brattleboro, 1885–98, and President of Andover Theological Seminary, 1901–8.

To Sidney Low, 22 December 1897
ALS: Dalhousie University

The Elms / Rottingdean / Dec 22 97.

Dear Low:

"Enclosed please find" these few cards which may or may not be of use.[1] I've written to the men concerned. F.N. Finney who is by way of being six varieties of Railway King may be a convenient man to know when you get west – at all events he can put you up to a heap of railway facilities. It's too early for a tour on the lakes but he owns a line of steamers there. Van Horne[2] of course you will catch through Parker[3] who has probably given you all hints needful. I can only say:

(a) never order wine at dinner or any meal. It's ruinous besides being indifferent.

Try to like their whisky.

Never travel with more personal luggage than you can carry in one hand, i.e. no rugs or wraps are needed in the cars; umbrellas are not much good. If it storms they are useless: and it doesn't much storm.

Nothing need go in the cars at all, unless for a night journey when a small hand bag (buy it *there*) will cover all your needs.

Do *not* drink the water in the cars – except qualified.

Travel as much as possible in an ordinary coach. American pullmans are full of English and these I take it you do not want to meet. Get by the stove where the conductor lives and listen, hard. Remember that the Century Club, where you will be put up, is *New York* which is not America. Norton – C.E. – you must see. He represents all that is best in the land – best but most ineffective so far as we can see. He will show you young America of the college type. Roosevelt is another kind – rabid anglophile *plus* an education to back him. He'll let you go round the docks at Washington and try all you know to see Cramp's Yard at Philadelphia.[4]

The Georgetown (Ontario card) is a "Kate."[5] There's a man there who has knocked about the big North West a good deal and may tell you something if you happen to stop over there for an hour or two. I don't know whether you will have time to see quiet home life of America (which is where the heart of the people beats) but it's difficult because they *will* pose for a stranger, being young and self conscious. This applies only to small towns.

Marshall[6] is a delightful man – a New York architect who knows every one worth knowing and should show you some of the quieter life that is characteristically American – American of the fifth generation which is yearly becoming rarer.

I can't think of any others that would be valuable – *within* the time at your disposal. If you were going over for a year it would be different.

To recapitulate

> Norton – for intellect
> Marshall – for social *men's* life – N.Y.
> Finney – railroad development in the West.
> Roosevelt – the Navy and anglophilia.
> Fraser – common ordinary man who has been in odd places.

Don't be surprised at anything that happens; and specially don't be surprised if nothing happens.

I've written to all these men when to expect you.[7]

With best wishes for a good time

Yours ever sincerely,
Rudyard Kipling.

Notes
1. Low was about to leave for a three-month visit to the United States.
2. Sir William Van Horne (1843–1915), American-born builder of the Canadian Pacific Railway. RK had met him in 1892: see *Something of Myself*, p. 198.

3. Sir Gilbert Parker (see 3–4 December 1893), a Canadian.
4. The shipyard founded by William Cramp (1807–89) and carried on by his son Charles Henry (1828–1913); notable for design and technical innovation, RK could have visited the yard in September 1889, but there is no evidence that he did.
5. Partridge, *Dictionary of Slang*, gives "skeleton key" as one of the meanings for this term, but RK seems to mean something like "option" or "extra".
6. Henry Rutgers Marshall.
7. All of these letters survive, all dated 22 December except that to Roosevelt, which is dated 21 December. RK wrote to Roosevelt that he wanted Low to "see *you* for many reasons – chiefly because he will enjoy himself and otherly because you'll teach him a lot" (ALS, Library of Congress). To Fraser, RK wrote that he wished Low "to learn about the big northwest and divers other matters on which you could enlighten him" (copy, Cornell); to Marshall saying that "you can show him more of the genuine New York life – the life that is of importance and value – than any one else" (ALS, Columbia); to Finney that "you could show him a few things in the railroad line that would make him open his eyes" (ALS, Dalhousie); and to Norton that "I want him to see the best man in America and from his lips to learn the hope and the promise of the land" (ALS, Harvard).

To Margaret Mackail, 6 January 1898
ALS: University of Sussex

The Elms / Rottingdean. / Jan. 6. 98

Dear Wop –

I read it again and I think all the charm remains[1] – except the peculiar smell of *Good Words*, in the hall. Bless you for the kind thought that bade you hand it on to the third generation. We're in all the agonies of the very last move but the bulk of the work will be over by noon. Love to you all from us both

Ever your cousin
Rud.

Note
1. Margaret's note on this letter says: "I sent him George Macdonald's Princess and the Goblins." The story appeared in *Good Words for the Young*, III (1870–1), a periodical edited by Macdonald. RK alludes to the story and to the bound volume of *Good Words* containing it in "Wee Willie Winkie": "Wee Willie Winkie had once been read to, out of a big blue book, the history of the Princess and the Goblins – a most wonderful tale of a land where the Goblins were always warring with the children of men until they were defeated by one Curdie" (Uniform Edition, pp. 261–2).

To A. P. Watt, 7 January 1898
ALS: Berg Collection, New York Public Library

The Elms / R'dean. / Jan. 7. '98

Dear Watt –

Just a personal and private note of thanks to you, ere I sail, for all you have done for me this past year. I can't write these things prettily so you must read between the lines – you and Alick[1] together.

All good luck attend you in your businesses. May things go as easily for you as you have made 'em go for me. I can't say more than that if I tried for four pages.

Yours very gratefully
Rudyard Kipling

Note
1. Alexander S. Watt (d. 1948), who worked with his father and ran the firm after the elder Watt's death in 1914.

To Frederick Norton Finney, 11 April 1898
ALS: Dalhousie University

The Vineyard[1] / Cape Town: / Easter Monday. '98

Dear Mr. Finney:

Your letter with its sad news about Mrs. Finney reached me while I was wandering about the interior of this vast continent – from Bulawayo to the sea.[2] Need we tell you how very grieved we all are to learn about it; and how sincerely we hope that by the time this letter reaches you the whole trouble will have gone away into the past. One doesn't mind being ill on one's own account. It's when the Partner in the Syndicate falls sick that the trouble begins.

We have had what you might call a truly monumental time. I went out to the North by myself and found a new people growing up by Bulawayo – the railway being laid from there on to the Zambesi. By the way I had a permit to ride on the loco and as a patriotic Englishman I was grieved to see so many Baldwins[3] on the road. However they fire beautifully and with the rank bad colonial coal used that is an advantage. I've been all over all the railway workshops I could get at; into all the round houses and generally have made myself a nuisance all along the road. It's only 3'6" guage but they pile on the heaviest locos and rolling stock that I have ever seen. If ever you have six months to spare you ought to come out here. It is nothing less than a new nation in the throes of birth – a nation with resources behind it of which it hardly dreams now: but in another quarter of a century it will have found its feet: I see by the papers you are going to walk into Cuba:[4] and my sympathies are with you. There is no place in the world today for worn-out nations.

    With all our best love and good wishes

believe me
Yours ever sincerely
Rudyard Kipling

Notes

1. The boarding-house at Newlands, Cape Town, where RK and his family stayed on this first visit. It was kept by an Irishwoman who "spread miseries and discomforts round her in return for good monies" (*Something of Myself*, p. 148).
2. RK left for Kimberley by special train on 5 March; on 9 March he left for Bulawayo; on the 14th he was in the Matopos, and on the 28th in Kimberley again, on the way to Johannesburg, where he arrived on 1 April. On 4 April he left for Cape Town, where he arrived on the 6th (CK diary; Grahamstown *Journal*, 2 April 1898; *Cape Argus*, 5 April 1898).
3. Products of the Baldwin Locomotive Works, Philadelphia.
4. War with Spain over Cuba was declared by the US on 25 April.

To James M. Conland, [early April 1898][1]

ALS: Library of Congress

The Vineyard / Cape Town

– Cape Town – Kimberley – Bulawayo – Kimberley again – Johannesberg – and so back to the Cape. You look those places up on the map and see if I haven't put in big work while I've been here. The wife and babies stayed at a hotel here – a quiet place surrounded by oaks under the shadow of Table Mountain – an ideal place to work at: but kept by three thoroughpaced female devils – one with a moustache and no figure – who have made things just as unpleasant all round for all the guests as the twelve hours of daylight would let 'em. But in spite of it all we got on very well; and as the news from Rottingdean reports 86 cases of measles at the local school as well as unlimited influenza we feel that we are well out of it. We sail on Wednesday by the *Norham Castle*. At present it is raining – not in a mere wet way but with the steady ceaseless downpour of the regularly appointed season for Rains – same as our Indian monsoon. The leaves are burning and there is a smell of autumn in the air. Every one is now talking about the "Winter"; and I feel as though I were standing on my head.

There isn't the least chance of my telling you all my adventures until we meet: but be sure that I have had a Royal Time – the best of good times. I have seen Diamond mining at Kimberley where the diamonds come out by hundreds from the washed gravel. They gave me a beauty of 3 ½ carats which, as you may believe, the wife has annexed. I have seen every type and breed of native south of the Zambesi in the huge guarded enclosures where the native labour is kept. Kaffirs steal diamonds (chiefly by swallowing them) and that is why they are put through a five days' course of purging before they leave the service of the mines (one chap put away 35/ carats of diamonds valued at $5,000 and his stomach didn't seem any the worse for it). Then I went a thousand miles north into Matabele land, over a new laid railroad across dry rivers, till I came to the city of Buluwayo, a town of 5,000 white men. They treated me like a prince. Then I went on into the Matoppos – a wilderness of tumbled rocks, granite boulders and caves where the white men fought the Matabele in '96. You never dreamed of such a country. Because I was in the heart of southern Africa, my travelling companion for 18 miles was a girl from Cayuga Co. Western New York who had married an Englishman. We talked America hard for two days. Then I met a man from Montreal – farming for Rhodes, who has only 60,000 acres up there. The land is shot full of gold and prospectors are coming in and going out every day with bags of samples. It's like a cross between a Kansas town, Cripple Creek and a bit of London. Ice is a scarce commodity up there. I left Kimberley with 200 lbs of it which the Diamond Fields Company had given me and it was rather more valuable than diamonds. On the banks of the Macloutsi river – 300 miles from anywhere in particular – I saw a prospector with a pack on his back chucking up green bile under a tree. He was pretty dead with fever and he had an Abra'm Lincoln beard. I stepped out of the train and gave him 20 grains of quinine. Then, like a fool, I offered him whiskey and that set him vomiting worse than ever. Then I thought of the ice: and got out a bottle of soda-water that had been *froze* into the ice for two days. *That* fetched him. "My God" he said "you're as good as an uncle" and he put it down in a minute. "Where do you come from?" says I. "Boston, Mass'chussetts" was the amazing answer. "And what are you doing here"? says I. "Pegging out claims an' dyin'" says he. Then the train went on. I kept my eye out for him on my return journey (I came down with the railway doctor and saw a good deal of fever in the low-country) and was relieved to find that he was safe at a town in Khama's country. I thought he would have been dead. Well. I had a great time at Buluwayo and returned to Kimberley where I saw the town-hall burn down and played about the diamond fields some

more. Then I went (50 hours rail) to Johannesbergh where they gave
me a banquet.[2] It is the one big city of S'Africa but the white man there
is a slave to the Boer; and the state of things turned me sick. They are
without votes: and forbidden to carry arms. The Americans (half the
mine managers are Americans) naturally want another revolution and
this time I don't think the revolution will be a fizzle. I preached a lecture
on success and failure which could be read two ways (I didn't want to
get my hosts into trouble by talking sedition and the place was full of
spies) and I wound up by giving the toast of America – and the white
man in the West.[3] An American mine manager replied and *he* talked
red-hot Revolution. [   ][4] a few hundred of the boys saw me off
at the station and nearly fetched the roof off. I was glad to get back to
the white man's country again. There was a diamond-rush on at
Hopetown as I passed and most of the population seemed crazy-drunk.
But what's the use of writing. I'll tell you when we meet.

The wife's health has most distinctly benefitted by her stay and so
have the kids. Elsie is now a most fascinating child of two; and John is
a sturdy kicking imp with an eternal grin on his face. I am vastly better
than I was; though now and again the black cloud comes down on me.
But I think it will come all right in the long run. Idleness never did me
any good yet.

With all our best feelings to you and Mrs Conland and Harry

Yours ever

Rudyard K

P.S.   this is a messy scrawl to acknowledge your two last long letters.

Notes
1. RK returned to Cape Town on 6 April and was on shipboard for the return voyage on
   12 April (CK diary); this letter was thus written between those dates.
2. At the Rand Club, 2 April.
3. I have found no report of this speech.
4. One line erased.

To Sir Donald Currie,[1] 7 May 1898
Text: Marischal Murray, *Union–Castle Chronicle* (1953) p. 321

The Elms, / Rottingdean. / May 7, 1898.

Dear Sir Donald Currie,
    This is merely a line to tell you how splendidly comfortable we have been on the *Dunvegan* and the *Norham*,[2] and how thoroughly we have been looked after in every detail as a family, including three children. I feel that we tested the resources of the Line most thoroughly, and the voyages were made wholly delightful to us. . . .

Very sincerely yours,
Rudyard Kipling.

P.S.   If it is a fair question *how* do you manage to build boats that do not complain in a sea way? We were rolled about a good deal in the Bay and the woodwork of the *Norham*, which they tell me is fifteen years old, never so much as creaked. This is a secret they don't seem to have mastered in the Atlantic trade.

Notes
1. Currie (1825–1909) was the founder of the Castle Steamship Company and, after its merger with the Union Steamship Company, head of the Union–Castle Line.
2. RK went out in the *Dunvegan Castle*, 5,958 tons, built in 1896, and returned in the *Norham Castle*, 4,241 tons, 1883.

To Charles Eliot Norton, 2[3][1] June 1898
ALS: Harvard University

The Elms / Rottingdean. / Thursday June 22. 98.

Dear Mr. Norton:
    I wanted *you* to know as much as any man not here, of Uncle Ned's death and the rest.[2] I do not know what Sally has heard or what may have been written to you from the Grange.
    It came, of course, most utterly unexpectedly – and the first news, on Thursday[3] morning last, was a telegram from Phil to the vicar here saying that his father had died that same morning. Even so, the thing seemed like some sort of ghastly hoax because we had been in correspondence with Aunt Georgie on small matters day by day and her last letter said that she was coming down with Ned in a few days.

Then, at midday, of Friday, came a letter – one of his wild, nonsensical "lark" letters – to me: a beautiful tissue of absurdities. He said he was a bit fagged working at the Avalon picture,[4] standing up all day and dozing in the evening when he wasn't dining out. That was posted about an hour before he died. As you know it was heart-failure of some sort or other. They called it angina-pectoris and it may have been so: but when a man has worked without rest for forty years, the failure may take any shape. It was clean, clear over work – as good a death on the field as ever man could desire. They two by good luck had their last evening alone. They dined alone, and talked and read together alone, and Ned was very happy. Then he went to bed, and about two o'clock called up Georgie with some word that he had a bad touch of heartburn. Before half-past two – before any one of his blood could come – he died in Aunt Georgie's arms and that was as it should be (I fancy he had complained of some uneasiness that afternoon: and his doctor looked him over and told him that there was nothing wrong with his heart). The mercy of it was unspeakable – when you think of all that vile crowded London life so near to them. He might have been struck down in public – at a theatre or dining out somewhere; instead of in his own place, quietly and shieldedly. And so he died – Avalon unfinished: and of course, a mass of other unfinished work waiting. There wasn't anything to be done at our end of the calamity but to wait – to sit still and wait and see what would happen. He was more to me than any man here: over and above my own life's love for him: and he had changed my life in many ways by his visits down here. The man was a God to me – as a workman I can't tell you about *that* side of it and it doesn't very much matter now.

Sallie knows the Rottingdean church where Margot was married and where his seven windows are. Last autumn he went for a walk and caught the Vicar – who is a good man but I should fancy a bit bewildered by Uncle Ned, who wanted, so he said, a "cozy place" for his ashes. The spot he chose was roughly where I have marked in the sketch here –

[sketch map of Rottingdean churchyard and green]

a little recess facing to North End House, in the arm, so to speak, of the S.W. buttress of the church – a place shut out from all the winds, and surrounded with a high border of valerian – purple and white spikes. It is rising ground and as I said, he can look straight across the green, a bare fifty yards, to the windows of North End house. He told us of the place, on the evening of the day of that walk, and explained – you know how he would – its advantages. There, then, the grave was made but, thank Heaven, it wasn't any yawning pit because he had left orders to be cremated.[5] That thing was done on Monday from the Grange – Edward Poynter and Phil going to Woking together: and from what I gathered there are a few points about cremation that may be improved. Nobody from the outside was aware of this first funeral – no body followed; no body stood about and stared except a few of the poor people from the houses across the road; and they, being better than gentle-folk, kept to their own thresholds. On Monday night they came down, Aunt Georgie, Margot and her husband and Phil to North End house; Aunt Louie and Uncle Alfred and Stan also came down to the Ridsdales across the green. We saw Aunt Georgie for a little and – I never had any doubt of her being a saint – but I knew it even for a greater certainty then. She was seeing and realizing all the glory and splendour of that death: but I don't think that the other realization had come to her – quite – the full meaning of the wreck and the loneliness. Margot's face was like pearl-shell and frightened me a little. She wouldn't break and one felt that the break was what they all needed. Phil was quite quiet and deadly changed. I am sorrier for Phil than almost for any one because I know how he and his father were men together and besides I love Phil very much. The little box of ashes was laid in front of the altar on his drawing table – no drapery, no nonsense – no nothing except four candles and there it was watching through the night – the night of midsummer eve – a hot, still grey night with no true darkness at all: but our northern twilight. Phil and Jack Mackail stayed from eight till twelve: then a friend of theirs, Harry Taylor, from twelve to two; Stan from two to four; I from four to six; and Uncle Alfred from six to eight. In Stan's watch just as the true dawn was breaking Aunt Georgie and Margot came in, all in white to watch a little and dear old Stan said he felt like a profane heathen and crept out till they called him back. I can believe it for her face in daylight was like nothing earthly. In my watch there came in the old, old Mr Ridsdale, father of Stan's wife, Cissy – rather an appalling figure at five a.m. – scrupulously dressed in black; looking rather like Father Time strayed in from among the tombs; and he stayed an hour. It was an unearthly night but for the life of me I could not connect the man who was three parts a God with the little oak box before me. The drawing table and the windows were much more *him*.

Tuesday was one long nightmare of which I don't remember much. People wandered about doing things in an aimless purposeless way. There was a good deal to be done, I know, and I tried to do some things but it was all no good. One couldn't stay to anything. Father came down from London (Mother and Aunt Edie stayed together at Tisbury) and with him came Aunt Aggie, Uncle Edward, Ambo – Fred Macdonald with two sons, and we all herded together in the Elms. There were a lot of other people in the churchyard and on the green but I can't say I took an extravagant interest in them. The simplicity and quiet of the arrangements had cut down all outsiders to the smallest number: but from my point of view one didn't need any more. At two the English burial service began in the church and Aunt Georgie was there with all the others. Then Phil and Margot themselves carried the box to the grave which was lined with moss and roses and themselves let it down at the last – so that no hands, except those of his own blood, touched him. The decency, the cleanliness and the sanity of it all were as he would have wished. I had had a horror in my mind of some bungling, hireling business with ropes and boards. All that thank God was done away with. Just at the end, I saw Uncle Crom – my Uncle Crom – near me – broken to pieces. You know how he and Ned had been together always. It was awful. I can tell you about Aunt Georgie when we meet. One doesn't want to write these things. She was standing with her eyes shut at the head of the grave and at the end she kneeled for a minute or two; and then we came away. North End House went in quietly to its own sorrow. There was no mobbing; no jabber; no idiotic condolences; and the rest of us of his kin, walked about our garden for awhile till it was time to get the carriages and go back to town.

That same evening Aunt Georgie and the others went up to town again. We saw the grave (only it wasn't a grave thank God) put in order: with some flowers from Ruskin and a wreath from Swinburne – no dirt on the edges: no mess – nothing but decency and order. Our gardener who has seen Uncle Ned of course from afar, said to me reflectively: – "Of course I hadn't anything to *do* with him: but what *did* strike me about him" (I use the man's own words) "was his humanity. There aren't many too humane men in the world today – are they?" That struck me as very curious. You see in point of space we are nearer to Uncle Ned even than North End House, because he is only just across the road and, being a dry season, Marten the gardener waters the grass on his own initiative for the sake of the "humane man." The village kept itself quite quiet. The regular omnibus which blows a disgusting horn round the green, kept away and (I know something about the common folk here) every one was *sorry* – really sorry for the loss. They knew in their several ways that he was the "humane man." Yesterday (Wednesday) was the memorial service in the Abbey to which Carrie and I went but I should *not* have gone if I had realized that all the English church could do in the way of a memorial would be to repeat practically the whole of the burial for the dead. There was fine music and a choir, a Dean in black and white and red (a little shrivelled figure against the background of gold) but I kept seeing the Rottingdean of the day before under my eyelids all the time. Everybody was there of those who had been to the funeral; and judging from the number in the abbey, I suppose the best of Babylon had turned out for the function.

One good sight was Angela and Dennis Mackail in white – but there were (inevitably I suppose) a heap too many people who stared about and rather enjoyed the show. Then we had lunch with Aunt Louie and came down again – broke – broke – broke. I can't cry. At least I don't seem able to have found out the way yet and I don't think it will come either. It's all a sort of a clot in my head because one has to realize that the man won't come back. Any body's grief is selfish in essence, of course; and mine probably more selfish than others because I am a selfish man. His work was the least part of him. It is him that one wants – the size and the strength and the power and the jests and the God given sympathy of the man. He *knew*. There never was man like to him who *knew* all things without stirring. Last autumn, he was good enough to talk to me after work – and he talked to me like an equal – as though I were also a workman. He could work more and harder and more sustainedly than a navvy – and it was *that* among a million things that I reverenced him for beside all my love for him. He was never at fault in his discernings: he made all allowances, just as a God would do; and he laughed like a God. You know, things had rather broken me up before I left America and this thing has snapped something else inside me. It's all in the day's work of course and one must hold on to the end of the day but, sometimes one gets a wee bit tired. That's my grief and by the side of the others it's a little one. I don't know how they'll come through but they will somehow – unless Aunt Georgie breaks as I sometimes fancy she may. She thinks she is going to stay on at the Grange – the Grange without Ned –.

Give our best love to your household – don't bother to answer this.

Always your affectionate
Ruddy.

Notes
1. Thursday was the 23rd of June in 1898.
2. Burne-Jones died on 17 June.
3. In fact Friday.
4. *The Sleep of Arthur in Avalon*, begun in 1881 and still unfinished at Burne-Jones's death. It is now in the Ponce Museum of Art, Puerto Rico.
5. Cremation was still a novelty in England, and had not been legal until 1884. The crematorium at Woking was the only one in the country.

To John St Loe Strachey,[1] [early July 1898]

ALS: House of Lords Record Office

The Elms, / Rottingdean, / Nr. Brighton.

Dear Mr. Strachey –

Many thanks for your kind little note. I wait tomorrow's *Spectator* with immense interest, but since one is always most unprejudiced before one has read the reply to one's argument I make haste to explain that I shall stick to my theory of the genesis of the *Tempest*[2] It is my first attempt at Shakespearian criticism and I am very pleased with it. Besides, the more I think it over the more am I persuaded that things fell out precisely as I have indicated. Consequently, and in advance of your brother's letter, I disbelieve altogether in William Strachey – unless, indeed, he was the original Stephano. *There was a human being and no document behind that play and very near to it.*

I am sorry to say that I shan't be up in town just now as I expect to be off with the Fleet[3] almost immediately.

Very sincerely yours,
Rudyard Kipling

Notes
1. Strachey (1860–1927) was editor and proprietor of the *Spectator*, 1898–1925. Strachey's politics were close to RK's, and they shared a keen interest in the question of national defence.
2. RK's letter to the *Spectator* on "Landscape and Literature" was published on 2 July 1898. In it he argues that Shakespeare must have got the story of *The Tempest* from sailors who had been shipwrecked in Bermuda. It was answered by Henry Strachey in the *Spectator*, 9 July; he suggested that Shakespeare's source was a pamphlet by William Strachey, Secretary to the Virginia Colony. RK returns to his idea in "The Coiner" (*Limits and Renewals*).
3. RK joined HMS *Pelorus* at Devonport on 1 September for manoeuvres off Ireland; he returned to The Elms on 12 September (CK diary). This was the occasion when RK, after reciting some of his verses at a ship's concert, was carried shoulder-high round the quarterdeck in triumph.

To Charles Roswell Bacon,[1] 9 August 1898
ALS: Library of Congress

The Elms, / Rottingdean, / Nr. Brighton. / Aug. 9. 98.

Dear Bacon –

Excellent! Hurrah! *Salaam! Râm-râm!* Bully for you! Likewise congratulations.[2] America is distinctly looking up; and you seem to be leading the procession. I suppose you'll enter him for the Navy – same as my boy John now all but a year old.

Haven't your views on matters imperial changed in the last few months? I sit here and chuckle as I read the papers over the water. The land seems to be taking kindly to the White Man's work. Of course the boys are doing well at Santiago and elsewhere.[3] The funny thing is to see the nation behind 'em – not understanding what America is committed to – wondering and blundering and trying to get out of her responsibilities. Remember, we've been at this little business for a matter of half a century. Only this spring we finished up the work of an army of 60,000 men who had been on the war-path on the Frontier for eight months; and we've twenty five thousand odd engaged in "busting" the heathen on the upper Nile at the present moment.[4] It is the fate of our breed to do these things – or rather to have these things forced upon us and it is a joy and gratification beyond words to me to see you 'uns swinging into line on your side of the world and getting to business instead of heaving rocks at one another and turning out the militia for railroad strikes. Your *real* work will begin after peace is declared. If you don't annex the Phillipines now, you'll have to do it all over again, precisely as we did in Egypt and you have fifteen years solid administration laid out for you in Cuba where, if you are wise, you will infallibly clean out the guileless Cuban. This has been a grand year for the White Man.

All goes well with us here. Please send our best love to your sister and with good wishes for you and the Man-child.

Yours ever

Rudyard Kipling

P.S.   You'll see that tale some day with your "quote" at the head of it.

Notes

1. Bacon (1868–1913) was a painter who had studied in Paris, kept a studio in New York, and lived in Ridgefield, Connecticut. Evidently he was known to CK and thus to RK through Wolcott Balestier. CK wrote to Bacon in 1893 that "I can fancy Wolcott delivering you a long lecture about all these things which you plan to do with your life and believing you would make much out of it. He liked and trusted your future" (25 October [1893]: ALS, Library of Congress).

2. A note on the letter says: "On the birth of our son, Henry".
3. Spanish resistance in the Spanish–American War ended in July, and Spain sued for peace at the end of the month.
4. A frontier war in the Swat Valley, North-West Provinces of India, ended in early 1898. Kitchener in the Sudan was advancing up the Nile against the Mahdists; they were defeated at Omdurman in early September and Khartoum was retaken.

To William Heinemann, 9 August 1898

ALS: Princeton University

The Elms, / Rottingdean, / Nr. Brighton. / Aug. 9. 88.

Dear Heinemann,

Many thanks. They are very noble and impressive but they are also entirely out of my beat. What you want for that type of "types"[1] is a few lines apiece from a man saturated with his London as I – am not. They are worthy of really good verses (they mustn't be frivolous or cheap in any way) and I don't know enough of the life of the little village to be able to do them justice. Why not try Henley? *He* ought to be the very person for the job. If you say so I'll send the "types" on to him if he doesn't know them.

Yours sincerely always
Rudyard Kipling.

Note

1. Drawings of London types – barmaid, clerk, porter, and the like – by William Nicholson; accompanied by verses by Henley these were published by Heinemann in 1898 as *London Types*: see 29 December 1898.

To George Cram Cook,[1] 19 August 1898

Text: Composite of copies in Berg Collection, New York Public Library, and Parkin Papers, Public Archives of Canada

The Elms / Rottingdean / Nr. Brighton / Aug. 19, '98

Dear Corporal Cook –

I can't tell you how honored I feel by your letter, – and at the same time how it touches me. What a glorious experience this will be to you, if you don't go and pick up typhoid, which seems to be the staple commodity of the South just now.

So far as I can make out they are going to disband the bulk of your army on the conclusion of peace:[2] and I hope they will have the savvy to start in with an enlarged, regular one. A quarter of a million won't be any too big for the regular work in hand – work that will be unromantic, necessary, inevitable, and with precious little Kudos in it.

I own I felt like Methuselah when I read your note – racially old beyond telling – a cave man as it were, listening to the chant of a new tribe. For, you see, you are on the threshold of your work which, thank God, is the White Man's work, the business of introducing a sane and orderly administration into the dark places of the earth that lie to your hand.

To you – we will assume for the purposes of argument that ex-professor Corporal Cook is 70,000,000 strong – it is a tremendous upheaval, a breaking with the past and a time of amazing self-realization. To me – for the purposes of argument I am rather more than eight hundred years old – it is the business whereto I was bred and trained. I send out yearly some 70,000 men to police 300,000,000 persons who have a taste for slaughter, infanticide and a few other genial weaknesses. I have only this spring called in 60,000 from an eight months old war amid the underheaps[3] of the Indian frontier: and 22,000 men are now going in to arrange matters with a merry barbarian down in the south of Egypt.[4] Behind all these men, who die or will die of fever, sun, cholera, the sword and syphilis, stand all my administrators who without hope of reward of public favor or any expressed approval will go out and die in strange places for the good of the various races they have taken under their wing. I have suppressed much evil in many lands; I have made two blades grow where but one grew before: I have brought peace where there was only war; I have abated famine and sent my picked men to fight pestilence. And this I have done, O Theophilus, not once in a year, but yearly for fifty years.

And my reward has not always been the sympathy or the comprehension of Corporal Cook, ex-professor 70,000,000 strong. He said in his papers – I exploited and ground down the heathen (this was before he had heathen of his own to play with) he said I was a robber (this was before he had to knock down another man's house to prevent a nuisance) and a burglar; a canting hypocrite and many other things. He bombinated in a vacuum[5] of twenty white men to the square mile, where so generous is the land and large that it didn't very much matter what any one did. He scoffed at my administrators; he misunderstood my methods; he did not believe in my ideals; he blasphemed against the means I employed

> "He said it very loud and clear
> He went and shouted in my ear"[6]

He went out of his way two years ago to get up a fight with me; and *it was no fault of his'n that he did not succeed –*[7]

But two years ago is a very long time and since then ex-professor Corporal Cook 70,000,000 strong has had his own experiences; not the least of which has been hearing the Continental races apply to him and his motives, every epithet and adjective that he ever hurled at me. The years will bring him more enlightenment as he really gets to work. At present he has hardly begun on the White Man's destiny.

To drop nonsense. Don't you see that *now* the States have justified 'emselves as White Men. They are worth talking to: they are equals (which for all their wealth they were not before) they understand things. Up till lately they were like a barren woman laying down the law on the control of children. And each year of administering alien races who have no rights, and for that very reason must be dealt with with an immense forbearance, will educate, stiffen and cleanse them. Sitting here, I could write down with almost absolute certainty a few problems that will confront your government a few years hence. They will strike your folk as absolutely new and unparalleled in the history of mankind. They are in reality, as old as black and white. The enthusiasm of your first conquest will die away: you will find yourselves brought face to face with a vast amount of hard work; you will blunder horribly; you will fail, succeed, fail and succeed again, but in the long run you will come out all right and *then* you will be a nation indeed. Does this sound patronising? Live another twenty years and you will see what I mean. The fighting is the least part of it. You will look back on scores of small fights before you come to die – expeditions by land and sea undertaken without hysterics or flag-wagging for a definite end, to be accomplished without fuss or excitement.

But if, as we tried to do in Egypt[8] – you evade your responsibilities toward the lower races: if you try to patch up some sort of ignoble compromise with half-breeds: if you cheat yourselves into the belief that written and paper constitutions can help races who have never conceived the western notion of liberty: if relying on these makeshifts you shirk and scuttle, the greater will be your condemnation, because you have our policies as a warning to guide you aright. In plain English, if you don't annex and administer the Phillipines, you ought to be hung.

Liberavi animam meam! and you will say that I have preached most inordinately.

As to my views on the tribe, the day is yet young and I may have room and time to alter 'em; but I can quite understand and sympathize with your feeling that I have not been just to you and yours as White Men. None the less I maintain (vide Captains Courageous) that I have come pretty close to understanding that section of the Tribe among whom I built my house and raised a couple of babies. I am not going to go round with butter in a ladle, not for a wilderness of Santiagoes or a ship-load of Hobsons,[9] but one of these days, maybe, you'll see me ablossoming into verse – "poetry Mr. Wegg."[10] Speaking of you now as an ex-professor, can you tell me anything about the impetus to your own bards that this war is likely to give? I am very curious to see how the younger singers will take hold of the affair and whether, out of the stress and strain of it all, some good literature will be born.

And now I will cease to pester you. In the language of our Immortal Williams, virtute puer marte[11] – go in and win. We – that is to say me and a few mates of mine who pay taxes for about 463 ships of sorts, have been standing guard over you 'uns with a shot gun while you went around pounding Dons; and it is intensely funny to see how instinctively and accurately all the continent has damned both sections of the Tribe as burglars; and how, in spite of Venezuela, all of us here with no word said, have mechanically moved up in support of your little performances. Someday, perhaps, the diplomatic side of the business will be made public and I think you will be interested.

You've come into the Tribe for keeps now and no one is more pleased than

Yours always sincerely
Rudyard Kipling

Notes

1. Cook (1873–1924) taught English literature at the University of Iowa and at Stanford, worked on newspapers, and published fiction and drama. He is remembered, with his wife, Susan Glaspell, as the founder of the Provincetown Players in 1915. At the time of this letter Cook was with the 50th Iowa Volunteers at Camp Cuba Libra, Jacksonville, Florida. RK's letter is a reply to one that Cook wrote to him on enlisting (Susan Glaspell, *The Road to the Temple*, 1941, p. 98).
2. The armistice in the Spanish–American War was declared on 12 August; the peace treaty was signed in December.
3. The Berg copy reads "amid the underheaps"; the Parkin Papers copy reads "amid under heaps"; neither seems to make sense.
4. RK means the Swat Valley campaign in India and Kitchener's campaign in the Sudan: see 9 August 1898.
5. Rabelais, *Gargantua and Pantagruel*, ii.viii: "whether the Chimera, buzzing in a vacuum [*in vacuo bombinans*], can eat its secondary causes".
6. Lewis Carroll, *Through the Looking-Glass*, ch. 6.
7. RK means the Venezuelan incident at the end of 1895.
8. RK presumably means the British abandonment of the Sudan after the triumph of the Mahdi in 1885 until Kitchener's expedition in 1896.
9. Lieutenant Richmond Hobson (1870–1937), following a daring but unsuccessful attempt to blockade Santiago harbour, was transformed into a war hero. He afterwards had a political career.
10. Dickens, *Our Mutual Friend*: "Wegg" ought to be "Venus", for it is Silas Wegg who "drops into poetry".
11. Thus in copy: possibly RK wrote "martis virtute puer": "a boy of martial courage". But that is a guess.

To Moberly Bell, [*c.* 12 September 1898][1]

ALS: Library of Congress

The Elms, / Rottingdean, / Nr. Brighton.

Dear Bell –

Oh you funk! Put it in as "sporting" in the *Times* and save twenty quid. It will be smothered in Literature.[2] The philistines will call it a "poem" and want to know whether it is founded on fact; which by the way, it is. I didn't want the American rights and I'm sorry now I didn't say so. I wanted the row in the *Times* and all the virtuous people who believe Russia to be civilized calling you names. However, if you use it for *Literature* can't you make its political meaning clear?

I like M.W.[3] but once when I was a newspaper correspondent he kept me dancing on the mat for half a day refusing me news. I'd like to pay him back for that little business – at Pindi in 1885.[4]

I shot my bolt about Egypt after Firket in some verses called "Pharoah and the Sergeant."[5] I'm sorry now I didn't hold it in reserve. It would just have fitted Omdurman.[6]

I'm just back from the Channel Fleet cruise[7] with mounds of work to get through and town is not for me.

Yours ever
Rudyard Kipling.

Notes

1. Dated from RK's statement that "I'm just back from the Channel Fleet cruise"; he returned on 12 September (CK diary).
2. RK is talking about his "The Truce of the Bear" (*The Five Nations*), which appeared not in *The Times* but in *Literature*, 1 October 1898.
3. Mackenzie Wallace, private secretary to Lord Dufferin as Viceroy of India, 1884–8. He was now director of the foreign department of *The Times*.
4. RK reported the meeting of the Viceroy of India and the Amir of Afghanistan at Rawalpindi in March–April 1885; see 30 July–1 August 1885.
5. Published in *The Graphic*, July 1897 (*The Five Nations*). The battle of Firket, June 1896, was the first retaliatory raid on the Mahdists after the death of Gordon in January 1885.
6. Kitchener's victory at Omdurman on 2 September 1898 put an end to the Mahdist state in the Sudan.
7. See [early July 1898].

To Theodore Roosevelt,[1] 13 September 1898
ALS: Library of Congress

The Elms, / Rottingdean, / Nr. Brighton. / Sept 13 '98

Dear Roosevelt –

I'm just back from a tour with the Channel Fleet round Ireland and such like. It isn't campaigning but it's rather hard work. I can't tell you how pleased I was to get your letter or how sorry to see that you are nominated for Governor this fall.[2] Why don't you leave that sort of skittles to Bryan[3] & Co. and go in for being a colonial administrator. God knows the country will need 'em pretty bad in a few years. I see your army has proved its lineal connections with ours by arranging transport and commissariat pretty much as we did in the Crimea.[4]

It isn't a thing to take too seriously to heart – except for the poor chaps who happen to be the victims. We slew about 30,000 with cold disease and starvation in '54.

Now go in and put all the weight of your influence into hanging on permanently to the whole of the Phillipines.[5] America has gone and stuck a pickaxe into the foundations of a rotten house and she is morally bound to build the house over again from the foundations or have it fall about her ears. All good luck go with you and yours. I've been watching your career somewhat closely and foresee a big future for you.

Ever yours sincerely and admiringly
Rudyard Kipling

P.S.   Don't go into politics yet awhile.

Notes
1. Roosevelt (1858–1919), Republican President of the United States, 1901–8, was before that a New York Assemblyman, a Civil Service Commissioner, a New York Police Commissioner, Assistant Secretary of the Navy, an author, and a soldier. He had just returned from the war in Cuba as a national hero. RK had met Roosevelt in the spring of 1895 in Washington, DC; his admiration for Roosevelt is expressed in *Something of Myself* and in his poem on Roosevelt's death, "Great-Heart" (1919).
2. Roosevelt was elected Governor of New York in November.
3. William Jennings Bryan.
4. The American Army was unable to provide adequate transport, supply, and medical service in the Spanish–American War. Of 5,462 deaths in the Army, only 1,983 were in battle or from wounds (Walter Millis, *The Martial Spirit*, 1931, p. 367).
5. The war in Cuba was undertaken in order to free the island from Spanish domination; the Philippines were regarded as a prize. Though there was much American sentiment against it, the treaty of peace with Spain ceded the Philippines to America.

To Frank N. Doubleday, 30 September 1898
ALS: Princeton University

The Elms, / Rottingdean, / Nr. Brighton. / Sept 30. 98.

Dear Doubleday –
   I have done more blaspheming over "The Day's Work" than is right or respectable. However, it's all over now and I don't care. As you say the Maltese Cat must have gone missing in the mail. The typed copy overtook me on the coast of Ireland, when I was having a lovely time with the Channel Fleet, and I had to sit down and correct it instead or larking about Bantry bay with landing-parties and [boat?] guns. I tell you our Fleet which lies mighty low and says nothing is no small kind of a Fleet. I've written an account of it for the newspapers – in order to make the public take an interest.[1]
   Today is the advertised date for the Day's Work this side. I hope the MacMillans have got it ready but they too have been rather sad.
   Strictly speaking (but I ain't going to confess this) I might just as well have turned in all proofs before I went to South Africa instead of waiting till May. So you see I forgive you the trouble I was the means of causing. Best salaams to S.S. [McClure] who I see has 400,000 readers behind him. It's curious to notice how "Recessional" is printed. It was sold by the *Times* for a solid year after it came out.
Yours ever,
Rudyard Kipling.

Note
1. The articles collected as *A Fleet in Being* first appeared in the *Morning Post* in November.

To Louisa Baldwin, 8 October 1898
ALS: Dalhousie University.

The Elms, / Rottingdean, / Nr. Brighton. / Oct: 8/98

Dear Aunt Louie –
   Never a glimpse of sun yet – only fat grey low clouds and a north-east wind. From Worcester[1] I came down with three young and wonderfully dressed sons of Belial – two of whom played poker all the way and the third (with a yellow-flowered waistcoat) talked about drinks. Just before we got into Paddington he solemnly opened his

dressing-bag – got out a mirror, an ivory brush with a silver monogram, and – brushed his suckling moustache, which was a pale straw colour. This breed of person is new to me.

I found my Carrie with nothing worse than a vehement cough – John with a small cold and the other two well. But it's pestiferous weather. Carrie as usual had superintended the execution of some dozen or two small jobs in the plumbing, carpentry and gardening line, while I had been away.

I went over to see Jenny Morris[2] at North End House and for all her trouble found her curiously unchanged. "The Day's Work" hasn't come in to me yet,[3] but as soon as it does you shall have a copy. Let me know if you have time to spare how "The Bees"[4] comes on. There's a heap in that tale, and it could be made most telling. We don't drink '47 Port in this house[5] but a merciful Providence is sending me George Wyndham this evening and I am going to deliver my little soul over Army and Navy whiskey about our foreign policy. I only wish Uncle Alfred were here.

With all love (need I say how I enjoyed my time at Wilden) from us both.

Your affectionate nephew
Ruddy.

Notes
1. The Baldwins lived at Wilden House, Stourport, near Worcester.
2. Jane Alice Morris (1861–1935), the elder of William Morris's daughters, suffered from epilepsy.
3. It was published on 30 September.
4. Evidently not published. The MS of the story is in the Baldwin papers now in the Worcestershire Record Office; the story turns on the tradition of "telling the bees" family news in order to keep them. In this case the news is of an illegitimate child.
5. Alfred Baldwin was a connoisseur of wine; no doubt something from his cellar is meant.

To Leonard Raven-Hill,[1] 31 October 1898
ALS: Cornell University

The Elms, / Rottingdean, / Nr. Brighton. / Oct: 31. 98.

Dear Mr. Raven-Hill –
I am glad to know that you are the illustrator of the school-tales; because I feel sure that the boys will appear as boys. *But* I do not see

why you or I should add to the already vast and variegated knowledge that boys possess of torture. I was at great pains merely to indicate the devilments my three used. I carefully cut out all details for moral and pious reasons; and here are you calmly proposing to illustrate the whole Inquisition![2] I refuse to give you the details because I know that your pictures would teach about five thousand young imps new and fascinating styles of breaking their enemies' hearts. All I will confide is that an "Agag"[3] is a person whose thumbs and big toes are tied together with fine string. He then walks delicately but his language is different.

Very sincerely
Rudyard Kipling.

Notes
1. Raven-Hill (1867–1942), an artist for *Punch* since 1896, illustrated seven of the nine *Stalky* stories as they appeared in magazines.
2. In "The Moral Reformers", *Windsor Magazine*, March 1899.
3. " 'Make him an Ag Ag, Turkey!' And an Ag Ag was he made, forthwith" ("The Moral Reformers", *Stalky & Co.*, p. 147). Presumably the allusion is to Agag in I Samuel 15:32.

To Alfred Baldwin, 18 November 1898
ALS: Dalhousie University

The Elms, / Rottingdean, / Nr. Brighton. / Nov. 18. 98

Dear Uncle Alfred,
   You've been married to a Macdonald for some time and I've been the son of one for a few years. They do not strike *me* as a very pliable breed. However – this is what we have arrived at.
   On the 22nd inst (not before) my mother comes up to town and with Trix goes into retreat at the Royal Palace Hotel for three weeks while Colenso and a *masseuse* work over her and she is dosed and dieted and generally looked after.[1] I tried to forestall the date but found that it didn't suit mother's arrangements. She has however given up a visit to a country house with which she purposed to enliven her time of waiting – and that seems to me one point gained. If she does not kill herself before the 22nd we shall at least have the satisfaction of knowing that she will then seriously enter upon the care of herself. I shall take steps then to introduce a specialist, because though I do not know precisely what kind of ass Colenso may be I incline to think he is many varieties. The main point is not to flutter the mother.
   I did not answer your last letter till I had some progress to report.

This gives you the situation up to date; and bless you for setting the machinery in motion. With love to Aunt Louie.

Always yours affectionately,
Ruddy.

Note

1. Trix had now begun to suffer from the mental illness that would afflict her, off and on, for many years. She made many "recoveries", but her condition, until late in life, remained unstable. An added difficulty was the reluctance of her mother to allow Trix to be treated as mentally ill: "nothing has been allowed to be done to cure her", CK wrote in 1900. "Mrs K will not have it, and so it's not done" (to Meta de Forest, 11 May 1900: ALS, Harvard). Yet Mrs Kipling clearly recognised the fact of her daughter's condition. She wrote to Georgiana Burne-Jones in 1899 that "my poor Trix is . . . still very, very far from being herself". At times her condition would be that of "mutism": this then changed "to almost constant talk – and of – my dear – nearly all nonsense. . . . There are times in every day when she is her own bright self and then she suddenly changes and drifts away into a world of her own – always a sad one – into which I cannot follow her" (6 March 1899: ALS, Sussex). In this first onset of her illness, Trix was put under the care of a Dr Robert Colenso, of 91 Cromwell Road; later she seems to have been taken to a nursing home and to have remained there for at least a year.

To Mrs Armitage,[1] 6 December 1898
ALS: Lieutenant-Colonel J. Harvey-Kelley

The Elms, / Rottingdean, / Nr. Brighton. / Dec. 6. 98.

My dear Mrs. Armitage

"Perhaps I will remember L.C. Dunsterville (No 10)." Forgive me quoting your own words but *don't* you see any likeness between "Stalky" and L.C. Dunsterville No. 10? We were only in the same form, same dormitory and same study for five and two years respectively. There was a time when Dunsterville-Beresford-Kipling were pronounced as one word at the U.S.C. and we fell into punishment as one boy. I last saw him in Mian Mir in 90 or 91, on a flying visit. His fame was great in the land then. Price tells me he is now married.[2]

Surely you have not forgotten the small matter of a dance at your Father's house about 2000 years ago – before I was bald and had six year old daughters! Can you give me Dunster's address that I may bring his ancient sins before him once more? I have a great belief in that boy as a tactician and a strategist and, when you have read all the stories in Stalky and Co, I think you will agree with me.

Yours very sincerely
Rudyard Kipling

1. The former May Dunsterville, one of Lionel Dunsterville's five sisters.
2. Dunsterville was married in November 1897.

To John St Loe Strachey, 25 December 1898
ALS: House of Lords Record Office

The Elms, / Rottingdean, / Nr. Brighton. / Dec: 25: 98.

Dear Mr. Strachey,

You will see by the copy of the *Cape Times* Xmas No. sent herewith that I am taking you at your word in sending you things that might suggest something.

Few people have hitherto taken notice of the vestiges (artistic and architectural) that remain of the Dutch occupation of the Cape and I can't help thinking that a proper and sympathetic knowledge of these may be of some importance at the present moment to English people who have not too many points of contact with the dutch.

The mine isn't a very large one but it seems to have been worked with a good deal of intelligence and artistic feeling by Mrs. Trotter[1] who can also draw. I wish I could give you some idea of the beauty and repose of the old Dutch houses at the Cape. So much of course depends on the clear air in which the least line or moulding shows for its full value, the heavy oak foliage about the stoops and the raw purple hills behind the roof that no photograph or pencil can render them fully. Looking at the houses one realizes how in spite of the usual Dutch bickerings the Cape had a quiet and dignified past in which the old houses took deep root.

So far as I know no attempt has hitherto been made to give any artistic account of the farms and homesteads where the old, narrow and very dear life of the leading families was lived. Every one knows about the Dutch E. India Company and how they desired the Cape as a sea-tavern – a house of call between Holland and Batavia – but every body does not realize how the carefully landed and strictly guarded Dutch agents and factors at the Cape – men hired to keep the "sea-tavern" and supply the needs of the ships, – insisted almost in the teeth of the "Seventeen,"[2] on laying vehement hands upon the country and colonizing it. Nor is it well enough known how they got the French Huguenots to help them.

The belief of the modern colonist is that a sheet of corrugated iron is, of necessity, the architectural unit of the Cape. It is no such thing. The Dutch colonists have set copies of convenient, roomy and dignified houses perfectly adapted to the climate and in artistic propriety far in advance of recent importations. These are small matters of course but if you ever have time to look through the number I fancy it will interest you. I believe Mrs. Trotter's article is merely the preliminary sketch. She is keenly interested in the subject and knows a good deal about it. I hope she'll carry it forward to a serious work before the dutch houses are all gone. They are good to live in – as I can testify.[3]

I see a very kindly review of the Fleet in Being in this week: and it is pleasant to see the *Spectator* commends my "tact" in not ventilating service grievances.[4] I ought to have some reward for the way in which I hardened my heart against the warrant officers (whom I like) and the Engineers (whom I love). Some day there will be an awful smash in our Navy if the Admiralty does not give better engineers and increased engine room staffs. It isn't a "service" grievance but a matter of national importance and I'd give much if I had special knowledge enough to bring it forward convincingly. Can't you find some one who will seriously and temperately attend to this matter? The day is coming when the engine room will govern the ship – and in those days newspapers will know a very great deal about technical terms. They will learn them as the beaver learned to climb – because he had to.

Sincerely yours
Rudyard Kipling

Notes
1. Aly Fane Trotter (1863–1961), wife of a government engineer at the Cape, where she lived, 1896–8. Her pioneering article on old Cape Dutch houses in the *Cape Times* was the basis of her *Old Colonial Houses of the Cape of Good Hope* (1900).
2. The central body of the Dutch East India Company.
3. Strachey noticed the article in the *Spectator*, 31 December 1898, p. 993.
4. *Spectator*, 24 December 1898, p. 952, giving "unstinted praise" for the "consummate tact" RK shows in the matter.

To William Ernest Henley, 28 December 1898

ALS: Morgan Library

The Elms, / Rottingdean, / Nr. Brighton. / Dec. 28. 98.

Dear Henley –

I'm glad Cornford explained: because I was expecting the "types"[1] but put down the delay to your trouble with the hand.[2] I went over and saw Cornford's copy of which I think the *Barnmaid*, the *Flower girl* and the *Beef-Eater* are the best versicularly considered but they're all mighty good. Doesn't it suggest to you that you should make a regular menagerie of 'em – all types – but not all necessarily sonnets. Take the City Man; the Clerk; the prostitute; the volunteer; porter, guard; and the whole show so that the thing may go on record as a living gallanty-show?[3] I want Nicholson to show me what he can do in mediums other than his present lumps of light and shade. But he seems wedded to what he does.

We've all been grieved sorely about the hand. What a fool Providence is. There are so many men in whom a crippled right hand would have been a blessing to the world, a salutary discipline and a real gain to literature that I can't understand why this should have come to you. How much longer is it likely to go on? Cornford tells me that some day or other you will truly make Brighton your head-quarters. I'll believe it when I see you careering down the front in a wild bath-chair but I wish you'd hurry up and begin.

Ever yours sincerely
Ruddy

Notes
1. See letter to Heinemann, 9 August 1898.
2. Henley had undergone one of many operations late in 1898, this one on his arm (Connell, *Henley*, p. 338).
3. A shadow-pantomime.

To John St Loe Strachey, 2 January 1899
ALS: House of Lords Record Office

The Elms, / Rottingdean, / Nr. Brighton. / Jan 2. 99.

Dear Mr Strachey –

I read from Grave to Gay[1] with deep thankfulness. Now that the *Saturday* has been dead four days,[2] and the *Academy* is the Lowther Arcade[3] of Literature and the Athenæum is, as always, "Golly what a paper!"[4] one is grateful for sane and temperate views of things decently put forward. Besides I wanted the R.L.S. studies and the notes on "The Boy" because I don't file my papers as I ought.[5]

What you say about the "poet as interpreter"[6] pleases me on one side of my head and annoys me on the other. It is too late now: but there was a happy time of some six or seven years when I was accepted as a story-teller and rhymester, in which I think I managed to get more work out of the type of man I wished to reach, than since people found out I was putting two meanings into my work. But you must always remember that I am only getting things ready for the real poet who will appear about the first quarter of the next century. He will appropriate everything he wants — perhaps six lines and half an idea – out of all that I and scores of others have done: he will add his own powers to it and then we shall have Browning's successor – not Browning but another. My own dream is that he will be born – perhaps he is born already – in one of our colonies. The Great War between 1905 and 15 will make him find himself: and about 1925 or '30 the people will know who he is. I am roughing out the work for that man – as Ferguson did for Burns: and I think if he hasn't appeared when I die I shall leave him a private letter of suggestions.

It's a great shame because if I had been born twenty years later I might have seen and understood the drift of the new century: it began in 1889 as nearly as I reckon but we are all bondslaves to our childhood and mine was mixed up with the '70s, which belong to a dead age, and I was under the care of people who drew from the '40s and '50s. Have you ever thought how all the people who talk about "the present" are every one of them at least thirty years behind it?

Sincerely yours
Rudyard Kipling.

P.S.   Of course my real poet will not interfere with the English-bred, English trained contemplative masters. They will always persist but he will severely shake up and influence the more fluid ones.

Notes
1. Strachey's *From Grave to Gay: Essays and Studies* (1897) is a collection of articles from the *Spectator*.
2. I cannot explain this remark.
3. Synonymous with children's toys and cheap jewellery.
4. From Stevenson and Osbourne, *The Wrong Box*, ch. 15.
5. Both in *From Grave to Gay*: "A Study of Louis Stevenson", pp. 73–114; "Every Boy in His Humour", pp. 246–75.
6. Strachey's "The Poet's Function as Interpreter" takes RK's verse as illustration of the poet's power to make "the nation realise itself" (p. 12).

To Cormell Price, 4 January 1899
ALS: Library of Congress

The Elms / Rottingdean, / Nr. Brighton. / Jan 4. '99

Dear Uncle Crom

As it turned out I was going down to see the Pater for a few days[1] and so I couldn't fix a date to dine with the Torreys. I am awfully sorry about it because I should like to have come up and seen Baker.

Aunt Georgie is very busy down here and I think she is getting her health back. The place seems as if it would do her good.

I've been corresponding with Griffiths (*mi*)[2] Anderson (*ma*)[3] and Dunsterville's sister.[4] The schoolboy stories seem to unearth all sorts of far away O.U.S.C.'s. Did I tell you how (H.G.) Green[5] called on me twice and J.A. Osborne[6] (Biscuits) once? I am a regular receipt of custom. *When* the Schoolboy tales come out I'm going to dedicate the book to you and it will cover (incidentally) the whole question of modern education. Ordained headmasters and people of the Weldon[7] and Farrar[8] types will weep and howl at it: but we of the genuine congregation will approve. I get the wildest sort of letters from school-masters, denying or confirming my simple narratives.

Ever your affectionate
Ruddy.

Notes
1. RK went to Tisbury on 6 January "to discuss Kim" (CK diary).
2. Griffith minor is probably Lieutenant-Colonel David Maitland Griffith (1871–?), at USC 1881–7, though perhaps RK means his brother George (see 18 December 1896).
3. Charles Lascelles Anderson (1863–?), at USC 1874–9.
4. Mrs Armitage: see 6 December 1898.
5. Herbert Green-Spearing (1849–1929) taught at USC, 1875–81; the boys called him "Barky" (Dunsterville, *Stalky's Reminscences*, p. 23).
6. J. A. Osborne taught French at USC, 1879: Beresford calls him "the most eccentric, unusual, fantastic, irritating, unwarranted, surprising schoolmaster in history" (*Schooldays with Kipling*, p. 177).
7. The Revd James Welldon (1854–1937), Headmaster of Harrow, 1885–98, and author of, among other things, *The Religious Education of Boys* (1891).
8. Dean Frederic William Farrar: see 13 October 1899.

To Robert Barr, 10 January 189[9]

ALS: University of Sussex

The Elms, / Rottingdean, / Nr. Brighton. / Jan. 10. '98

No. I've had about enough of grey skies and boiled potatoes.[1] I'm going over to where the sun shines and oysters is cheap. I shall have 'em on toast – likewise stewed, *and* roasted and fried; and I shall have grape-fruit for breakfast and nineteen different sorts of bread. Also biscuits. But we're only going over for a month or six weeks – just to cheer up Teddy[2] who is governor of New York and don't you forget it and I'm going to Washington and – what d'you mean about my

Goddamning America? See next McClure's for a poem about expansion which will make you rejoice.[3] We shall be back just in time for the sweet April weather of England; and anyhow I despise a man who uses the Rottingdean sea car[4] and then don't come in. I must have been away that day because the girl (as I know) doesn't know enough to lie decently to visitors.

I'm afraid I can't be up in town before we go but if you drift down in that third class carriage you're so proud of we will feed you and discourse.

Ever thine
R.K.

P.S. Think of oysters and Groton bread!

Notes
1. RK was preparing to leave with his family for New York.
2. Roosevelt, elected governor in November 1898.
3. "The White Man's Burden", *McClure's*, February 1899.
4. An electrically driven passenger car running between Brighton and Rottingdean on rails laid below the surface of the ocean. The car rose on steel legs 24 feet above the rails and ran on sixteen wheels. The rails were laid on concrete blocks placed on the sea bed. It opened in 1896, and soon proved to be impractical.

To Robert Barr, 19 January 1899
ALS: University of Sussex

The Elms, / Rottingdean, / Nr. Brighton. / Jan 19. 99

Dear Barr –

I didn't know there were any posthumous works of Robert Browning on the market[1] and I take your offer most kind. I presume from the title it is something in the nature of "Fifine at the Fair," and will come in handy when I am at the basin. *The Majestic* of the 25th is our boat.[2] I wish you were coming over too with us.

Sincerely ever.
R.K.

Notes
1. There were not. Browning left almost nothing for posthumous publication, and the Cambridge edition of 1895 collected most of the fugitive items. Barr must have referred to some current reprint.
2. They sailed from Liverpool and arrived, after a stormy crossing, in New York on 2 February.

To Francis Sherman,[1] 19 January 1899
ALS: University of New Brunswick

The Elms, / Rottingdean, / Nr. Brighton. / Jan. 19. 99

Dear Mr. Sherman –

Excellent! They are just what I wanted. You must have guessed that. They are singing of their own country and the things they know. This is vastly well and I chuckled to myself as I read, with delight. Now I am going to turn the whole thing over to a London Editor[2] who is not likely to know much about pines and the coming of spring in Canada; and I'm going to see what sort of deduction he'll draw from it.

I like your In the North and the Road Song in May very much indeed – especially the last for

> "toward the sound of waking mills
> swing the brown rafts in one by one."

That makes me sniff the smell of new sawn timber and crushed hemlock tops again. After that, as you know, comes the thin whine of band-saws on a hot July afternoon mixing in with the noise of the crickets – what's the name – grasshoppers? The noise like the heat of the day expressed in sound. Tell me, now, who is Theodore Roberts[3] because his "Hearth in the North" is mighty good.

I don't care so much for Bliss Carman's[4] Andrew Straton but I *do* like his "grey ships of St. John." Please give him my salutations when you run across him. It must be a gorgeous thing to be one of the band of new singers whose eyes are well opened on the country of their birth and love – new men in a land that is both old and new.

I'm only coming over for a few weeks and I fear that (whisper it low) our Lady of the Snows does not offer much shooting or fishing at present. At least, I don't call still-hunting for moose in the snow any sort of lawful sport for a man who spends all his time under a roof and I *won't* fish through ice for any consideration. Maybe, I'll see you if you're down in New York but if I don't please take my best thanks and give my heartiest greetings to all of you. You don't know how much of the making of Canada lies in your hands – and Canada doesn't either.

> Yours ever sincerely
> Rudyard Kipling

P.S.   Don't forget to send me more clippings. Send some real *vile* ones – the good old Lydia Languish sort that lonely women write in lonely places and send to small city papers. There is a heap of instruction in them; and sometimes one or two good lines.

RK

Notes
1. Sherman (1871–1926), poet and banker, born in Fredericton, New Brunswick; he had published three short collections of verse by this time: *Matins* (1896), *In Memorabilia Mortis* (1896), and *A Prelude* (1897).
2. Strachey: see 21 January 1899.
3. Roberts (1877–1953), journalist, editor, novelist, historian, and poet; born in Fredericton, New Brunswick. He published *Northland Lyrics* (1899).
4. Carman (1861–1929), poet and editor, like Sherman and Roberts born in Fredericton, New Brunswick. He spent most of his professional life on magazines in New York and Boston, and later lived in Connecticut. Of the poems RK mentions, "Andrew Straton" comes from *By the Aurelian Wall and Other Elegies* (1898); "The Ships of St. John" from *Ballads of Lost Haven* (1897). RK had met Carman in Washington, DC, in March 1895 (CK diary).

To John St Loe Strachey, 21 January 1899
ALS: House of Lords Record Office

The Elms, / Rottingdean, / Nr. Brighton. / Jan. 21 99

Dear Mr Strachey
(Of course not. You're the Senior or I'd drop the Mister myself.)

> I've a friend over the sea
> I don't know him and he don't know me

but he sends me clippings of Canadian verse in papers; and being a poet (His name is Sherman) he knows what I want when I bother him. I am trying to get samples of the same kind from Australia, N.Z. and that disappointingly slow-to-sing country, the Cape. This batch that I enclose seems to me very encouraging, and I send it on to you in the hope that it may perhaps make a "middle" called, say: – "The Genesis of National Poetry" which is a fine stodgy title.[1] Now I loathe too much insistence on Nationality which is apt to degenerate into rank provincialism but I do want you to see how these chaps are working each with his eye on the object – describing his own pines, the lights and shades of his own sun and the coming of his own spring. Out of these things, I think, a good and sane national poetry is born. Of course the men are only fore runners – *ferashes*[2] sweeping the floor and laying the carpets till the great poets come in: but their verse says what the Canadian born thinks and feels as he goes about his own land. Their similes are his similes and some day, may be, he will back his actions by quotation from verses like these.

There was once a beast – a Bloomsbury, bus-riding, Beast – in the *Athenæum* who went out of his way, and did much mischief thereby, to say that songs in the English tongue introducing an "alien flora and fauna left him cold."[3] I did my best to warm him up with "The Flowers" in *The Seven Seas*; but the harm was done and the young Colonial singers in all sorts of places were naturally hurt and discouraged.

One doesn't want to make the boys self-conscious more than they are: but don't you think that you could set forth the inner significance of the work they are doing?

I don't know who Theodore Roberts is but his "Hearth in the North" goes straight to the inside of people who know the snows and the return of the trappers; and Sherman's two lines

> – toward the sound of waking mills
> Swing the brown rafts in one by one –

gives the whole Canadian spring. One can smell the raw, new-sawed lumber and feel the squashy ground underfoot. Looking through the senses, one can see here and there how the men are working with a new background – and I am intensely curious to know what the upshot will be. It will differ from American poetry because there isn't the gross materialism in Canada that stains and distorts a good deal of what the Americans think noble and refined. It will be the poetry of free white men who have never had to face the actual bread-and-butter problem – men who have never lain down in the shadow of external fear – (think what that means) a race with nothing but open-space and ice between them and the North Pole! I don't know whether you can see the face of the unborn child in these clippings but I do think they'll interest you.

We're off on Wednesday to New York whence I hope to get up north a bit and round up some of these singers. They are a splendid lot and they'd answer a word of sympathy from head quarters (even if you named no names) as a well bred horse would answer the hint of a spur. I don't want to be a nuisance but you said I might send in anything unusual.

Sincerely
Rudyard Kipling.

Notes
1. Strachey does not appear to have taken up the suggestion.
2. Menial servants.
3. RK quotes the passage in question at the head of "The Flowers".

To James M. Conland, 6 February 1899
ALS: Library of Congress

[New York] Feb. 6 Monday. '99

Dear Conland,
  Hurrah!
The first because your topsails are lifting over the sky-line and the second because all our kiddies are down with bronchitis caught *en route* to America. Come down on Wednesday if you can – come and dine but come early – as early as you know how and we'll have a day together. I can't get away just yet but *you come*.[1]

Sincerely
Rudyard K.

P.S.   Come along on Wednesday.

Note
1. Conland arrived on 8 February (CK diary).

To James M. Conland, 16 February 1899
ALS: Library of Congress

[New York] Feb 16. 99

Dear Conland –
  I've just written down a rather colourless acknowledgement of that little document you forwarded me:[1] which I beg you to hand over to the good folk concerned. The clumsiness of the language must be forgiven. I haven't much experience in expressing thanks properly: and I don't use a lot of fine words. But, you may be sure, I feel it just the same. The weather here is something beyond description. Rain on slush with a freeze running through it. The kiddies are getting better and so's Carrie but it's slow work. Keep me posted on any happenings of interest up in Brattleboro, and I'll let you know when I am on the move for Boston. In haste, between engagements.

Yours ever
Rud.

You didn't tell me who started the idea of the letter so I don't know who to address the reply to: but I can depend on you to put it into the right hands. Thank 'em all personally from me.

Note
1. A letter signed by a number of prominent citizens of Brattleboro, welcoming RK back to the United States, offering him a banquet in Brattleboro, and hoping for his return to Naulakha (Charles S. Forbes, "Rudyard Kipling in Vermont", *The Vermonter*, April 1899, p. 150).

To Lionel Charles Dunsterville, 17 February 1899
ALS: University of Sussex

Hotel Grenoble. / New York. / Feb. 17. '99

Dear Old Man –

Hurrah! I'm raising 'em one by one like a scientific trout-fisher – O.U.S.C.'s from all parts of the world. Even Haslam wrote one from the wilds of New Zealand, on the strength of "In Ambush."[1] I've been hoping to fetch you sooner or later. Price told me about your marriage (you know we always keep touch with Bates.[2] He is running a cram-shop at 8 Powys Square and I don't think he's very successful. He's as big a dear as ever and he has married his house keeper, the pretty girl we used to know – and he has a son![3] There's news for you). Well, I knew that you wouldn't be easily accessible then and a little later I got news of you by a side-wind from a chap who was coming over to Brindisi. Since then you've disappeared: but I *did* think a man of your fertility of resource could find some better place than Mian Mir.[4] Funny how we all drift round and round Mian Mir!

Kay Robinson is in London doing turnovers and notes for the Globe. I see him from time to time. What are your chances of coming home for a while? You seem to have done yourself well in the matter of special leave. That Russian interpretership is a good idea and one that will be mighty useful in the days to come. I want you to get a staff-billet where your peculiar talents will have a full field. I think you're a bit too good to be stuck always with a native regiment – even with so crack a lot as the 20th P[unjab]. N[ative]. I[nfantry]. I wonder how you'd have got on with the Gippy army. Old (Satan) Young[5] is a full blown *Bimbashi* which, I take it, is some sort of festive Lieutenant Colonel. Now what news can I give you? When I was at Torquay at '97 (we took a house there for a year) old H.C. Stevens[6] turned up and he and his wife had a meal with us. He's just the same as ever – a little more grey but otherwise unaltered. Then we took a house at Rottingdean (four miles from

Brighton) and one day old H. Green walked in – Barker Green.[7] He'd changed his name to "Spearing" on account of some money left him but he was just the same as ever, asked me to do a heap of things for him which I took dam' good care not to do. He came two or three times: with the proofs of a book on yachting excursions in Norway. Well, after that, who should turn up but Biscuits – J. A. Osborn.[8] He'd been running a private school at the mouth of the Thames and had a row with his builder. He smacked his lips and jawed about geology just in the old sweet way. He told me that Crofts is now a photographer; Bode[9] is running a school; and so, I think, is or was little Evans.[10] Willes[11] is also running a school – if he isn't a parson in the midlands. I fancy it's a case of "once a school master – always a school-master." I do not despair of some day seeing Pugh,[12] who is also running a school. But I am annoyed with one thing. I saw the balance-sheet of the old Coll the other day. It's in an awful condition – only 70 or 80 boys and the bulk of 'em day-boarders. A fat man of God called Harris is in charge[13] and – *they – let – the – Coll buildings in the holidays for a holiday resort!* That just enables 'em to pay their way.

Well, that isn't all! The Chronicle still goes on and a recent issue discussing the Stalky tales, claimed *me* as an O.U.S.C. and wondered why I didn't write for "my own paper!" Cheek! don't you ever own that you belong to the Coll after Price left it. I have tried to make my position clear – and I think I have. We are the genuine original O.U.S.C.'s but, remember, we don't know anything of the Coll since Price left. I was present at the last prize-giving in '94 and I made a speech to the Coll.[14] You ought to have heard the boys cheer. It was in the old gym and I nearly broke down. It cut Price to the heart to be forced to go. He hadn't any money saved and of course he had no pension. Now, the school has gone to pot – and I wish to God it was finally wound up.

I rejoice to think that you like the "Stalky" yarns. All sorts of people write to the papers to explain that such boys as I described, could never exist and that the masters are equally impossible. I chortle to myself and do not reply. There will be six or seven tales altogether and then they will all come out in a book, a copy of which I will send thee, O Dunster. I don't know whether you read "Slaves of the Lamp" – but I fancy you didn't. Edwards (S.M.)[15] and Remington[16] and Morris IV[17] come into it. But you'll see 'em all in book form.

Curiously enough, the tales are immensely appreciated in America, so I suppose that the average percentage of undiluted devil in the young of the human animal is a constant quantity throughout the world. We came over here for a few weeks – a fortnight ago – with our three kiddies, two girls and a boy – so as to enable the wife (I married an American) to see her mother. We all have got colds and coughs and the weather is damnable. Our permanent address is *The Elms, Rottingdean,*

Brighton. It's a great nuisance to be a notorious and celebrated literary man. It makes me laugh a good deal but the bother and fuss of talking to a hundred people a day isn't good enough. I hear that old Beresford has joined the Fabian Society (He was always a bit of a socialist) and he also got a sunstroke in India. This Bates told me but I haven't seen G.C.B. since Westward Ho!

I don't know if you remember Phillips IV.[18] He lives at Rottingdean. Gilbert (ma.)[19] was also down at Brighton. He was a widower and he just married again! This makes me feel hideously old.

I got a note in from White[20] (he had the study below us and we poured fried bacon fat on his head). He is staying at the Holland house; and as soon as I can turn round I shall go and have a coll. *bukh*[21] with him. Also, by this mail, I got a note from Henderson[22] (can't remember which Henderson –) on his beam-end somewhere out west. As he began the letter "dear Sir" I incontinently dropped him.

I always meditate a big O.U.S.C. dinner in London, some day: but we are such a scattered and evasive lot that it's more difficult in our case than with any other school. I don't despair of managing it some day. The last time I saw Bates was at the funeral of my uncle (Burne-Jones) whose life-long friend he was. Old Bates was fearfully broken up. I wish to goodness we could do something for him. Anyhow, the Stalky book will be dedicated to him, and now I think I'll shut up. Write me a letter from time to time and if you're good I'll send you a coll cap. I got one in '94 from Scholefield:[23] and by dint of much patching and relining, it holds good to this day.

"The Weazel" is the only one of the original staff if you except Thomas[24] with the toes ("take fifty lines for not 'olding up your 'and before speakin', Mister Savile") left at Westward Ho! I'd dearly like to go down and see the place again but I'm afraid that the beast Harris would use it as an advertisement!

All this time I haven't congratuated you on your marriage. I can only hope you'll be half as happy in that relation, as I've been, old man. It is a good and an honourable position and it makes a man's character – let alone the deep and abiding joy one gets out of the kiddies. I've a small six year old who is all the world to me. But this is an unmitigated imposition on your time. Remember me to all O.U.S.C.'s of our rank and standing, giving my best salaams to your wife and believe me

Thine as ever
Gigger.

Notes

1. The second of the *Stalky* stories to be published: *McClure's Magazine*, August 1898.
2. "Bates", or "The Prussian Bates", was the name given to Cormell Price, for no known reason.

3. Price married Sarah Hopper, the daughter of his housekeeper at Westward Ho!; the daughter was called by the boys "La Pricienne" (Beresford, *Schooldays with Kipling*, p. 102). Their first child was C. E. W. Price (1898–1966).
4. Dunsterville was now adjutant in the 20th Punjabis, stationed at Mian Mir, the cantonments at Lahore.
5. Norman Edward Young: see 24 April 1883.
6. RK's mathematics master: see 18 December 1896.
7. See 4 January 1899.
8. French master at USC: see 4 January 1899.
9. Clement William Louis Bode (1854–?), joined the staff of USC in 1879.
10. H. A. Evans: see 9 May 1896.
11. George Willes: see 17 November 1882.
12. Matthew Pugh: see 18–27 February 1886.
13. The Revd Percy Harris: see 9 May 1896.
14. See 17 July 1894.
15. See 31 January–1 February 1882.
16. Joseph Cameron Rimington: see 9 May 1896.
17. Lieutenant-Colonel Charles James Ussher Morris (1865–?), at USC, 1876–83; he has not been identified with any of the characters in the *Stalky* stories.
18. Richard Mereweather Phillips (1870–1920), at USC 1882–8.
19. Lieutenant-Colonel Clarence Edward Lloyd Gilbert, Indian Medical Service (1862–?), at USC 1878–80.
20. Michael Alfred Edwin White (1864–1935), at USC, 1879–82 in Pugh's house. He published two books on Indian subjects, 1901 and 1912.
21. Chatter.
22. Perhaps William Douglas Henderson (1866–?), at USC 1879–82.
23. George Schofield (1839–1907), the school sergeant and gym instructor at USC, identified with Foxy in *Stalky*; his actual nickname was The Weasel.
24. Perhaps Stephen Thomas (d. 1903), drawing master at USC 1880–1900; but there were three other Thomases on the staff at various times.

To Charles Eliot Norton, 19 February 1899

ALS: Harvard University

[New York] Feb. 19. 99.

Dear Mr Norton –

Bless you for your kindly line. Yes, I do feel rather "Oh why left I my home" but the kiddies are slowly getting better and I suppose, some day, we may return to our so far away normal life.[1]

As to the Boston visit, I hope to be able to leave on a morning train on the 3rd March (Friday) and stay till Monday – if this does not conflict with your plans, and if there are no further developments among the kiddies. C. fears that she won't be able to come – at least not at present.

We are both anxious to see you all again. Sallie's visits were a blessing to us.

Yours ever affectionately
Ruddy.

Note
1. On the evening of the next day RK fell ill and barely survived the attack of pneumonia that developed. His daughter Josephine meanwhile grew worse and died on 6 March, just as RK was emerging from the crisis of his illness.

To [The Press],[1] 2 April 1899
ALS: Princeton University

Hotel Grenoble. New York. / Easter Day. 1899.

Dear Sir

Will you allow me through our columns to attempt some acknowledgement of the wonderful sympathy, affection and kindness shown towards me during my recent illness, as well as of the unfailing courtesy that controlled its expression? I am not strong enough to answer letters in detail, so I must take this means of thanking, as humbly as sincerely, the countless people of good will throughout the world who have put me under a debt I can never hope to repay.

Faithfully yours,
Rudyard Kipling

Note
1. This letter was widely printed in the United States and elsewhere. RK's illness had been a front-page story for a month.

To Frank N. Doubleday, 24 April 1899
ALS: Princeton University

Lakewood[1] / April: 24: 99: / Monday 8:30. p.m.

Beloved Effendi:[2]

It is about three days and a half since you left: and we feel every hour of it. But we are coming along not so bad after all. Be pleased to hear the record of the day's doings. After an indecently large breakfast Carrie, the Pater[3] and me at 10 a.m. went out for a drive of at least an hour and a quarter. At the end of it C. saw the kids on the horizon, picked them up for a drive back to Hoveys and the Pater and I walked (WALKED) from the end of Main Street to the hotel. True, I hung on the Pater's arm a little but I didn't cave in.

Miss Ryerson[4] sends her love.

Elsie asked for you today and when told you had "gone" said "will he come back when daddie calls out to him." You see she has perfectly grasped the necessity of her Doubleday.[5]

I think that is about all our small newses. C. has not coughed quite so much today but it comes on worst at night. The Pater is fat and happy. My Mother writes (she has just got his letter about me) saying that you are indeed a "heart of gold." This is stale news to us but she feels it acutely. There is a polo game every Sunday on the Guild polo ground. We'll go next Sunday and watch 'em. The Lakewood golf tournament begins on Thursday I think and . . . . the Ryerson[6] wants me to come to her. Our best love to Mrs. Doubleday and Dorothy[7] upon whom be all blessings.

Affectionately yours
Rud

P.S.   What *is* the statement that there is a new editor – one Finley[8] – for McClure's mag?

Notes

1. The resort where the Kiplings had been in 1896 (see 2 May 1896). RK was taken there for his recuperation by private railcar on 17 April.
2. "Effendi" is RK's play on FND, Doubleday's initials; Doubleday adopted it (it is a Turkish title of respect) and used it for the rest of his life. Doubleday had devoted himself to RK throughout his illness, had brought him to Lakewood, and continued to give indispensable help, even to accompanying RK on his return voyage to England.
3. RK's father had come over to help during RK's illness.
4. See 9 June 1899.
5. The two preceding paragraphs appear to be in CK's hand.
6. One of RK's nurses: see 9 June 1899.
7. Doubleday's daughter.
8. John Finley (1863–1940) had just taken over as editor not of *McClure's* but of *Harper's Weekly*, also a McClure property.

To Dr. William Peterson,[1] [1 May 1899]
Text: Daily Chronicle, 29 May 1899

I do not think I need say how honored I feel by the proposal of the
McGill University to confer on me the honorary degree of Doctor Laws,[2]
or how much more than pleased I should be to accept this distinction.
It is a matter of peculiar pride to me that the suggestion has come from
Canada, the Elder Sister of the new nations within the Empire. Unluckily
I see no reason to hope that my state of health will permit me to take so
long a journey as to Montreal in June. I am very sorry for this, because
nothing would have given me greater pleasure than a visit to Montreal;
which, indeed, I had contemplated before I fell ill. Will you convey my
sincerest thanks to the Convocation, and believe me, yours.

                                                     Rudyard Kipling.

Notes
1. Peterson (1856–1921) was Principal of McGill University, 1895–1919; he was knighted
   in 1915. This letter is said in an article in the *McGill News,* Spring 1936, p. 20, to have
   been written from Lakewood, New Jersey, on 1 May 1899.
2. RK was awarded the degree of LL D by McGill on 16 June 1899 *in absentia.* This was
   the first of his academic honours.

To Margaret Ryerson,[1] 9 June 1899
ALS: Princeton University

                                                     Cold Spring[2]/June 9. 99

Dear Miss Ryerson –
Many thanks for your letter. We are now at Cold Spring harbour in
the middle of what is the longest heat-wave that I remember but so far
the kiddies are quite well. John's war-song is "Swing Slow" which he
sings half the day – waving his arms and stamping his feet to the time.
I am very fairly well but now and again I get a small stitch in my side
when the temperature changes too much. I haven't been writing or
doing *any sort of work* at all and even now it seems a little strange to
have my pen in my hand.
Curiously enough, I met Miss Lee, your Mrs Lee's daughter at
Morristown[3] and she told me that she had heard of me from you.
Herewith I enclose the letter (official) which I only hope may be of
some use to you in your future.
I hope you are keeping well and resting yourself and that all goes
well with your family.

                                                     Very sincerely yours
                                                     Rudyard Kipling.

We hope to sail S S Teutonic, Fourteenth June.

P.S.   Do not forget to remember me to the small nephews and to express my regards to the toad – isn't it – that they christened for me.

Notes
1. One of RK's nurses. She attended him for ten weeks, until 10 May (CK diary).
2. Doubleday's house on Long Island, where RK and family went on 5 June (CK diary).
3. Where the Catlin family lived: RK was there between his stays at Lakewood and Cold Spring Harbor, 9 May–5 June (CK diary).

To James M. Conland, 13 June 1899
ALS: Library of Congress

Cold Spring / June 13. 99

Dear Conland,

I don't think much of the machinery of the U.S. Govt: and the arrangements for getting boys into the navy seem to be planned by a lunatic. I enclose a note from Hay which shows what sort of a dead-wall this nomination business is. Please return it when you've done with it. So far as I can see the only way is to go sway your member of Congress: but if you can think of any other way in which we might manage it, and in which I could be of any service, write at length and command me. Hay has evidently been to McKinley about it.

The weather is hotting up a little and promises to be warm tomorrow. However we have everything in shape for the voyage and the kids are very well. Yesterday aft. I went out in a racing cat, steered by a Cape-Codder, and we beat to smithereens another cat – captained by a Jersey man – a very pretty little bit of judgement and skill. Our skipper told me yarns of "Flat-foot" Baker of whom you may have heard. It was like a chapter out of Captains Courageous. Which reminds me I hope you have got the Sea to Sea books.[1] I sent 'em yesterday. You'll get a copy of the schoolboy yarns when they come out this fall.

And now goodbye! It was a joy and a delight to see you once more and I'm not likely to forget all you've done for me. Take care of yourself: keep a letter going once a month if you can, and fix your flint to come over and see us.

> Yours ever affectionately
> Rud.

Note
1. *From Sea to Sea* (1899), a collection of Indian sketches and travel letters, revised by RK before and after his illness, and now just published.

To Andrew Carnegie,[1] 25 June 1899
ALS: Library of Congress

The Elms / Rottingdean / June 25. 99.

Dear Mr Carnegie
     We are just back from the other side: and our thoughts turn swiftly to your princely offer of a farmhouse near Skibo in the fall.[2] Would it suit your dates and your general convenience if we came up between the *7th* and the *10th* of *August: for a month*? I know – none better – that you are a man of many affairs and I shouldn't be bothering you: but we felt that you really wanted us to come. And I want to convert you to Imperialism.
     With kindest regards in which Mrs Kipling joins, to yourself and Mrs Carnegie

Very sincerely
Rudyard Kipling

Notes
1. Carnegie (1835–1919), Scottish-born American steel millionaire and philanthropist. Carnegie had been introduced to RK in New York while RK was recuperating from his illness (F. N. Doubleday, *A Few Indiscreet Recollections*, privately printed, n.p., 1928, p. 8).
2. The Manse, Creich, near Carnegie's Skibo Castle estate in Sutherlandshire, on Dornoch Firth. See 8 August 1899.

To Sir Walter Besant, [1 July? 1899]
ALS: Dalhousie University

The Elms, / Rottingdean, / Nr. Brighton / Saturday

Dear Sir Walter –
     Herewith my letter.[1] Could I have proofs as soon as may be? It's an

embarrassing thing for Putty[2] and I feel I owe him a million apologies for not dying at the psychological moment when his "Edition" would have sold beautifully and I couldn't have protested.

The devil of it is, I believe he is going to try on this patent edition manaufacturing process on other authors. I only hope he won't try any fresh tricks on them. Isn't the idea of a secretary of the American Copyright League[3] smuggling non-copyright poems between the covers of a copyright book delicious. That and the fraudulent trademark, and the inclusion of the Day's Work are the main points in the argument.

I send you with this the documents in the case – letters that passed between Putnam and fellow publishers which will prove at least that we did *not* attack Putnam unawares. Also, a copy of G.H.P.'s priceless interview to the *Daily Chronicle* which I have not made the most of.[4] You see he has just married a second wife,[5] and I believe he is a sensitive little devil to boot and I have let him down as easy as I could.

Personally I don't think much is gained by threshing the case out in the papers. I want to get the Putnams under oath in the witness box and I want to get the N.Y. publishers to testify a little. They are not pleased with Putnam for having raised this row. One result of his action has been that I have flooded the markets with an edition of 300,000 vols (20,000 sets of my own books @ 15 vol a set) and the result is that the poor pirates can't compete with 'em.[6] But all authors can't do this and I hope by my action to be able to save his discrediting some chap who doesn't sell as well as I do but who is just as anxious to turn out good work.

Please return all the documents relating to the case.

As ever

Rudyard Kipling

Notes

1. A long letter published in *The Author*, 1 July 1899, pp. 30–4, complaining of the American publisher G. H. Putnam and his "Brushwood Edition" of RK's works. RK is described as "hard at work" on his letter to *The Author* on 29 June 1899 (CK to August Gurlitz, 29 June 1899: ALS, Sussex): the nearest Saturday to that date is 1 July, which I conjecture to be the date of this letter to Besant. Presumably the number of *The Author* containing RK's letter of protest, though dated 1 July, was in fact published somewhat later. At the beginning of 1899 Putnam brought out a so-called "Brushwood Edition" of RK's works; it was made up from unbound sheets of the American editions already widely circulated throughout the United States by RK's various authorized publishers. Putnam paid them the market price and so provided a royalty to RK, though he might easily have bought much of the material from unauthorized sources. RK brought suit against Putnam in federal circuit court in April to enjoin publication of the "Brushwood Edition" and to claim $25,000 in damages. He argued that Putnam had wrongly advertised the work as a new and authorized edition, that he had used RK's signature and elephant-head "trademark" without authorization, that he had injured the prospects of the authorized Outward Bound Edition, and that material not by RK was included. All of this is set forth in *The Author*. The case was decided against RK in

May 1901, the judge calling RK's arguments "fantastic" and directing the jury to find for the defendant (Kipling *vs* Putnam, US Circuit 'Court of Appeals, *Transcript of Record,* [New York, 1902] 200, 212). RK thereupon appealed, but in January 1903 the Court of Appeals affirmed the original judgment. It is very hard to see what RK could have expected in bringing an action against Putnam (who was genuinely surprised and indignant at having his dealings challenged). The "Brushwood Edition" was made with the co-operation of RK's publishers; it was not a piracy, and its promotion was well within the limits then accepted. *Publisher's Weekly,* 29 April 1899, drily remarked that it was "one of the most curious suits in the history of copyright". The Putnam suit was one of several that RK brought at this time in the United States in a desperate effort to stop the unauthorized publication of his work.

2. George Haven Putnam (1844–1930), son of the founder of G. P. Putnam and head of the firm; one of the most distinguished of American publishers in his time. He is the subject of RK's scurrilous "The Life of George Haven Putnam", 1900 (unpublished: see Harbord, *Readers' Guide,* v, 2563).

3. Putnam, who inherited the cause of international copyright from his father, organized the American Publishers' Copyright League in 1886 and served as its secretary.

4. RK's letter to *The Author* quotes Putnam in an interview with the Daily Chronicle, 13 May 1899, as having said of the "Brushwood Edition" that it was not an edition: "merely you had an harmonious binding" of books from different sources.

5. His first wife died in 1895; Putnam married Emily James Smith, first Dean of Barnard College, on 27 April 1899, three days after RK had brought suit against him.

6. This was the "Swastika Edition", Doubleday and McClure, 1899. The justices in RK's appeal of the Putnam decision noted that in bringing out the Swastika Edition RK himself was guilty of just such unfair competition against the Outward Bound Edition as he had alleged against Putnam (*Federal Reporter,* vol. 120, 637).

To Edmonia Hill,[1] 30 July 1899

ALS: Library of Congress

The Elms, / Rottingdean, / Nr. Brighton. / July. 30. '99 –

Dear Mrs Hill:

Thank you very much indeed for your kind note of the 13th. Yes, I got the picture of Elysium[2] but that was at a time when I was not allowed to do any writing. I opened it myself and recognized the handwriting on the outside, at once. Personally, I would have given a good deal to have let the From Sea to Sea alone:[3] but it was too well known and one or two firms had sent a man out to India to dig up as much of my old work as he could. So I put it out as you might say in self defence – it was better that it should be revised by me than by any one else. I tried to read the proofs of it when I was ill – or rather when I was getting better and that didn't do me any special good. I can remember the writing of almost every line of it. There isn't much news of Anglo-India in my life. Now and again I hear of an old name – but not often. It has all changed. The Curzons wanted me to come out and stay with them – but Viceroys are not exactly my line.[4] This fool-sickness of mine which had the bad taste to leave me and take my little Maiden (I wish you could have seen her) makes it, I believe, impossible for me to stay in England through the winters: so I suppose I may as well try India as any other place. Be thankful that you have never had a child to lose. I thought I knew something of what grief meant till that came to me.

My "fame" never was of any use to me anyway, and now it seems more of an irony than ever.

Will you let me thank you again for your kindness in writing to me [and perhaps when you have leisure and inclination you will send me a line, only don't associate me with that most notorious person Mister Rudyard Kipling.][5] I don't think it likely that I shall ever come back to America. My little Maid loved it dearly (she was almost entirely American in her ways of thinking and looking at things) and it was in New York that we lost her. Everybody was more than kind to us and to her but I don't think I could face the look of the city again without her.

Very sincerely yours
Rudyard Kipling.

P.S.   I am afraid this is rather badly written but the fact is that I don't do much writing nowadays.

Notes
1. Apparently the first communication between RK and Mrs Hill since late 1890 (see [early December 1890]).
2. In Simla.
3. As RK says in the "Preface" to *From Sea to Sea*, he was "forced" to publish by the operations of pirates. Since some of the material in the book had been circulating in pirated editions as early as 1891 the pressure cannot have been very urgent.
4. Curzon was appointed Viceroy and created Baron Curzon in 1898.
5. The sentence from "and perhaps" to the end has been deleted by RK but is recoverable. Mrs Hill has written on a copy of the letter that the words probably "struck him as a bit mushy" (Sussex).

To Brander Matthews, 4 August 1899
Text: Letter dictated, signed by RK, Columbia University

The Elms, / Rottingdean, / Nr. Brighton. / Aug 4: 99.

Dictated.
Dear Brander,
    Many thanks for your letter.
    I wish I could get the American papers just for once, as a change, to

print my case against Putnam in full,[1] but they are content with cable summaries of it. I notice the Putnams' reply is given very much in extenso; however I fancy I have spoked the polite gentlemen's wheel this side the water, and later on perhaps I may be able to get at them in New York. It's a matter that affects American authors just as much as English ones and that's a thing I can't get them to see.

Many thanks for your kind wishes: I am coming on pretty fairly.

Sincerely yours
Rudyard

Note

1. See [1 July? 1899].

To James M. Conland, 8 August 1899

ALS: Library of Congress

The Elms, / Rottingdean, / Nr. Brighton. / Aug. 8. 99

Dear Conland –

I was beginning to think that you'd given up writing for good and was on the edge of sending you a cable of an insulting nature to stir you up when your letter came.

[   ][1] I am going to write to Teddy Roosevelt about it. He isn't a dyed-in-the-wool politician *yet*, and he may see some way of getting round the impasse.[2]

Things here are going on with a quietness that must be seen to be believed. I've been sitting to my cousin Sir Phillip Burne-Jones for my portrait.[3] It's just me at my writing-table, and as like me as one pea to another, down to the flap of my pocket and the pipe at my side. All the same sitting is mighty hard work. After ten or fifteen minutes the most natural attitude in the world, if persisted in, becomes a sort of agonizing cramp and you want to scratch yourself. However I have managed to train myself to sit without a quiver for three quarters of an hour at a stretch! I'd like to send you a photo of the new picture when it's done. He is going to do me a picture of Carrie too[4] – and that's something I've wanted for ever so long.

Our scheme of going up to Carnegie's place in Scotland has come off after all. We go this afternoon to London – then all night in the cars which, in England, is an enormous journey – and arrive at Creich Manse, Bonar Bridge, at eleven tomorrow. The Manse is the Presbyterian minister's house about six miles from Carnegie's castle and half a mile from a trout-loch. I've got my rods and tackle into working order, as well as a choice collection of rainbow-coloured salmon flies (for there is a salmon river somewhere on the ground) and I only hope the fish will take half as much trouble for me as I've taken for them. Since we got back we've had a regular deluge of fine weather – six weeks of cloudless skies and what they call "heat" in England. It was as much as 76° in my bedroom! The kids go down paddling to the beach every day when John generally finds some excuse or other for falling into the deepest pool. They are exceedingly fit and brown, and very full of joy at the thought of Scotland. By the way Edith Catlin[5] is coming up to stay with us for awhile. She is a good fisherwoman. Our garden is now just at its loveliest: and I am rather sorry to quit it. I do hope that you'll go and see Julia DeFried while she is at Naulakha. I'd like to think of you tramping round the verandahs again, in the old place.

I've been lying low and doing nothing except going to sleep in the afternoon and getting to bed by ten p.m. All the same my head is full of notions for yarns, and when I get back from Scotland I think I shall have a shot at doing a little work again. Carrie keeps well and fit but as usual she seems to delight in doing the work of ten women. However, she has now a secretary[6] and so spends only a few minutes dictating replies to letters where she formerly spent hours at the desk. This gives her time to rest in the afternoon and now and again I can prevail upon her to get her breakfast in bed.

The Pater, too, will come up to Scotland for a bit. He reports that the heat (and English heat is much more exhausting than the same article anywhere else) has knocked him out of tune. My own notion is that he has been working too hard and needs a bit of a let up. I don't know whether he will ever make a salmon fisher.

Yesterday the Tiffanys[7] called on us. I was in bed worse luck but I heard their voices in the garden. They had been having a specially gay time in England and he has got over the malaria or whatever it was that had attacked him in the spring. With those exceptions, we have not seen anybody from the other side – and not many callers from here either.

Now I must go and take this to the post. The house has that peculiarly unhappy look that a swept and garnished place takes on on the eve of a journey. Our baggage is standing about the halls and the cart will come for it in a few hours. We both send our best love to you.

Ever yours affectionately
Rud

I'm glad to hear that Harry has gone on his cruise. Evidently black water is that young man's natural destiny.

Notes
1. Two lines erased.
2. Presumably about "getting boys into the navy": see 13 June 1899.
3. The portrait was begun on 8 July and is now in the National Portrait Gallery. It shows RK in left profile, seated at his work table, pen in hand and pipe at left elbow.
4. Painted in this summer and now at Bateman's.
5. One of the daughters of Mrs Catlin of Morristown: she married the architect Stowe Phelps in 1907. Her MS personal recollections of RK and CK are now at the University of Sussex.
6. Sara Anderson (1854–1942), the first of many secretaries that the Kiplings were to have; she arrived on 12 July (CK diary). As Carrington says, her story would be interesting, for she had been secretary to John Ruskin, George Meredith, and George Moore before coming to the Kiplings: but she never told it (Carrington, *Kipling*, p. 293). According to Sydney Cockerell, RK called her "a woman apart; all the others were just secretaries. She knew by the way I pronounced the word 'damn', just how to answer any letter. And she was utterly discreet" (Wilfrid Blunt, *Cockerell*, 1965, p. 120).
7. Louis Comfort Tiffany (1848–1933) and his wife; the son of the New York jeweller, he was an artist, most famous for his work as a glass-maker.

To Henry James, 19 September 1899

ALS: Harvard University

The Elms, / Rottingdean, / Nr. Brighton. / Sep. 19. 99.

Bless you for that lovely letter! Yes. Things are better with us all round and that month we've just spent in the Highlands all among Carnegie's pines and heather in the seclusion of a stone built manse with horse-hair furniture, did us a world of good.[1] How I wish you could have been there! Phil came up, to paint a portrait of Carrie – companion to same which he has done of me – and for five weeks we simply rioted in the Primitives. We did what we liked and when we liked and as we liked. There was an American girl there too – a Miss Catlin daughter of one who was most kind to us this spring in America. *She* was a type that Phil had never seen before and *he* was a type she had never, never seen before and their manoevrings around and about each other were very fine.[2]

To cap it all, one evening, sitting before a peat fire Phil (who really can read aloud) read us "a Bundle of Letters".[3] It was immense by reason that he was the only one who had not the key to both hemispheres and we made him read it all at one sitting. We used you to read aloud of evenings and you very nearly received just such another terrible telegram as we sent you once from here.

As to honest women we congratulate and envy you. Lawful matrimony (in real estate)[4] is ever the most honourable but what is one to do when three deboshed trustees will not permit us to make an honest woman of our little place. She exists now in a state of be-plastered harlotry. We want to rough cast her and clean out cows and hens etc. from her borders and generally to make her decent and they won't give us leave though we offer money with both hands. What a joyous time you ought to have when your marriage settlements are signed. She will be expensive but at least she won't rebuke you for extravagance incurred on her account. When you can draw a free breath (Literature isn't in it with house-warming) come down to us I pray you and we will match your lamb against our Southdown mutton. Our news is of course nothing. I'm not doing any work of any importance and am beating my convalescence out thin as a defence against the Impertinent. On mature thought, I don't think I shall ever be quite strong again – for social purposes which I dislike. Brighton and Rottindean are too close to town for a man to be robustly accessible to all the loafers of the place. But please come down and see us how we live and we'll talk.[5]

Carrie joins me in best love and I am, as ever, affectionately yours

Ruddy.

Notes
1. RK and his family returned to The Elms on 15 September (CK diary).
2. JLK reported a somewhat different impression: Phil, he wrote, was "philandering tepidly with Edith Catlin a somewhat plump and pleasing person, amiable and null" (to Sally Norton, 15 September 1899: ALS, Sussex).
3. James's short story, published in 1879.
4. James had leased Lamb House, Rye, in 1897, and was now buying it.
5. James came to Rottingdean on 17 October (CK diary).

To Moberly Bell, [28 September 1899]
Text: Copy, Library of Congress

The Elms, / Rottingdean. / Nr. Brighton. / Thursday 9.A.M.

Dear Bell

Herewith the verses[1] which my secretary is good enough to take up to town for me.

You may have information which may make its issue on Friday inexpedient or inopportune. In that case please return to bearer who waits the answer.

If however you publish on Friday please cable it this afternoon, points and all, to

Aidedecamp
New York.

Mark copy in Times *"Copyrighted by Rudyard Kipling in the United States of America."* By this means I shall save my copyright and also get the verses home in America where the crisis in the Transvaal is rather misunderstood.[2]

The thing is my contribution to the situation and so of course there is no charge.

> Sincerely ever
> Rudyard Kipling

Notes
1. "The Old Issue", *The Times*, 29 September 1899 (*The Five Nations*).
2. The poem appeared in the New York *Tribune* and the Boston *Globe* on 29 September.

To Dean Frederic William Farrar,[1] 13 October 1899
ALS: Library of Congress

The Elms, / Rottingdean, / Nr. Brighton. / Oct. 13. 99.

private
Dear Sir,

I am in receipt of your letter and can only express my sincere regret that the schoolboy's comments on *Eric* and *St Winifreds* should have pained you so much.[2] At the same time I would ask you remember that the two books are practically classics, that it would be impossible to write any sketch of schoolboy life of twenty years ago without in some way alluding to their influence; and also that there are boys – ignorant and vulgar minded it may be – who take less interest in the moral teachings of the two books than in their divergencies from the facts of school-life as boys know these today.

I can assert honestly that it was no part of my intention to try to injure you with gratuitous insult. Your years and your position in the English Church alike forbid the thought of that.

> Sincerely yours
> Rudyard Kipling.

Notes
1. Farrar (1831–1903), Dean of Canterbury, had been a master at both Marlborough and at Harrow before becoming Headmaster of Marlborough and then Rector of St Margaret's, Westminster. While he was at Harrow he published school stories, including *Eric, Or Little by Little* (1858), and *St. Winifred's* (1862).

2. *Stalky & Co.* had been published just a week earlier. *Eric* and *St. Winifred's* are derided in both "Slaves of the Lamp, I" and "An Unsavoury Interlude".

To Mr. Ritchie, 16 November 1899
ALS: University of Sussex

The Elms / Rottingdean / Sussex / Nov. 16. 99.

Dear Ritchie

Very many thanks for yours of the 14th. That uncle of mine is so busy with being at the head of the Methodist Conference[2] that I haven't been able to come across him: but I think that we have more or less established the fact that we come of the Skye peoples. Our Methodist forbears, I fancy, took more account of a man's religious convictions than his ancestry. One hears a good deal about their eloquence and piety and but little of their cattle-lifting fathers. We've been mourning for Creich ever since we left it. My wee maid Elsie saw me open your letter this morning and I told her it was from you at Creich. Said she: – "Then let's *all* go back to the manse tomorrow." She plays a little play of her own in which throwing stones into Migdale, walking over the heather and having tea in the open are all beautifully mixed – on the drawing-room floor. She bids me specially: "Send my love to Mary."

I've had a letter or two from the Laird[3] and, by the same token, he sent us a splendid donation (no conditions attached) to my boys reading-room here.[4] I fear he'd disapprove of our last venture – a boy's miniature rifle-range.[5] They're fell on shooting. Now I am glad to learn that you're in the way to get your reading-room tho' for the life o' me I can't see what the Libraries Act has to do with it one way or another.[6] Herewith I send my £5 (the same yearly for two years) and wish you all the best of success.

The days are short and grey with us but it's likely that you're having clear cold and may be snow. I thought of you the other day at the end of a two days s.w. gale, when a big steamer lay at two anchors just off our foreshore. She'd clean lost her propeller – as I could see when she lifted to the roll. The tug from Newhaven tried to pull her into harbour but she took charge of the tug and they had just time to drop their anchors and save her from going ashore.

As to pictures of myself, I'll send you one as soon as I can lay hands on a decent copy. I'm sitting for an oil-picture of myself and it's weary work.

We're all very well and fit – thanks to Creich, and this bears with it my wife's kindest regards, as well as heartiest greetings from Sir Philip who is at this moment getting ready to paint me. Pray remember me to the wet McPherson (I can see him twisting two pounders out of Migdale in the wet) and Mowatt and give the children's love to Mary.

Yours ever sincerely
Rudyard Kipling.

Notes

1. Evidently one of Carnegie's men at Skibo. In his letter to Carnegie of [18 September 1899] (ALS, Library of Congress), RK says that Ritchie accompanied them as far as Tain on their departure from Creich.
2 .Frederic Macdonald was President of the Wesleyan Methodist Conference in 1899.
3. Carnegie.
4. RK had been active in the Rottingdean Boys' Club at least since October of 1898 (CK diary, 28 October 1898).
5. This had just been established; encouraging rifle training was a major interest of RK's in the rest of his Rottingdean years.
6. The Public Libraries Act of 1892 gave the power of adopting the Act to local authorities rather than to the voters. Presumably this made a difference in Creich.

To Sarah Orne Jewett, [December 1899][1]

ALS: Harvard University

The Elms, / Rottingdean, / Nr. Brighton.

Dear Miss Jewett –

They are all beautiful[2] – with that exquisite silvery touch you have; but it seems to me that I recognize in "Bold Words at the Bridge" a new departure which I hope you will follow up. It's the very life and human nature itself: and it does me good (medically to the soul) to read the tales.

With love from us both

Yours ever
Rudyard Kipling

Notes

1. Receiving post office mark 8 January 1900.
2. *The Queen's Twin, and Other Stories*, published in November 1899.

Register of Names and Correspondents

A full index will be published at the end of the fourth volume. For the convenience of the reader in the interim this list is provided of RK's correspondents and contemporaries identified in this volume. The page references are to the notes in which the identifications are made.